Like Clay Under the Seal

By Pastor Dean Odle

"The earth is changed like clay into which a seal is pressed; And the things [of the earth] stand out like a [multi-colored] garment."

Job 38:14 AMP

Like Clay Under the Seal

By Pastor Dean Odle

ISBN: 978-1-54398-751-5

Second Printing

Revised & Expanded Edition

November 2019

Front and back cover art by Faye Fletcher

All Scripture quotations are from the
King James Version unless otherwise noted.

Acknowledgements

First, I want to thank our Lord Jesus Christ for saving me many years ago by His grace and for continuing to lead me into truth by His Holy Spirit. Secondly, I thank my wife Nancy who is the hardest working person that I have ever seen. Her love, loyalty, and dedication, first to Jesus and then to me and whatever the Lord wants us to do never ceases to amaze me.

I also want to thank our "junior-editor" Kelsey Himes, Jordan Winsor for contributing some research on the moon, Sal and Daniela Corona for making and delivering the best Indian food to get us through the last days of editing. A big thank you to Faye Fletcher for capturing and beautifully painting my vision for the front cover and then adding and executing your vision for the back. Thanks to Robert "Paint Tank" Moore for providing some inside artwork. And of course, a thank you goes to my friend Sam Botta who started me on this journey by sending me that first "flat earth" video by Scrawny2Brawny.

And finally, a special thanks to our Fire & Grace Church family both locally and abroad. None of this would have been possible without your prayers, fasting, and faithful financial support. The encouraging messages and testimonies really help us to keep pressing forward with gospel of Jesus Christ and all the truths found in the Bible.

Like Clay Under the Seal

Table of Contents

Preface

Introduction

Preface

A Note to Christians:

Toward the end of writing this book, I posted an open letter on Facebook entitled *"An Open Letter to Ministers, Pastors and Christians about Flat Earth."* It began as a response to a local pastor's wife who mocked the idea of a flat earth when a mutual friend posted my YouTube video entitled, *"The Bible DOES Say Flat Earth"* on her Facebook page. The last time I checked, this particular video had 670,000 views not counting the people who have mirrored (copied) it. The following letter is my response to the pastor's wife along with some additional thoughts. Needless to say, my post started a firestorm of attempted debunks and rude, condescending, and very uninformed comments, many from pastors and Christian leaders. Here is the letter that triggered their cognitive dissonance:

Open Letter to Ministers, Pastors and Christians:

"He that answereth a matter before he heareth it, it is folly and shame unto him" (Proverbs 18:13).

"O Timothy, keep that which is committed to thy trust, avoiding profane and vain babblings, and oppositions of

science falsely so called: Which some professing have erred concerning the faith. Grace be with thee. Amen" (1 Timothy 6:20-21).

A little more than 5 years ago, I was just like you. I had allowed years of government schools, Antichrist college professors, modern pseudoscience, media brainwashing and bad theology to blind me from seeing the entire truth in God's Word about creation. But in October 2015, the Lord led me to the truth and a much deeper study in the Bible on creation than I had ever done. I also did extensive research and several earth curvature tests across Mobile Bay with high zoom cameras and telescopes. We have had an engineer, a geometry teacher, and a retired Army Lieutenant Colonel with us on these tests. In short, we have mathematical, photographic and video evidence that the earth curvature is not there (as do thousands of others). It is flat and we have been lied to about almost everything. As it says, **"Prove all things: hold fast that which is good"** (1 Thess. 5:21).

What you don't know is that this Biblical truth and the many evidences coming forth have spawned a revival outside of almost all churches. This flat earth truth is leading atheists, agnostics and new age people back to the Bible and then to Jesus for salvation. I am almost done with a 300+ page book on this subject and one entire chapter is one testimony after another of atheists who have come to Jesus because of flat earth truth and evidence. And we are having a conference on October 4-5, 2019 at the Dixon Conference Center in Auburn, Alabama (450 seats total) and there will not be a seat left. People (saved and unsaved) are coming from all over the US, Canada, England, Switzerland, Brazil, Slovakia, and other places.

It is an awakening that just keeps growing. And like all revivals, God brings forth a truth from His Word that has been neglected or misunderstood or just totally buried by ignorance or bad teaching. Like the Pentecostal revival, God brought back the truth of the gifts of the Spirit, particularly tongues, and the mainstream Christians thought it was foolishness and the majority mocked it and rejected it. But the Pentecostal truth became a world-wide awakening that by-passed the vast majority of mainline churches. They missed the mighty outpouring of the Holy Spirit and the opportunity to learn about and experience the nine gifts of the Holy Spirit. That does not mean that those who missed out ceased being Christians or ceased being used of God, they just missed out on a powerful move of God that became the fastest growing segment of Christianity in the 20th Century. They missed out on an important truth that would help them win others to Jesus.

Most Christians missed that revival due to their pride and the fact that they refused to accept what the Bible taught about the gifts of the Holy Spirit. One very well-known pastor at the time of the Azusa Street Revival called it the *"last vomit of Satan upon the earth."* Sadly, the same thing is happening now with the truth about creation. The Holy Spirit has revived some very important Biblical truths and evidence to back it up. However, many Christian choose to believe government propaganda, astronauts, and atheist scientists rather than the Bible even when it has been proven that astronauts, scientists and governments have lied about almost everything.

So, to my fellow ministers and Christians: Can you show me in the Scripture where the Bible teaches that the Earth is a spinning ball, flying around the sun? Can you show me where the Bible calls the sun a star? Or did God create the sun, moon and stars as three different things? Jesus said the stars would fall to earth at His second coming, but if the stars are massive suns, wouldn't one star completely destroy the earth if it fell upon it? You may say that only means meteorites and asteroids. Where did you get that? From the Bible or man? Where did God say that He made meteors or comets or asteroids? Do you really know what those lights are in the sky? Jesus said the moon gives off its own light, but modern science says it reflects the sun's light? Who do you believe?

The Bible is clear that the earth is still and at rest (Zechariah 1:11) immovable and fixed (Psalms 93:1 and 1 Chronicles 16:30). The Bible does not teach that the earth moves, and true scientists proved this in the late 1800s. Furthermore, the Bible teaches that the sun moves in a circuit or circular path over the earth (Psalms 19 and Joshua 10). And in Job 38:14, God says that the earth was formed like clay pressed down flat under a seal ring (if you look up the original Hebrew words it is very clear).

The Bible also teaches that the firmament is a solid, molten glass-like structure over the earth with God's throne upon it and supporting the waters that are above (Genesis 1 and 7, Job 37:18, Ezekiel 1 and Revelation 15). Moreover, in Isaiah 40:22 where it says that God sits "upon the circle of the earth," that word "circle" is the Hebrew word *chuwg* and it means circle, not ball. In Isaiah 22:18, the word ball is used which in Hebrew is *duwr*. So, you can see that these are two different Hebrew words used for circle and ball. And God NEVER uses the word ball or *duwr* to describe the earth. So, before you call true Biblical cosmology (aka flat earth) error or ridiculous, you better do some deeper study and research, or you will be found defending and pushing the Satanic lies that are against the rightly divided Word of God.

Many are blinded to parts of God's Word because they have believed some of the lies of modern science and government "space" agencies. But you might as well believe that we came from monkeys if you are going to believe the anti-Bible heliocentric view of creation that came from occultists, Jesuit priests, former Nazi scientists and Freemasons. I implore you to stop the knee-jerk reactions that come from a lifetime of government and media brainwashing and get back to what the Bible actually teaches. Stop mixing the Bible with the doctrines and fables of men who claim they went to the moon.

"And they shall turn away their ears from the truth and shall be turned unto fables (fictitious tales)" (2 Timothy 2:4).

Sincerely,

Pastor Dean Odle

The Responses

One local Baptist pastor commented on my letter, *"Oh, my friend. I am so sorry. If you are truly serious, it is this type of ridiculous conjecture that causes many to question other aspects of our beliefs. This is even too far-fetched for science fiction."*

This was my response to Pastor Tom, and it was followed by crickets: *"Ridiculous conjecture? Wow! Must say that I'm not shocked. Most modern ministers believe Copernicus, and NASA more than their Bible. Tell me Pastor Tom did the sun and moon stop moving in Joshua 10 or did the earth stop spinning? Did those primitive prophets like Moses and*

Joshua (who were on the mountain with God and walking in and out of glory) not understand that the earth was spinning and orbiting the sun? The Bible says the sun stopped. Psalms 19 says it is the sun that moves in a circuit over the earth. Was David wrong too? Or do you even believe that every word of the Bible was inspired by God and means what it says? Do you even know what the firmament is?"

A pastor who lives in Montgomery, Alabama commented and gave an article from a "scholar" to explain away and dismiss the above Scriptures that plainly teach geocentric creation. In an attempt to diminish the passage in Joshua 10 that plainly says the sun and the moon stood still an entire day, the "scholar" says that the reasoning of Biblical flat earthers **"...violates one of the principles that we have discussed: a failure to account for audience's understanding."** That statement is nothing but the demonic doctrine of accommodation which most "scholars" believe. What the doctrine of accommodation basically says is that the Holy Spirit could not give those primitive, nomadic prophets like Moses, Joshua, Job, or Ezekiel the exact truth of how the sun and moon really worked or what the firmament really is because they just couldn't handle it. The doctrine of accommodation implies that God lied to them or allowed them to believe a lie about the nature of creation and then inspired them to write it down wrong in the Bible. Unbelievable!

A former Assemblies of God pastor responded, *"...I'm going to stick to the Gospel and refuse to get on the questionable fringes."*

My response to Pastor Glenn was this, *"The gospel of John starts out with presenting Jesus as the God of creation. The first book of the Bible starts out with creation. The book of Romans talks about creation in the first chapter as does Colossians. Ezekiel 1 describes the firmament and on and on it goes. The true nature of creation does matter. It is foundational to our faith. God said the sun moves and the earth is still and at rest (Zech. 1:11), fixed and immovable (1 Chron. 16:30). Modern science says the Earth is spinning at 1,000 mph, orbiting the sun at 66,000 mph, and flying through "space" at 500,000 mph (yet Polaris is always in the same spot and the other constellations move across the sky exactly the same every day)."*

Pastor Glenn's simple answer was *"Nonsense."* He also went on to say that my *"...Biblical interpretation and understanding is lacking"* to which I *replied, "Yes my Biblical interpretation is lacking the filter and premise of your cult of Copernicus and priests of NASA. I don't have to understand the Word of God through the nonsense of dark matter, dark energy, black holes, or other fairytales of men landing on the moon or putting a rover on Mars only to take a picture of a dead prairie dog on Mars. Oops."*

Biblical Hermeneutics

Since most Copernican Christians want to accuse Biblical Earthers of wrong interpretation or hermeneutics, I want to address the accepted laws of hermeneutics from true conservative Christian scholars. And just so the readers of this book understand, I have diligently studied the Bible for 32 years, but I also seek counsel from knowledgeable men. I was contacted in 2016 by a man who has a PhD from Fuller Theological Seminary in California. I confirmed his credentials before I interviewed him on our Prophecy Quake Radio Show. He reads his Bible in Hebrew and Greek and has led two different Bible colleges. We have had numerous conversations and I have asked him to check my hermeneutics and understanding of the original languages that I have presented in many sermons and he says that I am doing it correctly. Below are the laws of Biblical interpretation (hermeneutics) that I verified with him and now teach in our school of ministry. I have endeavored to follow these rules of Biblical interpretation for the last 32 years and I plan to continue.

1. **The most important law of Biblical hermeneutics is that the Bible should be interpreted literally.** We are to understand the Bible in its normal or plain meaning, unless the passage is obviously intended to be symbolic or if figures of speech are employed. But even when symbols and figures of speech are used, they are usually describing something that actually does exist. For instance, the seven headed, ten horn Beast of Revelation 13 is a symbol of a United Nations world government with seven main leaders and ten kings under them. We see this being literally fulfilled in the United Nations right now. In other words, taking the Bible literally simply means the Bible says what it means and means what it says. For example, when Jesus speaks of having fed "the five thousand" in Mark 8:19, the law of hermeneutics says we should understand five thousand literally—there was a crowd of hungry people that numbered five thousand who were fed with real bread and fish by a miracle-working Savior. Any attempt to "spiritualize" the number or to deny a literal miracle is to do injustice to the text and ignore the purpose of language (which is to communicate). And when it comes to creation, we cannot attempt to "scientize" passages to make them fit our indoctrinated, preconceived notions and theories from modern

"science." Biblical hermeneutics keeps us faithful to the intended meaning of Scripture and away from allegorizing, minimizing or scientizing Bible verses that should be understood literally.

2. **A second crucial law of Biblical hermeneutics is that passages must be interpreted historically. Interpreting a passage historically means we must seek to understand the culture, background, and situation that prompted the text.** For example, in order to fully understand Jonah's flight in Jonah 1:1–3, we should research the history of the Assyrians as related to Israel. When it comes to cosmology and the nature of creation, we must also look at history. For example, the writings of first century Jewish historian Josephus makes it clear that the Jews in Israel 2,000 years ago still believed in a solid crystalline, firmament dome set over the earth and that the sun, moon and stars moved in a circuit over the earth.

3. **Interpreting a passage grammatically requires one to follow the rules of grammar and recognize the nuances of Hebrew and Greek**. For example, when Paul writes of "our great God and Savior, Jesus Christ" in Titus 2:13, the rules of grammar state that God and Savior are parallel terms and they are both in apposition to Jesus Christ - in other words, Paul clearly calls Jesus "our great God." Additionally, studying how the same Hebrew or Greek words were used in other Bible passages also gives understanding of what the passage is saying. A good example of this is the word "elect" in Matthew 24. Those who teach the false pre-tribulation rapture doctrine claim that "elect" is a reference to the Jews

and not to Christians or the church in general. They claim this because Matthew 24 destroys their pre-tribulation rapture doctrine. However, when you look up all of the passages in the New Testament that use the word "elect" they are referring to the entire church (aka the body of Christ) in 8 out of 10 times. And of the remaining two uses, one refers to Jesus and the other angels. So, it is totally incorrect hermeneutics to say the word "elect" in Matthew 24 is a reference to the Jews. As Christians, we must use the same diligence with "firmament," "circle," "breadth," and many other words in the Bible or we will not properly understand Biblical topics and doctrines.

4. **A fourth law of Biblical hermeneutics is that Scriptures must be interpreted in context. Interpreting a passage contextually involves considering the context of a verse or passage when trying to determine the meaning.** The context includes the verses immediately preceding and following, the chapter, the book, and, most broadly, the entire Bible. A good example of this would be in Job 38:14 where God describes the shape of the earth as being like clay pressed down flat by a signet or seal ring. When we go back to the previous verses in the chapter, we see God answering Job out of the whirlwind. He begins a series of probing questions about creation which continue to the end of the chapter. So, we see that Job 38:14 is in the context of God Himself discussing the nature of creation before and after verse 14. Thus, using Job 38:14 to describe the shape of the earth is using the verse in context.

5. **A fifth law of Biblical hermeneutics is that Scripture is always the best interpreter of Scripture.** For this reason, we always compare Scripture with Scripture when trying to determine the meaning of a passage. On such subjects as the firmament, we do not take one passage or let some liberal theologian using corrupt texts give us their definition of a word. Neither do we filter what the Bible says through what we think is "science." We must look at ALL of the passages in the Bible that mention the firmament (or whatever subject we are studying) directly or indirectly from Genesis to Revelation and build our understanding and interpretation from that.

These are the rules of Biblical interpretation that are being used in this book. I have exhaustively covered what the Bible teaches about creation. I have also done my fair share of research into the people and organizations that have given us the popular false notions of our world. I will present a lot of Scripture, definitions of Hebrew and Greek words used in the Bible from multiple lexicons, history (both Biblical and secular), real science vs. pseudoscience, proof that space agencies have lied to us, our own experiments across Mobile Bay, long distance photography and videography, testimonies from high and low-ranking ex-military sources, math confirmed by engineers and geometry teachers, declassified government documents and military technical manuals that admit "a flat non-rotating Earth," and many testimonies of those who have come to trust the Bible and Jesus Christ as their Savior and Lord because they seriously looked into all of these things.

My prayer is that many more of my Christian brothers and sisters will break free from the years of demonic programming and return to a childlike faith in every word of the God-breathed, infallible, and supernaturally preserved Bible that we still have today. Here's how Jesus put it:

"At the same time came the disciples unto Jesus, saying, Who is the greatest in the kingdom of heaven? And Jesus called a little child unto him, and set him in the midst of them, And said, Verily I say unto you, Except ye be converted, and become as little children, ye shall not enter into the kingdom of heaven. Whosoever therefore shall humble himself as this little child, the same is greatest in the kingdom of heaven" (Matthew 18:1-4).

In Jesus Christ,

Pastor Dean Odle

Important Note

As much as you might be tempted to skip around based on the chapter titles, please read the chapters of this book in order. Each chapter builds on the previous one and certain dots must be connected to fully grasp the magnitude of one of Satan's biggest end-time deceptions.

Introduction

(For all the Athenians and strangers [Truthers] **which were there spent their time in nothing else, but either to tell, or to hear some new thing**.*) Then Paul stood in the midst of Mars' hill, and said, Ye men of Athens, I perceive that in all things ye are too superstitious. For as I passed by, and beheld your devotions, I found an altar with this inscription,* **To The Unknown God. Whom therefore ye ignorantly worship, him declare I unto you"** (Acts 17:21-23).

I sat amazed as I listened to speakers who were not even Christians take the stage at this unprecedented event and declare, *"They are hiding god!"* All of the speakers at the first Flat Earth International Conference on November 9, 2017 were known as "truthers" and yet the most important Truth of their lives had eluded the majority of them for one reason or another. I knew the Lord had placed me in that moment to boldly declare the identity and name of the One, True God of creation - Jesus Christ. He had started me on this journey just two years earlier and never could I have imagined the twists and turns it would take. Many people call it going down the *"rabbit hole,"* but in reality, it is God revealing Himself and the deceptions that have been set in motion to control us and turn us against God and His Bible.

The enemies of the God of creation (the Lord Jesus Christ) have worked for centuries to create this massive deception. Satan and his servants have devised a carefully crafted plan to deceive and enslave the world. But Jesus said to those who believe in Him, *"If ye continue in my word, then are ye my disciples indeed; And ye shall know the truth, and the truth shall make you free"* (John 8:31-32).

Jesus said to the Pharisees who rejected the truth, *"And because I tell you the truth, ye believe me not. Which of you convinceth me of sin? And if I say the truth, why do ye not believe me? He that is of God heareth God's words: ye therefore hear them not, because ye are not of God"* (John 8:45-47).

And of those who refuse to believe it was said, *"Behold, ye despisers, and wonder, and perish: for I work a work in your days, **a work which ye shall in no wise believe, though a man declare it unto you"*** (Acts 13:41).

There are times when God sends messengers to share incredible truths with a lost and wicked generation but because they are so immersed in lies, only a small portion can accept the revelation. Even the perfect, sinless Jesus could not get the majority of the people in His own religion, race, and culture to believe Him. Jesus spoke and did things in a way that had never been seen before. He spoke truth and gave evidence that He was their Messiah, and yet most still could not believe or accept that He was the Way, the Truth and the Life. They could not accept that the Bible prophecies they claimed to believe were happening and that God in the flesh was standing before them.

This happened with Noah's warning about the coming flood and Jeremiah's warnings of the Babylonian invasion.

For the most part, those who heard the incredible messages from God could not break free from their cognitive dissonance (the mental conflict that occurs when beliefs or assumptions are contradicted by new information). Years of indoctrination had become so integrated into who they were that it was impossible for most to humbly accept the truth that God was revealing.

Sadly, most people are no different today. Jesus warned that mass deception would be one of the main signs that we are in the last days before His return. And yet, so many refuse to see that what they now call "conspiracy theories" were actually foretold in the Bible just like the Messiah's coming. My prayer is that this book will help many break off deception and open eyes to the Truth that Jesus Christ is revealing in the exciting time we live in. He is revealing Himself!

"The heavens declare the glory of God; and the firmament sheweth his handywork" (Psalm 19:1).

Chapter 1

Satan's Global Deception

"And the great dragon was cast out, that old serpent, called the Devil, and Satan, **which deceiveth the whole world***: he was cast out into the earth, and his angels were cast out with him"* (Revelation 12:9).

"Now the Spirit speaketh expressly, that in the latter times some shall depart from the faith, giving heed to seducing spirits, and doctrines of devils; *Speaking lies in hypocrisy; having their conscience seared with a hot iron;"* (1 Timothy 4:1-2).

"Then I turned, and lifted up mine eyes, and looked, and behold a flying roll (scroll or cylinder shape). *And he said unto me, What seest thou?* **And I answered, I see a flying roll***; the length thereof is twenty cubits* (about 30 feet), *and the breadth thereof ten cubits* (15 feet). *Then said he unto me,* **This is the curse that goeth forth over the face of the whole earth:"** (Zechariah 5:1-3a).

"And in the days when NASA grants were paying my bills I never had this freedom to choose what I would study, and how I would study it." - Jesuit Astronomer Guy Consolmagno

"And there shall be signs in the sun, and in the moon, and in the stars; and upon the earth distress of nations, with perplexity; the sea and the waves roaring; Men's hearts failing them for fear, and for looking after those things which are coming on the earth: for the powers of heaven shall be shaken. And then shall they see the Son of man (Jesus Christ) *coming in a cloud with power and great glory"* (Luke 21:25-27).

"And many chiefs of the stars shall transgress the order prescribed. And these shall alter their orbits and task, and not appear at the seasons prescribed to them. And the whole order of the stars shall be concealed from the sinner, and the thoughts of those on the earth shall err concerning them {And they shall be altered from all their ways}, Yay, they shall err and take them to be gods. And evil shall be multiplied upon them and punishment should come upon them, so as to destroy all" (Enoch 80:6-8).

*"My history of the Jesuits is not eloquently written, but it is supported by unquestionable authorities, [and] is very particular and very horrible. Their [the Jesuit Order's] restoration [in 1814 by Pope Pius VII] is indeed a step toward darkness, cruelty, despotism, [and] death. ... **I do not like the appearance of the Jesuits. If ever there was a body of men who merited eternal damnation on earth and in hell, it is this Society of [Ignatius de] Loyola."***
- John Adams (1735-1826), 2nd President of the United States of America

26

Vatican astronomer Guy Consolmagno is a Jesuit priest with advanced degrees from MIT and the University of Arizona. He is a highly respected planetary scientist whose research focuses on meteorites, asteroids, and dwarf planets. He also spent several terms as a visiting scientist at NASA's Goddard Space Flight Center. Consolmagno is the author of several books including his 2014 book called, *Would You Baptize an Extraterrestrial?* He begins his book by rejecting Biblical creation in the first chapter entitled, *"Biblical Genesis or Scientific Big Bang?"* This representative of the Pope stated, *"...very soon the nations will look to aliens for their salvation."* This Jesuit deceiver, Guy Consolmagno appeared on FORA.tv on March 2, 2008 discussing the creationist theory of the origin of life and argued that the theory that rests on a literal interpretation of the Bible is not practical or correct. He went on to say that the Bible is just poetry and metaphorical. The following is part of what he said:

"A couple of years ago, I was asked to do a Bible study group in Houston with a bunch of astronauts... So, I wound up at a dinner evening with about 12 couples all of them astronauts and spouses. One of the guys (half of them were Catholic) came up to me and said, 'You know...I just want to let you know, I believe in the absolute truth that creation was made in the six days just as described in the book of Genesis and that's my religion. I just want to let you know that ahead of time.' And I'm thinking, 'Have you actually read Genesis where it says the world is flat, and it's covered with a dome and there's water above and below the dome? Where does the shuttle go? How come you don't get wet?"[1]

---
[1] https://www.youtube.com/watch?v=wUyiQufyiK0&feature=youtu.be

Would You Baptize an Extraterrestrial?

...AND OTHER QUESTIONS FROM THE
ASTRONOMERS' IN-BOX AT THE VATICAN OBSERVATORY

Guy Consolmagno, SJ
and Paul Mueller, SJ

The crowd that he shared this story with just laughed and laughed. But those are good questions Guy! This book will answer those questions and more like:

- Should we believe Biblical creation or scientism's big bang, heliocentric, spinning, flying ball?
- What is space?
- What and where are satellites?
- Does the aether exist?
- What did the Michelson-Morley experiments really discover?
- Did Einstein create the theory of relativity to cover up a major discovery that would have turned the entire Copernican revolution of a heliocentric universe on its head?
- Is there evidence the earth is flat and covered by a solid dome that the Bible calls the firmament?
- Is there evidence that the sun, moon and stars are much smaller and closer than we have been told?
- Has Satan (with his servants) deceived the entire world about God's creation and in doing so, turned millions

and millions away from trusting the Bible to be the inspired, infallible truth of the God of Abraham, Isaac & Jacob?

The Bible makes it clear that the leader of the fallen angels (known as Satan, Lucifer, the Dragon, the Serpent, the Devil) always wanted to be like God and put himself in the place of God. Isaiah 14:12-15 says, *"How art thou fallen from heaven, O Lucifer, son of the morning! how art thou cut down to the ground, which didst weaken the nations! For thou hast said in thine heart, **I will ascend into heaven, I will exalt my throne above the stars of God:** I will sit also upon the mount of the congregation, in the sides of the north: **I will ascend above the heights of the clouds; I will be like the most High.** Yet thou shalt be brought down to hell, to the sides of the pit. "* So, it should not surprise us that Satan and his fallen ones would try to usurp the creation and even disguise themselves as "aliens" to take credit for "seeding" mankind on earth. Some ancient astronaut theorists postulate that "aliens" terraformed earth or were the creators of our "planet."

How successful could you be in deceiving the world if you had supernatural power, an army of invisible angelic beings and evils spirits, knowledge of superior, ancient technology, the loyalty of the most wealthy and powerful humans on earth to assist you and were invisible? What if you could convince governments and world leaders to fund your deceptions with billions and billions of dollars from taxpayers? And what if your people own and control the media, the public schools, almost all of the centers of higher education, and the biggest religious institutions like the Vatican, Islam, and Judaism? Do you think that you could succeed in deceiving the entire world? Of course! An entity with that kind of power and network could succeed at most anything.

There are many warnings about deception in the Bible. The Holy Spirit of God gave the Apostle Paul this warning about the last days, *"Now the Spirit speaketh expressly, that in the latter times some shall depart from the faith, giving heed to seducing spirits, and doctrines of devils;"* (1 Timothy 4:1). The Lord Jesus Christ warned us that in the last days many false christs and false prophets would rise and deceive many. He said, *"For there shall arise false Christs, and false prophets, and shall shew great signs and wonders; insomuch that, if it were possible, they shall deceive the very elect"* (Matthew 24:24).

The term "false Christs" can also be translated "false saviors" or "false messiahs" which is very interesting when you recall what the Jesuit astronomer Guy Consolmagno said *"...the nations will soon look to the aliens for their salvation."* The Holy Spirit of Jesus Christ stated through the Apostle Paul that these end-time deceivers would *come "...after the working of Satan with all power and signs and lying wonders, And with all deceivableness of unrighteousness in them that perish; because they received not the love of the truth, that they might be saved"* (2 Thessalonians 2:9-10). It is important to note here that the phrase "lying wonders" in the original Greek is *pseudos* and means *"...a lie; a conscious and intentional falsehood."*[2] And the Greek word for "wonders" means *"...something so strange as to cause it to be 'watched' or 'observed'; hence, 'a sign in the heavens.'"*[3]

---

[2] https://www.blueletterbible.org/lang/lexicon/lexicon.cfm?Strongs=G5579&t=KJV

[3] Thayer's Greek-English Lexicon of the New Testament by Joseph H. Thayer published 1889

Of course, very few even consider that the magic shows of "space" agencies and their rocket men could be a part of these intentional falsehoods in the heavens that have caused people to stand in awe and wonder. Nor do they believe that Satan and his fallen angels along with the wandering stars of the heavens could be deceiving them with light shows and other alleged observed phenomena in our sky. The book of Revelation warns that an assistant to the Beast (the Antichrist) will do *"...great wonders, so that he maketh fire come down from heaven on the earth in the sight of men, And deceiveth them that dwell on the earth by the means of those miracles which he had power to do in the sight of the beast; saying to them that dwell on the earth,* that they should make an image to the beast, which had the wound by a sword, and did live"* (Revelation 13:13-14). This assistant is same individual that will push loyalty to the coming world government (aka the New World Order) of the Antichrist and the coming implanted mark of the Beast that will control all buying and selling.

So, what is this "fire from heaven" mentioned in Revelation 13? Could this "fire from heaven" be the NASA, SpaceX, or Roscosmos rockets? How about the appearance of UFOs, aliens (which are demons), falling stars (which are angels) or other manipulations in the heavens/sky? I believe that all of those things will happen just like the old television series *V* and Arthur C. Clarke's novel *Childhood's End* portrayed. They told us that the Vatican will work with the "visitors" (fallen angels and demons disguised as aliens) to deceive the world into worshipping the Antichrist, his world government and Satan with his fallen ones as they are hailed as gods and the creators of mankind. The seal of pledging allegiance to all of this will be what the Bible calls the mark of the Beast which is some form of microchip technology voluntarily implanted in the hand or forehead (see

Revelation 13 and 14). Be forewarned, the Bible states there is no salvation for the person who accepts this mark.

If you think the possibility of a Vatican and Satanic "alien" deception agenda is ludicrous, just read what some of their leading priests and even the Pope have said:

"The highest levels of the Vatican governance know what is approaching the earth and it will be of the upmost importance in the coming years." Father Malachi Martin

"Very soon we will not have to deny our Christian faith **but there is information coming from another world, and once it is confirmed it is going to require a re-reading of the gospel as we know it.** *"* Father Giuseppe Tanzella-Nitti Professor, Vatican University[4]

"There is an alien presence on earth now." Monsignor Corrado Balducci, Vatican Exorcist and Spokesman

[4] *Exo-Vaticana* by Chris Putnam & Thomas Horn ©2013 Defender Front Cover

"Intelligent beings created by God could exist in outer space." Father Gabriel Funes, Director of the Vatican Observatory[5]

And then take a look at this excerpt from a review of a new book that came out in January of 2019 called ***American Cosmic: UFOs, Religion, and Technology***.

*"A new book by D.W. Pasulka — professor and chair of the Department of Philosophy and Religion at the University of North Carolina Wilmington — **American Cosmic: UFOs, Religion, and Technology**, focuses not on grassroots investigative societies or marginal cults, but on UFO believers in the halls of power.*

***Her narrative begins on a drive through the hills with pioneering computer scientist, venture capitalist, and ufologist Jacques Vallee. 'Silicon Valley is full of secrets,' he tells her. It ends in the Vatican Secret Archives** (alas, not because the Ultimate Clue lies steganographically hidden in a Templar codex).*

*Along the way, Pasulka meets "Tyler," a biomedical technology mogul associated with the U.S. space program. Tyler is the most curious part of a curious book. Like most of the scientists, government researchers, and tech giants Pasulka quotes, Tyler's real name remains a secret. But Pasulka has presumably done scholarly due diligence on his background, which would otherwise be hard to believe: **Tyler has over 40 biotech patents to his name, many of which he believes were communicated to him by non-human intelligence. He works in a government program** where, according to him, the kind of intricate security-*

---
[5] http://news.bbc.co.uk/2/hi/europe/7399661.stm

clearance labyrinths one might find in an X-Files episode are the norm. '*I don't know who is responsible for putting me on these jobs. I think that somehow, <u>they</u> are responsible for it. My own direct boss doesn't know what I do. This is how the program works.*'

*Pasulka describes him breezing through airports without getting stopped by security: 'We arrived at the airport, and Tyler sailed right past security, past first class, past economy class, and out the other side. **He seemed to be literally beyond the law.' His name unlocks doors at the Vatican. In his official capacity as a researcher with the U.S. space program, one of his roles is merely to be at certain places at certain times — his superiors believe, apparently that his physical presence produces certain outcomes at experiments and rocket launches**...At one point, Pasulka travels to an unnamed site in New Mexico. Accompanying her are Tyler and Pasulka's own colleague "James," **an astrophysicist at a prestigious university, and not only a UFO believer, but a repeat contactee. (He finds the phenomenon unwelcome and describes it as something that in earlier times would be called 'demonic.')** The unidentified mesa is allegedly the site of a spacecraft crash many years ago. Tyler has obtained special permission for the two academics to visit and look for artifacts, on the condition that they travel blindfolded.*

"There are signs that alien belief is poised to become one of the world's ethical religions. *Alien beliefs often implicate the world in wickedness and call for repentance — many accounts of alien contacts include calls for an end to war and an increase in peaceful human cooperation. A recent New York Times op-ed used an alien invasion as a model for thinking about climate change...Perhaps, with fear and hope, its adherents will look to the skies for a* *promised return. Their worship will conclude with a reiteration of the sacred promise: **The aliens are coming. Maranatha.**"[6]*

This end-time "alien" deception is already taking root and will soon get much worse when the supposed "aliens" actually "show up." Many deceived people are going to rejoice and party just like they did in the 1996 movie *Independence Day* as they stood on the rooftops of skyscrapers welcoming "aliens" to earth. There will be a feeling of exhilaration because they are "not alone in the big universe." The Luciferian world leaders, NASA scientists, astronauts and government officials will "disclose" that they knew all along. Formerly classified documents about the "aliens" and close encounters will be opened for public viewing. This deception will take the world by storm and many weak, lukewarm Christians will fall away from their faith in the Bible and the Lord Jesus Christ because of this new revelation. How could something that sounds so bizarre happen? By getting people to first believe the Copernican and NASA deceptions of the Big Bang and heliocentric solar system and in turn completely disregarding the Biblical account of creation and the shape of the earth.

Even as I am writing this book (in September of 2019) there is a flurry of activity in the news over "UFO encounters" with U.S. Navy pilots. In 2017 the New York Times released three different videos taken from F-18s, but just days ago, the US Navy brass at the Pentagon confirmed that these stories and videos from the F-18 pilots are real. Tucker Carlson of FOXNEWS said that the videos *"...do, in fact, show aerial phenomena the Navy CANNOT explain*

---

[6] https://theoutline.com/post/7215/american-cosmic-review-aliens-are-extremely-real

and that, in fact, our understanding of physics CANNOT explain. " Tucker conducted an interview with Nick Pope (a UK "journalist" who once investigated UFOs for the British government) who was explaining how big this moment is and then Tucker said that the admission from the US Navy, *"...seems like a watershed moment"* (a turning point).

Then on my way to the hardware store, the "UFO encounters" were also being discussed on Glenn Beck's radio show. He and his guest were making comments like, "If there are aliens, I'm sure they are benevolent ones and don't want to kill everyone." The same line of conversation occurred on the Common Sense Show with Dave Hodges who is supposed to be a Christian alternative media truth source. It would appear that the talking points have been handed out from the top of Satan's control structure and it's time for "alien disclosure."

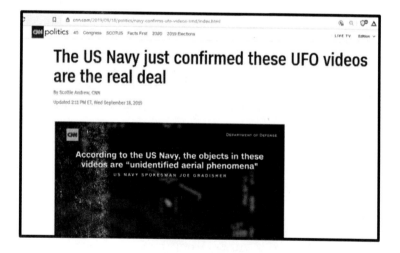

US Navy confirms multiple UFO videos are real

Believe it or not, the God of creation revealed that this UFO end-time deception would happen through the prophet Zechariah in 520 BC. *"Then I turned, and lifted up mine eyes, and looked, and behold a flying roll (scroll or cylinder shape). And he said unto me, What seest thou? And I answered, I see a flying roll;* the length thereof is twenty cubits (about 30 feet), *and the breadth thereof ten cubits* (15 feet). *Then said he unto me, **This is the curse that goeth forth over the face of the whole earth: for every one that stealeth shall be cut off as on this side according to it; and every one that sweareth shall be cut off as on that side according to it. I will bring it forth, saith the Lord of hosts, and it shall enter into the house of the thief, and into the house of him that sweareth falsely by my name: and it shall remain in the midst of his house, and shall consume it with the timber thereof and the stones thereof."** (Zech. 5:1-4).

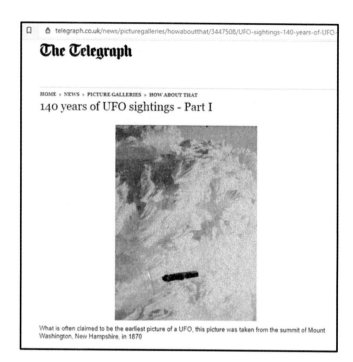

The Telegraph

HOME › NEWS › PICTURE GALLERIES › HOW ABOUT THAT

140 years of UFO sightings - Part I

What is often claimed to be the earliest picture of a UFO, this picture was taken from the summit of Mount Washington, New Hampshire, in 1870

God showed His prophet that there would come a day where flying scrolls or cylinder shapes would be a curse that ***"goeth forth over the face of the whole earth."*** That means these flying cylinders would be everywhere, but God warned that they are a curse (Hebrew word *alah*). They are evil. The LORD warned that everyone who steals, swears, and swears falsely by His name (claims to know Jesus but is not concerned with living a holy life for Him) shall be destroyed by this ***"flying scroll"*** curse. Zechariah 5 tells us that the wicked and the lukewarm, compromised Christians are going to be deceived and affected by this "flying cylinder" curse that will be going forth throughout the entire earth. It is going to affect their minds and beliefs. But without first convincing people of the "Big Bang," and a massive, universe with billions of galaxies and billions of planets, the "alien" deception wouldn't be possible at all. That is why Satan has been setting this up for centuries.

The Falling Away & the Antichrist

This is what the Holy Spirit inspired the Apostle Paul to right about the end-times, *"Now we beseech you, brethren, by the coming of our Lord Jesus Christ, and by our gathering together unto him, That ye be not soon shaken in mind, or be troubled, neither by spirit, nor by word, nor by letter as from us, as that the day of Christ is at hand. Let no man deceive you by any means: for that day shall not come, except there come a falling away first, and that man of sin be revealed, the son of perdition; Who opposeth and exalteth himself above all that is called God, or that is worshipped; so that he as God sitteth in the temple of God, shewing himself that he is God"* (2 Thessalonians 2:1-4).

The original Greek word translated "falling away" is *apostasía* and it is defined by the Strong's Greek dictionary as a *"...defection from truth* (properly, the state) ("apostasy"):—falling away, forsake." The Thayer's Greek Lexicon defines it the same way as *"...a falling away, defection, apostasy; in the Bible namely, from the true religion."* The Encyclopedia Britannica defines apostasy as *"...the total rejection of Christianity by a baptized person who, having at one time professed the Christian faith, publicly rejects it."*

Apostasy does not happen quickly in a true Christian's life. It begins as a slow erosion of the core foundations of faith in the heart of the believer. This principle also applies to the entire Christian church throughout the world. Sadly, the faith that many Christians had in the Divine inspiration of the Bible has already been eroded through Satan's elaborate attacks using false science and "magic shows" about NASA going to the Moon and Mars. He is quite the magician, and many have fallen for his sleight of hand, especially through the lies and agents of the Vatican.

A recent example of this erosion by false science is a high-profile Christian that recently announced on Instagram, *"I'm genuinely losing my faith, and it doesn't bother me. Like, what bothers me now is nothing. I am so happy now, so at peace with the world. It's crazy."* The Christian Post reported, *"Marty Sampson, a prolific worship music writer known for his work with Hillsong Worship, Hillsong United, Delirious and Young & Free, revealed he is losing his faith and believes Christianity is 'just another religion.'"* Among several reasons for his apostasy, Marty Sampson stated, *"Science keeps piercing the truth of every religion. Lots of things help people change their lives, not just one version of God. Got so much more to say, but for me, I'm keeping it real. Unfollow if you want, I've never been about living my life for others.'"*[7]

Another article points out, *"The Pew Forum on Religion and Public Life has noted that 39% of those currently unaffiliated who grew up as mainline Protestants now believe that "[m]odern science proves religion is superstition," and 31% identify this belief as an "important reason" they became unaffiliated."*[8] Of course, most of these people don't know how REAL science has actually proven the Bible to be true many times over with DNA research, the geology of the great flood, archaeology, and now earth curvature tests. Another thing that most people don't know is that a lot of so-called "modern science" (much of which originated during the Renaissance), particularly

---

[7] https://www.christianpost.com/news/hillsong-writer-reveals-hes-no-longer-a-christian-im-genuinely-losing-my-faith.html

[8] https://religionnews.com/2015/11/30/are-young-people-losing-their-faith-because-of-science/

having to do with the origin and nature of the cosmos and mankind, were Satanic, occult superstitions and philosophies.

The heliocentric (sun-centered) deception began with a Roman Catholic man from Poland that believed occult Hermetic philosophy and theology. Nicolaus Copernicus was one of the first to postulate that the earth was a moving planet which orbits the sun. He was clearly part of a Roman Catholic family. His uncle was a Roman Catholic Bishop who took Copernicus under his wing at age 10 after his father died. Copernicus' brother Andrew became an Augustine canon and his sister Barbara became a Benedictine nun. Copernicus studied in Italy and eventually received his doctorate in Canon law.

Some try to deny or downplay his connection to the Roman Catholic Church but let us not forget to whom Copernicus dedicated his book called *On the Revolutions of the Heavenly Spheres* which presented the heliocentric theory...Pope Paul III. And although some try to deny that Copernicus became a priest, The Catholic Encyclopedia states that his ordination to the priesthood was probable because in 1537 he was one of four candidates for the episcopal seat of Warmia, a position which required ordination.[9] Another clue that he did indeed become a Roman Catholic priest was that he never married.

However, the most disturbing fact about Nicolaus Copernicus was that his sun-centered universe theory actually came from the demonic writings of Hermes Trismegistus that regained popularity during the Renaissance. The occult philosophies of Hermes

---

[9] https://en.m.wikipedia.org/wiki/Nicolaus_Copernicus

Trismegistus can be traced back to ancient Egypt and a priest of the sun god by the name of Imhotep. An ancient inscription calls Imhotep *"(... 'the one who comes in peace' late 27th century BC) was an Egyptian chancellor to the pharaoh Djoser, probable architect of the Djoser's step pyramid, **and high priest of the sun god Ra at Heliopolis.** Very little is known of Imhotep as a historical figure, but in the 3000 years following his death, he was gradually glorified and deified. **Traditions from long after Imhotep's death treated him as a great author of wisdom texts...** The Hermetic literature among the Egyptians, **which was concerned with conjuring spirits and animating statues, inform the oldest Hellenistic writings on Greco-Babylonian astrology and on the newly developed practice of alchemy...***

The Hermetica is a category of papyri containing spells and initiatory induction procedures. The dialogue called the Asclepius (after the Greek god of healing) describes the art of imprisoning the souls of demons or of angels in statues with the help of herbs, gems, and odors, so that the statue could speak and engage in prophecy. In other papyri, there are recipes for constructing such images and animating them, such as when images are to be fashioned hollow so as to enclose a magic name inscribed on gold leaf."[10]

---

[10] https://en.wikipedia.org/wiki/Imhotep & *Egyptian Saints: Deification in Pharaonic Egypt* by D. Wildung ©1977 pg. 34

A research paper by Dr. Marina P. Banchetti, a professor at Florida Atlantic University in Miami, Florida entitled, *The Influence of Renaissance Hermeticism on the Scientific Revolution,* reveals the fact that Copernicus was not just influenced by sun-worshipping Egyptian hermeticism, but he also strongly believed in it. Copernicus even quoted Hermes Trismegistus directly in the first chapter of his revolutionary departure from the geocentric Ptolemaic understanding of the cosmos (which is the Biblical revelation of creation), sounding more like a priest of sun-worship than a scientist.

Long before Copernicus published his heliocentric cosmology presenting the idea of the sun holding a central place in creation, Egyptian sun-worship via hermeticism had already infiltrated the Renaissance through the writings of Ficino and other thinkers *"...who were influenced by the Neopythagorean and hermetic idea of the sun as divine. Since hermetic thought held the sun to be either itself divine or a manifestation of the divine in the physical universe,*

*Renaissance Platonist like Ficino, **who inherited these ideas from the hermetic tradition, held that the sun had both metaphysical and physical centrality in the cosmos. Ficino's Liber de sole (1487) makes the hermetic origins of sun-worship quite explicit.** He states: '...in the heavens, definite spaces are noted, in regard to the sun itself, within which the planets wander and regularly change their motions. At conjunction with the sun, they are at the highest point of their epicycles, at opposition they are at the lowest point, and in quadrature they are at mean altitude. **The Chaldeans, the Egyptians, and others all locate the sun, like a Lord, in the center of the world, although for different reasons so that the sun, which proceeds as a king, takes the middle way.'**

Despite the clearly religious and theosophical undertones of these ideas, one cannot overestimate the impact they had on the development of the heliocentric cosmology in the work of Copernicus and on its positive reception by such scientist as Kepler and Galileo. In fact, the general agreement between Ficino's ideas regarding the sun and those of Copernicus is not merely coincidental, nor is Copernicus advocacy of a central sign in merely coincidental agreement with Neil Pythagorean mysticism. In the first chapter of **On the Revolution of the Celestial Spheres** (1543), Copernicus is very explicit in his references to the Neoplatonic and Neopythagorean mystical traditions that were embraced by Ficino and other Renaissance Platonist and hermeticists. Here, the language used by Copernicus is not the language that one might expect from a scientist who is systematically and socially committed to strictly rational method, unencumbered by spiritual or mystical considerations. **Rather, in the first chapter of this groundbreaking work, Copernicus describes the sun by using this sort of language that one would expect from an***

Egyptian high priest or hermetic adept. He writes "...*in the middle of all sits the sun enthroned. In this most beautiful temple could we place this luminary in any better position from which he can illuminate the whole at once? He is rightly called the Lamp, the Mind, the Ruler of the Universe; Hermès Trismegistus names him the Visible God, Sophocles' Electra calls him the All-seeing. So, the Sun sits upon a royal throne ruling his children the planets which circle around him.*"[11]

This clearly exposes that the source of Copernicus' heliocentric, sun-in-the-center theory came from Satan's Egyptian sun-worshipping mystery religions instead of pure scientific observations. And when you consider that Newton and Kepler were also part of this hermetic occult philosophy, it becomes quite obvious that Satan and his fallen angels were directly involved in creating a model of the universe that would contradict and oppose the truth revealed by God to His prophets and apostles in the Bible. Therefore, it should be no surprise that the Vatican, known as the Great Whore or Mystery Babylon in the book of Revelation, has been involved in perpetrating the deceptions of false science from

---

[11] https://www.academia.edu/7072076/The_Influence_of_Renaissance_Hermeticism_o n_the_Scientific_Revolution

Copernicus to the Big Bang theory to the coming "alien" deception. The Jesuit astronomer Guy Consolmagno reminds us of their involvement in all this...

"But, in fact, astronomy was part of the original seven subjects of the medieval universities, and those universities were themselves founded by the Church. The 'father of geology' who first described and classified minerals was the Dominican monk known today as Albert the Great. The 'father of astrophysics' who first classified stars by their spectra was a Jesuit, Angelo Secchi. The modern big bang theory originated with a twentieth-century priest, Georges Lemaître. The Vatican had a direct practical interest in supporting astronomical research when it reformed the calendar in 1582—a work headed by the Jesuit mathematician Christopher Clavius. There's a prominent crater on the Moon named for him (as fans of the movie 2001: A Space Odyssey will recall) along with two dozen other craters named for Jesuit astronomers. No surprise; the fellow who drew the map and named the craters, the basis of all our modern Moon maps, was himself the Jesuit priest Francesco Grimaldi. (He also invented the wave theory of light)."[12]

In other words, much of so-called "science" is from Satanic occult, esoteric beliefs designed by the ultimate Deceiver to turn people away from believing the Bible and finding the true Creator, our Lord Jesus Christ. And (as you will see) this cult of Copernicus has been carried on not only by the sun-god worshipping Jesuit priests, but also modern Freemasons, former Nazi Vril/Thule Society members, and high-level   deep   state,   New   World   Order

---

[12] *Brother Astronomer: Adventures of a Vatican Scientist* by Brother Guy Consolmagno JS pg.2 ©2000 McGraw-Hill

Satanists/Luciferians in various governments and "space" agencies. And sadly, even many Christians choose to believe those Satanic liars over the Holy Spirit-inspired Word of Almighty God in the Bible.

But the God of the Bible, the true Creator foretold this conspiracy over three thousand years ago through His beloved King David, *"Why are the nations in an uproar [in turmoil against God], and why do the people devise a vain and hopeless plot? The kings of the earth take their stand; and the rulers take counsel together against the Lord and His Anointed (the Davidic King, the Messiah, the Lord Jesus Christ), saying, 'Let us break apart their [divine] bands [of restraint] And cast away their cords [of control] from us.'* He who sits [enthroned] in the heavens laughs [at their rebellion]; The [Sovereign] Lord scoffs at them [and in supreme contempt He mocks them]. Then He will speak to them in His [profound] anger and terrify them with His displeasure, saying, 'Yet as for Me, I have anointed and firmly installed My King upon Zion, My holy mountain. *I will declare the decree of the Lord: He said to Me, 'You are My Son; This day [I proclaim] I have begotten You. Ask of Me, and I will assuredly give [You] the nations as Your inheritance, and the ends of the earth as Your possession.* You shall break them with a rod of iron; You shall shatter them [in pieces] like earthenware.' Now therefore, O kings, act wisely; Be instructed and take warning, O leaders (judges, rulers) of the earth. *Worship the Lord and serve Him with reverence [with awe-inspired fear and submissive wonder]; Rejoice [yet do so] with trembling. Kiss (pay respect to) the Son (Jesus Christ), so that He does not become angry, and you perish in the way, For His wrath may soon be kindled and set aflame. How blessed [fortunate, prosperous, and favored by God] are all those who take refuge in Him!"* (Psalms 2:1-12).

The reason for their many deceptions and this sophisticated plot against the God of the Bible and His Anointed is simple: Satan and his servants want to keep everyone away from the truth of salvation and eternal life that is ONLY found in the Lord Jesus Christ of the Bible. They want to keep people from understanding the issue of sin and the penalty for sin against God (which is death and eternal damnation in hell for the wickedness and evil that we have committed). Satan does not want people to understand how God's love for us was demonstrated when He became a man to pay that death penalty for us on the cross. And he wants to prevent as many people as possible from knowing and accepting the truth that the ONLY WAY to be forgiven of our sins and enter into a right relationship with our Creator is to believe in Jesus and turn from our wicked ways. We must believe in who Jesus is and what He did for us on the cross and through His resurrection from the dead. That is why these deceivers have been trying to hide God by hiding the truth about creation – it is all a plot to keep us from the One True God and eternal life. God is not a distant Creator in a vast universe, He is closer than even most Christians realize.

Just to be crystal clear, the Jesus Christ of the Bible is NOT the New Age version that teaches Jesus was just a man who discovered the "Universal Christ Consciousness." Deceived people are flocking to the New Age philosophies of people like Eckhart Tolle, Oprah Winfrey, Deepak Chopra, Franciscan Friar Richard Rohr and 2020 Presidential candidate Marianne Williamson that claim we can all become "Christ" through eastern-style meditation and visualization. These deceptions are nothing new. One of the first lies that Satan told Eve in the garden was that she could become a god by disobeying the One True God, the Creator. The Lord Jesus warned about this specific last days deception when He was asked by His disciples about the signs of His coming and the end of the world and He responded, *"Take heed that no man deceive you.* ***For many shall come in my name, saying, I am Christ; and shall deceive many"*** (Matthew 24:4-5).

The Jesus Christ of the Bible is God Almighty who became a man to pay the penalty of our sin by His personal sacrifice on the cross. And then being God the Creator and Giver of Life, He rose bodily from the tomb after being dead for three days. The Jesus Christ of the Bible is God the Creator, the fullness of the Godhead bodily, the Word (Logos) made flesh, the Messiah, the Son of God, the High Priest, the Good Shepherd, the Door, the Alpha and Omega, the Beginning and the Ending, the Lamb of God, the Resurrection and the Life, the Way, the Truth, and the Light of the World. Isaiah 9:6 declares Jesus to be the Wonderful Counsellor, the Mighty God, the Everlasting Father and the Prince of Peace. The book of Revelation declares Jesus to be the King of kings and the LORD of lords. He is the ONLY way to find forgiveness of sins and eternal life.

*"In the beginning was the Word, and the Word was with God, and the Word was God. The same was in the beginning with God. **All things were made by him; and without him was not anything made that was made.** In him was life; and the life was the light of men. And the light shineth in darkness; and the darkness comprehended it not… **And the Word was made flesh, and dwelt among us, (and we beheld his glory, the glory as of the only begotten of the Father,) full of grace and truth.** John bare witness of him, and cried, saying, This was he of whom I spake, He that cometh after me is preferred before me: for he was before me. And of his fulness have all we received, and grace for*

*grace. **For the law was given by Moses, but grace and truth came by Jesus Christ"*** (John 1:1-5 & 14-17).

Chapter 2

The Vril Society & Operation Paperclip

*"So Saul died for his transgression which he committed against the Lord, even against the word of the Lord, which he kept not, **and also for asking counsel of one that had a familiar spirit** (a medium or channeler)**, to enquire of it; And enquired not of the Lord: therefore he slew him, and turned the kingdom unto David the son of Jesse"* (1 Chronicles 10:13-14).

"But evil men and seducers shall wax worse and worse, deceiving, and being deceived" (2 Timothy 3:13)

"We must be alert to the...danger that public policy could itself become the captive of a scientific technological elite." – President Eisenhower's farewell speech given January 17, 1961

When President Eisenhower was pressed by Herbert York (the first director of ARPA which later became DARPA) to clarify what or who he meant in the warning he issued in his farewell speech, without hesitation Eisenhower answered,

"Wernher von Braun (NASA) and *Edward Teller* (father of the hydrogen bomb)."[13] It doesn't take long when doing research on the Satanic plot to deceive mankind about the true nature of God's creation, to uncover the individuals and occult societies that have pushed demonic ideas such as aliens, distant galaxies, and space travel into the mainstream. When exploring this topic, it is important to realize that the demon-inspired philosophies and secret societies that spawned the wicked Nazi Party in Germany also ultimately forged the deeply held beliefs of its Nazi SS officers and scientists like Wernher Von Braun who were part of early rocket development. And for those who may not know, the Nazi SS was a German military branch that was brutal, evil and fiercely loyal to Hitler and the Nazi ideals. Occult groups like the Thule Society, Knights Templar/Freemasons, Vril Society and the SS Black Sun have all worked together to further Satan's agenda. Although some over the years have tried to discredit information regarding the occult roots of the Nazis, Heinrich Himmler (the leader of the SS and one of the main architects of the Holocaust) had the occult symbol of the Black Sun placed in the floor of his Wewelsburg Castle. Directly under the Black Sun was a swastika on the ceiling of the room below that was used for occult ceremonies and rituals.

---

[13] *Arms and the Physicist* by Herbert F. York ©1995 The American Institute of Physics Woodbury, NY

The Vril Society was formed in 1917 by two women who were mediums and four men. This group met at the Schopenhauer café in Vienna to discuss topics such as the coming New Age, secret revelations, the Spear of Destiny, and the magical, violet black stone. They spoke of making contact with the ancient Germanic and Babylonian deities like Ishtar, Astarte, and Osiris and of communicating with distant worlds in "outer space." The originating members of the Vril Society included the occultist Karl Haushofer, Baron Rudolf von Sebottendorf, WWI ace pilot Lothar Waiz, Prelate Gernot of the secret "Societas Templi Marcioni" *(The Inheritors of the Knights Templar)* and Maria Orsic, a medium.

Let's not forget that, *"...the Freemasons also have been connected with a mysterious order called the Knights Templar. These knights were (Roman Catholic) monks who took up arms in 1118 A.D. in order to protect Christian pilgrims traveling from Jaffa (a port city in Israel) to Jerusalem. According to legend, the Knights Templar discovered the greatest treasure in history buried in the ruins of King Solomon's temple. The Knights became rich— so rich, in fact, that they were the targets of envy and*

suspicion. *In 1307, King Philip IV of France had all of the Knights Templar arrested so that he could take possession of their great wealth.* **What happened to the Knights after their imprisonment remains a mystery, but some say they went into hiding and continued their work in secret, <u>only to reemerge in Europe during the 1700s as the modern Freemasons.</u>**"[14] So this makes it clear that one of the founders of the Vril Society was a high-level Freemason.

The term "Vril" and many of the occult concepts of the group came from an 1871 novel called ***The Coming Race*** by Edward Bulwer-Lytton. It is reported that Bulwer-Lytton was a member of the occult secret society of the Rosicrucians. *"'The book describes a race of men psychically far in advance of our own. They have acquired powers over themselves and over things that made them almost godlike. For the moment they are in hiding. They are said to live in caves in the center of the Earth. 'Soon they will emerge to reign over us.' While researching their classic book,* **Morning of the Magicians**, *authors Jacques Bergier and Louis Pauwels were given the above account by one of the world's greatest rocket experts,* **Dr. Willy Ley, who fled Germany in 1933. Dr. Ley said that the Vril Society - which formed shortly before the Nazis came to power - believed they had secret knowledge that would enable them to change their race and become equals of the men hidden in the bowels of the earth.** *Methods of concentration, a whole system of internal gymnastics by which they would be transformed.*

In Lytton's The Coming Race, the subterranean people use the Vril Force to operate and govern the world (a few

---

[14] https://science.howstuffworks.com/dictionary/awards-organizations/freemason1.htm

children armed with vril-powered rods are said capable of exterminating a race of over 22 million threatening barbarians). Served by robots and able to fly on vril-powered wings, the vegetarian Vril-ya are - by their own reckoning - racially and culturally superior to everyone else on Earth, above or below the ground. At one point the narrator concludes (from linguistic evidence) that the Vril-ya are "...descended from the same ancestors as the great Aryan family, from which in varied streams has flowed the dominant civilization of the world.'

The Vril Force or Vril Energy was said to be derived from the Black Sun, a big ball of 'Prima Materia' which supposedly exists in the center of the Earth, giving light to the Vril-ya and putting out radiation in the form of Vril. The Vril Society believed that Aryans were the actual biological ancestors of the Black Sun. This force was known to the ancients under many names, and it has been called Chi, Ojas, Vril, Astral Light, Odic Forces and Orgone.

In a discussion of the 28th degree of the Ancient and Accepted Scottish Rite of Freemasonry - called Knight of the Sun or Prince Adept - Albert Pike said, **'There is in nature one most potent force, by means whereof a single man, who could possess himself of it, and should know how to direct it, could revolutionize and change the face of the world.'** This is the force that the Nazis and their inner occult circle were so desperately trying to unleash upon the world, for which the Vril Society had apparently groomed Hitler. A manifestation of the 'Great Work' promulgated by the Adepts of secret societies throughout the ages."[15]

---

[15] https://www.bibliotecapleyades.net/sociopolitica/sociopol_vril01.htm

In December 1919, members of the Thule Society, Vril Society and other occultists rented a small lodge near Berchtesgaden, Germany. Maria Orsic and another medium who is only known as Sigrun, joined them. Maria claimed to have received telepathic/medium transmissions (what New Agers today would call channeling) in a language unknown to her containing technical information for building a flying machine that could reach distant galaxies (space travel). Vril documents mention that these telepathic messages originated in Aldebaran, a solar system 68 light-years away in the constellation Taurus. By 1943, Orsic claimed that subsequent messages from the "aliens" in Aldebaran revealed that there were two habitable planets orbiting that star and that the ancient Sumerians were linked to the aliens there.

As crazy as this Maria Orsic tale sounds, just before sitting down to write this chapter, I read a Yahoo News Business Insider article entitled, *"Earth-like planets in our home galaxy, new research reveals."* The articles states, **"Our galaxy could be littered with warm, watery planets like earth.** *That's the conclusion of researchers at Penn State University, who used data from NASA's Kepler telescope to estimate the number of earth-like planets in the Milky Way. Their results, published in The Astronomical Journal this*

*week, suggest that an earth-like planet orbits one in every four sun-like stars. Totaled up, that means there could be up to 10 billion earth-like worlds in our home galaxy. **The estimate is an important step in the search for alien life**, since any potential life on other planets would most likely be found on an earth-like world warm enough to hold liquid water.* "[16]

But how did they come to this amazing conclusion that there could be 10 billion earth-like planets with possible "alien" life in our home galaxy? Would you believe that they made this incredible claim based on seeing tiny dips in a star's brightness through a telescope? The articled continued, *"The researchers' estimate is based on data from NASA's Kepler space telescope. Launched in 2009, the telescope used what's known as the transit method to find worlds outside our solar system. **It watched over 530,000 stars for tiny dips in a star's brightness that could be caused by a planet passing in front of it — transits, in other words.**"* [17]

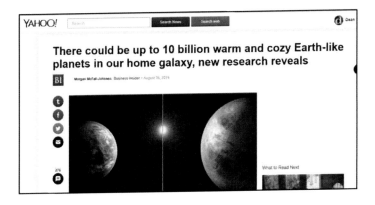

---

[16] https://news.yahoo.com/could-10-billion-warm-cozy-172800606.html
[17] Same as reference #11

Yes, a star twinkled and NASA "experts" and their space/fairytale-worshipping trainee students deduce that the dip in brightness is an earth-like planet with the potential for "alien" life. Then, NASA artists jump into creative mode to provide beautiful space art of what they IMAGINE the new planets look like. It is the same load of baloney that Maria Orsic channeled in 1919, but now people embrace it because the secret societies call it "science." As a matter of fact, Dr. Steven Greer of the Sirius Disclosure Project does the exact same thing when he takes people out in the desert and uses occult Buddhist meditation techniques to channel and contact "UFOs."[18]

Members of the Vril Society are said to have included Adolf Hitler, Alfred Rosenberg, Heinrich Himmler, Hermann Göring, and Hitler's personal physician, Dr. Theodor Morell. These were original members of the Thule Society that supposedly joined Vril in 1919. The NSDAP (National Sozialistische Deutsche ArbeiterPartei) was created by Thule in 1920. Dr. Krohn, who helped to create the Nazi flag, was also a Thulist. And it was this atmosphere of occult philosophies and science fiction about "space" travel and "aliens" that the young Wernher von Braun grew up in, later becoming a decorated Nazi SS officer (who used slave labor, torture, and death to build his V2 rockets for Hitler). Von Braun eventually became the head of the United States rocket program and the head of NASA and the so-called Apollo "moon missions."

Some try to blow off any talk about the Vril Society and Nazi occultism by saying it's just a conspiracy theory or a bunch of nuts that believed a stupid novel. However, leading Luciferian Theosophists like Helena Blavatsky, William

---

[18] https://siriusdisclosure.com/expeditions/

Scott-Elliot, and Rudolf Steiner accepted *The Coming Race* as a book based on occult truth. And I assure you that Ms. Blavatsky who was the founder of *Lucifer Magazine*, Lucifer Publishing Company and author of *The Secret Doctrine* (in which she declares Lucifer the Serpent to be God and the Holy Spirit) was not duped by something that was just a novel. Furthermore, the plot and occult beliefs in *The Coming Race* can clearly be seen in the twisted philosophy of Hitler and his Nazi officers from the superiority of the Aryan race to the mass extermination of the undesirable "barbarians."

It is alleged that the Vril Society established contact with the "Secret Chiefs" or the "Vril-ya" themselves, and secretly began working with certain German scientists in the late 20's. It is no coincidence that in 1936, Hitler started sending teams into caves and mines all over the world searching for the "Vril-ya." As usual, Hollywood mixed fact and fiction when they included this scenario in the plot of *Raiders of the Lost Ark*. In 1937 and 1938 the Nazis finally explored Antarctica extensively and then all of a sudden stopped searching and built secret bases there. It has been said that Antarctica is where they made contact with the "Unknown Superman" who lived in the fabled "Rainbow City." And it is extensively researched and documented that the Nazis did have and may still have secret bases in Antarctica where contact with the "aliens" is ongoing.[19] This would definitely explain all of the quick, covert visits to Antarctica by world leaders in the last few years.

This contact with "aliens" would also help shine light on these strange statements made by two well-known Nazi scientists:

Wernher von Braun said this in 1959, *"We find ourselves faced by powers which are far stronger than hitherto assumed, and whose base is at present unknown to us. More I cannot say at present. **We are now engaged in entering closer contact with those powers**, and within six or nine months time, it may be possible to speak with more precision on the matter."*

Dr. Hermann Oberth, who pioneered rocket design for the German Reich during World War II and later advanced rocket technology for the American manned space launches, cryptically stated, ***"We cannot take the credit for our record advancement in certain scientific fields alone; we have been helped."*** When asked by whom, he replied: ***"The people of other worlds."*** [20]

It is interesting to note here that Wernher von Braun participated in a U.S. government expedition to Antarctica in 1967.[21] Allegedly it was to search for meteorites, but I believe it was to make "contact" with those powers that he alluded to in 1959. And just to be clear again, I do not believe in "ETs" or "aliens" from other planets or galaxies far, far

---

[19] *Empire Beneath the Ice: How the Nazis Won World War II* by Stephen Quayle ©2015 End Time Thunder Publishers

[20] https://www.bibliotecapleyades.net/ciencia/ciencia_flyingobjects55.htm

[21] https://www.newworldencyclopedia.org/entry/Wernher_von_Braun

away. I believe that Satan, his fallen angels, and their half-breed offspring called the Nephilim or Rephaim are deceiving people into believing they are "aliens." They have loyal human accomplices that know exactly what they are but they lie and deceive right along with Satan and his evil entities. It is a plan that Satan has been unfolding for many years and although he has been announcing it through his people using various avenues, most don't see it.

In the 1998 *X-Files: Fight the Future* movie, Agent Scully is stung by a bee that infects her with an "alien" virus. Scully collapses and her partner Agent Mulder calls an ambulance. After loading Agent Scully into the ambulance, the driver shoots Mulder. Not severely injured, Mulder is able to slip out of the hospital to go find Scully. He meets a man that gives him her location and the vaccine. Mulder finds Scully in a large underground facility in Antarctica where humans are being kept in strange enclosures. They make it to the surface and escape just as a massive "alien" spaceship breaks through from beneath the ice and flies away into the sky, validating Mulder's lifelong search for "aliens." Was *Fight the Future* just a movie or was it Illuminati/Luciferian pre-programming for their coming grand finale of deception? I know what I believe.

Operation Paperclip

"After WWII ended in 1945, victorious Russian and American intelligence teams began a treasure hunt throughout occupied Germany for military and scientific booty. They were looking for things like new rocket and aircraft designs, medicines, and electronics. But they were also hunting down the most precious "spoils" of all: the scientists whose work had nearly won the war for Germany.

The engineers and intelligence officers of the Nazi War Machine.

The U.S. Military rounded up Nazi scientists and brought them to America. It had originally intended merely to debrief them and send them back to Germany. But when it realized the extent of the scientists knowledge and expertise, the War Department decided it would be a waste to send the scientists home. Following the discovery of flying discs (foo fighters), particle/laser beam weaponry in German military bases, the War Department decided that NASA and the CIA must control this technology, and the Nazi engineers that had worked on this technology.

There was only one problem: it was illegal. U.S. law explicitly prohibited Nazi officials from immigrating to America--and as many as three-quarters of the scientists in question had been committed Nazis.

Take for example, Nazi officer Arthur Rudolph, during the war, **Rudolph was operations director of the Mittelwerk factory at the Dora-Nordhausen concentration camps, where 20,000 workers died from beatings, hangings, and starvation.** *Rudolph had been a member of the Nazi party since 1931; a 1945 military file on him said simply:* **'100% Nazi, dangerous type, security threat..!! Suggest internment.'**

But the JIOA's final dossier on him said there was **'nothing in his records indicating that he was a war criminal or an ardent Nazi or otherwise objectionable.' Rudolph became a US citizen and later designed the Saturn 5 rocket used in the Apollo moon landings. In 1984, when** *his war record was finally investigated, he fled to West Germany.*"[22]

And guess who worked right beside Arthur Rudolf at the slave-labor/death Mittelwerk factory building Hitler's V2 rockets that indiscriminately killed civilian men, women, and children? None other than the golden boy of NASA, Disney star of "space" propaganda, and head of the American space/Apollo programs - Baron Wernher von Braun.

The 1963 book *"The Secret of Huntsville: The True Career of Rocket Baron Wernher von Braun"* by popular author and lawyer Julius Mader depicted von Braun as a passionate and enthusiastic Nazi. ***"On the dust jacket of the book, there was a drawing of von Braun wearing a black SS-Sturmbannfuhrer's uniform. Around von Braun's neck was the Knight's Cross."***[23] The Knight's Cross of the Iron Cross was given to recognize extreme battlefield bravery or successful leadership and was one of Nazi Germany's most prestigious and famous awards - the Western equivalent might be the US Medal of Honor.

---

[22] http://www.conspiracyarchive.com/NWO/project_paperclip.htm

[23] *Operation Paperclip* by Annie Jacobsen ©2014 Little, Brown and Company New York pg. 399

Annie Jacobsen, Princeton alum and author of the *New York Times* bestselling book *Area 51*, wrote the definitive exposé on *Operation Paperclip* and the Nazi scientists that formed our space program. Her research included exclusive interviews with dozens of Paperclip family members, colleagues, and interrogators, access to German archival documents (including previously unseen papers made available by direct descendants of the Third Reich's ranking members), files obtained through the Freedom of Information Act, and dossiers discovered in government archives and at Harvard University. Her book, *Operation Paperclip: The Secret Intelligence Program That Brought Nazi Scientists to America* follows more than a dozen Nazi scientists through their postwar lives. She reveals just how dark government can get in the name of national security.

"In the chaos following World War II, the U.S. government faced many difficult decisions, including what to do with the Third Reich's scientific minds. These were the brains behind the Nazis' once-indomitable war machine. So began Operation Paperclip, a decades-long, covert project to bring Hitler scientists (around 1,600) *and their families to the United States.*

Many of these men were accused of war crimes, and others had stood trial at Nuremberg; **one was convicted of mass murder and slavery.** *They were also directly*

64

responsible for major advances in rocketry, medical treatments, and the US space program."[24]

Annie Jacobsen also documents that Wernher von Braun was in charge of the Mittelwerk V2 factory in Nordhausen:

"The underground factory at Nordhausen had been in operation since late August 1943, after a Royal Air Force attack on the Peenemünde facility up north forced armaments production to move elsewhere. The day after that attack, Heinrich Himmler, Reichsfuhrer-SS, paid a visit to Hitler and proposed they move rocket production underground. **Hitler agreed, and the SS was put in charge of supplying slaves and overseeing facilities construction.** *The individual in charge of expanding Nordhausen from a mine to a tunnel complex was Brigadier General Hans Kammler, a civil engineer and architect who, earlier in his career, built the gas chambers at Auschwitz-Birkenau.*

The first group of 107 slave laborers arrived Mittelwork in late August 1943. They came from Buchenwald concentration camp, located fifty miles to the southeast. The wrought-iron sign over the Buchenwald gate read Jedem das Seine, 'Everyone gets what he deserves.' **Digging tunnels was hard labor, but the SS feared prisoners might revolt if they had mining tools, so the men dug with their bare hands.**

Notable among the staff, and important to Operation Paperclip, was the man in charge of production, a high school graduate named Arthur Rudolph. Rudolph's specialty was rocket engine assembly. **He had worked under von**

[24] Operation Paperclip by Annie Jacobsen ©2014 Little, Brown and Company New York cover flap

Braun in this capacity since 1934. *Rudolph was a Nazi ideologue; he joined the party before there was any national pressure to do so, in 1931. What he lacked in academic pedigree he made up for as a slave-driver. As the Mittelwerk operations director, Rudolph worked with the SS construction staff to build the underground factory.* **Then he oversaw production on the assembly lines for V-weapons scientific director Wernher von Braun.**

The prisoners worked twelve-hour shifts, seven days-a-week, putting together V-weapons. By the end of the first two months there were eight thousand men living and working in this cramped underground space. There was no fresh air in the tunnels, no ventilation system, no water, and very little light. 'Blasting went on day and night and the dust after every blast was so thick that it was impossible to see five steps ahead,' read one report. Laborers slept inside the tunnels on the wood bunkbeds. There were no washing facilities and no sanitation. The trains were barrels cut in half. The workers suffered and died from starvation, dysentery, pleurisy, pneumonia, tuberculosis, and phlegmasia from beatings. The men were walking skeletons, skin stretched over bones. Some perished from ammonia burns to the lungs. Others died by being crushed from the weight of the rocket parts they were forced to carry. The dead were replaceable. Humans and machine parts went into the tunnels. Rockets and corpses came out. Workers who were slow on the production lines were beaten to death. Insubordinates were garroted or hanged. After the war, war crimes investigators determined that approximately half of the sixty thousand men eventually brought to Nordhausen were worked to death. "[25]

---

[25] *Operation Paperclip* by Annie Jacobsen ©2014 Little, Brown and Company New York, pp. 13 & 14

The truth about the Nordhausen V2 facility should not be surprising to anyone familiar with WW2 history. The Nazi SS officers and soldiers were known for this kind of evil and brutality. However, many people don't know or ignore the crucial fact that Nazi SS officer Wernher von Braun was in charge of that underground torture chamber. He should have swung from the gallows at Nuremberg for his crimes, but he escaped justice. Years later, Wernher von Braun downplayed his Nazi past and a famous biography conveniently left it all out. The US government also helped keep it all quiet.

"The US military also was active in 'transforming' German Nazis into honest German scientist. The Joint Intelligence Objectives Agency (JIOA) had actually started collecting German scientist in May 1945 (even though President Truman didn't formally order to do so as 'Operation Paperclip' until August of that year).

Furthermore, when the President finally did give his order to create Operation Paperclip, it was with the understanding that any German who was even a member of the Nazi party or an 'active supporter of Nazi militarism' was to be excluded from the project. This would have made most of the

German rocket scientist including Wernher von Braun and others involved in both rocketry as well as nuclear research ineligible to bring to the US under the terms of the President's directive.

To circumvent the President's intent (as well as the requirements of the Allied Potsdam and Yalta agreements), the JIOA created false employment and political biographies for scientist, even going so far as to expunge their names from Nazi party membership lists. **With fake documents and newly cleaned records, the former Nazi scientists were granted security clearances to work in programs that would eventually become NASA.**"[26]

Consider the strangeness around the Nuremberg Tribunal that tried Nazi war criminals. *"Obvious war criminals like Reichmarschall Goring, Field Marshal Wilhelm Keitel, Army Chief of Operations Staff Colonel-General Alfred Jodl, are sent swinging from the gallows, or, in Goring's case, cheating the hangman by swallowing cyanide.*

Other Nazi bigwigs like Grand Admiral Karl Donitz, mastermind of Germany's devastating U-boat campaign against Allied shipping, or Minister of Armaments Albert Speer, or Finance Minister and Reichsbank President Hjalmar Horace Greeley Schacht, were imprisoned.

Missing from the docket of the accused, of course, were the Pennemunde rocket scientists headed by Dr. Wernher von Braun and General Walter Dornberger, already headed to America to take charge of America's ballistic missile and

---

[26] *Project Paperclip: German Scientists and the Cold War* by Clarence G. Lasby ©1975 Scribner as quoted by Steve Quayle in Empire Beneath the Ice, pp. 166 & 167

space programs along with a host of scientists, engineers and technicians under the then super secret Project Paperclip.

They, like their nuclear physics counterparts in Germany, had seemingly suffered from a similar 'bungler's malady,' for once having produced the first successful V-1 and V-2 prototypes comparatively early in the war, they suffered a similar lack of inspiration and ingenuity and (so the Legend goes) managed to produce only 'paper rockets' and theoretical study projects after that.

But perhaps most significantly, by joint agreement of the Allied and Soviet prosecutors at Nuremberg, missing from evidence in the tribunal was the vast amount of documentary evidence implicating the Nazi regime in occult belief systems and practice."[27]

Why did they hide *"...the vast amount of documentary evidence"* implicating the Nazi regime and their occult (Satanic) belief systems and practice? They hid those Satanic and secret society roots of the Nazi scientists because those inconvenient truths would not have gone over well with the far more conservative Christian America of the late 1940s and 1950s. But, the more sinister reason for hiding the occult beliefs was that the Satanic/Luciferian cabal in America (and Russia) had plans not only for weapons development, but a complex hoax. This scheme of theirs would turn many away from trusting the Biblical account of creation and ultimately keep them from finding Jesus Christ as the One True God, Creator, and personal Savior from sin and eternal judgment.

---

[27] *Reich of the Black Sun: Nazi Secret Weapons & the Cold War Allied Legend* by Joseph P. Farrell (c)2004 Adventures Unlimited Press, Ch. 1

This is what the spiritual war has been about since Lucifer rebelled against God and Adam and Eve were created.

Chapter 3

Parsons, Crowley & NASA's Freemasons

*"But there was a certain man, called Simon, **which beforetime in the same city used sorcery, and bewitched the people of Samaria, giving out that himself was some great one:** To whom they all gave heed, from the least to the greatest, saying, This man is the great power of God. And to him they had regard, **because that of long time he had bewitched them with sorceries"** (Acts 8:9-11).*

*"**The Masonic Movement is the custodian of the law; it is the home of the mysteries, and the seat of initiation.** It holds in its' symbolism the ritual of deity* (their god Lucifer aka Satan), *and the way of salvation is pictorially preserved in its work. The methods of deity are demonstrated in its Temples, and under the All-seeing Eye the work can go forward. **It is a far more occult organisation than can be realised, and it is intended to be the training school for the coming advanced occultists...***

There is no dissociation between the One Universal Church (the Roman Catholic Church and the

71

infiltrated/polluted part of Christianity) *the sacred inner Lodge of all true Masons, and the innermost circles of the esoteric societies. The Three types of men have their need met, three major rays are expressed, and the three paths to the Master are trodden, leading all three to the same portal and the same Hierophant.*"[28] – Alice Bailey (Disciple of Helen Blavatsky & Occultist Medium for the United Nations)

"And they worshipped the dragon (Satan/Lucifer) *which gave power unto the beast: and they worshipped the beast, saying, Who is like unto the beast? who is able to make war with him?"* (Revelation 13:4)

Is it a coincidence that the man that Wernher von Braun declared to be *"...the true father of the American space race"*[29] was also deep into Satanic occult beliefs and practices? I'm referring to John Whiteside "Jack" Parsons, the founder of the Jet Propulsion Laboratory and the Aerojet Engineering Corporation. He also *"...invented the first rocket engine to use a castable, composite rocket propellant and pioneered the advancement of both liquid-fuel and solid-fuel rockets."*[30]

"In 1939 Parsons became acquainted with the works of English occultist Aleister Crowley who referred to himself as 'The Great Beast 666,' and was referred to by the English media as the *'wickedest man in the world.'*

---

[28] *Externalisation of the Hierarchy* by Alice Bailey p. 511-513

[29] http://www.spacesafetymagazine.com/aerospace-engineering/rocketry/jack-parsons-occult-roots-jpl/

[30] https://en.m.wikipedia.org/wiki/Jack_Parsons_(rocket_engineer)

Crowley was the founder of the Thelemic religion whose practitioners lived by the motto *'Do what thou wilt.'* He had previously enjoyed some success as a mountaineer, having scaled K2 and Kanchenjunga, the 2nd and 3rd highest mountains in the world, respectively. During the Kanchenjunga expedition in 1905, Crowley's fellow mountaineers fell victim to an avalanche. They called to Crowley for help, but rather than assist his dying comrades he did what any good Englishman would do…he put his feet up, made a cup of tea. He then sat and watched them die on the mountain, later claiming that he had 'no sympathy' for his chums.

Afterwards, in 1910, hooked on mysticism and debauchery, Crowley was admitted to another secret society, this time into a group known as the Ordo Templi Orientis, or O.T.O. Crowley quickly rose through the ranks of the O.T.O. and became leader of the English-speaking fraternities. *Although the O.T.O. was originally modeled on principles of <u>Freemasonry</u>, with Crowley at the helm it quickly reinvented itself with the beliefs of the Thelemic religion at* *its core, along with its ideas of free love, debauchery, and 'Sex Magick.'*

Fast forward back to 1939… Parsons and his wife Helen joined the O.T.O.'s Pasadena chapter, known as the Agape Lodge, which was led by Wilfred Smith. He began correspondence with Crowley, and quickly became Crowley's American representative for the O.T.O.

Parsons pursued his occult interests and scientific interests with equal intensity. He purchased a large house on South Orange Grove Avenue, Pasadena, and created a commune, inviting actors, actresses, poets, and writers (including sci-fi master Robert Heinlein and ultimately, sci-fi minor L. Ron Hubbard) to participate in his wild parties. He nicknamed the house 'The Parsonage.' The police were frequent visitors to 'The Parsonage,' receiving reports of naked pregnant women dancing through fire in the garden, loud music, and consumption of illegal substances. Parsons always greeted them at the door and assured the officers that he was a respectable Cal Tech scientist, and therefore they had no cause for alarm, so they duly left him and his entourage in peace.

At work, Parsons was excelling in his rocket developments, and blending his newfound occultism with his work practices by dancing and chanting Crowley's "Hymn to Pan" before the launch of every test rocket. Nobody batted an eyelid at the time, and Von Kármán, who had just arranged government funding for the 'GALCIT Rocket Project' regarded him as a 'delightful screwball.'"[31]

---

[31] http://www.spacesafetymagazine.com/aerospace-engineering/rocketry/jack-parsons-occult-roots-jpl/

I wrote about the relationship between the Satanist O.T.O. leader Aleister Crowley, Jet Propulsion Laboratory founder Jack Parsons and Scientology founder L. Ron Hubbard in my 2012 book entitled *The Polluted Church: From Rome to Kansas City*:

"Aleister Crowley lived from 1875 to 1947 and was the most notorious and powerful practitioner of magic and occult arts of the early twentieth century. He was bisexual, experimented with drugs like peyote, and founded the religion of Thelema and the occult communal society called the Abbey of Thelema (which was a school for witches). Crowley wrote numerous books on occult rituals and witchcraft and was known in his time as "the wickedest man in the world." It is interesting to note that Crowley first became interested in the occult and magic in 1896 after his first homosexual experience that he claimed introduced him to an "immanent deity." Crowley went to India around 1901 and studied various Hindu practices. He then travelled to Egypt in 1904 where he conjured up a spirit that gave him his famous Book of the Law.

As the years passed, Crowley became more popular and is still recognized as the most influential occultists of all time. He spent time with Gerald Gardner who went on to found the religion of Wicca. Crowley also discipled a rocket scientist named Jack Parsons who discipled L. Ron Hubbard, the founder of Scientology. Jack Parsons and Merton's greatest influence, Aldous Huxley, were also friends...

*During my studies, I came across another false prophet that was in regular contact with a female "angel." L. Ron Hubbard was the founder of Scientology and a close friend of Jack Parsons (a disciple of occultist Aleister Crowley). Hubbard lived with Parsons for a time at his Mansion in California (referred to by the band the Eagles as the Hotel California in their song by the same name). Parsons told Aleister Crowley, "[Hubbard] is a gentleman; he has red hair and green eyes, is honest and intelligent, **and we have become great friends. He moved in with me about two months ago,** and although Betty and I are still friendly, she has transferred her sexual attention to Ron. Although he has no formal training in Magick, he has an extraordinary amount of experience and understanding in the field. From some of his experiences, I deduced that he is in direct touch with some higher intelligence, possibly his Guardian Angel. He describes his Angel as a beautiful winged woman with red hair whom he calls the Empress and who has guided him through his life and saved him many times.** He is the most Thelemic person I have ever met and is in complete accord with our own principles."[32]*

Jack Parsons, the "true father of the American space race"[33] and Wernher von Braun, the leader of the American rocket team were both clearly practicing occultists. It is

---

[32] *The Polluted Church: From Rome to Kansas City* by Dean Odle ©2012 Book Baby Publishing Ch. 6 & 11

[33] http://www.spacesafetymagazine.com/aerospace-engineering/rocketry/jack-parsons-occult-roots-jpl/

important to keep this in mind when looking at everything they were involved in, including rockets, "space" travel, "aliens," NASA and their hidden agenda.

The "Extraterrestrial" Occult Connection

It is also important to note that many years before Aleister Crowley and Jack Parsons joined forces, while in New York City in March 1918 Crowley began a series of occult rituals called the Amalantrah Workings. These rituals were performed by what Crowley dubbed "Sexual & Ceremonial Magick," with the intent to summon certain entities to manifest in physical form.

Not surprisingly, one entity did manifest to Crowley and his medium friend. "This entity either called itself 'Lam,' or was named 'Lam' by Crowley. Either way, he considered it to be of interdimensional origin, which was the term then for extraterrestrial…Crowley included the portrait of Lam in his *Dead Souls* exhibition held in Greenwich Village, New York, in 1919.

In that same year it was published as a frontispiece labeled *The Way to Crowley's commentary to Blavatsky's The Voice of the Silence.* Beneath the picture was the following inscription: *'LAM is the Tibetan word for Way or Path, and LAMA is He who Goeth, the specific title of the Gods of Egypt, the Treader of the Path, in Buddhistic phraseology.* Its numerical value is 71, the number of this book.'"[34]

---

[34] Aleister Crowley's Lam & the Little Green Men,
https://www.bibliotecapleyades.net/cienciareal/cienciareal07.htm

Aleister Crowley's sketch or drawing of this evil entity (demon) LAM looks just like the modern depictions of so-called "grey aliens." It also resembles the "alien" in Steven Spielberg's 1982 movie E.T. The Extra-Terrestrial. Be assured that this is no accident. The following is an excellent breakdown of the occult messages and alien deception in the movie E.T.

"Indeed, when Elliot first meets and finally parts with him, E.T. touches Elliot's "third eye." In Hinduism and esoterism, this is the spiritual eye that is awakened through the Kundalini power that is purportedly coiled at the base of the spine, which eventually reaches the third eye for 'enlightenment.' It is also directly connected to sexual potency and energy. You'll also notice that Venus was not left out, but referenced in the closet, with the clear imagery of the star of Venus, the eight-sided star. We also figure out that E.T. is reptilian, since there is a connection between Elliot freeing the frogs and his sympathy for E.T. This is also why E.T. can breathe underwater and resembles a cross between a frog and a turtle.

Further evidence of E.T. as a kind of familiar spirit is the fact that his reptilian "light" evokes Biblical imagery from

Genesis, with the serpent, as well as later New Testament texts where Paul describes the devil as a deceptive 'being of light.' In Hinduism, the Kundalini energy is the serpent energy, again evoking similar themes. Indeed, E.T. even dies, but appears to grant Elliot the power of resurrection, since Elliot's love causes E.T.'s heart to beat again. Indeed, in the DVD commentary, Drew Barrymore makes a bizarre comment that E.T. was like a 'guardian angel for them,' insisting that he was almost real. One of the more odd scenes surrounds the arrival of the government agents who have surveilled Elliot's house. When they arrive, they don't wear Hazmat suits, they arrive as Apollo Mission astronauts.

This is one of the more interesting aspects of the film. Why? After this scene, the doctors and scientists all wear Hazmat suits, and we never see anything like this again. There are several possibilities, but my speculation is that this is a reference to Kubrick. Just as we have seen planets evoked, particularly planets related to *2001: A Space Odyssey*, where Bowman encounters the monolith of the alien/gods, so here the 'man from the moon' come down and the Apollo astronauts suddenly appear so that we make the association. *Whatever one's view of the Space Program and the moon landing, there is evidence that trickery and deception were involved, as well as the use of Disney sounds stages for some shots. In fact, it is undeniable that Kubrick worked with NASA in some capacity. While the references to Crowley might seem a bit strained, recall that Crowley claimed he communicated with a 'spirit' that has famously been identified as an early image of what would become the modern archetype for the 'alien.'"*[35]

[35] E.T. The Extra-Terrestrial – Esoteric Analysis by Jay Dyer https://jaysanalysis.com/

And this "alien" concept is connected to more than just Crowley. Even L. Ron Hubbard, the founder of the Scientology cult incorporated an "alien" story into their creation theology after spending time with Aleister Crowley and Jack Parsons. Once a person reaches a certain level in Scientology, they learn about Xenu, the ruler of a "Galactic Confederacy" who 75 million years ago (to avoid being deposed from his throne) forged a plot of population reduction. Billions of Xenu's citizens were transported to earth to be exterminated by detonating atomic bombs inside of volcanos that the victims had been placed around. Those who died became disembodied souls called thetans who want to possess bodies.[36] To most people this story sounds completely ridiculous, but it is really no different than some of the ancient alien theories people are falling for today.

There are clearly anti-Christianity and anti-Jesus themes in Hubbard's "alien" theology (which is no surprise when one understands that the entire "alien" narrative is from Satan). Another interesting note is that Hubbard called earth "prison planet" which is the exact same phrase that Alex Jones (founder and host of a popular "alternative" media source) has used for years. And after seeing Jones push a similar "alien" creation theology on a Joe Rogan show (while wearing a NASA t-shirt), it is obvious that even Alex Jones is part of the Satanic cabal's "alien" deception.[37]

---

[36] https://en.wikipedia.org/wiki/Xenu

[37] Joe Rogan Experience #1255 - Alex Jones Returns!   https://youtu.be/-5yh2HcIlkU

Here is a funny side note about the show I mentioned above. On it, Joe Rogan and Alex Jones were arguing with Eddie Bravo (a non-Christian flat earther) against flat earth. They were pushing NASA, as they spoke of the crystal firmament and twisted Bible passages into their "alien" agenda. Then all of a sudden Jones mentions to Rogan **"...a weird, dumb preacher in Alabama making you mad."** I have no doubt that I am that preacher in Alabama that is making him mad, as I am one of the few preachers that has sermons on all of the subjects they were discussing.

I have no doubt that I have made a lot of people mad by exposing the Satanic "alien" deception and their attempts to hijack Biblical cosmology (aka flat earth). They are leading people astray into their New Age, occult philosophies and DMT-induced "God-consciousness" or what the Bible would call sorcery (the Greek word *pharmekeus*) induced deception and I am doing all I can to stop people from falling for it.

Again, I must point out the connection that all of these occult practitioners who were in contact with demon spirits (whether it be the Nazi Vril, Thule, Black Sun, the O.T.O. of

Aleister Crowley or Hubbard's Scientology) have is that they were all part of perpetuating the deceptions of the Copernican solar system and the Satanic lie of "aliens" from "outer space." And the key figures in the American "space" program have been involved with these occultists and adhere to their beliefs. But the trail of occultists does not stop with the Nazi scientists, Aleister Crowley, Jack Parsons or Joe Rogan and Alex Jones.

NASA's Freemasons

It is a known fact that, in addition to the Nazi scientists that led America's "space" and rocket programs, many of the early NASA astronauts and mission administrators were high-level Freemasons. Sadly, this damning little truth (even if known) usually flies right over the heads of the average person. Most people have been deceived into thinking that Freemasonry is just a private club for men to escape their families, smoke cigars and plan community service events. However, there is much more involved in Freemasonry, especially for those who reach the 32nd and 33rd Degrees.

To fully understand the depth of the occult rituals and Satanic power within Freemasonry, one must research Albert Pike and Manly P. Hall. Albert Pike (1809-1891) was the leading American Masonic scholar of the nineteenth century. In his days before Freemasonry (1833-1834), he taught school in Fort Smith, Arkansas while he studied law. He opened his law practice in 1834 and was politically active, joining the Freemasons in 1850.

"*At the beginning of the Civil War (1861-65), Pike, then living in New Orleans, Louisiana, was named commissioner of Indian Affairs for the Confederacy. He eventually was named a brigadier general and he organized several regiments from the Arkansas tribes. Unfortunately, some of his soldiers mutilated Union soldiers in a battle in 1862. Amid that controversy, he quarreled with his superiors and accused the Confederacy of neglecting its treaty obligation to the tribes. He was arrested for treason but released as the war effort collapsed. Now hated by both sides, he retreated to the Ozark Mountains.*

*It is possible that Pike's sojourn into the occult started during his days in hiding. **Rumors emerged that he was conjuring the devil and engaging in sexual orgies (charges discussed by Montague Summers in his History of Witchcraft and Demonology).** He had joined the Freemasons in 1850 and began working seriously on reforming what he thought of as worthless rituals. **He became accomplished in hermetic, Rosicrucian, and continental Masonic traditions and incorporated extensive esoteric content.** His monumental textbook, Morals and Dogma of Freemasonry, appeared in 1872.*

In 1873 he moved into the Temple of the Supreme Council of the Scottish Rite in Washington, D.C. The council offered him a stipend and he would remain there the rest of his life. **He dominated Scottish Rite Masonry for the next two decades.** *During this time, he wrote several additional books on Masonry (and left behind a number of manuscripts still unpublished) but is still remembered for his early text and reformed rituals. He died in Washington on April 2, 1891.*

In 1899 the Scottish Rites erected a statue of Pike in Washington. Ninety years later, civil rights activists brought up the old accusation of Pike having written the rituals of the Ku Klux Klan and demanded that it be removed. Lacking clear evidence of their accusations, they were unsuccessful."[38]

One of the most important things to recognize about Freemasonry is revealed in Albert Pike's book *Morals and Dogma*, he wrote, **"Every Masonic Temple is a temple of religion.** *"*[39] Furthermore, the Encyclopedia of Freemasonry written by two 33rd Degree Freemasons confirms this statement from Albert Pike, *"The tendency of all true Masonry is toward religion if it make any progress, it's progress is to that holding in. Look at its ancient landmarks, it's sublime ceremonies, it's profound symbols and allegories – all inculcating religious doctrine, commanding religious observance, and teaching religious truth, and who can't deny that it is eminently a religious institution."*[40]

---

[38] https://www.encyclopedia.com/people/history/us-history-biographies/albert-pike
[39] *Morals and Dogma* (Masonic Doctrine and Usage for Superior Degrees by Albert Pike 33° Grand Commander to the Supreme Council of the 33rd° of Freemasonry 1872 pg. 213
[40] *The Encyclopedia of Freemasonry* by Albert Mackey 33rd Degree and Charles T. McClenacjan 33rd Degree 1873 & 1878

Under the heading **Nimrod** in the Encyclopedia of Freemasonry it says: *"The legend of the craft in the old constitutions refers to Nimrod as one of the founders of Masonry."* And under the heading ***Egyptian Mysteries it says***: *"Egypt has always been considered as the birthplace of the mysteries it was there that the ceremonies of initiation first established. It was there the truth was first veiled in the allegory, and the darkness of religion were first imparted under symbolic forms."*

Albert Pike elaborates, *"All truly dogmatic religions have issued from the Kabbalah and return to it; everything scientific in grand in the religious dreams of all the Illuminati, Jacob Boheme, Swedenborg, Saint Martin, and others, is borrowed from the Kabbalah; **all the Masonic associations owe to it their secrets and their symbols"*** (Morals and Dogma Pg. 744).

On pages 733 and 734, after praising the Satanic Jewish Kabbalah and disparaging Christianity, Albert Pike writes, *"There is in nature one most potent force, by means whereof a single man, who could possess himself of it, and should know how to direct it, could revolutionize and change the face of the world.*

This force was known to the ancients. It is a universal agent, whose Supreme law is equilibrium; and whereby, if science can but learn how to control it, it will be possible to change the order of the Seasons, to produce in night the phenomena of day, to send a thought in an instant round the world, to heal or slay at a distance, to give our words universal success, and make them reverberate everywhere.

*This agent, partially revealed by the blind guesses of the disciples of Mesmer, is precisely what the Adepts of the middle ages called the elementary matter of the great work. The Gnostics held that it composed the igneous body of the Holy Spirit; **and it was adored in the secret rites of the Sabbat or the Temple, under the hieroglyphic figure of Baphomet or the hermaphroditic goat of Mendes**.*" (Below: Baphomet next to a Freemason statue of George Washington).

Dig a little deeper and you will soon discover that Albert Pike was a student of the Kabbalah teacher and occultist Eliphas Levi. In fact, the above quote is almost word for word what Eliphas Levi wrote in his occult writings. Interestingly, the man that wrote the novel about the Vril-ya, (which was integral in forming the Nazi party and their core beliefs) was also a student of Eliphas Levi: *"In The Coming Race, Bulwer Lytton used the word vril for the wonder-working force described in that story.* ***He was a profound student of the Kabbalah, magic and Rosicrucianism, and made use of his occult knowledge in coining this term, vril, which he describes in a manner that leaves no room for doubt that he had in mind the doctrine of Eliphas Levi, with whom he is known to have corresponded,*** *and with whom there is reason to believe he was more or less closely associated by membership in a certain society of occult students."*[41]

The fact that the Freemason Albert Pike quotes directly from Eliphas Levi and says that the power they seek is symbolized by the Goat of Mendes, reveals that it all leads back to Lucifer (aka Satan or the Devil). ***"In pre-Eliphas Levi Tarot decks like the Tarot of Marseille, the devil is portrayed with breasts, a face on the belly, eyes on the knees, lion feet and male genitalia.*** *He also has bat-like wings, antlers, a raised right hand, a lowered left hand and a staff. Two creatures with antlers, hooves and tails are bound to his round pedestal."*[42] Post-Eliphas Levi Tarot decks use Levi's very similar depiction of Baphomet (aka the Goat of Mendes) as the DEVIL card.

To further confirm that the "god" of freemasonry is Lucifer (aka Baphomet, the Goat of Mendes), Freemason and occult expert Manly P. Hall did not mince words or hide

---

[41] https://www.hermetik-international.com/en/media-library/occultism/the-life-power/part-1/

[42] https://en.wikipedia.org/wiki/The_Devil_(Tarot_card)

behind symbolism when he wrote, *"The day has come when Fellow Craftsmen must know and apply their knowledge. The lost key to their grade is the mastery of emotion, which places the energy of the universe at their disposal. Man can only expect to be entrusted with great power by proving his ability to use it constructively and selflessly.* **When the Mason learns that the key to the warrior on the block is the proper application of the dynamo of living power, he has learned the mystery of his Craft. The seething energies of LUCIFER are in his hands and before he may step onward and upward, he must prove his ability to properly apply energy.***[43]

Manly P. Hall

Of course, these higher-level Freemasons admit that they hide the truth of their occult symbols, rituals and secret worship of Lucifer from the lower initiates. Albert Pike wrote, *"In fact, what can there be in common between the vile multitude and sublime wisdom?* **The truth must be kept**

---

[43] *The Lost Keys of Freemasonry* by Manly P. Hall ©1923 Santa Monica, CA chapter 4

secret, and the masses need a teaching proportioned to their imperfect reason...Masonry, like all the Religions, all the Mysteries, Hermeticism, and Alchemy, conceals its secrets from all except the Adepts and Sages, or the Elect, and uses false explanations and misinterpretations of its symbols to mislead those who deserve only to be misled; to conceal the Truth, which it calls light, and draw them away from it. "[44]

Manly P. Hall put it this way, **"Freemasonry is a fraternity within a fraternity -- an outer organization concealing an inner brotherhood of the elect** ... *it is necessary to establish the existence of these two separate and yet interdependent orders, the one visible and the other invisible. The visible society is a splendid camaraderie of 'free and accepted' men enjoined to devote themselves to ethical, educational, fraternal, patriotic, and humanitarian concerns. The invisible society is a secret and most august [defined as 'of majestic dignity, grandeur'] fraternity whose members are dedicated to the service of a mysterious arcannum arcandrum [defined as 'a secret, a mystery'].* "[45]

In other words, the high-level Freemasons (who know that they have been initiated into the service and power of Lucifer) keep the important secrets from the lower plebes who are not yet able to be fully trusted with the details of Satan's plot to deceive mankind, destroy Christianity, and establish their antichrist New World Order. They are simply used as a "good face" to the outside world and ignorantly help fund this Satanic plot with their dues, fundraisers, and their estates when they die.

---

[44] *Morals and Dogma*, pp. 103-105

[45] *Lectures on Ancient Philosophy* by Manly P. Hall ©1929 p. 433

Now, enter into this mix the fact that all of the following NASA astronauts were Freemasons:

1. Edwin "Buzz" Aldrin (Apollo 11)
2. Leroy Gordon Cooper, Jr. (Mercury 9, Faith 7 & Gemini 5)
3. Don F. Eisele (Apollo 7)
4. John H. Glenn (Mercury 6 & Friendship 7)
5. Virgil I. "Gus" Grissom (Mercury 4 & Apollo 1)
6. James Irwin (Apollo 15),
7. Edgar D. Mitchell (Apollo 14),
8. Walter M. Schirra, Jr. (Apollo 7),
9. Thomas P. Stafford (Apollo 10),
10. Paul J. Weitz (Sky Lab 2 & Challenger STS 6)

And then let's not forget the 33rd Degree Freemason Kenneth S. Kleinknecht who was the Manager of the Apollo Program Command and Service Modules, Deputy Manager of the Gemini Program, and Manager of Project Mercury. Also, other notable NASA Freemasons are Clark C. McClelland with ScO Space Shuttle Fleet (1958-1992) who served with the Office of Naval Intelligence, Manhattan Project and early Computer scientist Vannever Bush who was with NACA (the predecessor of NASA) and James Edwin Webb[46] who served as the second administrator of NASA from February 14, 1961 to October 7, 1968. *"Webb oversaw NASA from the beginning of the Kennedy administration through the end of the Johnson administration, thus overseeing all the critical first manned launches in the Mercury through Gemini programs, until just before the first manned Apollo flight."*[47]

---

[46] http://freemasonry.bcy.ca/biography/spacemason/index.html
[47] https://en.wikipedia.org/wiki/James_E._Webb

The above photograph is supposed to show the actual flag-presentation. From left to right are depicted the Masonic "Sovereign Grand Commander" Luther A. Smith, Edwin E. Aldrin Sr., C. Fred Kleinknecht, Jr., C. Frederick Kleinknecht, Sr., and Buzz Aldrin himself.

Amazingly, the source that identified all these NASA astronauts and administrators as Freemasons is the website of the Grand Lodge of British Columbia and Yukon located at 8555 Government Street Burnaby in British Columbia, Canada. I called their phone number and verified that it is in fact a legitimate Freemason lodge. Their website is very extensive and full of information. They even have a page where they display a photo-scanned letter on official NASA letterhead from astronaut Edwin "Buzz" Aldrin addressed to the Illustrious Luther A. Smith, 33rd Degree, Sovereign Grand Commander of the Supreme Council in Washington, D.C. dated September 19, 1969.

NATIONAL AERONAUTICS AND SPACE ADMINISTRATION
MANNED SPACECRAFT CENTER
HOUSTON, TEXAS 77058

IN REPLY REFER TO: September 19, 1969

Illustrious Luther A. Smith, 33°
Sovereign Grand Commander
Supreme Council, 33°
Southern Jurisdiction, U.S.A.
1733 16th Street, N.W.
Washington, D.C. 20009

Dear Grand Commander:

It was a great moment in my life to be so cordially welcomed
to the House of the Temple on September 16, 1969, by you and Grand
Secretary General Kleinknecht, 33°, and also the members of your
staffs. My greatest pleasure, however, was to be able to present
to you on this occasion the Scottish Rite Flag which I carried on
the Apollo 11 Flight to the Moon--emblazoned in color with the
Scottish Rite Double-headed Eagle, the Blue Lodge Emblem and the
Sovereign Grand Commander's Insignia.

I take this opportunity to again thank you for the autographed
copy of your recent book, entitled "Action by the Scottish Rite,
Southern Jurisdiction, U.S.A.," which is filled with a wealth of
information about your Americanism Program sponsored by the Supreme
Council, participating activities and related activities of the
Rite.

Cordially and fraternally,

Edwin E. Aldrin, Jr.
NASA Astronaut

On their website the Grand Lodge of British Columbia and Yukon admit that this is NOT a complete list of all the Freemasons (occultists) that have been intimately involved with NASA, the ISS, ESA, or any of the other "space" agencies. As I read that, I was reminded of an ISS video I saw a while back in which one of the astronauts had an Egyptian "Eye of Horus" tattoo on his arm. I had to wonder how many are part of this Freemason/Illuminati "club." Nevertheless, I believe we have seen ample evidence to show a common theme from Copernicus to our present day technological/government "elite." It is the theme of Satanic, demonic, occult influences being involved in the lives of those who were the "fathers" and propagators of NASA and our "space" program like Jack Parsons, Wernher von Braun, other Nazi scientists, and Freemason astronauts.

Occultist/Theosophist Helen Blavatsky wrote in her book *The Secret Doctrine* (spoiler alert - her "secret" is that she believes Lucifer is really God), *"Mercury is called the first of the celestial Gods, the God Hermes ... to which God is attributed the invention of and the first initiation of men into Magic....Mercury is Budh, Wisdom, Enlightenment or `reawakening' in the divine science."*[48] It is no coincidence that Copernicus got his idea of heliocentrism from the writings and occult theology of Hermes Trismegistus (aka Hermes) or Hermeticism and NASA named their first manned "space" flight "Mercury" (otherwise known as Hermes). Their true mission was to initiate man into their magic and Luciferian "science" with alleged space missions and they have certainly bewitched mankind away from the Bible and the gospel of Jesus Christ.

Never forget that it was these occultists at NASA who gave us the fake moon landing and the fake/deceptive "photographs" of earth from "space." And these are the same Satanic, occult forces that influenced Copernicus, Kepler, and a whole host of "scientists" over many years. They have also been subtly changing the narrative that the evil spiritual entities of Satan are actually ancient "aliens" from other

[48]https://www.lucistrust.org/online_books/esoteric_astrology_obooks/appendix_sugge stions_for_students/the_planetmercury#Lucifer

"planets" and "galaxies." These ancient "aliens" also claim to be our creators and thus they are attempting to uproot the God of the Bible, our Lord Jesus Christ as the true Creator. They want to take the place of God which is what God revealed to us about Satan – he wanted to overthrow God and take His place (Isaiah 14).

But what is really sad is that the majority of modern Christians choose to believe these Satanic liars over what the Holy Spirit-inspired, Hebrew prophets and apostles of Jesus Christ revealed to us in the Bible about creation and the end-time conspiracy of Satan and his servants. Even solid Christian authors and researchers (that I highly respect) like the late Chris Putnam and Tom Horn have fallen into the trap of discounting the literal interpretation of Scripture about the nature of the cosmos and believing NASA. Here's what they wrote in their book Exo-Vaticana:

"It is important to note that the geocentric universe was a classical pagan (rather than a Christian) concept." Of course, this couldn't be further from the truth. The ancient Hebrew prophets of the Bible clearly taught a geocentric cosmos and as I have shown already that it was the heliocentric theory that emerged from pagan occultists. Putnam and Horn continue, *"Although Christians accepted it, the Bible does not really teach that the sun revolves around the earth* (actually it does...see chapter 12). *The writers of the Bible had a prescientific worldview and they described the way things appear to the naked eye. They used the language of phenomenon."* Sadly, this statement is a denial of the Divine inspiration and infallibility of God's Word. This is saying that the writers of the Bible were writing from their own understanding and not from the mind of God. But then they put the icing on the cake of deception when they stated, *"One way we can rest assured that the*

heliocentric model is correct is by the remarkable success of NASA's satellite missions, like Galileo to Jupiter, which are based on Kepler's laws of celestial mechanics founded on the heliocentric model. These rockets fly precise trajectories which would inevitably fail if the heliocentric model were not true. Yet, they do succeed, and we have the satellite photographs to prove it, so geocentric Creationism must be false."[49]

Unfortunately, Putnam and Horn were unaware that declassified NASA documents admit that their rockets and computer programs on rocket guidance have been based on a "nonrotating, flat earth" (aka a geocentric Biblical model of the heavens and the earth - see chapter 18). But this is why we should NEVER believe man, or his impressive rocket shows over God's Word found in the Holy Bible…it always leads to more deception and casts doubt on the Divine inspiration of Scripture.

---

[49] *Exo-Vaticana* by Chris Putnam & Thomas Horn ©2013 Defender pg. 278

Chapter 4

Could the Earth Really Be Flat?

"He that answereth a matter before he heareth it, it is folly and shame unto him" (Proverbs 18:13).

"There is a crisis in cosmology. Usually in science, if we are off by factor of two or a factor of ten, we call that horrible. We say, 'Something's wrong with the theory we're off by a factor of ten. However, in cosmology, we're off by a factor of 10 to the 120. That is 1 with 120 zeros after it. **This the largest mismatch between theory and experiment in the history of science.** *"*[50] - Michio Kaku, famous American Theoretical Physicist and Professor of Theoretical Physics at the City College of New York.

"In order to analyze the dynamics of damaged aircraft **the dynamic EQUATIONS of motion MUST PROPERLY REFLECT THE UNDERLYING PHYSICS...*In this paper, the rigid body EQUATIONS of motion over a FLAT, NON-ROTATING EARTH ARE*

---

[50] https://www.youtube.com/watch?v=olo_z6yZjbg Michio Kaku clip from the documentary *The Principle*

97

SSSR which was their first world record-breaking flight. They used a larger balloon and a much-improved version of Piccard's capsule/gondola to break his high-altitude record. They reached an altitude of 60,695 feet which was confirmed by the International Aeronautical Federation. Like Piccard's, this Russian flight was also written about in *Popular Science Magazine*. Though modern accounts of these balloon flights conveniently leave out the details of what these early pilots really saw, the old science magazines and newspaper reports of that time tell the truth. Here is what the article in the December 1933 edition of Popular Science states about the Russian balloon flight:

"Soaring in their airtight balloon gondola to a record-breaking height of 11.8 miles above the earth, the other day, ***three Russian aeronauts brought back the first scientific observations ever made at so great an altitude.*** *Above their heads, the sky provided a striking spectacle; its color had turned a soft, deep violet, and almost devoid of the light-reflecting haze found at lower levels.* ***Looking down, they tried in vain to detect any curvature of the earth's horizon.***"[53]

So here we have very similar accounts from multiple scientists and different countries that clearly state they could not see any curvature of the earth from those high altitudes. One even said that the earth appeared to be a flat disk with an upturned (not a downturned) edge. And yet, today the initial knee-jerk reaction of most people when they hear someone suggest that the earth might indeed be flat (instead of the perfect sphere we see in every NASA/space agency "image") is one of complete unbelief and incredulity. Those who react this way simply think the idea is ridiculous; they dismiss the person who suggested it and consider them a fool.

The first picture of earth taken from "space" (an altitude of 65 miles or 343,200 feet) was in 1946 from a camera mounted on a V-2 rocket that the United States confiscated from the Nazis after World War 2. It shows a perfectly straight or flat horizon. Later, they launched other V-2 rockets and claimed to reach an altitude of 100 miles. They immediately started producing and releasing composite images of pieced together photos showing the earth's horizon curving. However, when I superimposed a semi-transparent picture of NASA's piecemeal V-2 images from 100 miles high over a NASA picture from the International Space Station which claims to be 265 miles high, there was more curvature at 100 miles. It seems the government was trying to cover their tracts and didn't realize that someone might someday compare pictures that are over 70 years apart. I have also included a screenshot below from an old documentary about the high-altitude X-15 plane. It also shows a perfectly, flat horizon behind the aircraft after it reached 67 miles high or 354,200 feet.

In spite of these early scientific balloon missions that reached altitudes of 51,000 feet to over 62,000 feet resulting in testimonies from scientists that they could not detect any curvature of the earth, many people claim that they have seen the curvature of the earth from commercial airliners that fly between 30,000 to 40,000 feet. First, I have flown overseas and across America many times in a window seat and I have never witnessed or caught any earth curvature in a photograph. Second, I have a friend that has been a commercial pilot for almost thirty years, and he is now a firm Biblical, flat earth believer. He has shared many things about his years of flying that confirm a flat, non-rotating earth and that satellites in some vacuum of "outer space" do not exist. The curve that people are "remembering" is simply from NASA cartoon images and fisheye lens footage that has been branded into their brains for decades.

Once a friend on Facebook asked me to help him in a debate he was having with his brother over the subject of flat earth. His brother claimed to have seen the curvature of the earth while flying on the Concorde. For those of you who may not know about the Concorde, it was a British-French supersonic passenger jet that operated from 1976-2003. It flew at an average speed of 1,350 mph and had a cruising altitude of 56,000 to 60,000 feet.

So, when my friend asked me to help with his brother's arguments, I simply searched for a YouTube video of someone flying on the Concorde. I found a 1998 video of British Airways Flight 0002 from JFK to London, dated November 7, 1998. The video starts from takeoff and records the in-flight screen in the cabin showing them flying at 59,000 feet at Mach 2. The passenger frequently turned his video camera to the window where a perfectly flat horizon could be seen. **Just as Auguste Piccard and the Russian aeronauts stated, no curvature of the earth could be seen at 59,000 feet.**

Furthermore, I also checked footage from the last commercial flight of the Concorde BA002 from JFK to London. Below is the grayscale screen shot of the perfectly flat horizon of earth taken from a window seat from over 50,000 feet up just as the sun was beginning to rise.

106

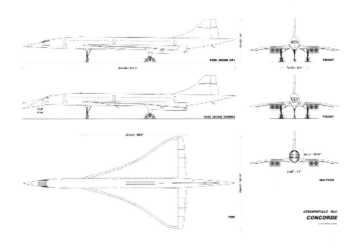

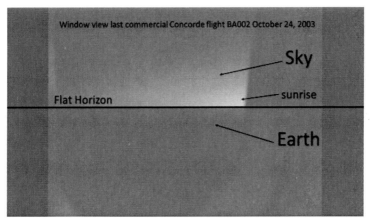

Window view last commercial Concorde flight BA002 October 24, 2003

Sky

sunrise

Flat Horizon

Earth

Moreover, both flights were between New York and London which according to Google Earth is 3,459 miles. The earth curvature formula for a sphere of 24,901 miles in circumference (what they claim the earth is) is 8 inches per miles SQUARED. For flights "across the pond" a 1,298-mile-high earth curvature bulge must be accounted for if they are flying around a ball. Also, flying at 1,350 mph means that the Concorde was covering 22.5 miles every minute. That 22.5 miles equates to 337 feet of alleged earth curvature that would have to be dealt with every minute by the pilot/plane to maintain a consistent altitude of 59,000.

That comes to having to nose down the aircraft 5,055 feet or nearly a mile every 15 minutes.

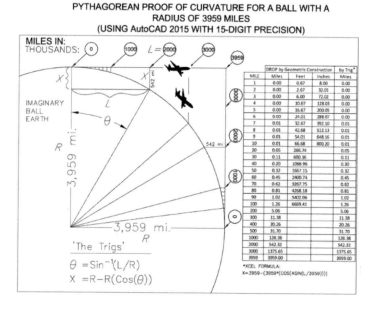

PYTHAGOREAN PROOF OF CURVATURE FOR A BALL WITH A
RADIUS OF 3959 MILES
(USING AutoCAD 2015 WITH 15-DIGIT PRECISION)

MILES IN:
THOUSANDS:

IMAGINARY BALL EARTH

R 3,959

'The Trigs'

$\theta = Sin^{-1}(L/R)$

$X = R - R(Cos(\theta))$

MILE	DROP by Geometric Construction			by Trig²
	Miles	Feet	Inches	Miles
1	0.00	0.67	8.00	0.00
2	0.00	2.67	32.03	0.00
3	0.00	6.00	72.02	0.00
4	0.00	10.67	128.03	0.00
5	0.00	16.67	200.05	0.00
6	0.00	24.01	288.07	0.00
7	0.01	32.67	392.10	0.01
8	0.01	42.68	512.13	0.01
9	0.01	54.01	648.16	0.01
10	0.01	66.68	800.20	0.01
20	0.05	266.74		0.05
30	0.11	600.16		0.11
40	0.20	1066.96		0.20
50	0.32	1667.15		0.32
60	0.45	2400.74		0.45
70	0.62	3267.75		0.62
80	0.81	4268.18		0.81
90	1.02	5402.06		1.02
100	1.26	6669.41		1.26
200	5.06			5.06
300	11.38			11.38
400	20.26			20.26
500	31.70			31.70
1000	128.38			128.38
2000	542.32			542.32
3000	1375.65			1375.65
3959	3959.00			3959.00

*XCEL FORMULA:
X=3959-(3959*(COS(ASIN(L/3959))))

A commercial airliner that averages 525 mph is covering 8.75 miles per minute or 131.25 miles every 15 minutes. There is 11,484 feet of earth curvature in 131.25 miles and dividing that by 4 means that a regular commercial pilot should be nosing his aircraft down 2,871 feet (or over half a mile) every 15 minutes. My friend who is a commercial pilot told me that he has never made any such adjustments to nose the airplane DOWN to maintain altitude over the fictitious ball earth. I have heard other pilots who have concurred that they fly only level paths across the earth.

Although these proofs are presented to people, more often than not cognitive dissonance kicks in. Then begins the reciting of years of media and public-school/government programming. Typical thoughts and/or responses include:

"How could any rational human being in this modern age actually believe the earth is flat? Haven't they seen the pictures and videos from space? Haven't they seen eclipses? What about the ISS? Haven't these flat earthers seen ships and boats disappear over the curve of the earth at the horizon? How about Magellan's circumnavigation of the earth? What about satellites and the moon landings? How do they explain day and night and the seasons?"

Of course, I could go on and on with the questions and challenges I have heard raised by those who reject the subject of flat earth as soon as it comes up. Like I mentioned above, we are all products of government programming through education and media. Then why have well educated engineers, PhDs, geometry and science teachers, commercial jet pilots, Army Rangers, former helicopter pilots, ex-NASA employees, basketball stars, Navy Missiles operators, an Army NATO officer in charge of radar detection of low-flying Russian attack aircraft, former atheists, and many others (who were also indoctrinated through education and media) come to believe that we have been lied to about the shape of the earth and the cosmos? Is it that there is real, tangible evidence that proves the earth to be flat and they are actually open to researching it? Could it be that there has been a Satanic conspiracy playing out over many centuries to hide the true nature of creation in order to turn people away from the God of creation who is the God of the Bible, the true Messiah and Savior our Lord Jesus Christ?

Before we delve deep into the Biblical side of this issue, let's answer the first question:

"Is there real scientific evidence/visual evidence/mathematical evidence that the Earth is flat?"

109

Now, when I use the phrase "real scientific evidence," I mean something that is observable, testable, and repeatable by the average person. In other words, tests done using the real scientific method, not the theoretical surmising and imaginative speculations taught by biased college professors or celebrity "scientists." I am not talking about something where I must just trust the word or testimony of some "expert" or astronaut who has allegedly witnessed something that I can never see or been somewhere I can never go. Believing something that you have not seen, experienced, or researched/tested for yourself is called walking in faith. Sadly, most people have built their entire belief system regarding creation and the shape of the earth on what others told them and not on what they have researched, tested, and observed themselves. That would mean their faith is in "science" and that can be as strong of a belief system as any religion in the world.

This massive resurgence of questioning the shape of the earth really took off in 2015. One of the main reasons that there has been such an explosion in the number of people who now know the earth is flat is because so many people have gone out and conducted their own earth curvature tests with high zoom cameras and telescopes. On March 2, 2015, Nikon announced their Coolpix P900 would soon be released. It is a "...superzoom digital bridge camera. With 83× zoom limit and a maximum 2000mm 35mm equivalent focal length, it was the greatest-zooming bridge camera at the time of its announcement, a record now held by its successor, the Nikon Coolpix P1000."[54] Placing this piece of technology in the hands of the average, everyday person has produced irrefutable evidence that we do not live on a sphere with a circumference of 24,901 miles and this is why...

---

[54] https://en.wikipedia.org/wiki/Nikon_Coolpix_P900

Eight Inches Per Miles SQUARED

The Pythagorean theorem is the math formula used to figure out the curve of the earth. It is really very simple. For a sphere with a circumference of 24,901 miles, the amount/rate of curvature comes to 8 inches per miles squared. That means the ball earth must curve or drop 8 inches in the first mile. However, the equation at two miles would be 8 inches x (2 x 2) which would be 8 inches x 4 equaling 32 inches. Three miles would be 8 inches x (3 x 3) which is 8 inches x 9 equaling 72 inches or 6 feet. At ten miles, the curve or drop would be 8 inches x (10 x 10) which is 8 inches x 100 equaling 800 inches or 66.6 feet. To put this in perspective, the average height of each story in a multi-story building is 10 feet. That means 66.6 feet would be higher than a six-story building.

Fig. 2.

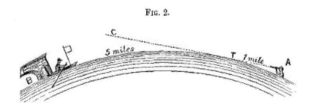

111

Our first curvature test was performed by me, a former member of our church, and Paul Kelley (graduated from LSU with an engineering degree) on April 30, 2016 from Fairhope, Alabama looking across Mobile Bay. From Fairhope we were able to look northeast at the Port of Mobile and the downtown city of Mobile, Alabama. We used a Nikon P900 and a telescope and checked distances by Google Earth and other maps. In that first test, we could see ships in the water at distances up to 12 miles away. That should be impossible if the earth is a globe.

Nikon P900 captures a boat across Mobile Bay (11-12 miles away) that should have been hidden behind at least 43 feet of earth curvature...

April 30, 2016

We also conducted tests from Fairhope on July 17, 2017, February 3, 2018 and April 19, 2019. Unfortunately, due to the atmosphere (surface heat, humidity, temperature, evaporation) we were unable to see a lot during our July 2017 test. However, the April 2016 and February 2018 tests both produced some amazing pictures and videos of things that we should not have been able to see due to the alleged curvature of the earth. For instance, in February 2018, we videoed (through the Nikon P900) the USS Alabama in Battleship Park in Mobile, Alabama from 12.4 miles away. As we panned the camera slightly to the right of the USS Alabama, we could see cars and trucks getting on HWY 98 and crossing the bridge over Mobile Bay.

Cars and trucks crossing I-10 Bridge
from over 10 miles away...

To confirm the heights of the bridges above the water, I called the bridge division of the Alabama Department of Transportation (ALDOT). I asked for the height of the bridges we could see from across Mobile Bay, measuring from the water to the bottom of the bridge. According to ALDOT engineers, the height of the HWY 98 bridge is 25 feet and the I-10 bridge is 16 feet. Using the Pythagorean theorem to calculate the amount of curvature we should experience across 12.4 miles; it comes out to an average curvature of 7.98 inches or approximately 8 inches per miles SQUARED. When we factored in the height of the camera at 5 feet, there should have been 62.25 feet (more than a six-story building) of earth curvature blocking our view of the cars and trucks going across the HWY 98 bridge out of Battleship Park. In fact, we could see at least 12-15 feet under the bridge which means that we were only missing 10-13 feet due to distance perspective issues of atmospheric conditions and the vanishing point (the visual limits of our eyes or any magnification device).

We also recorded video that day of cars and trucks moving across the I-10 bridge from 10.12 miles away. That bridge is only 16 feet off the water and our view of it should have been blocked by over 36 feet of earth curvature. It was crystal clear without any distortion and we were monitoring both the air and water temperatures so none of this was due to refraction or inverted superior mirages. We also saw small fishing boats in the water at distances of 10-13 miles which is way past where they disappear to the naked eye at the horizon. If those boats had disappeared over the curvature of the earth, there is no way that a high zoom camera or a telescope could pull those boats magically back into view.

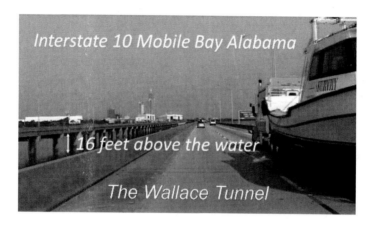

I came across this testimony in the 1899 book *Zetetic Cosmogony* that corroborates our seeing ships in the water at the distance of 12 miles. *"To the Editor of Earth Review. Sir,--In August last I, with several other friends, being in Oban for a holiday, took a trip for a day in a small yacht on Loch Lorne, and being a glorious sunshiny day and so calm that not a ripple was seen, and being becalmed for an our about mid-day, **we observed a good many sights of various kinds. Amongst other things that we saw was a yacht, which the captain told us was at 12 miles distant.** We saw all the mast and part of the hull, and to get a better view of her we took our binocular opera glass (a good one). Now, sir, wouldn't it require a funny curvature table either with or without the odd fractions to explain how we saw the hull of that vessel twelve miles off? **According to the table***

114

furnished by the present Astronomer Royal recently, it ought to have been 66 feet below the line of sight; but the 'table' that we saw it from was the side of our yacht, and we concluded the sea was level."[55]

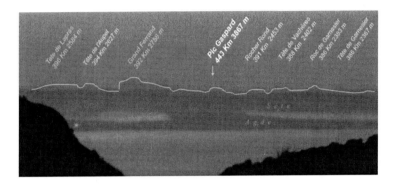

These kinds of tests with high zoom cameras and even lasers have been done over long distances by thousands of people all over the world. And recently, some researchers have started using infrared lenses and filters to see even greater distances with their equipment. On July 16, 2016, Marc Bret provided proof that the earth is flat without even trying as he set the world record for distant landscape photography.

The picture was of Barre des Ecrins in the French Alps taken from Pic de Finestrelles, a distance of 440 km (273.4 miles). Bret's picture was taken from an altitude of 2,820 meters as the sun rose behind the mountain range making a silhouette. The height of Barre des Ecrins is 4,102 meters. According to the math, 4,920 meters (3 miles) of earth curvature should have been blocking this photographer's view of the French Alps. That means the Barre des Ecrins

[55] Zetetic Cosmogony by Thomas Winship ©1899 Durban Natal pg. 27

should have been hidden by 819 meters (2,687 feet which is over half a mile) of earth curvature.[56]

Another great example of long distance and time-lapse photography that absolutely proves the earth to be flat is the work of the non-flat earther Josh Nowicki. Many of his photos and time-lapse videos of the Chicago skyline are taken from Grand Mere State Park near Stevensville, Michigan and Warren Dunes State Park in Sawyer, Michigan (which according to Google Earth is 52 miles across Lake Michigan). Using the math of a sphere that is 24,901 miles in circumference (8 inches per miles squared) and factoring in the camera height of six feet above the surface of the water, the amount of earth curvature that should be there is 1,601 feet or almost one third of a mile. According to Wikipedia, the tallest building in Chicago is the 108-story Willis Tower (formerly the Sears Tower) standing at 1,451 feet.

Needless to say, the Willis Tower should be hidden from view by the 150 feet of left-over earth curvature. That also means that none of the skyscrapers in Chicago, like the Trump International Hotel, the Aon Center or the famous landmark 875 N. Michigan Avenue, should be seen from Michigan…but they are.

---

[56] https://www.google.com/amp/s/beyondhorizons.eu/2016/08/03/pic-de-finestrelles-pic-gaspard-ecrins-443-km/amp/

116

View of #Chicago from Grand Mere State Park in Stevensville #Michigan. 4/28/15 @yourtake #ItsAmazingOutThere

9:34 PM · Apr 28, 2015 · Twitter Web Client

Of course, those who attempt to debunk these long-distance sightings of skylines, boats, and mountains will either make a false claim about the math or that refraction or atmospheric lensing causes the images to be pulled up over the curve of the earth. Sometimes, they claim that the image is a superior mirage. However, after consulting with a former Air Force weather expert and conducting four earth curvature tests across Mobile Bay at different seasons of the year, it became easy to tell when atmospheric or surface temperatures were distorting images. There is always some distortion when the surface temperature is higher than the air temperature. But, as we observed on February 3, 2018, the moment the water temperature and air temperature both reached 54 degrees Fahrenheit, all haze and distortion across the bay vanished. It was crystal clear viewing for our high zoom cameras and telescopes. Our view of the Port of Mobile and downtown Mobile from Fairhope, Alabama became more and more clear as the air temperature went a few degrees higher than the water/surface temperature. Furthermore, we were out there for hours in changing conditions and the view of distant objects never changed after the temperature inversion. We did not witness any superior mirages or atmospheric lensing after that.

Surface temp hotter than air above caused distortion and mirages   Surface temp cooler than air above gave clear views from 12 miles

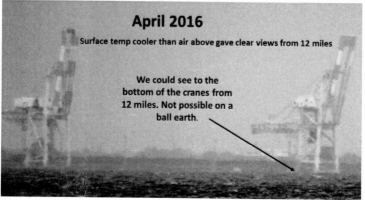

Another great earth curvature test came from a couple in Utah. The man and his wife had a high-zoom camera set up on Utah Lake right outside of Provo, Utah. The man was on the east side of the lake while his wife went to Eagle Park which is on the west north west side of the lake. According to Google Earth, the distance between them was 7.53 miles and the man showed in the video that his camera was 30.5 inches off the surface of the water (which was frozen at the lake's shore). The earth curvature bulge that should be there if the earth is a sphere is 20.75 feet. The man's wife had a bright flashlight. He videoed her walking down to the shore of the lake, then standing there with her light about 4 feet off the lake's surface. The man had her turn the light on and off to verify that it was her. Once confirmed, she then placed the flashlight on the frozen lake at her feet and he could still see the light from 7.53 miles away. The 20.75 feet of earth curvature was not there.[57]

The main rebuttal from those who want to deny this amazing evidence of flat earth is "refraction." Many people claim "refraction" like it is a trump card as to why we see farther than we should on a spherical earth. However, many people who cry refraction do not have a clue as to what they are talking about and sadly, most flat earthers don't know how to address it.

First of all, the very definition of refraction is the *"...deflection from a straight path undergone by a light ray or energy wave in passing obliquely **from one medium (such as air) into another (such as glass) in which its velocity is different.** "*[58] Did you catch that? Light waves are deflected or made to slightly change direction when passing from one medium (like air) into another (such as glass). So, let's state for the record that these earth curvature tests that are done across lakes or oceans or canals are not too great of distances where the weather condition would be drastically different. These tests usually take place over just several hours with minimal changes in temperature and humidity. Furthermore, the light waves from distant objects are moving through one medium which is air. The light waves are not passing from one medium through to a completely

[57] https://www.youtube.com/watch?v=0hv127-2vl8&feature=youtu.be
[58] Merriam-Webster.com

different one. And though there may be some pockets of air that have slightly different densities (in one location like Mobile Bay or Lake Michigan), the amount of refraction is minuscule when compared to what is needed to bend an image up over hundreds of feet of earth curvature. Here's an example:

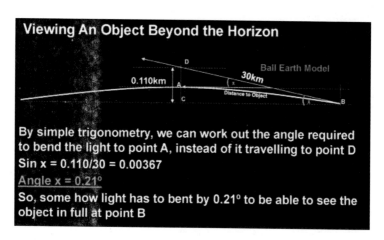

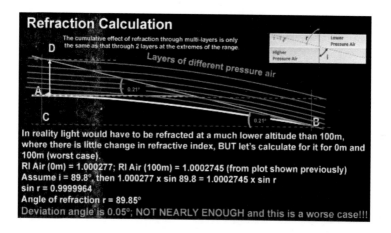

Conclusion

- Refraction is the Globe Earthers' main line of defence for observing distant objects when they should be below the horizon
  - Most don't understand curvature and certainly do not understand refraction
- Refraction simply can not explain these observations
  - It's affect on light in the lower atmosphere is tiny in comparison to what is actually needed to bend the light sufficiently to see objects that should be hidden under the horizon (by curvature)
- A lack of curvature is a much more plausible explanation

Another attempted rebuttal is the issue of temperature inversion and how that can distort images and create superior mirages. However, many people seem to misunderstand this concept. Even Dr. Danny Faulkner got it backwards in one of his flat earth debunk attempts. But according to the experts on a Smithsonian Channel episode, the right conditions for mirages, distortion, and the atmosphere bending light waves down (not up over the curve) is when surface temperature is higher than the air temperature above it.

To quote them, *"Just now the ground is much warmer than the air above it. This creates a gradient of hot to cold air. And since cold air is denser or heavier than warm air, the two air masses create distinct layers. Those layers act like a lens, bending and distorting our familiar reality."*[59] Yet, in this Smithsonian episode where they are using a helicopter in a desert as an example, you can still see the helicopter in the distance perfectly. The only thing affected by the surface temperature being warmer than the air temperature is that you lose sight of part of the ground under

---

[59] https://www.smithsonianchannel.com/videos/titanics-final-mystery/16859/playlist/1085686?auto=true

the helicopter as it lands on the desert surface. The ground under the helicopter becomes a mirror and looks like water. The only part that was obscured by this surface mirroring effect is the bottom of the helicopter landing skids. Consequently, when the surface temperature is lower than the air temperature, distortion and refraction almost disappear completely. Our teams have witnessed and documented this fact by doing multiple tests across Mobile Bay in different seasons and temperatures.

Survey Says

A surveyor in the late 1800s, Mr. T. Westwood, wrote *"In leveling, I work from Ordinance marks, or canal levels, to get the height above sea level. The puzzle to me used to be, that over several miles each level was and is treated throughout its whole length as the same level from end to end; **not the least allowance being made for curvature**. One of the civil engineers in this district, after some amount of argument on each side as to the reason why no allowance for curvature was made, said he did not believe anybody would know the shape of the earth in this life."[60]*

Engineer, W. Winckler wrote regarding the earth's supposed curvature, *"As an engineer of many years standing, I saw that this absurd allowance is only permitted in schoolbooks. No engineer would dream of allowing anything of the kind. **I have projected many miles of railways and many more of canals and the allowance has not even been thought of, much less allowed for. This allowance for curvature means this - that it is 8" for the first mile of a canal, and increasing at the ratio by the square of the distance in miles; thus a small navigable***

[60] Earth Review Magazine January 1896

canal for boats, say 30 miles long, will have, by the above rule an allowance for curvature of 600 feet. Think of that and then please credit engineers as not being quite such fools. Nothing of the sort is allowed. We no more think of allowing 600 feet for a line of 30 miles of railway or canal, than of wasting our time trying to square the circle. "[61]

"The distance between the Red Sea at Suez and the Mediterranean Sea is 100 statute miles, the datum line of the Canal being 26 feet below the level of the Mediterranean, and is continued horizontally the whole way from sea to sea, there not being a single lock on the Canal, the surface of the water being parallel with the datum line. **It is thus clear that there is no curvature or globularity for the whole hundred miles between the Mediterranean and the Red Sea**; had there been, according to the Astronomic theory, the middle of the Canal would have been 1,666 feet higher than at either end, whereas the Canal is perfectly horizontal for the whole distance. The Great Canal of China, said to be 700 miles in length, was made without regard to any allowance for supposed curvature, as the Chinese believe the earth to be a Stationary Plane. I may also add that no allowance was made for it in the North Sea Canal, or in the Manchester Ship Canal, both recently constructed, thus clearly proving that there is no globularity in earth or sea, **so that the world cannot possibly be a planet.** "[62]

"Let those who believe it is the practice for surveyors to make allowance for 'curvature' ponder over the following from the Manchester Ship Canal Company (Earth Review, October, 1893) 'It is customary in Railway and Canal constructions for all levels to be referred to a datum which

---

[61] Earth Review Magazine October 1893

[62] Terra Firma: The Earth Not a Planet by David Wardlaw Scott ©1901 London pg. 134

is nominally horizontal and is so shown on all sections. It is not the practice in laying out Public Works to make allowances for the curvature of the earth...

In projecting railways on a globe, the datum line would be the arc of a circle corresponding to the latitude of the place. That the datum line for the railway projections is always a horizontal line, proves that the general configuration of the world is horizontal. To support the globe theory, the gentlemen of the observatories should call upon the surveyor to prove that he allows the necessary amount for 'curvature.' But this is what the learned men dare not do, **as it is well-known that the allowance for the supposed curvature is never made...**

One hundred and eighteen miles of LEVEL railway, and yet the surface on which it is projected a globe? Impossible. It cannot be. **Early in 1898 I met Mr. Hughes, chief officer of the steamer 'City of Lincoln.' This gentleman told me he had projected thousands of miles of level railway in South America, and never heard of any allowance for curvature being made. On one occasion he surveyed over one thousand miles of railway which was a perfect straight line all the way...**

It is well known that in the Argentine Republic and other parts of South America, there are railways thousands of miles long without curve or gradient. **In projecting railways, the world is acknowledged to be a plane, and if it were a globe the rules of projection have yet to be discovered. Level railways prove a level world,** *to the utter confusion of the globular school of impractical men with high salaries and little brains...*

*That in all surveys no allowance is made for curvature, which would be a necessity on a globe; that a horizontal line is in every case the datum line, the same line being continuous throughout the whole length of the work; **and that the theodolite cuts a line at equal altitudes on either side of it, which altitude is the same as that of the instrument, clearly proves, to those who will accept proof when it is furnished, that the world is a plane** (FLAT) **and not a globe.***"[63]

Flatter Than A Pancake

It's obvious that surveyors believe their work and the railways and canals they plan depend on the earth being as "flat as a pancake." But did you know that there are many very large places (hundreds of square miles) on earth that are literally "flatter than a pancake?" This should not be possible on a sphere with a 24,901 miles circumference. However, the Departments of Geography at both Texas State University and Arizona State University did a study to see if the state of Kansas was flatter than a pancake. Their results:

"The topographic transects of both Kansas and a pancake at millimeter scale are both quite flat, but this first analysis showed that Kansas is clearly flatter. Mathematically, a value of 1.000 would indicate perfect, platonic flatness. The calculated flatness of the pancake transect from the digital image is approximately 0.957, which is pretty flat, but far from perfectly flat. The confocal laser scan showed the pancake surface to be slightly rougher, still.

Measuring the flatness of Kansas presented us with a greater challenge than measuring the flatness of the

[63] Zetetic Cosmogony by Thomas Winship ©1899 Durban Natal pp. 23, 107, 109 & 126

pancake. The state is so flat that the off-the-shelf software produced a flatness value for it of 1. This value was, as they say, too good to be true, so we did a more complex analysis, and after many hours of programming work, we were able to estimate that Kansas's flatness is approximately 0.9997. That degree of flatness might be described, mathematically, as "damn flat."[64]

Kansas has a width of 410 miles and a length of 213 miles. That comes to 82,278 square miles of land that is "flatter than a pancake." The earth curvature bulge that should be across the 410-mile width of Kansas if we live on a ball comes to a 9,261-foot-high arc. So how could the entire state of Kansas be "flatter than a pancake" or as the geography departments of two universities said, "perfectly flat?" But to make matters worse for the spherical earth religion, a 2014 article by The Atlantic sites another study by *"... geographers at the University of Kansas, who just published a paper, "The Flatness of U.S. States," in Geographical Review, a peer-reviewed journal published by the American Geographical Society."* The article entitled, **'Science: Several U.S. States, Led by Florida, Are Flatter Than a Pancake,'** goes on to admit, *"Once they'd developed their algorithm, Dobson and Campbell processed elevation data, gathered from NASA's Shuttle Radar Topography Mission, for the contiguous U.S.—48 states and the District of Columbia. (Why not Alaska and Hawaii? "We knew the answer for those well enough," Dobson told me; "we knew they weren't going to be the flattest.)"[65]* In fact, Kansas came in 9th behind Florida #1, Louisiana #2, Illinois #3, South Carolina #4, Minnesota #5, Delaware #6, North Dakota #7 and Texas #8. All of which begs the question, "How many

[64] https://www.usu.edu/geo/geomorph/kansas.html
[65] https://www.theatlantic.com/technology/archive/2014/03/science-several-us-states-led-by-florida-are-flatter-than-a-pancake/284348/

massive flat places can you have on what looks like a perfect sphere from every alleged picture of earth from NASA?"

There are also other places on earth that clearly defy the alleged curvature of the earth. For instance, the Bolivian salt flat called Salar de Uyuni is the world's largest salt flat measuring 4,086 square miles (80 miles across). The top layer of salt is several meters thick and has *"extraordinary flatness with the average elevation variations within one meter (3 feet) over the entire area of Salar...Following rain, a thin layer of water transforms the flat into the world's largest mirror."* According to the math (8 inches per miles squared), a sphere with a circumference of 24,901 mile should curve or drop just over 455 feet. That is the height of a 45-story skyscraper, and yet the flatness of the ENTIRE 4,086 square miles of Salar de Uyuni varies less than 3 feet. As the old saying goes, *"Houston...we have a problem."*

Another scientific fact that can easily be observed is that water always finds its level. That's why rivers flow and empty into the oceans. It is the reason water is used in construction levels. It is also why the oceans are said to be at sea level, not sea curve. Undisturbed water is level and needs a container. These facts may seem elementary and logical, but they are testable, observable and repeatable (otherwise known as the true scientific method). So, if water is level (and it is) and if 71% of the earth is water (and it is), then that should be enough to prove the earth is indeed flat. However, when the obvious facts contradict the heliocentric, sun-worshipping model of the scientism priests, they immediately cry "GRAVITY" (a mysterious force that is still only a theory). And if gravity doesn't work for the scenario then they say, *"The earth is too big to see the curve"* (though they have claimed to see the curve from 40,000 feet). Or they have to come up with magical and mysterious forces like "Dark Energy" and "Dark Matter" which once again cannot be tested or proven.

Neil deGrasse Tyson is a famous astrophysicist and winner of a 2004 NASA award. The following comments he made on his StarTalk radio podcast expose the esoteric sophistry these "experts" claim is science. When asked the question, *"What is gravity?"* Neil deGrasse Tyson immediately answered, *"We have no idea. Ok...next question."* His co-host that asked the question just says, *"Wooooow."* Then he adds, *"Here's the difference...we can describe gravity. We can say what it does to other things. We can measure it, predict with it. **But when you start asking like '...what it is...' I don't know.** In an Einsteinian answer, we would say that gravity is the curvature of space and time."*[66] But Tyson's earlier admission that he did not know what gravity is means that he has no idea what "curvature of space and time" means.

How is it that gravity is so powerful that it can hold the oceans down to the earth and allegedly make them curve to form our spherical earth, but a cloud can hold rain in it in the air, a rabbit can hop, and a bumble bee can fly? Wouldn't electromagnetism and density vs. buoyancy explain these things more realistically? Coulomb's law, or Coulomb's inverse-square law, is a law of physics that describes force interacting between static electrically charged particles. Coulomb's law can be used to derive Gauss's law, and vice versa. The law has been tested extensively, and all observations have upheld the law's principle. And would you be surprised to find out that *"...Coulomb's law (which was first published in 1784 by French physicist Charles-Augustin de Coulomb and was essential to the development of the*

---

[66] https://www.youtube.com/watch?v=Efh4bu4rcbs

*theory of electromagnetism) **being an inverse-square law, it is analogous** (or almost exactly the same) **to Isaac Newton's inverse-square law of universal gravitation?**"*[67]

But what if I told you (and document) that even NASA and the rest of our military industrial complex admit in their technical manuals that they design aircraft, missiles, other long-range projectiles, and radio waves to fly over a "non-rotating, flat earth"? Would you believe that you have been lied to and brainwashed your entire life if you could see that they must build things (like supersonic aircraft) to work the way things truly are? Believe it or not, these manuals and declassified document do exist. The first government document that I came across that admitted a flat, stationary earth (as the Bible has always taught) was NASA Reference Publication 1207 from 1988. It is entitled ***"The Derivation and Definition of a Linear Aircraft Model."*** It states in the summary and the conclusion of a manual full of very complicated, mathematical equations:

*"This report documents the derivation (mathematical origin) and definition of a linear aircraft model for a rigid aircraft of constant mass **flying over a FLAT, NON-ROTATING EARTH."***

In laymen's terms, that means that aircraft are designed to fly over a FLAT, NON-ROTATING EARTH. So, if the earth is a sphere/ball, why would any NASA engineer/rocket scientist even bother or waste time writing a reference manual with pages and pages of mathematical equations on the derivation and definition of aircraft flying over a flat, non-rotating earth? Why compute for something that doesn't

---

[67] *Electricity and Magnetism (3rd ed.)* by Purcell, Edward M.; Morin, David J. ©2013 Cambridge University Press. ISBN 9781107014022.

exist? Of course, some have put forth the idea that these "flat earth equations" are to simplify the math, but I must call bull on that lame excuse. Aren't these NASA people MIT, Harvard, Yale, Stanford, Georgia Tech aerospace engineers? Why do they need to simplify the math down to something that they claim doesn't exist? Aren't they trained and paid to do that kind of math? And with things like rockets, Mach 4 aircraft, and even "Space" Shuttle landings, you would think that they would ALWAYS have to calculate for the alleged curvature of the earth. So why waste time with "flat earth equations"? It's like saying that we must simplify the math down to "Thor Hammer equations" before we can design a log splitter to work with hydraulic pressure. If it doesn't exist, why use it for anything? But as I will address later in this book, NASA document 1207 is just the tip of the iceberg when it comes to government documents that admit the earth is flat.

Jesus said this, *"If I have told you earthly things, and ye believe not, how shall ye believe, if I tell you of heavenly things?"* (John 3:12)

And the Apostle Paul preached, *"Beware therefore, lest that come upon you, which is spoken of in the prophets; Behold, ye despisers, and wonder, and perish: for I work a work in your days, a work which ye shall in no wise believe, though a man declare it unto you"* (Acts 13:40-41).

Many things are being revealed in these last days. Will you believe the evidence and then believe God's Word? Or will you keep believing the liars of scientism who claim that all of this beauty and order came from a massive explosion and that we evolved from monkeys on a spinning, flying ball?

Chapter 5

The 2015 Awakening

*"Now in the first year of Cyrus king of Persia, that the word of the LORD spoken by the mouth of Jeremiah might be accomplished, the LORD **stirred up** the spirit of Cyrus king of Persia, that he made a proclamation throughout all his kingdom, and put it also in writing, saying, Thus saith Cyrus king of Persia, All the kingdoms of the earth hath the LORD God of heaven given me; and he hath charged me to build him an house in Jerusalem, which is in Judah. Who is there among you of all his people? The LORD his God be with him and let him go up"* (2 Chronicles 36:22-23).

Jesus said, *"**And ye shall know the truth, and the truth shall make you free**"* (John 8:32).

*"**The flat earth brought me to the truth of Christ.** Before, I was into yoga, Hinduism, and aliens. The truth that the earth is flat brought me to the Bible and the issue of demons. I realized I had been under demonic possession since birth. **Jesus set me free**."* - Lillian Hubbard (social media comment)

131

"I was blown away when the truth of flat earth hit me. I am now a follower of Jesus Christ." - Patrick Dodd (social media comment)

The LORD God of the Bible (also revealed as Jesus Christ), allowed His people in Israel to be taken into Babylonian captivity for seventy years for their wickedness and rebellion toward Him. The Lord sent prophets to warn them and to call them to repentance, but they would not listen. So, the Lord allowed Nebuchadnezzar, the King of Babylon, to destroy His Temple that He had directed King Solomon to build about three hundred years earlier. In the process, the King of Babylon took most of the surviving Israelites into captivity in Babylon. However, God did not leave them without hope. He gave them a very specific time in which He would end their punishment and bring them back to their homeland. Seventy years later, when that time of restoration and deliverance came, there had been a lot of changes in the kingdom of Babylon. The Medes and Persians had conquered it and at that time, Cyrus the Great was king of Persia and ruled from Babylon. It was then that God stirred up the spirit of Cyrus (a pagan, Gentile king) to bless His people and to fulfill the prophetic message that He had given through Jeremiah the prophet.

I share this passage to make a very important point: God Almighty can and will use anyone He wants to awaken and bless His people and bring His prophecies to pass. He can use people who don't know Him at all, and even use people who serve other gods. God can stir anyone's heart to do His will or fulfill His purposes in the earth. And this is exactly what He started doing in 2014 and 2015. God began to stir up some non-Christians and Christians to look into some very important Biblical truths that had been buried by what the Bible defines as *"science falsely so-called"* (1 Timothy

6:20). These truths had been hidden by alleged journeys into "space" by the early Russian satellites, cosmonauts, and later the United States government known as the CIA and NASA (made up of former Nazi scientists and Freemason astronauts). It is interesting to note that the original Hebrew word for "*stirred up*" in 2 Chronicles 36:22 is *uwr*: a primitive root that conveys the idea of opening the eyes. It means to awaken from sleep or to arouse, incite, or provoke. And that is the best way to describe what started happening...an awakening!

Our little church had been praying for revival since we started in January of 2009. We were all a bit weary from the many battles, even though there were small victories here and there. We knew deep down that there had to be more that God wanted to do. We knew that according to Bible prophecy we were nearing the time of great tribulation preceding the second coming of Jesus Christ. In our prayer meetings, we cried out for God to pour out His power, glory and truth upon the lost (people who do not know Jesus Christ as their Lord and Savior), the church, and our nation. We prayed that God would deliver people from Satan's deceptions by the power of His Spirit and the truth of His Word the Bible.

Unprecedented

In a time of prayer on December 31, 2013, the Lord Jesus spoke to me the word "unprecedented" in reference to the coming year. I immediately shared that word on Facebook and in our church service the following Sunday. Within a week North America experienced what meteorologists referred to as unprecedented cold temperatures as 49 states broke low temperature records. Just a month later, I discovered that we were not alone in our unprecedented weather when I saw a Jerusalem Post article on February 10, 2014 entitled, *"Israel Experiencing Unprecedented Drought Conditions."*[68] And then on March 6, 2014, The Guardian reported, *"Queensland drought spreads to an unprecedented 80% of the state: Drought-declared area is now the largest in the beleaguered state's history as state minister works to tap federal help."*[69] On May 2, 2014, Accuweather.com posted, *"Unprecedented: 100% of California is in a Drought"*[70]

Another unprecedented occurrence was the increase in great earthquakes. Of course, Jesus Christ prophesied the rise of great earthquakes in the last days leading up to His return, *"And great earthquakes shall be in divers places, and famines, and pestilences; and fearful sights and great signs shall there be from heaven"* (Luke 21:11). CBS reported: "If you think there have been more earthquakes than usual this year, you're right. A new study finds there were more than twice as many big earthquakes in the first quarter of 2014 as compared with the average since 1979." "We have recently experienced a period that has had one of the highest rates of great earthquakes ever recorded," said lead study author Tom Parsons, a research geophysicist with the U.S. Geological Survey (USGS) in Menlo Park, California. The average rate of big earthquakes -- those larger than magnitude 7 -- has been 10 per year since 1979, the study reports. That rate rose to 12.5 per year starting in 1992, and then jumped to 16.7 per year starting in 2010 -- a 65 percent increase compared to the rate since 1979. This increase

---

[68] https://www.jpost.com/Enviro-Tech/Israel-experiencing-unprecedented-drought-conditions-341003
[69] https://www.theguardian.com/world/2014/mar/07/queensland-drought-spreads-to-an-unprecedented-80-of-the-state
[70] https://www.accuweather.com/en/weather-blogs/weathermatrix/unprecedented-100-of-california-is-in-a-drought/26247776

accelerated in the first three months of 2014 to more than double the average since 1979, the researchers report."[71]

I continued to see the word "unprecedented" in newspapers and on television throughout 2014, but there was one unprecedented event that slipped under the radar toward the end of the year. On November 9, 2014, a strange New Age guy by the name of Eric Dubay published his book along with a documentary entitled, *"The Flat-Earth Conspiracy."* In these works, he shared arguments that were presented in the late 1800s and early 1900s by Zetetic (Flat Earth) Christians like Samuel Rowbotham, David Wardlaw Scott, and Lady Elizabeth Anne Mould Blount. Dubay even included a chapter on the Bible entitled, *"The Flat Earth Bible."*

This led to another non-Christian by the name of Mark Sargent (who I now believe was a preemptive, controlled-opposition plant) to investigate this seemingly ridiculous flat earth idea. Early in 2015, Mark Sargent released a series of YouTube videos called *"Flat Earth Clues."* In these "clues" he explored the possibility that we are inside of a "Truman show"-like, enclosed system that is hidden from the general public. As people began to share videos by Dubay and Sargent, the idea that the earth could be flat (as the Bible has always said it was) and we have been deceived started spreading like wildfire!

However, I believe one of the most credible witnesses that stepped forward to confirm the truth of flat earth was a man named Sean McCrary. I spoke with Sean on the phone in February of 2019 for over an hour and a half, and he is a

---

[71] http://www.cbsnews.com/news/big-Earthquakes-double-in-2014-but-scientists-say-theyre-not-linked/

great guy. In 2015, at the time of his interviews, he was a United States Navy Missile System Instructor. Prior to that job, McCrary was a NATO Sea Sparrow Surface Missile System operator who went through very rigorous electronic training, troubleshooting, with very detailed schematics on how the system worked. He stated in a public interview on Truth Frequency Radio on November 4, 2015, *"...that with my missile system, we have the ability to track something 50 nautical miles (57.539 statute miles) away with our radar that we use for this missile system."* He stated that his line-of-sight, tracking radar was a 2-degree pencil beam that stayed continually locked on target. He explained that his tracking radar could track an enemy aircraft flying 100 feet off the surface of the water from 45-50 nautical miles away. This should be impossible on a spherical earth with a circumference of 24,901 miles. The amount of earth curvature that should be blocking that tracking radar (even when you calculate the height of the radar at 120 feet above the surface of the ocean) is 455 feet. That means the aircraft would have to be flying above 455 feet to be detected and continually tracked by that missile system radar.

Navy Missile Instructor McCrary also confirmed, *"There is absolutely no circuitry designed into the engineering of our missile system that accounts for anything closely resembling the Coriolis Effect"* (the spin of the earth). This from a man who was trained on every aspect of this missile system and operated this weapons system for ten years. And he is not the only military veteran who has noticed some things just don't add up.

Missiles Over the Curve?

At our fourth earth curvature test across Mobile Bay, I had the privilege to meet and spend the day with Lieutenant Colonel (retired) Bryan Read. He is a 20-year U.S. Army veteran. Bryan served as a Missile Defense Commander and an Airspace Tactical Control Officer for NATO in Germany. Additionally, he served as the Defense Attaché to the United States Embassy in Tashkent, Uzbekistan and later as a Foreign Area Officer attached to the United States Army Special Operations Command in the Central Asian Theater. Bryan also served as a professor at the United States Military Academy at West Point.

The Lieutenant Colonel emailed me months before the test stating, *"I was a Tactical Control Officer and commander for US Army Missile Defense units in Germany. I now realize that our radars did not need to factor in curvature -- our Improved Continuous Wave Acquisition radar (ICWAR) could see up to 45 miles. The ICWAR was used to pick up low-flying, high-performance aircraft and helicopters. We were concerned about the NAP Earth flight paths of enemy aircraft; meaning their use of geographical features to hide their approach to our missile site or airbase."* (Nap-of-the-Earth is a type of very low-altitude flight course used by military aircraft to avoid enemy detection and attack in a high-threat environment).[72] He later shared on our August 20, 2019 episode of Prophecy Quake radio show that they were able to track low-flying aircraft (50 to 100 feet high) with their line-of-sight radar at a distance of 45 miles. The ICWAR system itself is only about 8-10 feet tall. Doing the math of our alleged sphere of 8 inches per miles squared, there should have been 1,128 feet of earth curvature blocking

---

[72] *Helicopters at War* - Blitz Editions ©1996

the line-of-sight of that radar system. Even if you elevate the radar to 50 feet high, that still comes to 880 feet of earth curvature that should be blocking the ability of the ICWAR to track nap-of-the-earth aircraft and helicopters.

One of our ministry school students sent me and interesting article from DefenseNews.com that backs up what the Lieutenant Colonel shared. It is entitled, *"When it comes to missile-killing lasers, the US Navy is ready to burn its ships."* The article is about the HELIOS laser weapon that is being developed by Lockheed Martin and is scheduled to be deployed by 2021. The Article states, *"With the progress on HELIOS,* **the Navy is getting closer to fielding a laser that could help it knock down Chinese and Russian anti-ship cruise missiles at very close ranges,** *said Bryan Clark, a retired submarine officer and analyst with the Center for Strategic and Budgetary Assessments... 'The laser being able to shoot down cruise missiles: That will happen,' he said...***Ideally, an incoming missile wouldn't get within 100 miles of its intended target.** *'"*[73]

[73] https://www.defensenews.com/naval/2019/05/23/when-it-comes-to-missile-killing-lasers-the-us-navy-is-ready-to-burn-its-ships/

After reading the Defense News article, I looked up some information on cruise missiles. I discovered that Russian cruise missiles like the Kalibr series have a flight ceiling (highest altitude) of 1,000 meters but, they only fly 20 meters (or around 65 feet) above the surface of the water as they approach a targeted ship.[74] Lasers are straight, line-of-sight weapons so there is no way the Navy could use a laser to shoot down a Russian cruise missile over 100 miles away if the earth is a sphere. The amount of earth curvature bulge that should block line of sight on a Russian cruise missile at 100 miles away is 6,666 feet (1.2 miles). What if we add 80 feet to the height of the laser weapon because of it being mounted on a Navy ship? The amount of earth curvature bulge that should be blocking the line-of-sight is still 5,287 feet, which is over a mile high. In fact, with the laser mounted 80 feet above the water on a ship, they could not hit a Russian cruise missile at even a range of 50 miles due to 1,016 feet of earth curvature bulge. So, a retired Navy officer talking about hitting a Russian cruise missile from over 100 miles away with a laser is either absolute crazy talk, or it proves that the earth is flat.

[74] https://www.janes.com/images/assets/147/70147/Game_changer_Russian_sub-launched_cruise_missiles_bring_strategic_effect_edit.pdf

The Impact

Articles like the one in Defense News, along with videos and books from people like Dubay and Sargent made people realize that they should question the trustworthiness of NASA and other government "space" agencies. Testing whether the earth is a sphere and observing reality is simple, and yet most have never even thought to question what we are told. The release of improved high zoom cameras (like the Nikon P900) and the ability for everyday people to conduct high altitude balloon tests and laser tests has fueled a massive growth in the number of flat earth believers over the last few years. The math simply doesn't lie (although some "debunkers" lie about the math). We can see things at distances that we should not be able to see if we lived on a sphere with a circumference of 24,901 miles.

The narrative of the fake news media says that "flat earthers" are just science deniers or fundamental religious nuts. However, average people (not government agencies) performing real science experiments (observable, measurable, and repeatable tests) have convinced millions of people that we have been lied to about the shape of the earth and the true nature of the sun, moon, and stars. And when people began to see that the Bible taught these truths about creation all along, they began returning to faith in the Bible and the God of the Bible.

Here are just a few testimonies that I received from people who were lost, but came to God once they saw these truths:

"Dean Odle, I would like to thank you for this video. I recently found God almost two months ago. I used to believe in the ancient astronaut theory and that we were a small

speck in a huge universe hurdling through space. I came across a flat earth video on YouTube and decided to check it out because I was curious what the fuss was about. Since that video I researched for weeks on end why Nasa would be lying to everyone. I finally saw God's fingerprint when I was 100% convinced the earth was flat and that everything, we know has been a lie and that God's word is more true than we know. I cried when I found God. Why? Well, I finally had understanding, life made sense now. I no longer question God's word and if we are alone in the universe. I'm thankful for you and this video and to help as many people as we can realize the truth of God's word. I have subscribed to your channel and would like to attend through YouTube since I'm in South Carolina. I know so many people who cannot see the truth or that think I'm crazy but I know now that God's word is true and I believe he used the flat earth theory to show me that he is real before the end of days. He works in mysterious ways. I was brought up in a family that had several different beliefs, so I never knew God as good as I wanted to. Please help me get to know him better and I appreciate you and everything you're doing! God Bless you and thank you!!!" - Wes from South Carolina.

"I was raised in a home with a Catholic mother and a Protestant father, but neither of them were believers in Jesus Christ or God. My parents were sinners all their lives and I grew up in an environment of alcoholism, adultery, physical, and psychological abuse. When I left the house after finishing university, I was somewhat of an atheist and totally disconnected from God. Having no spiritual background or protection, I easily fell victim to Satan and all his temptations (fornication, drugs, alcohol, etc.). Despite all my suffering and pain, I always felt like there was a silent voice telling to me to stop, and I often cried tears of despair and prayed, calling out for His help.

I believe the Lord touched me 4 years ago. After leading a reckless party lifestyle of alcohol, fornication and cocaine addiction, one day I decided enough was enough and I quit EVERYTHING - cold turkey. No therapy, no AA, no outside help. I left that whole sordid life behind, and now I realize that my change of heart and direction in life was thanks to the blessings of my Lord and Savior Jesus Christ. I was sure that some Divine force was helping me, and He was. Nevertheless, I still felt an emptiness inside that I couldn't explain.

In 2016 and 2017, I researched all the conspiracy facts and started to unravel the lies and deception of the Satanic/Luciferian system that we live in (banking fraud, counterfeit religions, corrupt governments, secret societies, pedophile rings, MK Ultra mind control, etc.). This started to really wake me up to the fact that a deeply sinister force was at work in our world.

I started following New Age spirituality, but I quickly realized that it was a dangerous mix of occult practices and symbolism, Freemasonry, and Eastern mysticism. Still searching for answers, I started watching videos on mudfossils and the Flat Earth and I studied this deeply. It made complete sense, and I remembered what I had learned as a young girl in Sunday school: that the Lord created all things in Heaven and Earth, including us!

Your video "The Flat Earth Can't Save You...Only Christ Jesus!" miraculously appeared as I was watching videos about the Flat Earth. Pastor Odle, your sermon changed my life forever. I am proud to say that today, I am a Born-Again Christian thanks to the grace and mercy of the Lord Jesus Christ and your passionate service to his cause on earth." - Melani from Canada

On one of my YouTube videos (Longing for Revival), Cate commented, *"I was woken up to the truth about flat earth whilst searching for the truth of this world. It has completely changed me. I am now born again and am studying The Holy Bible and have bought the series on DVD to listen to the Word of God in the car and at home whenever I can. I am drawing close to Jesus in these last days. Unfortunately, my family also think I am crazy and my husband has told my brother he thinks I have some sort of deluded personality disorder. It has become so difficult, as we have 4 children together. I am praying to God for strength."*

Robert Moore (aka Paint Tank) testified on my Longing for Revival video on YouTube, *"You have no idea what a blessing your videos and MP3s are. I was a Christian slowly sinking into entertainment as my god. Rock music, endless movies, TV shows, reading The Lord of the Rings again (3rd time), etc. My soul (mind) and spirit were becoming more and more filled with the garbage of this world as ENTERTAINMENT. All the old tricks of enjoying movies and music was fading and leaving me empty. I kept praying for God to draw me closer, but I continued to binge watch shows and enjoy falling asleep listening to ZZ Top, RUSH, and Van Halen.*

When I discovered the Flat Earth, Jesus woke me up and answered the "draw me closer" prayer. It was over. God was not OUTSIDE the universe in some DISTANT spiritual palace, he was only a few miles away (100-4000 or so?). He was close, VERY close. He was watching me. He wanted me to have a relationship with him, NOT my electronic devices. I was busted, exposed for the entertainment and worldly junkie I had become. *I stumbled onto your channel, Pastor Dean Odle. God gave me a new*

143

direction. I became filled with the Holy Spirit. Jesus became real to me. I started reading my Bible again. I read the book of Enoch. I started praying. Your sermons and Alexander Scourby's King James Bible MP3s replaced my rock music on my phone. I "broke up" with the Devil and gave him all of his stuff back (destroyed/burned over $4000 worth of stuff).

My wife, family, and some friends think I am nuts. Others have been awakened by me and are GRATEFUL for the Flat Earth Revelation. *Keep doing what you are doing EXPOSING (not ENTERTAINING, as a former addict of that sort, I KNOW the difference) the evils of our world. If you have not done so already, I think looking at THE TRUTH IS STRANGER THAN FICTION You Tube channel will be of help to you (RESEARCH) in these last days. I want to make the trip from Myrtle Beach, SC to you church soon. May Christ Jesus richly bless you this day and every day till we see him split the firmament and call us to his side. Amen."*

I could go on and on sharing the testimonies of non-Christians, atheists, agnostics, ancient alien believers, and lukewarm Christians who came to true faith in the Bible and our God and Savior Jesus Christ after they saw the evidences of the flat, stationary, enclosed earth, the nearness of the sun, moon, and stars and that the Bible revealed these things thousands of years ago. And as a minister of Jesus Christ for over 32 years, I have never seen any other Bible truth (outside of the simple gospel message) bring more atheists and agnostics to faith in the Bible and salvation through faith in the atoning death and resurrection of the Lord Jesus Christ. And when I ask people when God started opening their eyes to this truth of creation, a great majority say 2015. There is no doubt in my mind that this revelation of flat earth and true Biblical cosmology is a sovereign move of God to

144

combat the unbelief and Bible skepticism created by the many deceptions of Satan on this last generation.

In every true revival, there has been a restoration of some lost, ignored or misunderstood truth in the Bible. The Reformation under Martin Luther restored the truth of justification by faith without needing the trappings, rituals and works of the Roman Catholic system. The revivals under John Wesley in the 1700s and Charles Finney in the 1800s restored the truths of the responsibility of men and women to exercise their free-will to respond to the gospel of Jesus Christ by choosing to believe and repent of sin. The Azusa Street Revival of 1906 restored the truth of the gifts of the Holy Spirit given to the church on the day of Pentecost. And in these last days the Lord has revived His truths about His creation in order to free people from the antichrist scientism religion. I call it a religion because it is truly an exercise of faith to believe in "science" when much of it is actually unproven theories and wild speculations (that always seem to be contrary to God and His Bible).

For instance, consider this antichrist statement from Lawrence Krauss (an American Canadian theoretical physicist and cosmologist who is a professor in the School of Earth and Space Exploration at Arizona State University and a former professor at Yale University and Case Western Reserve University):

"The amazing thing is that every atom in your body came from a star that exploded. And, the atoms in your left hand probably came from a different star than your right hand. It really is the most poetic thing I know about physics: You are all stardust. You couldn't be here if stars hadn't exploded, because the elements — the carbon, nitrogen, oxygen, iron, all the things that matter for evolution — weren't created at

145

*the beginning of time. They were created in the nuclear furnaces of stars, and the only way they could get into your body is if those stars were kind enough to explode. **So, forget Jesus. The stars died so that you could be here today.**"*[75]

This is the kind of antichrist, made up nonsense that several generations of people have been brainwashed with since birth. And God in His mercy and love for mankind, is revealing the truth about His creation, truths that can be observed and tested with true science (observable, measurable, and repeatable). Here are some of the Bible truths that are being restored to mankind by the One True God of Creation:

1) The earth is not a sphere but rather it is flat (as the Bible has stated for thousands of years).

2) The earth is covered by molten glass-like dome called the firmament.

3) Above the firmament is a massive ocean of water (that can be seen through the glass-like dome) and not the vacuum of space or stars and planets.

4) The sun, moon, and stars are not far away in "outer space." They are inside the firmament dome and move in a circuit over us just like the Bible told us in Genesis 1 and Psalm 19.

5) The earth is stationary. That means the earth is not spinning, orbiting the sun, or flying through a vast universe at 600,000 mph.

---

[75] https://sciencebasedlife.wordpress.com/2012/03/11/stars-died-so-that-you-could-live/

6) When the Lord God of the Bible made the earth, He engraved a circle (not a ball) on the flat earth and that act made a boundary all the way around the outer edge to hold the oceans. That outer edge is what we call Antarctica and it is the ice wall at the *"...ends of the earth."*

7) The North Pole is the only magnetic center of the circle of earth.

8) There is no South Pole which is why compasses don't work the same in the "Southern Hemisphere."

9) The planets are not other terrestrial spheres in "space." They are the "wandering stars" that do not follow the same course as the other stars.

10) The stars are not giant suns that are millions of light years away, but instead, they are much smaller and closer to us (which is why they can and do fall to earth sometimes).

11) NASA and other government leaders and agencies all over the world have conspired to hide certain truths of God (particularly about creation) in an Antichrist plot against the Lord Jehovah and His Messiah Jesus Christ.

12) When Jesus Christ returns to this earth (very soon), the firmament sky will be rolled back like a scroll and the stars will fall like figs shaken from a fig tree by a mighty wind.

The world is getting further and further from God because of their wickedness and Creator-denying, alien-loving "science." And yet, in His great patience and mercy, the Creator of heaven and earth still continues to draw people to Him. And He is doing it with Truths that remind us that He is near, He loves us and is concerned with our day to day coming and going.

Chapter 6

Atheists Come to Jesus

"The fool hath said in his heart, 'There is no God.' They are corrupt, they have done abominable works, there is none that doeth good. The Lord looked down from heaven upon the children of men, to see if there were any that did understand, and seek God"* (Psalms 14:1-2).

*"For the invisible things of him from the creation of the world are clearly seen, being understood by the things that are made, even his eternal power and Godhead**; so that they are without excuse:** Because that, when they knew God, they glorified him not as God, neither were thankful; but became vain in their imaginations, and their foolish heart was darkened. **Professing themselves to be wise, they became fools"*** (Romans 1:20-22).

"In the beginning was the Word, and the Word was with God, and the Word was God. The same was in the beginning with God. All things were made by him; and without him was not anything made that was made. In him was life; and the life was the light of men. And the light*

149

shineth in darkness; and the darkness comprehended it not... **And the Word was made flesh, and dwelt among us, (and we beheld his glory, the glory as of the only begotten of the Father,) full of grace and truth.** *John bare witness of him, and cried, saying, This was he of whom I spake, He that cometh after me is preferred before me: for he was before me. And of his fulness have all we received, and grace for grace.* **For the law was given by Moses, but grace and truth came by Jesus Christ"** (John 1:1-5 & 14-17).

When someone's eyes are opened to the truth of God's stationary, enclosed, flat earth, it eventually leads them to at least consider what the Bible has to say about creation. The phrases in the Bible like *"the four corners of the earth...the ends of the earth...the stars of heaven fell unto the earth...or the moon will not give HER LIGHT, "* take on a new meaning. The Bible story of Joshua telling the sun and the moon to stand still finally makes sense. The Scriptures about the earth being still and motionless and the sun moving in a circuit path over the earth also make sense. In fact, many passages in the Bible really come alive when your eyes are opened to the evidence and you start connecting the dots.

Of course, these passages have always been in the Bible, but most people (including myself for many years) have seen them through Copernican, heliocentric theory "colored glasses." Thus, many relegate them to the convenient file cabinet of metaphors or fairytales. And as previously stated, it was the Copernican/Big Bang/Darwinian "science falsely so-called" that has caused many to throw out the Bible as the inspired words of the Creator. The following is what an atheist said during a debate with a Christian:

"As science has grown, Christianity has shrunk. Many fundamental things in Christianity were obliterated
150

centuries ago and Christianity hasn't quite realized it. It's *sort of the walking dead in my opinion. Let me give you some examples...with the development of astronomy, the Biblical system of the universe collapsed.* **The Bible describes a three-story universe. Heaven is a solid hemisphere that arches over the earth, the raqiya in Hebrew, the firmamentum in Latin, the firmament in the King James Bible.** *There was water above there, that's why the sky is blue and somewhere above that is the abode of God and the angels. We are down here on this flat earth, the Bible is definitely a flat earth book and below us in the sub-cellar is sheol or hell.*

Now, with the development of telescopes and the discovery that the earth goes around the sun and that the earth is a sphere, some very important Biblical ideas were shattered. *Heaven, for example, which was a physical thing up there, heaven has gotten lost...nobody knows where it is. It has moved outside the realm of space and time. It is in some other dimension I suppose. And like heaven, hell too has been displaced. It is no longer down in the basement...Nobody knows where the hell, hell is. Now, as long as we had this three-story universe with the physical heavens to which the sun, the moon and the stars were attached, the Magi could very easily have followed a star which was not many thousand feet above them, they could follow the star to the birthplace of Jesus. But without the firmament and the stars many light-years away, the Magi could not do that.*" (I wonder how sailors have used the stars to guide them for centuries, but I digress. Let's get back to Mr. Atheist). He continues, *"The ascension of Jesus for example in light of what we really have that we are a planet* *flying through outer space, the ascension of Jesus now is seen not to be a miracle, but a simple absurdity."*[76]

This is just one illustration of the position atheists and agnostics take and why they do not believe the Bible. It comes back to believing the lies, exaggerations, and false theories of the Copernican/Kepler/Galileo/NASA revolution. Sadly, many Christians have also adopted these beliefs of false science instead of taking a stand against the lies. Simple earth curvature tests have proven that the earth is not a sphere, and you will see in a later chapter that some honest scientists accidently demonstrated that the earth does not spin or orbit the sun. Yet, many Christians still don't believe the full Biblical account of creation and some even say, *"What does it matter?"* Well, beside the fact that ALL of God's Words should matter to a Christian, here are some reasons this issue of the shape of the earth and the true nature of the sun, moon, and stars matters:

Josh M. wrote, ***"I was not sure about the existence of God. I was a science junky. The Lord showed me the many lies of the world, then flat earth towards the latter part of my waking up. It sealed the deal for me. I know the Bible is truth and I will never again question the existence of our Lord Jesus Christ."***

Here is an email from a mechanical engineer in Sweden named Paul Logdberg. He is a former 39-year atheist that flew to Alabama to be water baptized at our church in 2017:

"Dear Pastor Dean,

---

[76]https://www.youtube.com/watch?v=LydGoPkwywE&list=PLbJUUs6PRfAD6RftPXNdrM ZrR4v8lY9nH&index=16

I am from Sweden, a country with ~80% atheists, and I grew up in a typical upper middle-class home where my dad worked a lot and my mother worked part time. The state took care of my indoctrination (aka education) and everyone in my greater family were (and still are) atheists. Of course, I didn't want to be an odd ball so naturally I was an atheist too. I believed all the scientism, space, evolution, NASA, and that the Bible was just a fairy tale. I did get "confirmed" at the age of 14 (in 1989) but it was mainly because my mother thought it was a nice tradition and also because I wanted that CD-player that my parents had promised me. I remember asking the Protestant pastor regarding communion: "is it true that it is the real blood of Jesus that is in the cup?" with a teenager's haughty arrogance to which the pastor replied "no, no, it's just an act of symbolism. It's not literal." Of course, the main take away from that brief episode in my life was that the Bible is only symbolic and not to be taken literally. I was never a very spiritual person and my purpose in life, when I ever contemplated it, was to get an education, get a job, get a wife, have kids, raise the kids, and make money so that my kids don't end up living under a bridge somewhere. And of course, to have fun and travel the world. Life is short, right?*

I lived quite a lonely life in my late teens, and I felt comfortable with it. I had a few closer friends rather than many superficial friends. I never had the desire to be popular or the quarter back hero at the school. I could feel slightly that there was something wrong with the world particularly when looking at the TV and all the surrealistically brain-dead reality shows, Eurovision song contest and the degree to which people are willing to degrade themselves in order to be on that TV.

In my youth, two seeds were planted: most politicians are a bunch of liars and capitalism is a wonderful thing. My parents were both hardcore anti-socialists and due to the fact that Sweden has had socialist rule 80% of the time during the last 100 years, it was natural that this anti-socialist ideology was synonymous to being anti-state.

But then, after graduating from the university with a master's degree in mechanical engineering, I (willingly, I guess) got entangled with the pleasures of this world for a decade: career, apartment, car, etc and it wasn't until my first daughter was born 2010 that I started questioning the paradigm that I had been born into. Since my wife was and is "poor as a church rat", as the saying goes here, I wanted to know how to invest money for the future, so my daughter and wife don't end up under that bridge somewhere. I turned off the TV in 2010 and when I opened the financial newspapers and the BusinessWeek's of the world, I felt more confused than informed. I then stumbled upon a YouTube video about the FED and the enslaving consequences of fiat money, which led to the Bilderbergers and the whole Alex Jones world, fake media and trolls/shills, the origins of our "education" system, false flags, 9-11, Illuminati, aliens and the pyramids of Egypt, and then free energy. **This was around 2014 and I was still an atheist or an agnostic at best.**

When I started looking into the lies of this world back in 2011 and heard someone mention God I would roll my eyes and think **"Oh boy, here come the Bible crazies again"**, but after having heard enough references to God, after a while I started to think "OK, they believe in God; I don't, but I'll listen to what he or she has to say anyway".

I did stumble upon the moon landing hoax back in 2012, but back then I thought it was simply a debt creation scheme by the "evil banker elites". Little did I suspect that there was a deeper purpose behind the moon landing hoax. Flat Earth surfaced on my radar in March April 2015, but I wouldn't even click the link to the video because I thought it was just 'too much.' I reasoned that it must be something put out by the TPTB to discredit those who question our paradigm. But after a month, I looked at it anyway, thinking that it would be fun to see something crazy and ridiculous. I started off with Math Powerland, Mark Sargent and Eric Dubay and to my shock, the arguments were not tinfoil-hattery, or crazy. *I spent 5 months on it and about 1 hour per day. Realizing that the earth is flat made me interested in the Bible.* What is it all about? And I quickly realized that there is a lot of disinformation regarding this topic too.

I then looked into the satanic forces that roam our earth, founding nations, installing rulers and control systems, rewriting history and thereby came to the conclusion that God is real, there is a firmament above us, Satan is evil, the Bible is literally true and we are living in the end times.

If someone would have told me in 2009 that in 8 years from now, you will believe in God, the Bible and Jesus as Savior, I would have called him or her a complete lunatic. But here I am now. I picked up my (Swedish) Bible in 2015 for the first time in 26 years and read on the inside of the cover what the pastor had written: Luke 22:32. (But I have prayed for thee, that thy faith fail not: and when thou art converted, strengthen thy brethren)… So in my face.

In my youth, I never really gave God a chance. I guess He knocked on my door a few times, but I was too deep inside the matrix. God knows me better than I know myself. God knew that if he had thrown the flat earth at me from the start it would've dripped off me like water off Teflon. I am so grateful that He did not give up on me. ***I am immensely grateful that Jesus Christ offers salvation from this deeply sick and twisted world that becomes more and more saturated in wickedness with every passing week.***"

On August 9, 2019 Thomas Schaan from Germany commented on the Dean Odle Ministries Facebook page and wrote, *"This ministry is filled with the Holy Spirit. Here you get the whole Truth.* ***This Pastor led me with his teaching of Biblical Cosmology from atheism to our Lord Jesus Christ, God in the flesh.*** *People, pray for this ministry, the pastor, and the church."*

Thomas Robertshaw shared, ***"I found Jesus and God through flat earth. It changed my life."***

Rannick testified, ***"All the preaching in the world could not pull me out of atheism. Once I realized the earth was not a spinning ball, it was about 2 seconds later when I realized the Bible is true and my lifelong atheism was toast. I understand the gospel is the most important thing, and it is...but if you want to turn an atheist around 180 degrees, flat earth does it faster than anything else. Atheists are always demanding proof of a creator. Flat Earth is that proof."***

Howard Massicotte wrote, ***"After over 1,000 hours of research of the flat earth, I found Christ and I believe the Bible."***

Lillian Hubbard commented, ***"The flat earth brought me to the truth of Christ. Before, I was into yoga, Hinduism, and aliens.*** *The truth that the earth is flat brought me to the Bible and the issue of demons. I realized I had been under demonic possession since birth.* ***Jesus set me free."***

Patrick Dodd wrote, ***"I was blown away when the truth of flat earth hit me. I am now a follower of Jesus Christ."***

Jenny Webb testified, ***"I always knew that the Bible and mainstream science could not both be true,*** *so for most of my life I chose to trust in learned men about the origins of the earth, and the universe, and everything else.* ***The flat earth led me to God and His Son, my Savior.*** *God's word is, literally, true and all men are liars."*

Former agnostic Brian Nielsen wrote, ***"Flat Earth solidified it for me, that, "Jesus is the way, the truth and the life."***

Two years ago, Marky Marxx commented on The Truth Is Stranger Than Fiction YouTube Channel, *"I have been*

157

awakened for 2 years now. I was a believer until my late teens, I am 50 now. **Flat Earth brought me back to God whom I was questioning for years**. I asked God to save me out loud, looking up just last year. I am so confident in Jesus my Lord, and it is a wonderful feeling."

Tiffany Contreras commented on my YouTube channel, ***"Jesus saved my life, but flat earth turned my life back to him. When I found out the earth might be flat, I decided to read the bible for the 1st time at 45 years old. Finding out the Bible said the earth was flat showed me the Bible could be trusted.*** *Reading the Bible put Gods word in my heart and changed me in a way I never imagined. God became more tangible knowing he was right above me on his throne. I never could grasp where God was and he seemed so far away in some distant galaxy. Now I get before him humbly on my face in prayer and I know he can hear me. I sing loudly on my deck up in the mountains cuz I know he can hear me. I LOVE JESUS. He saves AMEN"*

Liz Henry wrote, ***"Flat Earth has opened my eyes. I never believed in God*** *really, definitely was taught that the Bible is fiction. I believed that science was truth. What a gigantic hoax they have done! **Jesus Christ is my salvation. I love Jesus!** The book of Enoch! **The Bible is true.** I am the last person who would have believed it, until I saw with my own eyes and camera. There is a dome! The earth is not a globe."*

I received this email from Richard Carrel in the UK, *"I am 41 now and up until I was 39, I was an atheist; I was suicidal after losing both my parents and my best friend and life going against me in general. I had no belief in Jesus at all, was 100% believer in science and the 'Big Bang',* until one day a stranger running past me whilst I was walking the dogs (Thinking about ending it all!) and the man ran back and said do you mind if we talk. I said yes and he proceeded to tell me that he felt compelled to speak to me for some reason!!! He ended up praying for me, which I was apprehensive about as it wasn't what I believed. Nevertheless, the man was kind and very thoughtful and to be honest in the mood I was, it came as a relief and actually felt like a weight had been lifted from my shoulders and had light in my life!*

From there, I went on this obsessive truth mission which I can only say was something else guiding me on. I had some knowledge of "Conspiracies" but nothing to out the box if you know what I mean! I would wake at 7am and go to bed at 1-2am and this was so for 6 months!!! Something or someone wanted me to know this, there is no way I would have had the passion for this myself, somebody wanted me to see something!!!

Then I got hit with a metaphorical steamtrain!!! It was the culmination of all the truths that had been revealed to me... FLAT EARTH!!! Literally broke down crying.... It was like I saw/felt God, the Father, the Creator!!! Flat Earth SAVED my life, my soul and I have turned away from my life of old...I want to give everything to Jesus!"

159

Allen Buchanan commented on my video *Flat Earth Saved My Life*, *"I believed ancient aliens crap. I lay in bed one night and said, 'God. If you are real and my everlasting soul is at stake, then show me you're real. I deserve that much.'* **The very next night he showed me flat earth**. *I've NEVER been a conspiracy theorist. I mocked them. I couldn't have been more asleep! Blew my mind! And He showed me all the lies and deceit in the world. Then 2 years later, I met Him. He came into my life and actually spoke to me and filled me with the Holy Spirit.* **I was atheist/agnostic for 41 yrs. Now at 45 I'm a Spirit filled, born again Christian."*

▶ YouTube   Flat Earth saved my life

Unworthy Servant of Jesus Christ 5 months ago (edited)
Amen my testimony is very similar to this. If it wasn't for true biblical cosmology, on a night when i gave up on life and was thinking of ending my life, i would never have cried out to Jesus Christ. Once i knew true biblical cosmology i knew someone created it and that someone was Jesus Christ. All credit to the Holy Spirit He lead me to the truth and the truth set me free from addiction and hatred and the wicked lifestyle i lived. Addiction and depression lead me to being alone in my room depressed and jobless. When i watched my first flat earth video, i knew right away there was something true i was hearing. It lead me to searching it out day and night for hours upon hours. I was a "flat earther" for a while before i came to know Jesus and on a night when i didn't want to live anymore because of the true biblical cosmology i cried out to Jesus Christ and never have been the same since. After that night i woke up for this new found desire for the word of God that i use to say was just a fairy tale. For 27 years i lived my life with no care for God and would probably call my self an agnostic and believed in aliens and science. But hearing about true biblical cosmology it erased all of that indoctrination and truly awakened me. I now glory in my tribulations and the pain i experienced that lead me to Jesus Christ. I am so grateful for the tribulations i experienced that lead me to be a Holy Spirit filled born again Christ. All praise and glory to Jesus Christ.

Bruce Carrel shared this with Nathan Roberts, of FlatEarthDoctrine.com *"Thank you Nathan for all that you do, yourself and Dean have really helped me on my journey from atheism to Jesus Christ*. *All glory must go to Jesus Christ as without Him none of this would be possible. He woke me up 2 years ago from the brink of death and showed the evil entities we live with* **and then He showed me His Biblical creation** *(aka flat earth). Everything in a split second merged into one and I saw and felt everything."*

Flat Earth Saved My Life

Early in 2019, a brother named Jake Holdsworth visited our church here in Alabama. During his two-week visit, I was privileged to get to hear his testimony. His story was so amazing that I decided to interview him for our viewers. He was a staunch atheist all of his life, until he came across flat earth. At first, he thought it was ridiculous, but after researching it thoroughly for several months, he was convinced that the earth is flat and that we have been lied to about almost everything. That realization made him ask the next question… *"WHY the deception?"* He testifies that as he pondered that question, "God hit me. I was in my living room. I was hit with a ton of bricks and I found myself on my knees just balling my eyes out, weeping. God hit me and told me, 'I'm here.' I just instantly knew that there was a Creator and that this is THE deception (heliocentric, big bang lies), that we have been lied to. God said, 'All these things are lies to keep you from Me and here I am.'

Jake continues, *"I was just beside myself. I was just weeping. I didn't know how to pray. I didn't know how to do anything. I had no idea. I had no Bible and I had no idea how to get hold of one. It was like nine or ten o'clock and I'm just a mess, balling. I went and flushed all my weed down the toilet. I broke my pipes. I got rid of my cigarettes. I just had this urge that I had to make up for 37 years of not believing God is real.* ***I was like I need a Bible. I need something to start.*** *I was racking my brain (my buddy owns a motel) I'm like 'Motels have Bibles.' So, I got on the phone, 'Hey do you have a Bible? I just need a Bible right now.' He arrived at my house in like 10 minutes and I was waiting at the door. Before he could even get out of his truck with the Bible,* ***I was at the door with tears pouring down my face, telling him, 'The earth is flat! There is a God!'"***[77]

[77] Flat Earth Saved My Life https://www.youtube.com/watch?v=eWwhLO-nkBw&t=345s

From there Jake started reading the Bible. He read Genesis first and could not believe how anyone could get a heliocentric spinning ball out of Genesis 1. Finally, he got to the New Testament and became a born-again Christian through faith in what Jesus did on the cross and His bodily resurrection from the dead. But it was the revelation and evidences of God's flat earth that brought Jake to the Bible and faith in Jesus Christ.

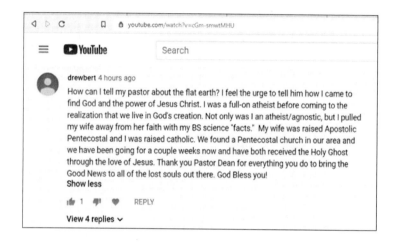

Another amazing testimony was sent to me as I was writing this chapter. Timothy from Long Island, New York sent me his amazing story. Here is an excerpt:

"So, some weeks had gone by, and I had managed to stay clean off the dope for a small time, using the medicine I had been prescribed. One day my friend and his girlfriend picked me up to go on a cigarette run at the nearest Indian reservation.

"Guess what, you'll never believe what my brother thinks." *'What's that?' I said.*

'He's completely lost his mind; HE THINKS THE EARTH IS FLAT!!!!'

'You've gotta be joking me?!? Are you serious?? It's 2017 and there are still people who think the world is flat??!!'

After joking about it for some time and making it back from the Indian reservation, I brushed it off as utter nonsense and fell back into my worldly cares.

One night a few weeks later, I couldn't sleep, and suddenly I remembered the conversation. It echoed in my head for a few minutes until I finally decided that I was going to look it up and debunk it, just so I could let it go and not think about it anymore. My first video was "The History of Flat Earth by Eric Dubay" 7 hours later the sun came up and I was still watching videos, completely blown away by what I was learning. 'It can't be, this has got to be some kind of internet joke.... but they're making some pretty undeniable points.'

Three weeks of sleepless nights later, I had a cognitive dissonance breakdown. I mourned the globe and everything I thought I knew about reality. **It CAN'T BE!!!!, BUT YET THERE IT IS!!!! oh my God, it's TRUE!!!! THE EARTH IS REALLY FLAT!!!!**

After more research, I started to understand why they would lie about something this big. But I had been caught up into Eric Dubay's school of eastern flat earth mysticism. I started believing what he was saying, and it reinforced all my past occult beliefs.

I managed to stay clean off heroin with the help of the medicine, but when it ran out, and I didn't have enough money to refill the prescription, I knew I would go right

163

back. I continued to do research on flat earth, until I came across the YouTube channel, 'The Truth Is Stranger Than Fiction.' I was fascinated by what he had to say, and he always brought it back to the reason why they were lying was to hide the God of the Bible, and the validity of scripture which had said it all along. Something began to change in me. I knew this man was speaking truth because it resonated so much to me. But I still had my hang-ups with Christianity from my past and did not want to accept it right away.

That's when my family moved from NY down to Florida, where the Holy Spirit continued to work on me, through the research I had been doing. **With no old friends to distract me, and no places to find any drugs, I concentrated solely on my job during the day, and researching flat earth and also the Bible at night.**

After running from the truth for so long, my mind's eye started to imagine me running straight to Jesus. The Holy Spirit had become a living, breathing presence in my life, probably for the first time ever that I had been consciously aware of.

It was on a chilly December night that I finally decided to trust Jesus as my Lord and savior, and I never looked back. *It suddenly dawned on me that the night I overdosed and died, Jesus had sent an angel to keep me from death, for the very purpose that I would give my life to him, and become a man on a mission for the kingdom of God.*

Flat Earth really did CHANGE EVERYTHING.... IT STILL BLOWS MY MIND... *"*

Timothy goes on to say…

164

"So, when people ask, 'What does flat earth matter?' Tell them IT LITERALLY CHANGES EVERYTHING. While we were once blissfully and hopelessly LOST, we now have an opportunity to be FOUND, and be REDEEMED, and made WHOLE again in the sight of God and all the Holy angels of Heaven.

Never again will we be just growing older but GROWING UP. Where we once were ever learning new ways to sin, Now, we're coming to the saving knowledge of the TRUTH we hold by the grace and mercy of our God who loves us. SO MUCH it breaks my heart because we don't deserve it! He has been so PATIENT, waiting for us to come home. And thanks to the true knowledge of creation, we've gained the wisdom to know the EXACT way, through our Lord and savior Jesus Christ!"

In my 32 years of ministry and following trends and revivals in the church, I have never seen another subject bring more atheists and agnostics to belief in the Bible and Jesus Christ as their Savior. This is truly a move of God and most of the church is missing it because they believe scientists, "Bible scholars" that explain away Scripture and the "space and rocket magic show" over what God's Word clearly teaches. This is why flat earth matters.

Chapter 7

The Flat Earth Pastor

*"...yea, **let God be true, but every man a liar;** as it is written, That thou mightest be justified in thy sayings, and mightest overcome when thou art judged"* (Romans 4:3).

"Let no man deceive himself. If any man among you seemeth to be wise in this world (Greek word aion meaning age or time), *let him become a fool, that he may be wise. **For the wisdom of this world** (**Greek word kosmos**) **is foolishness with God. For it is written, He taketh the wise in their own craftiness"*** (1 Corinthians 3:18-19).

*"Then **opened HE their understanding**, that they might understand the Scriptures"* (Luke 24:45).

In Luke 24, Jesus appeared to two of His disciples that were walking on the road to Emmaus. When He appeared to them the Scripture says that **"... *their eyes were holden that they should not know him"*** (Luke 24:16). They had walked with Him and believed in Him during His ministry, but they had doubts about Jesus being alive because they saw with their own natural eyes what happened at His crucifixion. It was hard for them to believe the reports that He had risen from the dead, even though they had witnessed Jesus raising others from the dead. I'm sure the dramatic and brutal image of Him hanging on the cross and dying right in front of them was still fresh in their minds. And those graphic images made it very difficult for them to see and believe His promise of rising from the dead on the third day.

This story shows that even disciples of Jesus can be partially blinded to certain Biblical truths due to cognitive dissonance. For those not familiar with that term, *"...in the field of psychology, cognitive dissonance is the mental discomfort (psychological stress) experienced by a person who simultaneously holds two or more contradictory beliefs, ideas, or values. This discomfort is triggered by a situation in which a person's belief clashes with new evidence perceived by that person. When confronted with facts that contradict personal beliefs, ideals, and values, people will find a way to resolve the contradiction in order to reduce their discomfort."*[78]

The disciples were holding to contradictory beliefs that they could not resolve. Their particular problem was that they had been taught their entire lives that the Messiah would save them from their enemies and establish His eternal kingdom from Jerusalem. So, how could He be dead? They saw Him heal the sick, cast out demons, open the eyes of the blind and the ears of the deaf, and raise the dead. They believed that He was the Messiah, but their knowledge of the Scriptures was incomplete. They were never taught the rest of the story about the suffering and atoning death of the

---

[78] https://en.wikipedia.org/wiki/Cognitive_dissonance

Messiah foretold in Isaiah 53, Psalms 16 & 22, and other places. Therefore, they were unable to see and believe all that the prophets had spoken concerning Jesus the Messiah. It took an additional encounter with Jesus where He opened their understanding so they could comprehend the Scriptures like never before. This is exactly what happened to me in 2015 about God's creation.

Like most true born-again Christians (who honestly believe and know the Bible is the inspired, infallible Word of the One True God and Creator Yahweh), I never considered the possibility that I really didn't believe ALL of the Bible. It wasn't willful unbelief, but like the disciples on the road to Emmaus, I had just been blinded to parts of the Bible. I allowed misled Bible teachers, sincere but sincerely wrong pastors, years of public-school and university brainwashing, the entertainment industry's "space" propaganda and a lifetime of NASA/government lies to influence my beliefs. I suffered from a clear case of cognitive dissonance, especially when I read about the sun and moon standing still in Joshua chapter 10 and even creation in Genesis chapter 1.

My Story

I was truly born again in 1979 in a small Baptist church in Alabama. After falling away from God and church during my teenage years, I repented and fully rededicated my life to the Lord Jesus Christ in the summer of 1987. Shortly thereafter, I had a powerful open vision of Jesus Christ standing at the right hand of the glory of the Father in heaven with the wings of the Holy Spirit hovering over Him. It was during that encounter with God that He called me to the ministry and later commissioned me to be a prophet. It was in 1987 that I became a diligent student of the Bible and history.

Since that time, I have served as a youth pastor, single's pastor, evangelist, teacher, church planter, and senior pastor of several churches. I have preached the gospel of Jesus Christ in Israel, the Island of Mauritius, Nigeria, and all over the United States. I have authored several books and received an honorary PhD in the Philosophy of International Evangelism and Missions. (In 2002 the faculty and staff of Pilgrims University decided that I had earned a PhD. They took into account my 15 years of very active and dedicated ministry as well as teaching seminary students every morning for a month in Aba, Nigeria. They considered my book *Grace Abuse* to be my "thesis." This was a fulfillment of something the Lord told me early on when I was seeking Him about attending a Bible school or seminary. He let me know that He was going to teach me His way and I would receive recognition from Him.) I have seen many saved, healed, baptized in the Holy Spirit, and delivered from demons by the power of God in my 32 years of ministry.

I have always believed and still believe the Bible to be the inspired, inerrant words of Almighty God. I have always believed that the Bible must be taken in context and literally unless it is very clear that a parable or symbolic language was used in a passage. I have also endeavored to live as a true New Covenant disciple of Jesus Christ just as the Bible teaches. So, had anyone walked up to me and told me that I did not believe everything written in the Bible, I would have vehemently denied that accusation. Almost immediately after returning to the Lord in 1987, I began teaching things from the Bible that most ministers ignore, twist, or are ignorant about. I have taken a stand against popular false teachings and false teachers. I have known the truth about the giants and the coming "alien" deception since the late 1980s. In my sermons I regularly expose the United Nations, the Illuminati and the NWO by teaching end-time Bible prophecy. I have known the truth about 911 and the Bush family. And I was never fooled by evolution or a moon landing. How could there be a major truth of the Bible that I was blinded to?

Now, I'm not trying to imply that I thought I knew everything about the Bible. I always prayed to God that He would give me His Spirit of wisdom and revelation in the knowledge of Him, that the eyes of my understanding would be enlightened. I would ask God to open my eyes to His Word because there is always more to learn about God and His Bible. So about two months before my flat earth awakening, I sensed in my spirit that there was something big stirring. Then I heard the Holy Spirit say to me that He had something else to reveal and it was a big deal.

The big day for me was October 24, 2015. About four years earlier, I had reconnected through Facebook with an old friend I grew up with but had not seen since high school. Sam was living in Hollywood and from seeing his pictures I knew that he was very "connected." That's why I was so surprised to discover that he was a Christian and enjoyed listening to my sermons online. He shared some amazing inside information about people in Hollywood and we would discuss the evil things going on in the world, the deeper things in the Bible, and how the second coming of Jesus was drawing closer and closer. So, I knew there was something to it when Sam sent me a link to a YouTube video and asked, *"Does firmament earth ring a bell?"* He was a researcher and usually on the trail of some truth.

171

Now, I must admit that I had no idea what he was talking about. ***"Firmament earth??? What is he asking?"*** I clicked on the video link in my email without even looking at the title; it didn't take long before I could sense the Holy Spirit moving upon me. As the video began to show the fakery of NASA, fisheye lenses that create a fake curve of the earth, the high-altitude balloon footage, the clouds behind the sun, and ships coming back into view with a high zoom camera after they had allegedly disappeared over the curve, I had the complete revelation before the video even said flat earth. It was a spiritual download from the Holy Spirit that Satan had deceived the entire world about the shape of the earth and true nature of the cosmos.

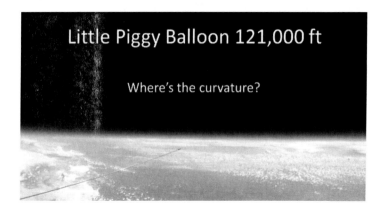

Finally, as the video reached the point where it began to systematically lay out the Scriptures that backed up what had been presented, I was overwhelmed by the fact that, once again, the Holy Spirit was leading me into truth. I felt as if a massive burden had been lifted off my shoulders. Things in the Bible like Joshua commanding the sun and the moon to stand still for a whole day (Joshua 10) finally made sense! It was like a key that unlocked a prison door that I didn't even realize had me in a measure of darkness. The joy of the Lord began to fill me as I opened my Bible and started looking up the verses about creation that I had previously only seen through the lens of a flying, spinning, spherical world.

I enjoyed a very blessed and powerful time in the presence of God as He opened my understanding to the Scriptures. It was also very humbling and convicting when I realized that I had believed men over what God's Word plainly said. How could I have accepted the narrative of public schools, governments, and their "space" propaganda that so blatantly contradicted what the God-breathed Scripture taught? I had to confess this sin of unbelief and accepting Satan's deception about creation to the Lord and ask for His forgiveness. I realized that the same men who told me the earth is a spinning ball that orbits the sun that is 93 million miles away, and is in a galaxy that is flying through an ever expanding universe at 600,000 MPH (even though the North Star never moves) also told us that we evolved from monkeys after a big bang that supposedly happened billions of years ago. I had never believed their theory of evolution so why did I accept their nonsense about the rest of creation?

WE MOVE IN A VORTEX

THE SUN

Modern science nonsense!

Perfect, circular, time-lapse star trails prove the reality of a stationary Earth.

I spent the next few weeks in deep study and research. I went through my Bible re-studying every verse that mentioned anything about creation and looked up the words in those passages in multiple Greek and Hebrew lexicons. I cross-checked many translations of the Bible and pulled out my copy of *The Complete Works of Josephus* to discover what the first century Jews believed about the firmament and the sun, moon, and stars.

A Funny Thing

During my research I watched a documentary called, *A Funny Thing Happened on the Way to the Moon* by Bart Sibrel.[79] This video contains the most damning evidence ever leaked from NASA as it shows the Apollo 11 crew faking the shot of the earth by trickery. The crew turned the lights off in the cabin (because "space" is black), backed the camera up, and filmed the round window. They lied and said that the camera was up against the window and that this partial view of earth was the entire "globe." It would have been much more convincing if someone's arm hadn't disrupted the façade, but once the lights were turned back on, it was obvious where the camera was and what they had done.

I also read, *We Never Went to the Moon* by Rocketdyne employee, Bill Kaysing and *NASA Mooned America* by Ralph Rene. I watched hours of NASA footage from Shuttle missions, "space" walks, ISS feeds, and the moon landings

[79] A Funny Thing Happened on the Way to the Moon, Bart Sibrel, https://youtu.be/xciCJfbTvE4

and compared NASA images of the earth and the moon. My investigation led me to Operation Paperclip, Operation Fishbowl, Operation Deep Freeze into the Antarctica with Admiral Byrd, the Antarctic Treaty and much more. My conclusion was simple: God's Word, the Bible is true from Genesis to Revelation and Satan and his loyal followers have created and continue to perpetuate the most elaborate deception in history in order to turn mankind away from believing the Bible and finding Jesus as their Lord and Savior.

As these weeks of research and study continued, I had absolutely zero doubts that the earth was flat, stationary, covered by a molten glass dome with God's throne and heaven just above it. I knew that the sun and moon are much smaller and closer than we have been told, that the sun, moon, and stars are inside the firmament and move in a circuit over an immovable earth. I also had no doubts that NASA and other space agencies have been lying to us. The purpose of this deception is to hide the God of the Bible and set mankind up for the Antichrist, his world government (through the United Nations), and his cashless money system controlled by an implant in your hand or brain (Daniel 7 and Revelation 13). I also believe that a major part of Satan's great deception will be the appearance of his fallen angels and their offspring posing as "aliens" from a far-away galaxy (that really doesn't exist). And when you discover that all of these lies about "space," moon landings, the shape of the earth, and the cosmos have come from Nazis who were deep into Satanic Secret Societies and world leaders that admit they worship Lucifer, then your eyes are opened to the end-time conspiracy foretold in Bible prophecy.

Initial Confirmations of the Biblical Creation

One of the things that really shook me in the first flat earth video I watched was a video clip of the clouds clearly behind the sun. Shortly thereafter, I came across some videos showing clouds behind the moon as well. Of course, this could not be possible if the sun is really 93 million miles away and the moon is 240,000 miles away. There should NEVER be a visible cloud behind the sun or moon because there are no clouds in "space." So, I started paying more attention, especially when clouds were in the sky. On a trip back from Birmingham, Alabama it finally happened! My wife and youngest daughter were with me, and we clearly witnessed clouds behind the sun for ourselves. It was unbelievably clear, and I couldn't believe I had never noticed it before. Soon after, while doing some contracting work at someone's home, I walked outside to get some air right before dusk and the moon was almost full in the blue sky. I watched as clouds moved in front of it and behind it. Those two incidents confirmed the Word of God which says that the sun and moon are inside the solid firmament dome with the clouds.

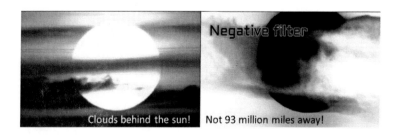

Clouds behind the sun!   Not 93 million miles away!

Here are some Bible passages that address this observable truth of a close sun being in the firmament where the clouds are:

"And now men see not the bright light which is in the clouds: but the wind passeth, and cleanseth them" (Job 37:21). The Gesenius' Hebrew-Chaldee Lexicon defines "bright light' in this verse as *"...the splendid, bright; of the sun."*

"And God made two great lights; the greater light to rule the day, and the lesser light to rule the night: he made the stars also. And God set them in the firmament of the heaven to give light upon the earth, And to rule over the day and over the night, and to divide the light from the darkness: and God saw that it was good" (Genesis 1:16-18).

"The heavens declare the glory of God; and the firmament (solid dome tent over the earth*) sheweth his handywork. Day unto day uttereth speech, and night unto night sheweth knowledge. There is no speech nor language, where their voice is not heard. Their line is gone out through all the earth, and their words to the end of the world. In them hath he set a tabernacle* (tent) *for the sun, Which is as a bridegroom coming out of his chamber, and rejoiceth as a strong man to run a race. His going forth is from the end of the heaven, and his circuit unto the ends of it: and there is nothing hid from the heat thereof"* (Psalms 19:1-6).

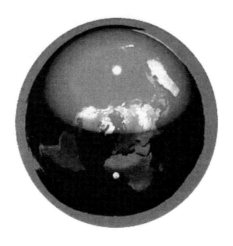

There is just so much I could talk about in these verses alone, but the Bible makes it clear that the sun is inside the firmament dome with the clouds. The firmament is the tabernacle or tent for the sun and the sun makes a circuit from one end of heaven (the dome tent) to the other end. In other words, it is the sun moving in a circle over a stationary earth, not the earth spinning or orbiting around a stationary sun. The Holy Spirit of God even drops this truth bomb through King David, *"...and NOTHING is hid from the heat of the sun."* That means NOTHING! The Bible says that the heat of our sun touches everything in creation. How could there be planets and galaxies millions and billions of light-years away where the heat of our sun could not reach? Hint: Someone is lying and it's not the God of the Bible.

What to do with all of this?

After I was completely convinced that a flat earth was both Biblical and backed up by observation, evidence, experiments, and plenty of solid reasons to question the government/space narrative, I wondered if I should go public with what I had discovered. Should I preach about God's flat earth, the firmament of His power, and the ends of the earth, or would it just be considered too crazy and detract from the ministry that God had called me to? Would this topic be so controversial and conspiratorial that everyone would just dismiss me as a nutcase? These were my questions to God as I earnestly prayed about it. I was willing to do whatever the Lord said to do. As I prayed and asked the Lord if I should preach on all of this, I heard Him say, *"Have I ever told you to hold back any of My truth?"* I answered, "No Lord, you have not." He said, *"Then you have your answer."*

At that time in 2015, I had been following Jesus whole-heartedly for 28 years. I had learned to discern God's voice and the leading of His Spirit. I also knew to trust Him. If He wanted me to share these Biblical truths about creation and the evidences that existed for a flat, enclosed, stationary, geocentric earth, then I knew it would set captives free from the lies and strongholds of Satan. Of course, along with that, I also knew there would be some Christian brothers and sisters who would not be able to accept these things, and there would be some lost relationships because of that. I have never made decisions to censor or leave out things in the Bible because it might offend people. I have always had the belief that every word in the Bible is important and that God put them there to help someone. Seeker-sensitive, build-a-megachurch philosophy was not what Jesus or any of His apostles or true prophets ever did so it is not what I do.

So, I got busy preparing a long PowerPoint presentation called *Lucifer's Greatest Global Deception*. I didn't tell anyone what the message was about except my wife and one elder. I shared it on social media and invited people to come to our church to hear the most controversial sermon that I would ever preach. Most people could not imagine what it could be because I was never one to shy away from controversy or stirring the pot with strong Bible truths. I did

179

not broadcast that first flat earth sermon LIVE on any social media or internet radio platform. I felt that I owed it to my congregation to let them hear about it before I went public. I told them beforehand that they might think I had gone crazy or they might not want to agree, but they would not be able to say that my message was not Biblically sound doctrine.

It was an amazing service and eyes were truly opened to the truth of God's Word and how we have been deceived by NASA, our government, and much of academia. Our church received these truths with amazing unity. I think that we may have lost only one family over this subject (I say "may" because they never said why they stopped coming). About a month later, I added some slides to the PowerPoint presentation and preached it publicly to our longtime online listeners. The response over the next few months on YouTube and Facebook was 95% positive and only 5% negative. I couldn't believe it. Then, I started receiving dozens and dozens of emails and new YouTube subscribers saying, *"You are the first pastor in a church that I have heard preaching and teaching about flat earth and what the Bible really says about the firmament and the sun, moon, and stars."* Many thanked me for my courage to stand up for such controversial Biblical truths. Many said, *"You are now my pastor."* But over and over I would receive a message or phone calls saying, *"You are the first pastor that I have heard talking about these things."* One phone call was a brother with a PhD from Fuller Theological Seminary who called and said, *"You are my hero."* I asked him if I was wrong about any of the Hebrew and Greek definitions that I used and he said, "NO."

Depiction of Biblical Flat Earth Cosmology by Robert "Paint Tank" Moore

As expected, it didn't all go well. My own brother (who I led to the Lord Jesus in 1987) did not agree with me at all. Even though he has been a dedicated Christian for decades, he could not get past his secular education and his years of teaching public middle and high school science. He quietly began to distance himself from me on social media even though he had previously joined me on our weekly Prophecy Quake radio show from time to time. When I confronted him about the snub, he admitted that it was about flat earth. He told me that I was wrong and when I asked for Scriptures to prove where I was wrong, he didn't give me one. Finally, I emailed him a list of verses from the Bible with definitions and some of the evidence and asked him to provide his verses for a flying, spinning, spherical earth. Unfortunately, I never received his list and he refused to turn loose of the years of brainwashing and believe the Bible. We are still divided over this truth, but Jesus foretold this too:

"Think not that I am come to send peace on earth: I came not to send peace, but a sword (His Word of TRUTH). *For I am come to set a man at variance against his father, and the daughter against her mother, and the daughter in law against her mother in law. And a man's foes shall be they of his own household.* He that loveth father or mother more than me is not worthy of me: and he that loveth son or daughter more than me is not worthy of me" (Matthew 10:34-37).

Someone once interviewed me and asked, *"How does it feel to be the first Flat Earth pastor?"* I had not really thought of myself that way because I know there have been many ministers in the past who believed that the earth is flat just as God said. But by 2017 after sharing more sermons on the subject and giving interviews, I started receiving emails and YouTube comments from atheists, agnostics, New Agers, and ancient alien believers that said researching flat earth had led them to the Bible and then to find Jesus Christ as their Savior. I know that God made me the "Flat Earth Pastor" and placed me in the middle of the awakening, so I could share even more truths from God's Word with people all over this flat earth. I have been able to share about salvation, deliverance, healing, the baptism of the Holy Spirit, Bible prophecy, end-times and much more. This is why God told me to preach this flat earth revelation that He gave me in 2015…because *"this is good and acceptable in the sight of God our Savior; Who will have* (desires) *all men to be saved, and to come unto the knowledge of the truth"* (1 Timothy 2:3-4).

182

Chapter 8

The Firmament & Dishonest Creationists

"The heavens declare the glory of God; and the firmament sheweth his handywork" (Psalms 19:1).

*"And the **likeness of the firmament** upon the heads of the living creature was as the colour* (Hebrew word ayin means outward appearance) *of the terrible crystal, stretched forth over their heads above. And under the firmament were their wings straight, the one toward the other: everyone had two, which covered on this side, and everyone had two, which covered on that side, their bodies"* (Ezekiel 1:22-23).

*"Hast thou with him spread out the sky, **which is strong, and as a molten looking glass?**" (Job 37:18)*

*"And I saw another sign in heaven, great and marvellous, seven angels having the seven last plagues; for in them is filled up the wrath of God. **And I saw as it were a sea of glass mingled with fire**: and them that had gotten the victory over the beast, and over his image, and over his mark, and*

183

over the number of his name, **_stand on the sea of glass_,** *having the harps of God"* (Revelation 15:1-2).

"And God said, **'Let there be a firmament in the midst of the waters, and let it divide the waters from the waters.'** *And* **God made the firmament and divided the waters which were under the firmament from the waters which were above the firmament:** *and it was so"* (Genesis 1:6-7).

"The Navigation Officer was giving his presentation (see the photograph below) **the theory assumes a 'height' of the stars above the flat world.** *I was quite shocked.* **The math assumes a flat plain with a certain height of the 'celestial dome,' pretty incredible.** *"* - Jay Tolan, Electrical Engineer, current US government technical advisor on Electronic Warfare, former Raytheon employee who worked on RADAR and cold war surveillance and reconnaissance.

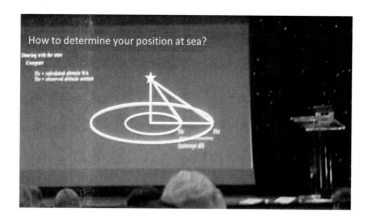

God first mentions this thing called the firmament in Genesis 1 when He creates it. It is in the very first book of the Bible and yet most Christians, including pastors have probably never studied it and don't have a clue what it really is. Recently, I watched a video in which a man called random pastors, rabbis, and priests asking them to explain to him what the firmament is. That question stumped most of them, and the ones who gave an answer didn't seem very confident. So, when the man asked what "dividing the waters that were under the firmament from the waters that were above the firmament" means, it became embarrassing for these "experts." The way they struggled to answer his simple Bible questions and some of their crazy responses blew my mind. One pastor said the firmament is earth. The caller then pointed out that Genesis 1:14-15 says that the sun, moon and stars were in the firmament to give light upon the earth, and that poor pastor began mumbling to himself.

Although I laughed at the video, I must admit that even though by 2015 I had studied the Bible for 28 years, I did not know what the firmament really was. I had heard Dr. Carl Baugh postulate his theory that the firmament was a vapor canopy (some even claimed ice) that surrounded the earth in the upper atmosphere. Dr. Baugh claimed that this vapor canopy firmament was very thick until it condensed and collapsed to cause the flood of Noah's time. He devised elaborate theories of how this event changed the oxygen levels on the earth and caused the dinosaurs to become extinct. His theory also claimed that the vapor canopy shielded man from harmful solar radiation which explains why mankind no longer lived to be hundreds of years old after the flood.

Of course, being in my twenties and fully indoctrinated in the heliocentric universe of my public-school education, Dr. Baugh's canopy theory sounded plausible and somewhat Biblical. Like so many others, I just blindly accepted his explanation without really digging into it myself. In fact, I never studied the subject of the firmament after that and like most Christians still do, I tried to interpret Bible passages through the Copernican model that modern science told me was reality. Looking back, the brainwashing of the globe earth and heliocentric solar system was strong. I could see through the lies, silliness, and impossibilities of Darwin's theory of macro evolution. However, I simply could not see through the very similar lies, silliness, and impossibilities of a spinning, water ball earth flying around the sun at 66,000 mph while also flying through the ever-expanding universe at almost 500,000 mph. All of this happening while the view of the constellations in our night sky has not changed after thousands of years of this alleged flying. Polaris is always in the same spot with the other stars circling perfectly around it, but I was completely blind to it.

As I have already shared, this flat earth revelation made me do another in-depth Bible study about creation and especially the firmament. One of the first things that I discovered was Psalms 148:2 which states, *"Praise him, ye heavens of heavens, and ye waters that be ABOVE the heavens."* This was a Holy Spirit-inspired word written 1,500 years AFTER the flood of Noah's day. This verse clearly debunks the vapor canopy theory as it states that there is still water ABOVE the firmament. And if there is still a massive amount of water above the firmament (which supports it), then NASA and other "space" agencies are lying about where their rockets go and what "space" really is. To me one of the most disturbing discoveries was not that NASA and other governments of the world have lied about the firmament, but that the so-called Christian creation ministries have lied. Granted, some of them may just be deceived themselves, but they are not providing the truth about the Hebrew definition of the word "firmament" and how it is used in the Bible. So, whether they are ignorant, deceived or intentionally dishonest, they are spreading deception that directly conflicts with God's Word.

Firmament Does Not Mean "Empty Expanse"

One creation ministry that has waged war against the recent resurgence of flat earth truth is Creation Ministries International, and one of their main Flat Earth "debunkers" is Dr. Danny Faulkner. He and his group attempt to hold to the Bible while holding on to heliocentric, Copernican/NASA cosmology and it has exposed their willingness to be dishonest with the original language of Scripture. They even deny the well documented history of what the ancient Hebrews in first and second century AD believed about the firmament and the nature of the sun, moon, and stars. For instance, early second century church father Theophilus of Antioch (who lived 115-181 AD) was known as a true shepherd of Christ's flock that fought hard against heresies and heretics such as Marcion. He became the leader of the Church of Antioch where Barnabas and Paul first served before being called out by God to their missionary journeys. Theophilus was a diligent student of the Scriptures and passed on Biblical Christianity and sound doctrine about how God created the heavens and the earth to his generation and the ones to follow. Theophilus wrote:

"For man, being below, begins to build from the earth, and cannot in order make the roof, unless he has first laid the foundation. But the power of God is shown in this, that, first of all, He creates out of nothing, according to His will, the things that are made. 'For the things which are impossible with men are possible with God.' **Wherefore, also, the prophet mentioned that the creation of the heavens first of all took place, as a kind of roof,** *saying: "At the first God created the heavens"—that is, that by means of the "first" principle the heavens were made, as we have already shown. And by "earth" he means the ground and*

187

foundation, as by "the deep" he means the multitude of waters; and "darkness" **he speaks of, on account of the heaven which God made covering the waters and the earth like a lid. And by the Spirit which is borne above the waters,** *p. 100 he means that which God gave for animating the creation, as he gave life to man, 574 mixing what is fine with what is fine. For the Spirit is fine, and the water is fine, that the Spirit may nourish the water, and the water penetrating everywhere along with the Spirit, may nourish creation. For the Spirit being one, and holding the place of light, was between the water and the heaven, in order that the darkness might not in any way communicate with the heaven, which was nearer God, before God said, "Let there be light."* **The heaven, therefore, being like a dome-shaped covering,** *comprehended matter which was like a clod. And so another prophet, Isaiah by name, spoke in these words:* **'It is God who made the heavens as a vault, and stretched them as a tent to dwell in.'** *The command, then, of God, that is, His Word,* **shining as a lamp in an enclosed chamber, lit up all that was under heaven,** *when He had made light apart from the world."*[80]

Did you see all of that? The dishonest creationists will say that the early church and even the ancient Hebrew prophets did not teach a solid, dome firmament/sky, but they did. Theophilus called it **"...the roof."** He also said that God covered the waters and earth **"...with a lid"** and that heaven was **"...a dome-shaped covering."** Then, he adds that the heavens were a vault stretched (*raqiya* spread out plates) like a tent and finished off calling earth an **"...enclosed chamber."** And all of this was less than 100 years from the

---

[80] Ante-Nicene Fathers, Vol II: THEOPHILUS: Chapter XIII. —Remarks on the Creation of the World

apostles and over a hundred years BEFORE the Roman Catholic Church came into existence.

However, dishonest Creation Ministries International (and Dr. Danny Faulkner in particular) wrongly teach that the Hebrew word *raqiya* which is translated "firmament" in the King James Version means "an expanse." This could not be further from the truth. Faulkner chooses to use this definition that comes from the corrupted Alexandrian text stream that was used to create inaccurate translations of the Bible like the New American Standard, The Revised Standard Version, the New International Version, and so on. He uses the word "expanse" because it goes better with his faulty Copernican belief system. He uses it to twist the Copernican heliocentric theory into appearing Biblical when it is completely opposite of what the Bible actually teaches.

I listened to Danny Faulkner teach this nonsense on the Cornerstone Television Network Show called *Origins* with Donn Chapman.[81] Over and over Faulkner kept saying *"...expanse, expanse, expanse..."* in the place of the word "firmament" as he went through Genesis 1. And though he did include the Hebrew word *raqiya* (translated "firmament") in his slide presentation, he intentionally left out the actual definitions of *raqiya* from multiple Hebrew lexicons. He purposefully left out what the Hebrew prophets and ancient Israelites all the way up to the time of Flavius Josephus (the famous first century Jewish historian) actually believed about the nature of the firmament. His conclusion was that the firmament or as he wrongly calls it, "the expanse" is "outer space." Then, to try to deal with the Biblical issue of "waters above the firmament," Faulkner

---

[81] *Origins* with Donn Chapman on the Cornerstone Television Network with guest Dr. Danny Faulkner 2016 https://youtu.be/RG_SiZ8m0CM

postulates that the universe must have an edge and waters above that edge. What ridiculous nonsense! Why not just accept what the Bible ACTUALLY says and what the prophets like Moses, Ezekiel, Isaiah, and John said it was?

There is no doubt that the firmament was first depicted in the book of Genesis as something that separates a massive heavenly ocean above it from the earthly waters below. It is described as having windows that must be opened to allow that water inside. It was this massive ocean above the firmament that helped to flood the earth in the days of Noah. The modern idea that the firmament is or was some kind of vapor canopy over the earth next to the powerful vacuum of "space" is just as ridiculous as it is un-Biblical. And the same goes for the idea that the firmament is just an empty expanse.

The original Hebrew word translated "firmament" in Genesis 1, Ezekiel 1, Psalms 19:1 and so on is *raqiya* and is defined by Brown-Driver-Briggs Hebrew and Blue Letter Bible Lexicons this way:

"An extended surface, (solid) expanse (as if beaten out; compare Job 37:18); — absolute רְ *Ezekiel 1:22* +*, construct* יְ *Genesis 1:14* +*; —* ᵐ5 *στερέωμα,* ᵛ9 *firmamentum, compare Syriac below* √*above; —*

1. (flat) expanse as if of ice (a solid), *compare* כְּעֵין הַקֶּרַח), *as base, support (WklAltor. Forsch. iv. 347) Ezekiel 1:22,23,25(gloss ? compare Co Toy), Ezekiel 1:26 (supporting* יְ'*s (God's) throne). Hence (Compare Ezekiel 1:22)*

2. The vault of heaven, or 'firmament,' regarded by Hebrews as solid, and supporting 'waters' above it, Genesis

1:6,7 (3 t. in verse); Genesis 1:8 (called שָׁמַיִם; all P), Psalm 19:2 יֹּהֶר הָר),(הַשָּׁמַיִם)("" Daniel 12:3; also ר הַשָּׁמַיִם׳ Genesis 1:14,15,17, ר עַלְמֹּנֵי׳ הַשׁ׳ Genesis 1:20 (all P). **רְקִיעַ עֻזּוֹ Psalm 150:1 (suffix reference to ׳).

The Gesenius Hebrew-Chaldee Lexicon defines *raqiya* as "...*the firmament of heaven, spread out like a hemisphere above the earth, like a splendid, pellucid* (translucently clear, transparent, crystalline, glassy, allowing the maximum passage of light, as glass; translucent) *sapphire* (stone), *to which the stars were supposed to be fixed, and over which the Hebrews believed there was a heavenly ocean* (see Gen. 1:7, 7:11; Psalms 104:3, 148:4)."

These definitions agree with Job 37:18, " *"Hast thou with him spread out the sky,* **which is strong, and as a molten looking glass?** " And they also agree with the most respected first century Jewish historian named Flavius Josephus. In his Book I, chapter I entitled, *The Constitution of the World and the Disposition of the Elements,* Josephus wrote: **"After this, on the second day, He (God) placed the heaven over the whole world, and separated it from the other parts; and He determined it should stand by itself. He also placed a CRYSTALLINE [firmament] round it, and put it together in a manner agreeable to the earth,** *and fitted it for giving moisture and rain, and for affording the advantage of dews...On the fourth day, He (God) adorned the heaven with the sun, the moon, and the other stars;* **and appointed them their courses,** *that the vicissitudes of the seasons might be clearly signified."*[82]

Furthermore, the *Theological Wordbook of the Old Testament* published by Moody Press with over 40

---

[82] The Complete Works of Josephus Translated by Wm. Whiston pg.25

Evangelical scholars as contributors defines *raqiya* as *"...literally "an expansion of plates" i.e. broad plates beaten out.* The root word and the verb version of *raqiya* is *raqa* which *"...acquires the sense of beating out precious metals, and of the spreading that results, to hammer out; spread into plates, make broad plates.*"[83] *Raqa* is the word used in Isaiah 42:5 and 44:24 to denote how God spread forth the tangible, physical earth. Thus, God beat out/spread out something like molten glass to form the solid firmament sky dome over the earth. Some want to argue about how He did it, but God calls the firmament His handywork that He stretched out over the earth like a tent for us to dwell in (Psalms 19: & Isaiah 40:22).

Additionally, the Hebrew scholars that translated the Old Testament into Greek during the reign of Ptolemy II Philadelphus between 285 and 248 BC, translated the Hebrew word *raqiya* (firmament) using the Greek word *stereōma*. Thayer's Greek Lexicon defines *stereoma* as *"...that which has been made firm; the firmament, the arch of the sky, which in early times was thought to be SOLID; a fortified place."* The Strong's Concordance Greek Dictionary states that the root words of *stereoma* are *stereoo (to solidify)* and *stereos* which means *"...stiff i.e. solid, stable, steadfast, strong, sure."* And it's actually pathetic to watch these dishonest creationists squirm when someone brings up this word *stereoma* which is used in the Septuagint. Some even stoop to the level of falsely accusing the translators of the Septuagint of picking the wrong Greek word for the firmament or they say they were influenced by the culture of that day.

---

[83] Theological Wordbook of the Old Testament, Volume 2, Moody Press 1980

If studied out honestly, there is no doubt or ambiguity that this is what the Bible teaches and what the Hebrew prophets knew to be true about the solid firmament dome over the earth. The prophet Ezekiel wrote that the firmament had the color (or Hebrew word meaning outward appearance) of *"terrible crystal"* upon/above which sat the sapphire throne of God, ***"And above the firmament that was over their heads was the likeness of a throne, as the appearance of a sapphire stone****: and upon the likeness of the throne was the likeness as the appearance of a man above upon it" (Ezekiel 1:26).* For those who may not know, sapphire gemstones are translucent blue. This passage does not in any way give the impression that the firmament over their heads was just an empty expanse.

Another passage mentions a paved work of sapphire stone under the feet of God when Moses, Aaron and his sons, and the seventy elders saw God, *"Then went up Moses, and Aaron, Nadab, and Abihu, and seventy of the elders of Israel: And they saw the God of Israel****: and there was under his feet as it were a paved work of a sapphire stone, and as it were the body of heaven in his clearness"*** (Exodus 24:9-10). The Hebrew word for "paved" is *libnah* and is defined as "whiteness from transparency." So, this passage in Exodus is saying that under God's feet there was something like a transparent blue gemstone that also acts as *"...the body of heaven."* The Hebrew word for "body" here is *etsem* which is defined in the Strong's Greek Dictionary as "...a bone (as strong); by extension the body or the substance." In other words, this paved, transparent blue, glass-like sapphire work under God's feet is like the bones in a human body that provide structural support. Our bones are the strongest physical part of our body and this pavement under God's feet is the strong, physical part of the heavens (or the *shamayim*).

Part of what is known as the heavens is our sky. Is this why the sky is blue? I believe so.

The Sky Stones

So, we now know what the Bible says, but is there physical and scientific evidence of this blue sky-stone mentioned in the Bible? The shocking answer to that question is yes. Here's the article published by AncientCode.com entitled, *'A Researcher Claims to Have Found a 55,000-year-old Artifact Made of Oxygen:'*

"In 1990 an Italian "geologist" named Angelo Pitoni was visiting Sierra Leone, in the vicinity of the border with Guinea Conakry, to verify if a certain region of the country known as Kono was indeed, a rich deposit of diamonds that could be exploited by the company that had hired him and sought to obtain the concession of exploitation in exchange for building a number of houses for the government.

While studying the region, Pitoni came across an incredible discovery that was for some reason left out in the cold. In an area between Sierra Leone, and Conakry, after removing a few inches of soil a Fullah Chief showed Pitoni one of the most mysterious stones Pitoni had come across in his career. A blue stone with mysterious white lines on its surface.

The tribal chief told Pitoni an ancient legend, which according to them, explains why the area was so rich in diamonds.

The chief Fulah-deeply embedded in the teachings of the Koran told Pitoni how in the mists of time, God found that among his angels a revolt was about to break.

The Angels were expelled to earth where they became statues, but these did not arrive at earth alone, according to legend, a great portion of the "sky" and "stars" fell with the angels on earth. In the eyes of the natives, this explains why the region is rich in so many minerals and diamonds.

*Pitoni examined the mysterious rock and thought it was some kind of very pure turquoise, but it is known that there is always some sort of impurities, **while this blue, mysterious stone was pure**.*

*After returning to Europe, Pitoni took the blue stone to the Institute of Natural Sciences of Geneva and the University La Sapienza in Rome for analysis. To his surprise, tests showed that the stone was not a turquoise, and it wasn't even officially cataloged. **The blue stone he had discovered not only does not correspond to any known mineral, but the "same" material was also recently located in Morocco by British geologist named Anne Grayson.***

The most intriguing thing is that the color of the mineral is not justified by the composition of the stone; Researchers do not understand from what the stone obtains its tonality even though several universities and laboratories have analyzed the artifact; All of them have failed to answer where the color comes from.

*Mysteriously, at the University of Utrecht, the stone underwent several tests with acids but none of the acids managed to damage or modify the stone. **It was heated to 3.000 degrees Celsius and its composition wasn't altered.***

195

The most interesting part is that when a small piece of the stone was pulverized and viewed under the microscope, it had no color. So far the only thing researchers know is that it has not been made by nature, and it has not originated on earth.

Some researchers believe that this mysterious blue stone was actually manufactured by an advanced civilization that has been lost in history. We know that there are numerous findings across the planet that cannot be explained. This mysterious blue stone is surely one of them.

One of the analyses that deepened the mystery of the "Sky stone", as it has been called, is when a fragment of the stone was subjected to rigorous examination to determine the composition of the stone and their respective proportions.

According to the analysis, 77.17% of the stone was made of OXYGEN. The remaining percentage is divided between carbon (11.58 per 100), silicon (6.39 per 100), calcium (3.31 per 100) and other elements whose presence was almost anecdotal.

But wait a minute, how can oxygen make up a stone? **Further tests were performed in Spain by several laboratories where the mysterious "Sky Stone"** underwent five different kinds of test: X-Ray analysis, plasma spectrometry, gas chromatography, mass spectrometry and finally infrared-spectrometry **yielding more mysterious results that left researchers clueless.**

In preliminary tests with X-rays it was determined that the blue stone was composed mainly of calcium hydroxide -Ca $(OH)_2$-, calcium carbonate, and calcium silicate -$CaCO_3$- -Ca_2SiO_4-, but mysteriously, none of these were able to *explain how the stone obtained its incredible blue color. Scientists speculated that copper or another transition material could be responsible for the tone, but they were unable to detect any materials in sufficient quantities to confirm their theory.*

The plasma spectrometry analysis reduced the oxygen level to 50/100 or 55/100 at most, which apparently is normal in any rock. More mysteries popped up when the stone was submitted to gas chromatography which tried to locate an organic compound in the rock, looking for some sort of "ink" that gave the stone its blue color.

Researchers decided to crush one piece of the rock and mixed it with acetone, hexane, and methylene and enhanced the extractions with ultrasound. Finally, researchers were able to detect an organic compound that was unknown to science. The Sky Stone does, in fact, have a non-mineral element in its composition but it does not reveal much since it is unknown.

The organic compound present in the sky rock is believed to be between 15,000 – 55,000 years old"[84]

Another article published by the UK news source *The Independent* in 1996 entitled, **'Rock from Road Stall Confounds the Experts Geologists'** discusses the "blue mineral" purchased by geologist Anna Grayson in 1981 at a Moroccan roadside merchant. Here's an excerpt from that article:

---

[84] https://www.ancient-code.com/researcher-discovers-a-55-000-year-old-artifact-made-out-of-oxygen/

"A piece of bright blue rock now puzzling mineralogists in the Natural History Museum may mark one of the rarest events on earth - a tourist getting the best of a deal with a Moroccan trader.*

When Anna Grayson, a geologist, came across the fist-sized lump of rock at a roadside souvenir stall in Morocco 15 years ago, its seller assured her that it was lapis luzuli - well-known for its blue colour and exotic associations.*

The stallholder sold it to Mrs. Grayson for the equivalent of a few pounds, confident that he had passed on a piece of the relatively common mineral to one of the millions of visitors who buoy up Morocco's economy. **But Mrs. Grayson realized she had found something unusual, though her scientific training could not identify it. Until last year, she had left it at her home in Watford, labelled 'unknown blue mineral.'**

Then a year ago, during National Science Week, she took it to the Natural History Museum, which was offering to identify mysterious objects. **It proved tougher than most - and the experts soon found that the mineral's structure and composition, a mixture of calcium, iron, aluminium, silicon, oxygen and a pinch of sulphur, was not listed among the 71,000 officially registered minerals.**

'We are still trying to work on the structure of the crystals,' said Dr Gordon Cressey, deputy head of the mineralogy department yesterday.

'We are trying X-ray diffraction and scanning electron microscopes, which takes you pretty close to the atomic level. The crystals are very, very small. And it's so blue that *when you look at light transmitted through it, it's like seeing a miniature stained-glass window.'"[85]*

So, is this blue sky-stone a piece of the firmament? The Bible reveals that the firmament is a solid crystalline structure (i.e. the terrible crystal). Ezekiel says that God's sapphire throne is above the firmament and Isaiah 40:22 makes it clear that God sits on that strong structure looking down at us. When Moses and the elders of Israel saw the God of Israel, they saw that "...*there was under his feet as it were a paved work of a sapphire (blue) stone, and as it were the body of heaven in his clearness.*"

When a piece of the blue sky-stone was heated to 3,000 degrees Celsius (5,432 degrees Fahrenheit), its composition did not change. Scientists could not figure out why the stone is blue and when a small piece was crushed and put under a microscope, the pieces had no color. The stone is created so that light can pass through it and they say it is not "earthly." Interestingly, the word 'terrible' written by the prophet Ezekiel in the original Hebrew is *yare* and it means "*...to fear, to inspire reverence, godly fear, and AWE.*" I believe the blue-sky stone is indeed a piece of the firmament that Ezekiel might describe as "terrible" or awe-inspiring.

The Solid Domed Sky

The Bible could not be clearer on the subject (no pun intended), the firmament is God's solid glass-like, sapphire gemstone-like dome over the earth. And here in the last days, we have physical and scientific evidence of a blue sapphire-like stone with amazing properties that has been tested and

---

[85] https://www.independent.co.uk/news/rock-from-road-stall-confounds-the-experts-geologists-1342797.html

found to not be of earthly origin. Is that a coincidence? Or is this yet another amazing detail about creation and the true Creator (the God of the Bible) that proves God told Moses, the Hebrew prophets, and His New Testament Apostles thousands of years ago EXACTLY what to write in His Bible?

Amazingly, (and accurately I might add) some Bible translations even use the word dome in place of the word firmament. Here are a few of them:

*"And God said, **Let there be a SOLID ARCH stretching over the waters, parting the waters from the waters.** And God made the arch for a division between the waters which were under the arch and those which were over it: and it was so. **And God gave the arch the name of Heaven.** And there was evening and there was morning, the second day"* (Genesis 1:6-8 BBE).

*"God said, '**Let there be a DOME in the middle of the water**; let it divide the water from the water.' **God made the***

DOME and divided the water under the dome from the water above the dome; that is how it was, and God called the DOME 'Sky.' *So there was evening, and there was morning, a second day"* (Genesis 1:6-8 CJB).

*"And God said, **'Let there be a VAULTED DOME in the midst of the waters, and {let it cause a separation between the waters}.'So God made the vaulted dome, and he caused a separation between the waters which [were] under the vaulted dome and between the waters which were over the vaulted dome.*** *And it was so.* **And God called the VAULTED DOME 'heaven.'** *And there was evening, and there was morning, a second day"* (Genesis 1:6-8 LEB).

Another thing to keep in mind is that the Bible teaches there are three heavens (not seven, ten or any other number from a demonic Gnostic or Jewish fable). The first heaven, which Genesis 1:20 calls the "open firmament of heaven," is our atmosphere where the clouds are, and the birds fly. The second heaven is the solid firmament dome over the earth to which the stars are attached like figs to a fig tree. In Genesis 6:8, God called the firmament dome "heaven." The third heaven is the place of God's throne. The Apostle Paul stated that he was caught up to the "third heaven" into paradise and heard things that are not lawful for a man to utter (2 Corinthians 12:1-6). The third heaven is the present home of those who died with a real born-again heart through faith in what Jesus did on the cross and His resurrection from the dead on the third day. It is also the home of all the babies who died before they were born (miscarriages and abortions) and children who died before they could come to understand who Jesus is, what He did, and why they need Him.

Once you understand this Biblical truth about the heavens and the molten glass-like firmament crystal over our heads, then verses like this one from the Apostle Paul make even more sense:

"Charity never faileth: but whether there be prophecies, they shall fail; whether there be tongues, they shall cease; whether there be knowledge, it shall vanish away. For we know in part, and we prophesy in part. But when that which is perfect is come, then that which is in part shall be done away. When I was a child, I spake as a child, I understood as a child, I thought as a child: but when I became a man, I put away childish things. For now we see through a glass, darkly; but then face to face: now I know in part; but then shall I know even as also I am known" (1 Corinthians 13:9-12).

Unfortunately, some dishonest and deceived theologians have wrongly taught that the "perfect" in this passage came in the form of the finished Bible and thus, the gifts of the Spirit have ceased. However, they are completely wrong because it is clearly referring to the second coming of Jesus Christ when we will see Him **face to face**. Even Thayer's Greek Lexicon bears this truth out. According to Thayer, the Greek word in this passage for "perfect" is *teleios* and it means, **"...the perfect state of all things to be ushered in by the return of Christ from heaven."** Thus, the Holy Spirit through Paul tells us that now (before the second coming of Jesus), there is a glass barrier that obscures a clear view of His face. But the Bible says that He is going to roll back the firmament like a scroll and every eye will see Him seated on His throne:

*"And I beheld when he had opened the sixth seal, and, lo, there was a great earthquake; and the sun became black as sackcloth of hair, and the moon became as blood; **And the stars of heaven fell unto the earth, even as a fig tree casteth***

202

her untimely figs, when she is shaken of a mighty wind. And the heaven departed as a scroll when it is rolled together; and every mountain and island were moved out of their places. And the kings of the earth, and the great men, and the rich men, and the chief captains, and the mighty men, and every bondman, and every free man, hid themselves in the dens and in the rocks of the mountains; And said to the mountains and rocks, Fall on us, and hide us from the face of him that sitteth on the throne, and from the wrath of the Lamb (Jesus Christ): For the great day of his wrath is come; and who shall be able to stand?" (Revelation 6:12-17).

Some New Agers and Christians that might as well be New Agers argue that those things in the Bible are just metaphors and figures of speech. They say that Jesus is not going to actually peel back a solid sky and physically return to the earth. To them His second coming is only spiritual and represents the coming of the Christ-consciousness in all of us which is the next stage in our "evolution." Many believe that Christ will come in a man who will be a great world leader and he will unite us in love and unity. To them, Christians like me are fundamentalists and foolish Bible-literalists that just cause division with our literal Bible interpretations and insistence that you must love and follow Jesus Christ, the One True God to spend eternity in heaven. Many are preparing for the "Golden Age" that they believe can be created from within themselves when they should be preparing to meet their Creator, God.

The God-breathed Scriptures make it clear that Jesus Christ WILL physically return to earth and the solid firmament is not a metaphor, but instead a very real part of God's creation. Revelation 15:1-2 says, *"And I saw another sign in heaven, great and marvellous, seven angels having the seven last plagues; for in them is filled up the wrath of*

God. *And I saw as it were a sea of glass mingled with fire: and them that had gotten the victory over the beast, and over his image, and over his mark, and over the number of his name, **stand on the sea of glass**, having the harps of God.*" As we read before, Ezekiel saw the throne of God established on top of the firmament (or "terrible crystal") and then in Revelation 15, the Apostle John saw people (who would make it to heaven in the future) standing on a sea of glass, praising God before His throne with harps. Here we have Old and New Testament Scripture confirming exactly where God's throne is located, and it is not in a galaxy far away.

Another passage that confirms that the firmament will be "departed as a scroll" to reveal the Lord Jesus Christ is Isaiah 25:7-8. It says, *"**And He (God) will destroy in this mountain the face of the covering cast over all people, and the vail that is spread over all nations.** He will swallow up death in victory; and the Lord God will wipe away tears from off all faces; and the rebuke of his people shall he take away from off all the earth: for the Lord hath spoken it.*" The Hebrew word for "covering" is *lowt* and it means "vail." The Hebrew word for "vail" in this passage is *maccekah* which the Strong's defines as *"...a pouring over i.e. a fusion of metal (especially a cast image) a coverlet (as if poured out) a molten covering.*" The Gesenius Hebrew-Chaldee Lexicon defines this word as *"...the casting of metal"* which is the same picture and definition that we get from the word *raqiya* translated "firmament" in our English Bibles and its root word *raqa*.

Hence, the vail or covering over all the nations of the world is the solid, molten glass, firmament dome that God Himself beat out and fixed over us. It is the terrible crystal, the sea of glass, the glass floor to God, and the glass ceiling to us. Glass ceiling, does that sound familiar? Remember Hillary Clinton saying, *"I know we have still not shattered that highest and hardest glass ceiling, but someday someone will and hopefully sooner than we might think right now."*[86] They know what is over our heads and they hint at it all the time. If you don't think so just start paying attention to television shows, commercials and movies and it will become clear.

The False Doctrine of Accommodation

Even with all of these very clear Bible passages, dishonest creation ministries and their "experts" make blatantly false claims that the Bible and the ancient Hebrew prophets did not teach or believe that the firmament was solid. But I have to give credit where credit is due; Dr. Michael Heiser (Ph.D., Hebrew Bible and Semitic Studies and Scholar-in-Residence at Logos Bible Software) at least admits that the Hebrew prophets of the Bible taught a flat earth, covered by a solid molten glass dome, with God's throne situated upon it and hell under the earth.

The really sad thing about Dr. Heiser is that he DOES NOT believe what the Bible teaches about the shape of the earth, the firmament, and the true nature of the cosmos. He admits that the Bible teaches about a flat earth with a solid firmament, but then runs (probably because of the fear of man) to the demonic doctrine of accommodation. This doctrine teaches that God is so transcendent from us that He cannot communicate to us as equals. Instead, God has to "stoop to our level" so to speak and say things in a way we can understand instead of telling the complete truth. He had

---

to tell lies and make up stories because the truth would have totally freaked out those primitive shepherds like Moses and David. Frankly, I can't think of a more demonic doctrine than this one. It attacks the Divine inspiration and authority of the Word of God just like Satan did with Eve in the Garden of Eden. This false doctrine also attacks the plain interpretation of what God gave us in the Bible and the purpose of the Scriptures which is to communicate truth to mankind. Here is an excerpt from Dr. Heiser's 2017 article posted on Logos Talk where he admits what the Bible teaches:

"We find an Israelite understanding of the heavens in Genesis 1:6–8, which describes it as an expanse, with waters above and below: "And God said, **'Let there be an expanse (רקיע, raqia') in the midst of the waters, and let it separate the waters from the waters.'** . . . **And it was so. And God called the expanse (רקיע, raqia') Heaven.** "

The sky, thought to be a solid firmament, separated the waters above from the waters below: *"When he established the heavens, I [Wisdom] was there;* **when he drew a circle on the face of the deep, when he made firm the skies above,** *when he established the fountains of the deep"* (Proverbs 8:27–28).

The firmament dome surrounded the earth, *with its edge meeting at the horizon— "the boundary between light and darkness" (Job 26:10). It was supported by "pillars" or "foundations," thought to be the tops of mountains, whose peaks appeared to touch the sky. The heavens had doors and windows through which rain or the waters above could flow upon the earth from their storehouses (Gen 7:11; 8:2; Pss 78:23; 33:7)."*

God was thought to dwell above the firmament, as described in Job 22:14: *"Thick clouds veil him, so that he does not see, and he walks on the vault of heaven."*[87]

The Whole Firmament

Amazingly, even a Russian scientific document (formerly marked TOP SECRET by the CIA) has the Russians explaining how they photographed ***"...the whole firmament at the same time"*** at one of their bases near the North Pole. Also consider that this document was dated 1959 which was two years after Sputnik. Did they not know that the earth is a sphere and they couldn't possibly photograph the entire firmament at the same time from one location on the ball? The heading on this particular document was entitled, *"Scientific Station at Bukhta Tiksi Built Especially for Auroral Studies."* It states:

"A scientific research station was created specially for observations of auroras during the IGY in the area of Bukhta Tiksi. It is situated almost in the center of a large depression, surrounded on three sides by mountains. Nikolay Ivanovich Tyabin is head of the observatory. A whole scientific settlement has developed in this location. The site was chosen specially because it was far away from industrial interference. The low station building faces the Arctic Ocean. One of the side walls, with narrow windows, is directed toward the hurricane-force northeast winds.

About 100 meters from the laboratory building is a massive metal tripod, supporting the original S-180 instrument, i.e., a system of mirrors with an automatic

---

[87] https://blog.logos.com/2017/02/ancients-guide-galaxy-israelites-viewed-god-universe/

*camera. **The S-180, and invention by Prof A. I. Lebedinskiy at Moscow State University, photographs the whole firmament at the same time on a sensitive motion-picture film.** Yuliy Nadubovich, graduate of Kiev University, operates this instrument.* "[88]

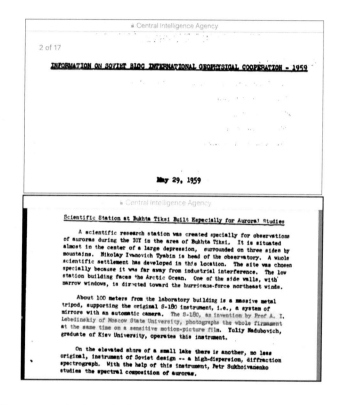

Let me ask the obvious question again: How could the Russian scientists photograph the whole (or entire) firmament at the same time from one central location on a big sphere? Wouldn't they be missing a huge portion of the so-called "expanse of the sky/firmament" due to it being on the other side of the ball? Yes, the only way to photograph the whole firmament at once from the central North Pole is

[88] https://www.cia.gov/library/readingroom/docs/CIA-RDP82-00141R000200690001-7.pdf

that we live on a flat earth with the firmament dome above us and 360 degrees around us.

So, for the Christians out there who say they believe the Bible is the inspired and infallible words of Almighty God, you have a problem (and yes, a big part of it is in Houston). You simply cannot claim to believe in the Divine inspiration and inerrancy of Scripture and then say that you believe the CGI pictures and claims of NASA about creation because they completely contradict one another. I know that the programming from childhood and up is hard to break free from. I also know that it is very difficult to admit and accept having been a victim of deception on this level. The mind races and the cognitive dissonance fights even the possibility that Satan and his servants could have deceived us with such a massive hoax.

However, if you can overcome the initial shock and break free from the comfortable lies, then you can start looking at the evidence with unbiased eyes. You will see that the true reality of the world we live in actually matches what the Bible has said all along. And then you will begin to understand the command of Scripture *"…let God be true and every man a liar…"* (Romans 3:4a).

Chapter 9

The Flat Circle of the Earth

"When he prepared the heavens, I was there: **when he set a compass upon the face of the depth:"** (Proverbs 8:27)

"It is he that sitteth upon the circle of the earth, *and the inhabitants thereof are as grasshoppers;* **that stretcheth out the heavens as a curtain, and spreadeth them out as a tent to dwell in:"** (Isaiah 40:22)

"It's cold out here..." *"Yeah it is...it's like the South Pole..."* **"It's like the deep South Pole...if there was one...there isn't though."** - Just Friends (2005 movie)

I can't tell you how many times I have heard, *"Not one verse in the Bible says the earth is flat!"* or *"The Bible says the earth is a sphere in Isaiah 40."* And though most sincerely believe those statements, in reality, they are totally false. They originate from indoctrination or mimicking debunking talking points and a lack of study into the original languages of the Bible. You may wonder how the original languages can impact the meaning of something that much, so let's use the four horsemen of Revelation as an example.

Revelation 6 tells of a white horse, red horse, black horse, and a pale horse. These are the colors that were translated from Greek in most of our English translations of the Bible. However, when we look up the word "pale" in various Greek lexicons, we discover that the original Greek word there is *chloros* and it actually means "green." This is the same Greek word used in the New Testament for green grass and green trees, but translators probably didn't think green horse made sense. However, these are spirits, not actual horses. Once we understand the original Greek word, then we can accurately identify the evil spirit and ideology that the green horse represents (which is Islam). And, this is the way that we must approach any subject of study in the Bible, especially the controversial ones. So, this was my method as I began researching flat earth.

I must admit that the Lord immediately had my attention as I watched that first flat earth video back in October of 2015. But toward the end when it started giving Scripture references one after another, I was really blown away. I immediately pulled out my Bible and read those verses. I began looking up key words in the passages in Hebrew and Greek and that was the "icing on the cake." I could not deny what I was seeing for the first time. I could not deny that the Bible teaches a flat, stationary, non-rotating, non-orbiting earth that is covered by a molten glass dome called the firmament.

*"And the brethren immediately sent away Paul and Silas by night unto Berea: who coming thither went into the synagogue of the Jews. These were more noble than those in Thessalonica, in that **they received the word with all***

212

readiness of mind, and searched the Scriptures daily, whether those things were so. Therefore, many of them believed; also of honourable women which were Greeks, and of men, not a few" (Acts 17:10-12).

"*Study to shew thyself approved unto God, a workman that needeth not to be ashamed, **rightly dividing the word of truth** "* (2 Timothy 2:15).

God Told Job the Shape of the Earth

Over the next several months, I continued to study my Bible and research these truths about creation. The more I studied the Bible and researched NASA's many lies and fake pictures, the more I became convinced that the earth is truly FLAT! The first verse I saw that perfectly illustrated the earth as a flat disk was Job 38:14. "*It is turned **as clay to the seal**; and they stand as a garment.*" As I will address in more detail later, the Hebrew words in that verse gives the picture of clay being pressed down flat with a signet or seal ring.

Then, on July 2, 2016, while preparing to preach a message on the Marriage Supper and the Millennial Reign, the Lord Jesus opened my eyes to another confirming passage about the shape of the earth. As I read Revelation 20:9, I noticed an odd word used to describe the earth. It was a word that I had never looked up in the Strong's Greek

Dictionary until that day. The Apostle John by the Holy Spirit wrote:

"And they went up on the BREADTH of the earth, and compassed the camp of the saints about, and the beloved city: and fire came down from God out of heaven and devoured them." I thought, "Why didn't he just say 'they went up on the earth?"

I looked up the word "breadth" (#4114) in the Strong's Greek Dictionary. It is the Greek word *platos* which immediately reminded me of our word "plateau." *Platos* is defined as "width or breadth." However, the Strong's Greek Dictionary says *platos* comes from the root word #4116 which is the Greek word *platys* (pronounced pla-toos). *Platys* is defined as "SPREAD OUT FLAT (plot) i.e. broad: ---wide."

So, next I looked up the etymology of the word "plateau" and found the following:

"Elevated tract of relatively LEVEL land," from French plateau "table-land," from Old French platel (12c.) "FLAT piece of metal, wood, etc.," diminutive of plat "FLAT SURFACE OR THING," noun use of adjective plat "FLAT STRETCHED OUT" (12c.), perhaps from Vulgar Latin *plattus, from Greek platys "flat, wide, broad."[89]

The origin of "plateau," which means "flat land", is from the Greek word *platys* which is also the root of *platos* used in Revelation 20:9 to describe the earth. So, just like "pale horse" in Revelation 6 is technically correct but could have been more accurately translated "green horse," Revelation

---

[89] elevated tract of relatively LEVEL land," from French plateau "table-land," from Old French platel

20:9 should read, *"And they went up on the FLAT EARTH."*

Of course, there are always detractors and attempts to debunk anything that contradicts the status quo. One person said that the use of the Greek word *ge* for "earth" could mean land and because of that, I was not being honest with the text. But according to the Greek lexicon based on Thayer's and Smith's Bible Dictionary plus others this word *ge* pronounced "ghay" means *"...1) arable land 2) the ground, the earth as a standing place 3) the main land as opposed to the sea or water 4) the earth as a whole 5) the earth as opposed to the heavens 6) the inhabited earth, the abode of men and animals 7) a country, land enclosed within fixed boundaries, a tract of land, territory, region."*

The word *ge* was used 252 times in the King James Version New Testament and was translated "earth" 188 times. It was translated "land" only 42 times. And this Greek word *ge* is the word the translators of the Septuagint used for the Hebrew word *erets* or "earth" in Genesis 1 and elsewhere. And *erets* according to Brown-Driver-Briggs' definition means, *"...the whole earth as opposed to part"* which would be how it was used in Genesis 1 at the creation of the entire earth. Thus, it is safe to say that "FLAT EARTH" is a legitimate translation/definition of the phrase *"...breadth of the earth"* in Revelation 20:9.

Furthermore, the Bible says, *"In the mouth of two or three witnesses shall every word be established"* (1 Corinthians 13:1). Most scholars believe Job was one of the first books of the Bible to be written. The Book of Job has a lot of information about the true nature of creation, the attributes of God, and the angelic host. And it also confirms the shape

215

of the earth and how God formed it. The clear context of Job 38 is God speaking about when He created the earth.

"Then the LORD answered Job out of the whirlwind, and said, 'Who is this that darkeneth counsel by words without knowledge? Gird up now thy loins like a man; for I will demand of thee, and answer thou me. Where wast thou when I laid the foundations of the earth? declare, if thou hast understanding'" (Job 38:1-4).

God begins to question Job and in doing so He gives some clues about the creation of the earth. A couple of those descriptors are in verses 13 and 14:

"That it might take hold of the ends of the earth, that the wicked might be shaken out of it? It (the earth) *is turned as clay to the seal; and they stand as a garment"* (Job 38:13-14).

The Complete Jewish Bible translates Job 38:14 this way: ***"Then the earth is changed like clay under a seal,** until its colors are fixed like those of a garment."*

The Amplified Bible translates Job 38:14 this way: ***"The earth is changed like clay into which a seal is pressed**; And the things [of the earth] stand out like a [multi-colored] garment."*

Both translations are correct because the Hebrew for "turned" means "changed." An example would be: "I turned or 'changed' these potatoes into potato pancakes by mashing them down." To make certain this is correct, I did a word study through multiple lexicons and researched how the word was used in other verses in the Bible. For instance, the Gesenius' Hebrew-Chaldee Lexicon says *haphak* or "turn" in Job 38 means *"**to convert or to change**."* It gives Leviticus 13:3 as an example of *haphak* meaning to change something as when ***"...the hair in the plague is TURNED (haphak) white."*** So, the word "turned" or *haphak* means to change something when the rest of the verse denotes something changing forms or character.

Furthermore, the word for "seal" in the original Hebrew is *chowtham* and **means "a signature-ring, seal or signet."** The Gesenius' Lexicon defines it as a *"...a seal, a seal-ring."* These type of seal rings or signature rings were used to mash a piece of clay or wax FLAT leaving the distinct features of the ring pattern standing out. This was done as a personal signature to identify the originator. Thus, in Job 38:14, God gave the description to Job of how He formed/shaped the earth during creation.

God's Word says the earth was changed as a lump of clay under a signet/seal ring. This is a word picture that beautifully illustrates the earth being pressed down flat with the contours of the ring standing out. Even the detail of an upturned edge as a border is given with this illustration. Skeptics can cry "metaphor" or "figurative language" until they turn red and pass out, but the fact is that God gave that description of the earth being formed or changed like clay pressed under a seal ring. In doing so, He provided the very important truth about the shape of the magnificent earth that He created. God's description matches the flat earth, not a spinning, flying ball. He was not giving us empty or meaningless poetry in His Holy Bible!

The Face of the Earth

Another phrase in the Bible that reveals the shape of the Earth is the phrase *"...the face of the earth."* This phrase appears 29 times in the King James Version of the Bible...28 times in the Old Testament and 1 time in the New Testament. Here are several of those verses:

"And the Lord said, I will destroy man whom I have created from the face of the earth; both man, and beast, and the creeping thing, and the fowls of the air; for it repenteth me that I have made them" (Genesis 6:7).

"For thou art an holy people unto the Lord thy God: the Lord thy God hath chosen thee to be a special people unto himself, above all people that are upon the face of the earth" (Deuteronomy 7:6).

"Behold, the eyes of the Lord God are upon the sinful kingdom, and I will destroy it from off the face of the earth; saving that I will not utterly destroy the house of Jacob, saith the Lord" (Amos 9:8).

Please note that the Lord could have left out *"the face of"* and just had His prophets write, *"I will destroy it from off the earth"* instead of *"...from off the face of the earth."* I don't believe this is just poetic language or God wasting His words. God was deliberate and purposeful about everything He included in the Bible. The Holy Spirit put this phrase in the Bible 29 times to further show us the truth about the shape of the earth.

The Hebrew word for "face" in these verses is *paniym* and it simply means, *"face or part toward the front."* It can also refer to the presence of God and the shewbread (literally the bread of His Presence) used in the Tabernacle of Moses and then later in Jewish temples. The shewbread or showbread was twelve pieces of unleavened bread that had to be stacked in two even stacks on a special table. These factors would suggest that the shewbread was flat.

Additionally, most people would assume a person's face to be rounded, but, in reality, our faces are very flat compared to the top and back of our head. According to this BBC article, *"The face of a modern human is almost uniquely flat and extraordinarily expressive."*[90] A National Geographic article states, *"Flat-Faced Early Humans Confirmed"*[91] and the Daily Mail article questions, *"Why the Flat Face?"*[92] Now I don't suggest these articles as a real source of truth because they get into their evolutionary nonsense; I am just making the point that it is well acknowledged that our faces are very flat compared to the rest of our head.

Also, in math and geometry, a face is defined as *"...any flat surface."*[93] The 11th Edition of Meriam-Webster's Collegiate Dictionary defines "face" this way, *"In solid geometry, a face is a flat (planar) surface that forms part of the boundary of a solid object."* Smartick teaches, *"The faces of a polyhedron are the flat surfaces on the outside*

[90] http://www.bbc.com/Earth/story/20170214-your-face-is-probably-more-primitive-than-a-neanderthals

[91] https://news.nationalgeographic.com/news/2012/08/120808-human-evolution-fossils-homo-nature-science-meave-leakey-flat/

[92] https://www.dailymail.co.uk/sciencetech/article-3348997/Why-FLAT-face-delicate-features-oddity-caused-loss-bone-explains-don-t-big-noses-skulls-Neanderthals.html

[93] https://www.ck12.org/geometry/faces-edges-and-vertices-of-solids/lesson/Faces-Edges-and-Vertices-of-Solids-MSM6/

of the polyhedron."[94] So, in math and when considering the shape of our heads, a face is pointing to flatness not a ball.

Furthermore, the same Hebrew word *paniym* was used in the Old Testament phrases *"...face of the deep"* and *"...the face of the water."* And we know that water is level or flat, not curved by the make-believe force called gravity. People want to claim that gravity curves the massive oceans into a ball shape and holds them on a sphere earth, yet the water in a glass, pool, pond, lake and even Mobile Bay (that I have personally tested) is completely flat. Supposedly, gravity curves the big oceans, but not smaller and less heavy bodies of water? It is simply ridiculous to believe in the water ball and gravity's selective force!

Water is flat and level and the Bible says that, *"The earth is the Lord's, and the fulness thereof; the world, and they that dwell therein. For he* (God) *hath founded it upon the seas and established it upon the floods"* (Psalms 24:1-2). The Hebrew word for "founded" is *yacad* and it means "to set or establish; to sit down; settle or lay the foundation." The Hebrew word for "established" is *kuwn* and means "...to be firm, be stable, to be fixed, to be firmly established, to be erect, to stand." So, God set the earth (the dry land) upon the water and they are both clearly flat! He didn't wrap a ball earth in a curved water blanket.

For the One Millionth Time: Circle Not Ball!

Speaking of ball, whenever the subject of Biblical cosmology (aka flat earth) comes up among Christians, the usual go-to-verse to prove the earth is a sphere is Isaiah 40:22. They say, *"See, the Bible says that God sits upon the*

---

[94] https://www.smartickmethod.com/blog/math/geometry/solid-geometric-shapes/

CIRCLE of the earth and that means the earth is a sphere." However, what they fail to realize is that a circle is not the same as a ball. When I play ball with my daughter I don't say, "Throw me that circle." And God in His great knowledge of words actually chose two different words in Hebrew for circle and ball. Do you think He knew what He was doing? Of course! In fact, God used the Prophet Isaiah to give us two passages that reveal there are two different Hebrew words for "circle" and "ball."

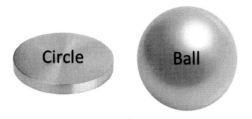

The Hebrew word for *"circle"* in Isaiah 40:22 is *chûwg (pronounced khoog) and it means "a circle: —circle, circuit, compass."* The Hebrew word for "ball" in Isaiah 22:18 is *dûwr* (pronounced dure) and it means *"a circle, **ball or pile:** —**ball,** turn, round about." "He will surely violently turn and toss thee **like a ball** into a large country: there shalt thou die, and there the chariots of thy glory shall be the shame of thy lord's house"* (Isaiah 22:18). In Proverbs, the Lord revealed that He engraved a circle on the face of the deep when He was fashioning the earth. In this passage the Wisdom of God is speaking (Jesus Christ is called the Wisdom of God in the New Testament) and says:

*"While as yet He had not made the earth, nor the fields, nor the highest part of the dust of the world. When He prepared the heavens, I was there: **when He set a compass upon the face of the depth:"** (Proverbs 8:26-27).

The Hebrew word for "set a compass" in this passage is *châqaq* (pronounced khaw-kak') and the meaning is, "*a primitive root; properly, to hack, i.e. ENGRAVE (Judges 5:14, to be a scribe simply); by implication, to enact (laws being CUT IN STONE or metal tablets).*"

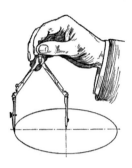

The Amplified Bible translates Proverbs 8:27 this way, *"When He established the heavens, I [Wisdom] was there;* **When He drew a circle upon the face of the deep."**

The Complete Jewish Bible translates Proverbs 8:27 this way, *"When He established the heavens, I was there.* **When he drew the horizon's circle on the deep."**

According to the etymology of the word "horizon," it is much more than just the limits of our vision. Wikipedia defines the term horizon as follows: The word horizon derives from the Greek word *kyklos* which means *"separating circle"* from the verb *horizo, "to divide", "to separate"* and that from *(oros) "boundary, landmark."*

So, this verse shows that God drew/engraved the circle boundary of the earth at creation. And that circle boundary of the earth is where the firmament dome comes down and meets the earth just beyond the ice wall that we call Antarctica. In the Biblical Flat Earth model, the North Pole is the only magnetic center of the circle and Antarctica is the ice wall, circle boundary that holds the oceans in at the edge or ends of the earth.

"He hath compassed the waters with bounds, until the day and night come to an end" (Job 26:10).

Many Bible passages confirm these truths as the Word of God uses phrases like *"...the ends of the earth"* and the *"...bounds (boundary limit) of their habitation."* Proverbs 8 even refers to the *"...habitable part of His earth."* All of these phrases specifically indicate in the original Hebrew and Greek languages an edge, boundary, or extremity of the earth, and these passages reveal that there is more land or earth beyond that boundary. From these Scriptures and others, I believe that God formed the earth originally as a square, cube-like structure just like the description of New Jerusalem in Revelation. Then, God drew/engraved the circle boundary into the flat surface of that cube.

Navigation

Could the fact that the earth is a circle with boundaries be why ship navigation is called - ***Great Circle Sailing?*** Here's how they define great circle sailing, *"A great circle is defined as a circle on the earth's surface the plane of which passes through the centre of the earth. For navigation purposes, the great circle track is the shortest distance between two places on the earth's surface.* ___**The great circle**___ ___**track appears as a straight line on Gnomonic (great circle)**___ ___**charts.**___ **The vertices of a great circle are the two points nearest to the poles which have a course on the great circle track due EAST/WEST. To follow a great circle track, the navigator needs to adjust the ship's course continuously** *because the great circle track is a curve when plotted on a Mercator Chart. Therefore, it is not really practicable to sail on an exact great circle route.*

*In order to take advantage of the shorter steaming distance of the **great circle track**, mariners usually divide a **great circle track** between the initial position and the destination into smaller segments (way points) of about one to two day's steaming time and make course adjustments at noon. The total distance is therefore the sum of the distances of those segments calculated by means of Mercator Sailing.* "[95]

In fact, one of the earliest instruments used to navigate the oceans was the first rudimentary computer called the astrolabe. It was a very accurate device used for celestial navigation, telling time, and predicting the movements of the sun, moon, and stars across the sky. An expert on astrolabes said in a TED Talk that to understand how this ancient instrument works, you must imagine the earth is at the center of the universe. The base of the astrolabe is a flat, circular disk with an upturned edge (yes, you read that correctly). The center of the circular, disk astrolabe corresponds to the North Star (or Polaris) and the paths of the sun, moon and stars are represented by offset circles on the astrolabe. The man giving the TED Talk said that the *"...real genius of the astrolabe was that it brought together two coordinate systems PERFECTLY."* As he explained how to use it, he laid the circular astrolabe flat in his hand and made a domed-shape motion over it with his other hand, while he said, ***"I have here a model of the sky that corresponds to the real sky. It is, in a sense, holding a model of the universe in my***

---

[95] http://www.coastalboating.net/Resources/Navigation/Calculators/greatcircle.html

hands."[96] It's amazing what happens when you look at creation the way God actually made it and not the way the Satanic cult of the ball has portrayed it. Things make sense!

God's Word (the Bible) teaches that the earth is a circle. Godless antichrist, scientists and occultists tell you that it is a ball. The LORD made it clear that He…

…Engraved a circle on the face of the deep.
…Stretched out the firmament over it like a tent for mankind to dwell.
…Sits upon the circular vault of heaven and watches the people like men view grasshoppers.
…Surrounded the waters below the firmament with a boundary He calls the ends of the earth.
…Placed His throne above and it sits on the glass-like firmament.

The real question (especially for Christians) becomes - Whose report will you believe?

---

[96] https://www.youtube.com/watch?time_continue=264&v=NKd2gFQ0bbI

Chapter 10

The Ends of the Earth

"Hear attentively the noise of his voice, and the sound that goeth out of his mouth. **He directeth it under the whole heaven, and his lightning unto the ends of the earth"** (Job 37:3-4).

"God understandeth the way thereof, and he knoweth the place thereof. **For He looketh to the ends of the earth, and seeth under the whole heaven;"** (Job 28:23-24).

"Hast thou not known? hast thou not heard, that the everlasting God, the Lord, **the Creator of the ends of the earth,** *fainteth not, neither is weary? there is no searching of his understanding"* (Isaiah 40:28).

"The adversaries of the Lord shall be broken to pieces; out of heaven shall he thunder upon them: the Lord shall judge the ends of the earth; *and he shall give strength unto his king, and exalt the horn of his anointed"* (1 Samuel 2:10).

The end of the earth is an idea that is often mocked when discussing the flat earth. People laugh and say, "If the earth is flat why hasn't anyone fallen off the edge (end)?" And yet, the phrase *"ends of the earth"* occurs 28 times in the King James Version (KJV) of the Bible and *"end of the earth"* (referring to a specific place) is used 12 times. The phrase *'uttermost parts of the earth"* occurs 7 times in the KJV and *"ends of the world"* referring to a specific location occurs twice. Altogether, this place called the *"ends or uttermost parts of the earth"* was included in the Bible a total of 49 times. In comparison, the word "firmament" or *raqiya* in Hebrew was only used 15 times (not including references like the molten, glass sky in Job 37:18, or sea of glass) and God calls the firmament a demonstration of His power. I would say the Biblical phrases about "the ends of the earth" are significant and cannot be downgraded to metaphors or figures of speech.

The Strong's Hebrew word for *"...ends of the earth"* in Deuteronomy 33:17 (the first use of the phrase in the Bible) is *ephec* and it means *"cessation, i.e. an end (especially of the earth); often used adverb, NO FURTHER; also the ankle*

228

(in the dual), as being the EXTREMNITY of the leg or foot: —ankle." The same Hebrew word **"...for ends of the earth"** is used in Psalms 72:8, **"He shall have dominion from sea to sea, and from THE RIVER unto the ENDS of the earth."** This verse gives a specific place in the world as an end point of measurement. He didn't just say, *"...unto the ends of the earth,"* but specifically from THE RIVER to the extremity of the earth where you can go no further.

Another Hebrew word used for the *"ends of the earth"* is *qatseh.* It means **"...an extremity: —× after, BORDER, BRIM, brink, EDGE, end, (in-) finite, frontier, outmost coast, quarter, shore, (out-) side, × some, ut(-ter-) most (part)**."

Here are two verses it is used in:

"Sing unto the Lord a new song, **and his praise from the end of the earth,** *ye that go down to the sea, and all that is therein; the isles, and the inhabitants thereof"* (Isaiah 42:10)

"From the end of the earth will I cry unto thee, *when my heart is overwhelmed: lead me to the rock that is higher than I"* (Psalms 61:2). Of course, these are just two verses of many that use this word.

Yet another Hebrew word that is translated *"end of the earth"* in our English translations is *kânâph.* The Strong's Greek Dictionary definition is **"...an edge or extremity**; *specifically (of a bird or army) a wing, (of a garment or bedclothing) a flap, (of the earth) a quarter, (of a building) a pinnacle:— bird,* **border,** *corner,* **end,** *feather(-ed), × flying, (one an-) other, overspreading, × quarters, skirt, × sort, uttermost part, wing(-ed)."* The Gesenius Lexicon defines this word as *"...the extreme bounds of the*

229

earth, the edge or extremity and also the highest summit of the temple. " Again, we have a Hebrew word for the "ends of the earth" defined as the limit, edge, or border while also stating it is the highest. The Bible makes it very clear that there is a definite edge, end and extremity (the furthest point or limit of something) of the earth. And this edge, end, or extremity simply cannot exist on a sphere.

Right before our Skyfall conference in 2018, Jordan Winsor (one of our Fire & Grace School of Ministry students) pointed out an amazing verse in the book of Job. The LORD was speaking to Job and asked him, *"Doth the hawk fly by thy wisdom, and stretch her wings toward the south?* (Job 39:26). Most people would just immediately assume that God was just talking about how birds fly south for the winter, but that is not what He was pointing out. When a bird stretches forth their wings, the wings are not pointing in the direction the bird is flying. In fact, their wings are pointing in opposite directions, yet God says that the hawk stretches her WINGS TOWARD THE SOUTH. How do two wings pointing in opposite directions both point south? This is how:

"Doth the hawk fly by thy wisdom, and stretch her wings toward the south?" (Job 39:26)

Let's go back to the verse about the river, " *"He shall have dominion from sea to sea, and from THE RIVER unto the ENDS of the earth"* (Psalms 78:2). I believe "the river" mentioned here is at the North Pole, which is the center of the circular, flat earth. If you turn one hundred eighty degrees in any direction from that center it is due south. When you head south to the uttermost ends of the earth it will take you to the 200-foot-high Antarctica ice wall. And just as the Hebrew word *kânâph* indicates, Antarctica is known to have *"...the **highest** average elevation of all the continents."*[97]

Polar explorer Admiral Richard Byrd, (one of the few men of his time to have explored both the Arctic and the Antarctic) made this statement in a documentary narrated by a very young Mike Wallace, *"The North Pole is at the center of a deep ocean whereas the South Pole is the center of **a high plateau that averages 7000-8000 feet in altitude...There is no life whatsoever beyond the EDGE of the world**...When we left on this expedition, we were, to put it very mildly, extremely anxious to see whether it existed."*

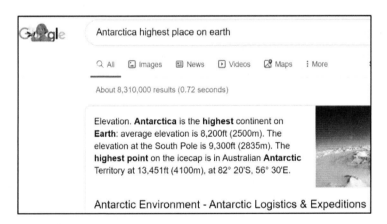

Of course, Biblical cosmologists do not believe Antarctica is a "continent" in the traditional sense of the word. But it does meet the requirements for a continent according to the Google definition which *is "...any of the world's main*

[97] http://www.dna.gov.ar/la-ant%C3%A1rtida

continuous expanses of land." Antarctica is the highest continuous land mass on earth. We believe that this highest land mass encircles all of the oceans and continents of the world. It is the "upturned edge" that Auguste Piccard described in 1931. It is the place where God set the borders of the earth or as Job put it, ***"He hath compassed the waters with bounds..."*** (Job 26:10). More on this verse later but think about that - God surrounded the waters with a boundary unlike the continents that are surrounded by water.

Is that why the United Nations uses the flat earth map as their logo? The only land mass missing on the UN map is Antarctica. Why would an organization that claims to want to unite the entire world in peace and unity leave out an entire "continent" in its symbol of the world? Maybe because the intertwining olive branches in the UN Azimuthal Equidistant projection map (the most accurate flat earth map) represent Antarctica as the high border around our flat earth? Of course, I believe that the United Nations is the satanic beast-world government in Bible prophecy, and they must submit to God's rule of showing truth to all. The UN logo is the truth in plain sight.

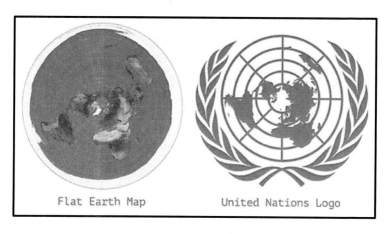

Flat Earth Map   United Nations Logo

The Design
The original UN logo was created by a team of designers during the United Nations Conference on International Organization in 1945. The design team was led by Oliver Lincoln Lundquist.

The United Nations Emblem
The design is "a map of the world representing an azimuthal equidistant projection centred on the North Pole, inscribed in a wreath consisting of crossed conventionalized branches of the olive tree, in gold on a field of smoke-blue with all water areas in white. The projection of the map extends to 60 degrees south latitude, and includes five concentric circles" (original description of the emblem).

UN Photo/John Isaac The flag of the United Nations, with its white emblem on a light blue field, flies from a pole in front of UN Headquarters in New York.

Interestingly, when I was studying this subject of the *"ends of the earth"* and the *"uttermost part of the earth,"* I came across another New Testament Greek word that also defines "the uttermost part of the earth" as the "highest place on the earth." Mark 13:26-27 says, *"And then shall they see the Son of man* (Jesus) *coming in the clouds with great power and glory. And then shall he send his angels and shall gather together his elect from the four winds, from the uttermost part of the earth to the uttermost part of heaven."* The Greek word translated "uttermost part" is *akron.* The Blue Letter Bible study app gives the "Outline of Biblical Usage: the farthest bounds, uttermost parts, end, highest, extreme;" all of which would accurately describe Antarctica. The Strong's Greek Dictionary defines #206 *akron* as *"the extremity (which Google defines as the furthest point or limit of something)—one end...other, tip, top, uttermost participle."* Thayer's Greek Lexicon defines *akron* as *"...highest, extreme; to top-most point, the extremity, the farthest bounds, uttermost parts, end, end of the earth."* So, the New Testament word used for the uttermost or end of the earth also means the highest part of the earth. This connects Antarctica to what the Bible calls the "ends of the earth" in a very specific way!

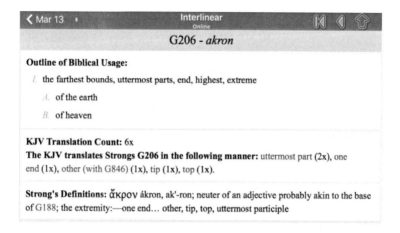

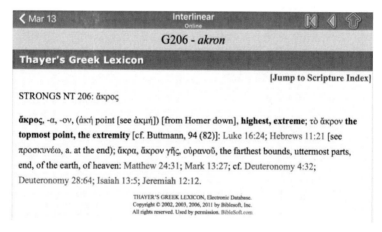

Admiral Byrd always made a clear distinction between the natures of the extreme North and South. And it is certainly unusual language to call any place on a ball "the EDGE of the world" or the "EDGE of the earth." Yet Byrd is not alone because we hear this language about Antarctica all the time, but we never hear that terminology used for the northern Arctic region. While discussing Antarctica in another famous interview, Admiral Byrd continually ran his finger around the outside edge of a saucer plate that was sitting in front of him on the table.[98] Was he giving hints?

LONGINES CHRONOSCOPE WITH RICHARD E. BYRD

It is not just Admiral Byrd and "flat earthers" that call Antarctica *"the ends of the earth"* or even *the "edge of the earth."* In my research at CIA.gov, I came across a FOIA declassified document entitled, ***"Argentina-Chile: Dispute at the Ends of the Earth."*** It was produced by the Central Intelligence Agency National Foreign Assessment Center in November 1978. This document presented the issues over a disputed Antarctic claim. One portion reads, *"An additional Argentine concern is that the International Court ruling will adversely affect their Antarctic claim which overlaps that of Chile."[99]*

---

[98] https://www.youtube.com/watch?v=PrdSal9uH28

[99] https://www.cia.gov/library/readingroom/document/cia-rdp08c01297r000800090009-8

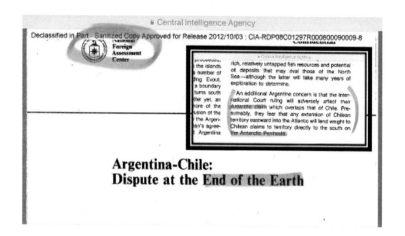

Argentina-Chile:
Dispute at the End of the Earth

Geographical UK posted an article in 2017 about a bogus climate change documentary by Huffington Post. In the documentary they traveled to Antarctica to "prove" climate change and how the melting ice is going to cause the oceans to rise. (Side note: The other day I filled a glass with ice and poured it full of good ole southern sweet tea. I went back to writing another chapter of this book, next thing I knew hours had passed. I looked over and the ice in my glass had completely melted and somehow my watered-down glass of iced tea didn't overflow. That's called reality as opposed to fake science and scare tactics.) Anyway, the point being that they entitled their climate change propaganda documentary *"End of the Earth"* in reference to Antarctica.[100]

National Geographic published a book by Peter Matthiessen in 2014 called ***End of the Earth: Voyage to Antarctica.*** It's description is worth noting, *"End of the Earth brings to life the waters of the richest whale feeding grounds in the world, the wandering albatross with its 11-foot wingspan arching through the sky, and the habits of every variety of seal, walrus, petrel, and penguin in the area,*

---

[100] https://geographical.co.uk/nature/polar/item/2392-end-of-the-Earth

all with boundless and contagious inquisitiveness. Magnificently written, the book evokes an appreciation and sympathy for a region as harsh as it is beautiful." [101]

Another interesting description of Antarctica comes straight from research scientists at the National Snow & Ice Data Center. *"Scientists from NSIDC have spent two Antarctic field seasons studying one of the little-known megadunes areas of the continent."* They called this research project: ***"Antarctic Megadunes: Research at the Edge of the Earth."*** [102]

I understand where someone might use the phrase "ends of the earth" as a modern euphemism for a distant or remote area, but "edge of the earth"? Why would anyone refer to Antarctica as the *"edge of the earth"?* The definition of the word "edge" states, ***"the outside limit of an object, area, or surface; a place or part farthest away from the center of something.*** " This word better describes the flat earth model (aka Biblical model) rather than the globe earth model. Another reference to the Antarctic being the "edge of the earth" comes from the memoir by Polar explorer Ben Saunders. He describes what it's like *"...to walk to the edge of the earth and live to tell the tale."* [103] He and another person claim that they walked from the shore of Antarctica to the South Pole and back. Why didn't he call it the walk to the bottom of the ball?

The Calvert Journal shared an article by Carole Devine entitled ***"Antarctic circle: living with Russian scientists at the edge of the world."*** Sharing her experience as a

---

[101] https://www.goodreads.com/book/show/10667.End_of_the_Earth

[102] https://nsidc.org/cryosphere/antarctica/megadunes

[103] https://www.huckmag.com/art-and-culture/bensaunders-scottexpedition/

volunteer in Antarctica she said, "I was leading the Canadian side of the Joint Russian Canadian Ecological Project in collaboration with the Russian Antarctic Expedition, which manages science programmes at its base on the vast continent. We were a group of 54 volunteers helping the Russians clean up over that austral summer season. **All stations had to quickly adopt rigorous new ecological regulations under the Madrid Protocol on Environmental Protection, part of the Antarctic Treaty designating the continent a 'natural reserve, devoted to peace and science.'"**[104]

An NBC affiliate in Minnesota KTTC reported in 2017, **"Spring Valley man captures new perspective from the Edge of the Earth***... SPRING VALLEY, Minn. (KTTC) — Joshua Swanson from Spring Valley is all about adventure and living life on the edge. In the late 1990s, when he was offered a chance to live and work in one of the harshest places on earth — Antarctica — he snapped it up. But it's a hobby he started there during the dark winter months that's giving us a chance to see Antarctica in a new light — **a new perspective from the edge of the earth."**[105]

As you can see, Antarctica is referred to as the "edge of the earth" by people all over this flat earth. It's just more truth in plain sight.

[104] https://www.calvertjournal.com/articles/show/5275/antarctic-cooking-and-cleaning-carol-devine-bellingshausen

[105] https://kttc.com/news/2017/02/07/spring-valley-man-captures-new-perspective-from-the-edge-of-the-Earth-9/

No One Is Falling Off the Edge of the Earth

Now, let's be clear…no one is falling off the edge of the Biblical flat earth even though that is the picture that is always put forth when this truth is being ridiculed. The Book of Job clearly states that God put a circle boundary around the oceans, *"He hath compassed the waters with bounds, until the day and night come to an end"* (Job 26:10). The Gesenius' Hebrew-Chaldee Lexicon defines the word for "compassed" as *"…to draw a circle with a compass."* That same lexicon also defines "bounds" in this verse as *"…a defined limit."* Psalms 74:17 says, *"Thou hast set all the borders of the earth: thou hast made summer and winter."*

The New Testament also mentions this circle boundary. In Acts 17:24-26, Paul wrote, *"God that made the world and all things therein, seeing that he is Lord of heaven and earth, dwelleth not in temples made with hands; Neither is worshipped with men's hands, as though he needed anything, seeing he giveth to all life, and breath, and all things; And hath made of one blood all nations of men for to dwell on all the face of the earth, and HATH DETERMINED the times before appointed, and the BOUNDS of their habitation."*

The Greek word for *"hath determined"* is *horizo* which happens to be the root word for "horizon." *Horion* is the root word for horizo and means *"…the separating circle boundary."* The Strong's Greek Dictionary defines it as a *"bound or limit; a boundary-line."* And the Greek word for *"bounds"* in this passage is *horothesia* which means *"…a limit-placing, boundary-line."* Thayer's defines *"bounds"* as *"…definite limit."* Of course, the habitation spoken of here is the habitation for all men which is the entire earth,

239

but there is a limit, a circle boundary line where men can go no further. It is called the ice wall of Antarctica that is the outside edge of the circle that God cut into the earth. And this is the place that the solid firmament comes down and meets the earth.

Enoch (whose book/prophecy is quoted in the Bible and found among the Dead Sea Scrolls) described that place after God showed it to him:

"I saw the treasuries of all the winds: I saw how He had furnished with them the whole creation and the firm foundations of the earth. And I saw the cornerstone of the earth: I saw the four winds which BEAR [the earth and] the FIRMAMENT of the heaven. And I saw how the winds stretch out the vaults of heaven and have their station between heaven and earth: these are the pillars of the heaven. I saw the winds of heaven which turn and bring the circumference of the sun and all the stars to their setting. I saw the winds on the earth carrying the clouds: I saw the paths of the angels. **I SAW AT THE END OF THE EARTH THE FIRMAMENT OF HEAVEN ABOVE"** (Enoch 18:1-5).

I actually discovered in my research that the firmament dome was photographed by George Rayner during an expedition to Antarctica from 1928-1930.[106] When you compare the sky in Rayner's photographs of Antarctica, it is clear that couple of them catch the sky with the appearance of a solid, crystalline wall with texture. This sounds very much like Ezekiel's description of the firmament having the appearance of "terrible crystal" in Ezekiel 1:22.

---

[106] https://collections.museumvictoria.com.au/items/393656

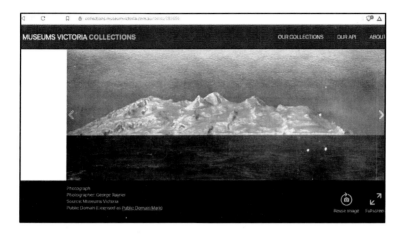

Amos 9:6 confirms that the "vault of heaven" (firmament) was bound to the earth. The King James Version says it like this, *"It is he that buildeth his stories in the heaven, and hath founded his troop in the earth; he that calleth for the waters of the sea, and poureth them out upon the face of the earth: The Lord is his name."* As is the case at times, the KJV translators were not technically wrong with their English word choices, but sometimes they made a verse difficult. This is one of those verses that you must look up the original Hebrew words in this passage, if you want to understand what it is saying.

The Hebrew word for "stories" is *ma'alah* and the Gesenius lexicon defines it as a **"...lofty place or upper room"** that you reach by steps or stairs. In fact, the KJV translates *ma'alah* as stairs 15 times. Amos 9 is literally talking about a stairway to heaven or what connects heaven (the firmament and God's throne) to earth. Do you think that high-level Satanists like Led Zeppelin know the truth when they write songs like, "Stairway to Heaven"? I do.

The Hebrew word for "founded" in Amos 9:6 is *"yacad"* and the Strong's Hebrew Dictionary defines it as

"...setting or laying a foundation." The Gesenius lexicon defines *yacad* like this, "...to found (a building), to place a building, to place a foundation stone." The Hebrew word translated "troop" in the KJV is *aguddah*. The Strong's defines *aguddah* as "...to bind, band, bundle, knot or ARCH." The Gesenius defines *aguddah* as **"...arched or vaulted work, used of the vault of heaven as in Amos 9:6."** This verse bears out that the Lord built a vaulted arch that makes both a story or stairway to His chamber above, but this vault or dome is also founded or bound to the earth like a building is set upon a foundation. As I was writing about this stairway, I was reminded of another "truth in plain sight." In the Truman Show when he finally realized that his "reality" was not real, Truman sailed to the edge of his world and climbed a stairway next to a "sky wall" to get out of the enclosed system. The truth is everywhere!

The Complete Jewish Bible gives a good translation of Amos 9:6, **"He builds his upper rooms in heaven and establishes his sky-vault over the earth.** *He summons the waters of the sea and pours them out over the earth. Adonai is his name."* Another good translation of this verse is from the Amplified Bible, **"It is He who builds His upper chambers in the heavens And has established His vaulted dome (the firmament of heaven) over the earth,** *He who calls to the waters of the sea And pours them out on the face of the earth—The Lord is His name."* Hence, the firmament dome comes down and meets the earth somewhere just beyond the coast of Antarctica. So don't worry, no one is falling off the edge.

The Ice Wall and the Molten Sea

I saw someone comment on social media the other day, *"There is no evidence that this ice wall in Antarctica even exists."* That statement was one of either pure ignorance or just outright dishonesty. There are many pictures, videos and older historical references to the Antarctic ice wall. I even discovered a declassified CIA document that acknowledges the ice wall while still denying what Antarctica really is. The document from January 1956 is entitled, ***"National Intelligence Survey: Antarctica"*** *and it states, "Most coasts of Antarctica are covered by great depths of snow and ice that extends seaward toward the shoreline **and terminate in vertical cliffs approaching 200 feet in height.**"*[107]

a Central Intelligence Agency

westerly winds produce a surface current that sets to the east or northeast.

Most coasts of Antarctica are covered by great depths of snow and ice that extend seaward beyond the shoreline and terminate in vertical ice cliffs approaching 200 feet in height. Where the sheet of snow and ice extends many miles out to sea it is called shelf ice. Along the coasts where the ice cliff stands nearly on the shoreline, cliffs or headlands of bare rock interrupt the vertical ice cliff. On the back side of the headlands, or where the ice edge has retreated inland, the edge of the ice sheet commonly terminates against a low ridge or bank of rocks and rock fragments called a mo-

and the ex 1954–55. coasts and the USHC and the U 1943, H.O. 1955. Otl tions to th Photogeog Scott Expe maps and In gener lacking in configurat

The testimony of James Clark Ross confirms the ice wall of Antarctica and another important detail. *"On October 5th, 1839 another explorer, James Clark Ross began a series of Antarctic voyages lasting a total of 4 years and 5 months. Ross and his crew sailed two heavily armored warships thousands of miles, losing many men from hurricanes and*

---

[107] https://www.cia.gov/library/readingroom/document/cia-rdp97-00952r000200250001-2

icebergs, looking for an entry point beyond the southern glacial wall. Upon first confronting the massive barrier Captain Ross wrote of the wall, '...extending from its eastern extreme point as far as the eye could discern to the eastward. It presented an extraordinary appearance, gradually increasing in height, **as we got nearer to it, and proving at length to be a perpendicular cliff of ice, between one hundred and fifty feet and two hundred feet above the level of the sea, perfectly flat and level at the top,** *and without any fissures or promontories on its even seaward face. We might with equal chance of success try to sail through the cliffs of Dover, as to penetrate such a mass.'"*

Antarctica is the ice wall boundary round the oceans...

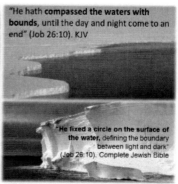

"He has inscribed a circular limit (the horizon) on the face of the waters at the boundary between light and darkness" (Job 26:10). Amplified Bible

"He hath compassed the waters with bounds, until the day and night come to an end" (Job 26:10). KJV

"He fixed a circle on the surface of the water, defining the boundary between light and dark" (Job 26:10). Complete Jewish Bible

The translators of the Amplified Bible wrote Job 26:10 this way, *"He has inscribed a circular limit (the horizon) on the face of the waters at the boundary between light and darkness."* They should have left out horizon in the parenthesis because the horizon is not the CIRCULAR LIMIT around the oceans; however, the phrase "circular limit" was a very good way to translate a boundary that surrounds something. The fact is this: God created a lip or wall to hold the oceans in our flat earth. Like Him, we have created dishes and bowls with sides to hold our milk when we want to have some cereal. We create the walls or sides of a swimming pool to hold the water. We buy fish tanks with walls or sides to hold water so we can have our pet fish. But somehow, we have abandoned this basic principle of water needing a container when it comes to the earth which happens to be 71% water.

Speaking of this circular wall or fence, even the Hebrew letters in the word "compassed" bears out that God made a fence around the earth. In my studies of the Bible and the original languages, I came across a book by Dr. Frank Seekins entitled *"Hebrew Word Pictures."* In his book, Dr. Seekins shows the evolution of ancient languages, particularly Hebrew. He explains how each letter represented a picture and thus gives more understanding of the meaning of a word. For instance, the Hebrew letter "aleph" was represented by the picture of the ox which depicted strength and leading the way. The Hebrew letter *"bet"* was pictured as a tent and meant a household. Those two letters together *"aleph bet"* or *"ab"* is the word "father" in Hebrew. The letter pictures depict, a father is the strong leader of the tent or home or household.

According to the Gesenius Hebrew-Chaldee Lexicon, the Hebrew word "גוח chûwg, (pronounced khoog) means "...*to describe a circle or draw a circle with a compass.*" Reading right to left are three letters "Chet," "Vav," and "Gimel." The ancient picture for the letter "chet" is a fence or tent wall, "vav" is a tent peg that secures the tent to the earth and "gimel" is the picture of a camel standing up or lifting up. So, the circle border that surrounds the oceans is a fence or wall that God lifted up higher and secured to the earth. Yet another perfect description of the firmament tent over the earth being secured to the ground at the "ends of the earth."

Vav 6	Hey 5	Dalet 4	Gimel 3	Beyt 2	Alef 1
Y	♀	ᴛᴛ	ᴸ	ᴌ	⅄
Nail Secure Add/and	Behold Reveal Breath	Door Move Entrance	Foot Camel Pride	House Family in	Ox Strength Leader
Lamed 30	Kaf 20	Yod 10	Tet 9	Chet 8	Zayin 7
∪	⅏	﹄	⊗	ꙮ	ᴄ
Shepherd Staff/Teach To/from	Palm To open Allow/tame	Arm/hand Work/deed Worship	Basket Snake Surround	Wall Fence Separation	Plow Weapon Cut off

I discovered another Biblical illustration of the circle of the earth and God creating a lip or wall around the circumference to hold the oceans while looking up Bible passages for this chapter. The thing to remember is that Hebrews 8 tells us that Moses was told to make things for the first Tabernacle according to the pattern that he saw when he was with God on the mountain. It is evident by reading 2 Chronicles chapters 1-4 that God imparted to Solomon exactly how He wanted the Temple and all of the different parts constructed. This brings me to the Bible passage that just blew my mind. It has to do with the "molten sea" that Solomon had made for the outer court of the LORD's temple, *"Also he made a molten sea of ten cubits from brim to brim, round in compass, and five cubits the height thereof; and a line of thirty cubits did compass it round about. And under it was the similitude of oxen, which did compass it round about: ten in a cubit, compassing the sea round about. Two rows of oxen were cast, when it was cast"* (2 Chronicles 4:2-3).

The moment I read this, it was clear that this molten or brass sea with the oxen foundation was a representation of the earth and its oceans being a circle with an outer wall to contain the water. The twelve oxen represent the pillars that God placed the earth and the seas upon. And when I started researching this molten sea further, I discovered that going back many centuries the Jews have believed and taught that the Molten or Brazen Sea of Solomon was a depiction of the world. Here's what it says in the Jewish Encyclopedia, *"The symbolism of the brazen sea is described in detail in the Midrash Tadshe.* **The sea represented the world.**" Here's an illustration of what the molten sea looked like:

THE BRAZEN SEA OF SOLOMON'S TEMPLE.—WITH VIEW OF SECTION.
(Restored according to Calmet.)

I believe that the illustration of the Molten Sea taken from the description in 2 Chronicles 4 speaks for itself. Considering how the rest of the Bible describes creation, it is quite evident that the top of the Molten Sea represents the circle of the earth with the outside being Antarctica with its ice wall and mountains to hold in the water of the seas. The area underneath the oxen represents the great deep and the underworld or sheol (hell).

As I stated before, the twelve oxen represent the foundation or pillars on which the circle of the earth with its oceans are set, *"He raiseth up the poor out of the dust, and lifteth up the beggar from the dunghill, to set them among princes, and to make them inherit the throne of glory: **for the pillars of the earth are the Lord's, and he hath set the world upon them"*** (1 Samuel 2:8). Those twelve oxen also foreshadow the twelve apostles of the Lord Jesus. The book of Revelation confirms this in the description we get of the future New Jerusalem, *"And he carried me away in the spirit to a great and high mountain, and shewed me that great city, the holy Jerusalem, descending out of heaven from God, Having the glory of God: and her light was like unto a stone most precious, even like a jasper stone, clear as crystal; And had a wall great and high, and had twelve gates, and at the gates twelve angels, and names written thereon, which are the names of the twelve tribes of the children of Israel: On the east three gates; on the north three gates; on the south three gates; and on the west three gates. **And the wall of the city had twelve foundations, and in them the names of the twelve apostles of the Lamb"*** (Revelation 21:10-14).

The Waters Wrapped in a Garment

And this verse in Proverbs really seals the deal, *"Who hath ascended up into heaven, or descended? who hath gathered the wind in his fists? who hath bound the waters in a garment? who hath established all the ends of the earth? what is His name, and what is His Son's name, if thou canst tell?"* (Proverbs 30:4).

Of course, the One who ascended and descended was the Lord Jesus Christ (John 3:13, Ephesians 4:8-10) and He is also the Son mentioned in this verse. The gathering of the wind in His fists is a major clue about the ends of the earth that we will look at in the next chapter. But when the writer of Proverbs asked, *"Who hath bound the waters with a garment?"* he was reiterating the picture of creation and the ends of the earth as a place that surrounds the waters like a garment. A garment goes around the OUTSIDE of your body. Thus, once again, we are given the example of God putting a boundary around the outside of the circle of earth and its oceans. Profound and yet so simple a child can understand it.

Chapter 11

The Secrets of Antarctica

Lt. Kaffee *"I want the truth!"* Col. Jessup *"You can't handle the truth! Son, we live in a world that has walls, and those walls have to be guarded by men with guns. Who's gonna do it? You? You, Lt. Weinburg? I have a greater responsibility than you could possibly fathom."* - A Few Good Men

*"**The Norwegian adventurer who made an unauthorized trip to Antarctica with a New Zealander on board has been arrested off the coast of Chile**...A spokesperson for M. Andhoy, Rune Olsgaard, told Morning Report **the Chilean navy has confined the crew to the boat and three armed guards are making sure they don't leave the naval base.**"* - Radio New Zealand report April 2, 2012[108]

*"Who hath ascended up into heaven, or descended? **who hath gathered the wind in his fists? who hath bound the waters in a garment? who hath established all the ends of***

---

the earth? what is his name, and what is his Son's name, if thou canst tell?" (Proverbs 30:4).

When the subject of Biblical cosmology (aka Flat Earth) comes up in a group setting the running joke among non-flat earthers seems to be, *"Show me the edge!"* Then, there's the meme that says, "...if the earth was flat, cats would have already knocked everything over the edge." The more serious scoffers will say, "Why don't you flat earthers put together an expedition to Antarctica and settle this thing once and for all?" Well, the answer to all that is simple...no one just picks up and goes to Antarctica without governmental authorization.

For Americans, we must submit form DS-4131 to the U.S. Department of State three months prior to intended travel to Antarctica. Expedition details must be sent to all parties of the Antarctic Treaty of 1959. Americans also need an approval from our Environmental Protection Agency *"...to ensure compliance with 40 CFR (Code of Federal Regulations) Part 8, Environmental Impact Assessment (EIA) of Nongovernmental Activities in Antarctica, as well as with other relevant U.S. agencies."* Also, ***"Certain expedition information may be posted on the National Science Foundation's and the Antarctic Treaty Secretariat's Web sites in order to facilitate notification of and access by all Parties to the Treaty."***[109] This public notification is required just in case an environmental group or obscure government agency wants to protest or sue you before you even get a chance to finish organizing your expedition.

---

[109] https://eforms.state.gov/Forms/ds4131.pdf

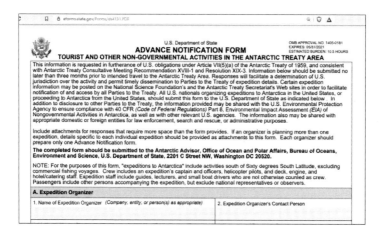

If a group of flat earthers were able to get approved for an Antarctic expedition, the next hurdle would be how to make that journey of thousands of miles round-trip into the coldest temperatures and wind on earth. For a journey that long, you would need a lot of supplies and some form of transportation. Vehicles, snowmobiles, and even sled dogs are highly regulated. Also, there are areas of Antarctica that are considered even more "special" and protected so access would be limited in order to ensure those sensitive areas are not disturbed. In other words, only very well vetted people get to go beyond flybys and cruise ships (where no one disembarks).

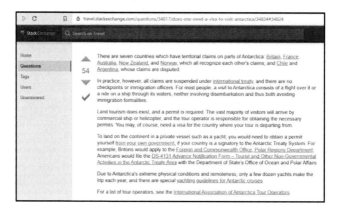

Here is part of an article about an unauthorized expedition to Antarctica: *"**The Norwegian adventurer who made an unauthorized trip to Antarctica with a New Zealander on board has been arrested off the coast of Chile.** Jarle Andhoy and his four crew were arrested in waters near the border of Chile and Argentina. **They were escorted to a nearby naval base at Puerto Williams and their sailing permit has been revoked.** Mr Andhoy's lawyer Nils Jørgen Vordahl told Radio New Zealand's Morning Report programme the arrest was made after a request from New Zealand authorities. However, the New Zealand Ministry of Foreign Affairs and Trade says the men are not under arrest as far as it knows. **A ministry spokesperson says the Government alerted Chilean authorities to the unauthorized expedition and has been encouraging Norway to take action against Mr Andhoy.** Norwegian newspaper Aftenposten is quoting the Chilean naval commander as saying the yacht was taken into custody because the skipper gave the wrong name of the boat when contacted on naval radio. Crew reported to be fine.*

*In January this year, Jarle Andhoy left New Zealand for Antarctica on the yacht Nilaya in search of missing sailboat Berserk, which sank in McMurdo Sound on his previous unauthorized expedition. Three people died in the sinking. Norwegian authorities had asked New Zealand to stop the latest expedition, but the Nilaya left Auckland in a hurry on 23 January after Mr Andhoy was served with a deportation notice. Mr Andhoy abandoned the search for the Berserk in February and the crew decided against sailing back to New Zealand, fearing they would face prosecution for not getting permission to sail to Antarctica. Mr Andhoy's lawyer Nils Jørgen Vordahl says the crew of the Nilaya are fine, but are still waiting to see official papers detailing why they have been arrested. A spokesperson for Mr Andhoy, Rune Olsgaard, told Morning Report **the Chilean navy has***

254

confined the crew to the boat and three armed guards are making sure they don't leave the naval base."

I have traveled to Europe, Israel, Nigeria, and the Island of Mauritius, and I have never seen anything like what it takes to visit Antarctica. They don't seem to mind the average person seeing the coastline from a cruise ship or airplane, but they don't want just anyone venturing further on their own. Why? Do they have something to hide? Many believe that they discovered where the firmament dome meets the earth and are suppressing this discovery because it would be solid evidence that the Bible is true, and the God of the Bible is the Creator. I believe this is what the Apostle Paul was referring to in Romans when he spoke about men suppressing the truth of creation even though God had shown it to them. Here's the passage:

"For the wrath of God is revealed from heaven against all ungodliness and unrighteousness of men, ***who hold*** *(Greek hold down, suppress)* ***the truth in unrighteousness;*** *Because that which may be known of God is manifest in them;* ***for God hath shewed it unto them. For the invisible things of him from the creation of the world are clearly seen, being understood by the things that are made, even his eternal power and Godhead; so that they are without excuse****: Because that, when they knew God, they glorified him not as God, neither were thankful; but became vain in their imaginations, and their foolish heart was darkened. Professing themselves to be wise, they became fools"* (Romans 1:18-22).

What invisible thing from the creation of the world could God have shown to men? And why would they suppress it? God calls the firmament a manifestation of His power, *"Praise ye the Lord. Praise God in his sanctuary:* ***praise***

255

him in the firmament of his power. *Praise him for his mighty acts: praise him according to his excellent greatness"* (Psalms 150:1-2). And Romans 1 says that the thing God showed them revealed His eternal power and Godhead and it left them without excuse. It says that when they knew it was of God, they did not praise Him or glorify Him as God. They hide the firmament and don't glorify God because they serve Satan and his agenda.

I believe they found the firmament during either operation Highjump (1946-1947) or Operation Deep Freeze (1955-1958) and they are guarding it…among other things. In fact, the Encyclopedia Americana 1958 Edition states, *"In December 1955, the task force left New Zealand to set up two base stations in the Ross Sea area* (Antarctica). *Little America V was established at Kainan Bay, about 30 miles east along the Ross Ice Shelf from the Bay of Whales, and an air operations base was constructed at Hut Point on Ross Island in McMurdo Sound. Four United States planes flew from New Zealand to McMurdo Sound on Dec. 20, 1955, and made exploratory flights over unknown parts of the continent until Jan. 18, 1956, when they returned to New Zealand. These flights proved the inland areas to be featureless in character, with a dome 13,000 feet high at about latitude 80 degrees South and 90 degrees East."*[110]

---

[110] *Encyclopedia Americana* ©1958 by Americana Corporation "Antarctica."

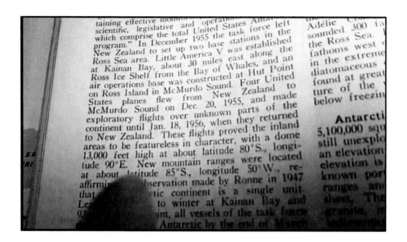

taining effective *mon...*
scientific, legislative and *opera...*
which comprise the total United States *An...*
program." In December 1955 the task force left
New Zealand to set up two base stations in the
Ross Sea area. Little America V was established
at Kainan Bay, about 30 miles east along the
Ross Ice Shelf from the Bay of Whales, and an
air operations base was constructed at Hut Point
on Ross Island in McMurdo Sound. Four United
States planes flew from New Zealand to
McMurdo Sound on Dec. 20, 1955, and made
exploratory flights over unknown parts of the
continent until Jan. 18, 1956, when they returned
to New Zealand. These flights proved the inland
areas to be featureless in character, with a dome
13,000 feet high at about latitude $80°S$., longitude $90°E$. New mountain ranges were located
at about latitude $85°S$., longitude $50°W$., re-
affirm... ...servation made by Ronne in 1947
that ...tic continent is a single unit
...to winter at Kainan Bay and
...int, all vessels of the task force
Antarctic by the end of *March*

Adélie ...
sounded 300 f...
the Ross Sea.
fathoms west ...
in the extreme
diatomaceous
found at grea...
ture of the ...
below freezin...

Antarcti...
5,100,000 squ...
still unexplo...
an elevation...
elevation is ...
known por...
ranges an...
sheet. Th...
...

Is it a coincidence that NASA was founded in 1958, right after these major operations in Antarctica? It was also in 1958 that Lewis Strauss, then chairman of the United States Atomic Energy Commission, opposed doing high-altitude nuclear tests.[111] That means discussion was already underway in 1957-1958 regarding what later became Operation Fishbowl in 1962. Why would the United States government call a high-altitude nuclear detonation Operation Fishbowl? Because they were trying to break open the "fishbowl" they had recently discovered in Antarctica? And to make things even more obvious, Operation Fishbowl was part of a bigger operation whose code name was Dominic which means "of the LORD." Put this together and you have – "Fishbowl of the LORD." More truth in plain sight!

---

[111] *Defense's Nuclear Agency 1947-1997* by Defense Threat Reduction Agency ©2002 pg. 139

Conflicting Accounts of Distances

"During Captain James Clark Ross's voyages around the Antarctic circumference, he often wrote in his journal perplexed at how they routinely found themselves out of accordance with their charts, stating that they found themselves an average of 12-16 miles outside their reckoning every day, some days as much as 29 miles. Lieutenant Charles Wilkes commanded a United States Navy exploration expedition to the Antarctic from August 18th, 1838 to June 10th, 1842, almost four years spent "exploring and surveying the Southern Ocean." In his journals, Lieutenant Wilkes also mentioned being consistently east of his reckoning, sometimes over 20 miles in less than 18 hours."[112]

"James Weddell, (born Aug. 24, 1787, Ostend, Austrian Netherlands—died Sept. 9, 1834, London), British explorer and seal hunter who set a record for navigation into the Antarctic and for whom the Weddell Sea is named. Weddell commanded the sealing brig "Jane" on three Antarctic voyages, the success of the first (1819–21) permitting him to buy a share in the vessel. On the second voyage (1821–22) he visited the island of South Georgia, east of the tip of South America, as well as the South Shetland Islands. In February 1822, he visited and named the South Orkney Islands. On his third voyage (1822–24), he surveyed the South Shetlands and the South Orkneys and then sailed southward in search of new land. Aided by unusually open ice conditions, he reached 74°15′ S in the sea that was later named for him, exceeding Capt. James Cook's record of southernmost exploration by more than three degrees. He left a record of his exploration in A Voyage Towards the South Pole (1825)."[113]

While reading a second edition copy (1827) of the 1825 book, *A Voyage Toward the South Pole* by James Weddell, I discovered many instances (once they were well into the southern "hemisphere") of him continually finding his ship to be out of reckoning with the logs based on a spherical model of the earth.

---

[112] *The Flat Earth Conspiracy* by Eric Dubay ©2014 ISBN: 978-1-312-66448-7

[113] https://www.britannica.com/biography/James-Weddell

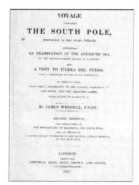

Weddell recorded in his captains journal, *"On the 11th in the morning the wind shifted to south west by south and we stood to the Southeast.* ***At noon our latitude by observation was 65° 32' that of account 65° 53' and the chronometers giving 44 miles more westing than the log…(pg.33)***

On the 15th at noon our latitude observed was 60° 44' by account 69° this difference of 16 miles in latitude with easting given by chronometers, makes a current in four days of North 53° East 27 miles. In the forenoon, with the ships head South by West, ***I took a set of azimuths, to which my great astonishment gave the variation but 1° 20' East.*** *In the afternoon, I took a second set, which gave 4° 58'.* ***As I have taken great pains in making the observations, and the instruments were good, however and accountable this great difference was, I could not do otherwise then abide by the result…*** *(pg.34)*

On the 18th, the weather was remarkably fine and the wind in the S.E…With the ship's head S.W. by S. at about 8:30 in the morning, I took a set of azimuths which gave variation of 13° 23' east. At noon, our latitude my observation was 72° 38' my account 72° 14'; ***hence with chronometer difference of longitude, we had been set in three days S. 62° W., distance 30 miles.*** *In the afternoon, I took a long set of*

*azimuths, which gave variation 19° 58'. <u>This increase in so</u>
<u>short a distance seemed unsatisfactory</u>; which account I
neglected no opportunity of making observations in order
to reconcile these irregularities. I had all the compasses*
brought up on the deck and found them to agree but rather
in active in traversing. "[114]

During his voyage into the southern "hemisphere," poor
Captain Weddell continued to be frustrated day by day.
However, it is good for us that he recorded these "variations"
between his logs and the actual readings. This is proof that
the distances on the spherical model of earth do not match
reality when navigating deep into the southern region. It also
confirms the reports of other voyages to Antarctica that
discovered these discrepancies. Sadly, some did not make it
back to tell us their story.

The Albatross

"In the southern hemisphere, navigators to India have
often fancied themselves east of the Cape when still west,
and have been driven ashore on the African coast, which,
according to their reckoning, lay behind them.   This
misfortune happened to a fine frigate, the Challenger, in
1845.   How came Her Majesty's Ship 'Conqueror,' to be
lost? How have so many other noble vessels, perfectly sound,
perfectly manned, perfectly navigated, been wrecked in calm
weather, not only in dark night, or in a fog, but in broad
daylight and sunshine - in the former case upon the coasts,
in the latter, upon sunken rocks - from being 'out of

---

[114] *A Voyage Toward the South Pole* by James Weddell F.R.S.E 2nd Edition London 1827
pp. 33-35

reckoning,' under circumstances which until now, have baffled every satisfactory explanation."[115]

"Yes, but we can circumnavigate the South easily enough,' is often said by those who don't know, **The British Ship Challenger recently completed the circuit of the Southern region - indirectly, to be sure - but she was three years about it and traversed nearly 69,000 miles - a stretch long enough to have taken her six times round on the globular hypothesis. "** [116]

This greater distance around Antarctica has been confirmed by the research of migration habits of the Albatross "around" Antarctica. The migration of the Albatross is one of the few bird migrations that include a *"circumnavigation of the earth."* They use the strong wind currents that circle in the south region to fly great distances. Albatross spend most of their life in the air. Documented research and witnesses have given us accurate distance data for this "circumnavigation" over a sabbatical year. After looking at that data, we will compare it with measurement data taken from Google Earth.

[115] *The Gallery of Nature: Tour Through Creation* by Rev. Thomas Milner London ©1860

[116] *One Hundred Proofs the Earth is Not a Globe* by William Carpenter Library of Congress ©1886 pg.78

Remember, we are told that coastline of Antarctica is 11,165 miles or almost 18,000 kilometers. Scientific reports at nature.com states that the Albatross "circumnavigates" Antarctica 2 to 3 times, covering more than 120,000 km in a single sabbatical year.[117] That means that in just one trip around Antarctica, they travel over 40,000 km or more than double the coastline of Antarctica. There are very detailed recordings of the path the Albatross take in their circumnavigation of Antarctica. However, when you map out the flight path of the Albatross migration on the Google Earth globe model, you get 28,564 km. If you multiply that by 3 then you have 85,692 km (53,246 miles) which is over 20,000 miles shorter than the actual data. Thus, the results indicate that the migration of the Albatross spans a much greater distance than would be expected using a round earth as our measuring device. If the flat earth model is used, it makes more sense and the distance complies with the documented data from the albatross researchers. This is huge confirmation that shows that the Albatross migration is happening on a flat earth model, not the globe earth model. Once again, things make sense when dealing with the reality God created and instead of the deception.

Another interesting anomaly concerning the length of the shoreline of Antarctica can be found on Flightradar24. For those not familiar with it, Flightradar24 is a "global" flight tracking service that provides real-time information about thousands of aircraft around the world. When you zoom out to see the entire world map, it is apparent that coastline of Antarctica stretches from the tip of South America all the way around the circle until you arrive back. It is shown to equal the distance around the so-called equator of the ball Earth. That would be at least 24,901 miles, not 11,165 like

---

[117] https://www.nature.com/articles/srep08853

we are told. Also, on the Flightradar24 map, Antarctica makes the other continents look very small. In fact, on this map it appears that all of the other continents would fit inside the massive land mass called Antarctica.

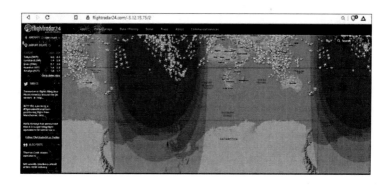

Furthermore, I have watched Flightradar24 and similar flight tracking sites many times and never have I seen a flight over Antarctica due south to fly under the ball to the other side. Neither have I seen any direct/non-stop flights from places like Santiago Chile to Sydney or Melbourne, Australia or Johannesburg, South Africa to Perth, Australia. And if you check out regular flight paths for the major airlines, they make far more sense on a flat earth map than a globe map. For instance, *"A woman who gave birth on a plane to the US has been deported home to Taiwan without her baby and may be ordered to pay $30,000 for diverting the flight, according to Chinese and Taiwanese media. The China Airlines flight, from Bali to Los Angeles, was forced to make an emergency landing in Alaska after the woman's water broke six hours into the 19-hour flight."*[118] The article states that this happened six hours into a 19-hour flight.

---

[118] https://www.telegraph.co.uk/news/worldnews/asia/taiwan/11946928/Woman-who-gave-birth-on-plane-deported-from-US-to-Taiwan-without-baby.html

After talking to my friend who is a 30-year commercial pilot, we can accurately estimate that the Chinese airliner was averaging 500-525 mph. Taking the higher range of 525 mph, six hours of flight time would put them at the approximately 3,150 miles over the Pacific Ocean. Using Google Earth, it is easy to see that on the alleged globe earth model the nearest airport would have been in Hawaii - not Anchorage, Alaska. In fact, my calculations on Google Earth show that Hawaii was 3,200 miles ahead while Anchorage, Alaska another 4,700 miles farther. Why would any pilot choose to fly an extra 1,500 miles or an extra 3 hours of flight time if you have an emergency? You wouldn't. However, if you chart a flight from Bali to Los Angeles on a flat earth map, you would fly right next to Anchorage, Alaska.

The Bible and Antarctica

*"When he uttereth his voice, there is a multitude of waters in the heavens, **and he causeth the vapours to ascend from THE ENDS OF THE EARTH; he maketh lightnings with rain, and bringeth forth the wind out of his treasures"*** (Jeremiah 10:13).

***"He causeth the vapours to ascend FROM THE ENDS OF THE EARTH**; he maketh lightnings for the rain; he bringeth the wind out of his treasuries"* (Psalm 135:7).

God told His prophets that He causes **"...*the vapours to ascend from THE ENDS OF THE EARTH*;** *he maketh lightnings with rain,* **and bringeth forth the wind out of his treasures"** (Jeremiah 10:13). The original Hebrew word that was translated "treasures" in this verse is the word *owtsar*. The Strong's Hebrew Dictionary defines it as a **"...*depository—armory, cellar, garner, storehouse,*** *treasure house."* A depository, armory, garner, storehouse, and treasure house are all places where an abundance of something exists. The Bible is very specific in these verses and others that the "ends of the earth" is connected with an abundance of wind. It just so happens that Antarctica is windiest place on the earth. According to the *Guinness Book of World Records and the Eighth Edition of the National Geographic Atlas*, Commonwealth Bay, Antarctica is the windiest place on earth. The winds there regularly exceed 150 mph with an average annual wind speed of 50 mph. Is that just a coincidence or did the God of creation reveal something to His Middle Eastern prophets that was impossible for them to know on their own?

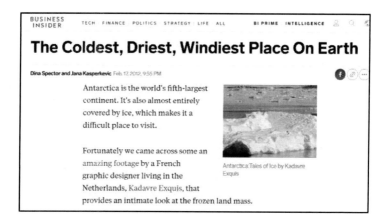

Another confirmation to the unique nature of the winds in, above, and around Antarctica came from searching through the CIA FOIA Reading Room for documents about Antarctica. I came across a report from 1959 entitled, ***"Information on Soviet Bloc International Geophysical Cooperation -1959."*** It stated, *"Parallel areological observations in the Arctic and Antarctic, first organized in connection with IGY, showed that mobile cyclones in the Antarctic are of great intensity and have a frontal structure similar to Arctic cyclones.* ***In addition, essential***

266

peculiarities of stratospheric processes in the Antarctic, not observed in other regions of the earth, were determined."[119] Through all of the vast research and expeditions of the Russians to Antarctica (including high-altitude rockets and balloons), they came to the conclusion that stratospheric processes there (one of which is stratospheric winds for carrying balloon "satellites") are not observed in any other regions of the earth. In other words, they found that the winds of Antarctica are abundant, very strong and totally unique which goes right along with the Bible calling "the ends of the earth" the treasury/storehouse of the winds.

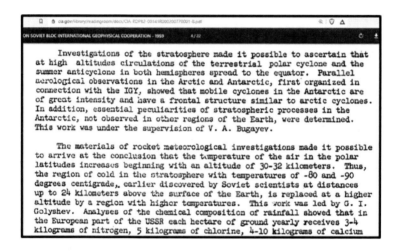

NASA has also admitted that the Antarctic winds are something very special. This is why they release the vast majority of their high-altitude balloon "satellites" there instead of Florida or Texas. They depend on the strong, circular winds of Antarctica to orbit their "satellites." A 2012 article on NASA's website states, ***"The Long Duration Balloons (LDB) site was established at Willy Field, McMurdo Station in order to take advantage of the***

---

[119] https://www.cia.gov/library/readingroom/docs/CIA-RDP82-00141R000200770001-8.pdf

stratospheric anticyclone wind pattern circulating from east to west around the south pole. The stratospheric wind circulation combined with the sparsely populated continent of Antarctica allows for long duration balloon flight at altitudes about 100,000 feet. One circumnavigation of the pole takes approximately 14 days."[120]

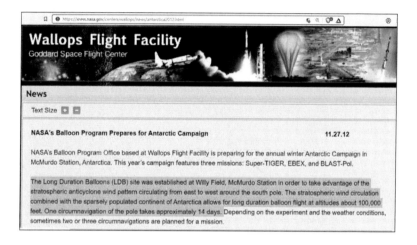

Vapors Ascending

Also, while researching volcanos in Antarctica, I came across some articles about the 91 volcanos that have been discovered there. This is in addition to Mount Erebus *which "...is currently the most active volcano in Antarctica and is the current eruptive zone of the Erebus hotspot. The summit contains a persistent convecting phonolitic lava lake, one of five long-lasting lava lakes on earth.* Characteristic eruptive activity consists of Strombolian eruptions from the lava lake or from one of several subsidiary vents, all within the volcano's inner crater. *The volcano is scientifically remarkable in that its relatively low-level and unusually persistent eruptive activity enables*

---

[120] https://www.nasa.gov/centers/wallops/news/antarctica2012.html

long-term volcanological study of a Strombolian eruptive system very close (hundreds of metres) to the active vents, a characteristic shared with only a few volcanoes on earth, such as Stromboli in Italy.*"[121]* In other words, consistent and persistent volcanic vapors are venting from the ends of the earth and ascending into those strong Antarctic wind currents (just like the Middle Eastern prophets of the Bible who never traveled to Antarctica revealed).

This Guardian article reveals that *"Scientists have uncovered the largest volcanic region on earth – two kilometres below the surface of the vast ice sheet that covers west Antarctica. The project, by Edinburgh University researchers, has revealed almost 100 volcanoes – with the highest as tall as the Eiger, which stands at almost 4,000 metres in Switzerland. Geologists say this huge region is likely to dwarf that of east Africa's volcanic ridge, currently rated the densest concentration of volcanoes in the world."[122]*

[121] https://en.wikipedia.org/wiki/Mount_Erebus

[122] https://www.theguardian.com/world/2017/aug/12/scientists-discover-91-volcanos-antarctica

So, what we learned from this article is that Antarctica has 47 volcanos and scientists recently discovered 91 more under the ice. Once all of this is confirmed and studied further, scientists believe that Antarctica will have the highest concentration of volcanos anywhere on earth. Also, Antarctica already has continuous volcanic eruptions and activity that releases vapor into the air and that unique high-altitude wind that circles the earth. And according to the USGS, *"By far the most abundant volcanic gas is water vapor, which is harmless. However, significant amounts of carbon dioxide, sulfur dioxide, hydrogen sulfide and hydrogen halides can also be emitted from volcanoes. Depending on their concentrations, these gases are all potentially hazardous to people, animals, agriculture, and property."*[123]

I find it interesting that the end-time Bible prophecy in Acts 2:17-21 says, **"And it shall come to pass in the last days, saith God**, *I will pour out of my Spirit upon all flesh: and your sons and your daughters shall prophesy, and your young men shall see visions, and your old men shall dream dreams: And on my servants and on my handmaidens I will pour out in those days of my Spirit; and they shall prophesy:* **And I will shew wonders in heaven above, and signs in the earth beneath; blood, and fire, and vapour of smoke: The sun shall be turned into darkness, and the moon into blood, before the great and notable day of the Lord come:** *And it shall come to pass, that whosoever shall call on the name of the Lord shall be saved"* (that name you call upon to be saved from your sin and eternal damnation is the Lord Jesus Christ of Nazareth).

Does that prophecy possibly foretell a massive eruption of the volcanos that have been discovered underneath the ice at the "ends of the earth"? The verses that mention the vapors

---

[123] https://volcanoes.usgs.gov/vhp/gas.html

at the ends of the earth say, "… *and He* (God) *causeth the* *vapours to ascend from THE ENDS OF THE EARTH."* Right now, we may only be seeing the beginnings of the vapors that will soon ascend from the ends of the earth (Antarctica). And considering the fact that the Luciferian "elite" (including heads of state) guard Antarctica to suppress the truth and have made many mysterious visits there over the last several years, this verse makes perfect sense, *"The adversaries of the Lord shall be broken to pieces; out of heaven shall he thunder upon them: the Lord shall judge the ends of the earth;* and he shall give strength unto his king, and exalt the horn of his anointed" (1 Samuel 2:10).

"When he uttereth his voice, there is a multitude of waters in the heavens; **and he causeth the vapours to ascend from the ends of the earth: he maketh lightnings with rain, and bringeth forth the wind out of his treasures"** (Jeremiah 51:16).

In talking about God causing vapors to ascend from the ends of the earth, this verse also says, *"…he maketh lightnings with rain, and bringeth forth the wind out of his treasures."* So, Antarctica is not only connected to vapors (from volcanos) but also weather (lightning, rain and wind). Of course, there is weather in every part of the world, so the Bible mentioning this means that there is something significant about weather and the ends of the earth.

By now, it shouldn't surprise anyone that I found another declassified TOP SECRET CIA document from 1958 that confirms this passage in the Bible. The document talks about the United States concern over Russia's interest in Antarctica. Even back then, the CIA document stated, *"The results of such scientific research are important to a variety of fields of vital concern to the USSR. For example, **the Antarctic may be an important factor in global weather**,*

271

including that of the Northern Hemisphere…Antarctic activities might also contribute to studies of WEATHER CONTROL, in which the Soviets are taking an active interest."[124] These concerns with the Soviet agenda caused the United States to push for the creation of a "multinational regime" to govern and control Antarctica. This came to pass a year later with the signing of the Antarctic Treaty of 1959.

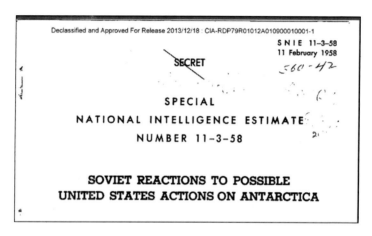

Declassified and Approved For Release 2013/12/18 : CIA-RDP79R01012A010900010001-1

S N I E 11–3–58
11 February 1958

SECRET

560 - 42

SPECIAL

NATIONAL INTELLIGENCE ESTIMATE

NUMBER 11–3–58

SOVIET REACTIONS TO POSSIBLE UNITED STATES ACTIONS ON ANTARCTICA

https://www.cia.gov/library/readingroom/docs/CIA-RDP79R01012A010900010001-1.pdf

We believe that a major concern is the collection of scientific data in a wide variety of fields, including basic research.

13. *Scientific Interests.* The USSR has a long established and highly developed program for accumulating scientific data in all the earth sciences including the geophysical fields. Such a program requires a multitude of observations during a long period and over wide areas. We believe that a major cause for the extensive Soviet Antarctic activity is the acquisition of data for this program while at the same time serving political and prestige needs. The results of such scientific research are important to a variety of fields of vital concern to the USSR. For example, the Antarctic may be an important factor in global weather, including that of the Northern Hemisphere. Long range forecasting is of importance to the Soviets as it relates to such matters as agricultural production in marginal lands and the availability of the Northern Sea Route. Antarctic activities might also contribute to studies of weather control, in which the Soviets are taking an active interest.

military activities in the Antarctic area either in connection with the IGY program or independently. While it is possible that the Soviets will develop an interest in using the Antarctic for missile testing, submarine and aircraft basing, or as part of a military communications net, we believe such possibilities to be unlikely. There is also the possibility that the area will be of value in monitoring earth satellites and space vehicles used for reconnaissance and other military missions.

16. *Economic Interests.* The Soviets have been whaling in Antarctic waters since 1946, and this activity will increase as new whalers and auxiliary ships now under construction are completed. In addition, results of current prospecting for minerals may possibly lead to increased Soviet interest in Antarctica. However, the difficulties of access, extraction and production are great. We do not believe that economic interests will be an important factor in Soviet decisions affecting the area.

17. *Political Interests.* To date the USSR has neither made any territorial claims nor recognized the claims of any other power. The

[124] https://www.cia.gov/library/readingroom/docs/CIA-RDP79R01012A010900010001-1.pdf

In all of my studies and research about Biblical cosmology and flat earth, I have done a lot of research on Antarctica. One thing that stands out almost immediately in what I have seen is the tremendous mountain range called the Transantarctic Mountains. It stretches for thousands of miles. Apart from that, there are other mountain peaks scattered about. They are beautiful and imposing. Something else that I have noticed is how calm the ocean is around the coastline of Antarctica. I'm not talking about the water miles away from shore, but the water next to the shore. The ocean that meets at the base of the ice wall and Antarctic mountains near the shores of Antarctica are as still as the water on a large lake or pond on a calm day.

There are simply no waves pounding the shore in Antarctica like they do in the Gulf of Mexico, Hawaii, or California. To make sure of this, I pulled up video after video containing footage of Antarctica and sure enough (apart from being in the middle of a big storm), the ocean is very still and there are no noisy waves crashing the ice wall or the mountainous shoreline.

Notice the mirror reflections of the mountains and the cruise ship in the water. This cannot happen on undulating ocean swells or water producing constant waves. It takes still water.

Then, just a few days ago as I was going over the Scriptures that talk about the ends of the earth, I reread Psalms 65. It is a Psalm of King David and the heading in my Bible says, *"Thanking God for Nature."* The Holy Spirit of God inspired King David to write this down over 3,000 years ago, *"By terrible things in righteousness wilt thou answer us, O God of our salvation;* **who art the confidence of all the ends of the earth, and of them that are afar off upon the sea: Which by His strength setteth fast the mountains; being girded with power: Which stilleth the noise of the seas, the noise of their waves,** *and the tumult of the people. They also that dwell in the uttermost parts are afraid at thy tokens: thou makest the outgoings of the morning and evening to rejoice"* (Psalms 65:5-8).

Speaking of the *"...ends of the earth,"* David confirms that this place is **"...afar off upon the sea,"** not a place near to Israel like the Mediterranean Sea. He goes on to describe the ends of the earth as a place where God by His strength *"...setteth fast the mountains,"* which clearly describes what we know and see in Antarctica. And then David writes that the ends of the earth is a place where God *"...stilleth the noise of the seas* (plural or all of them) and specifically **"...the noise of their waves."** This blew my mind and put me in deeper awe of the Lord and His Holy Bible. The Bible

274

is like no other religious writing in the world. It is very specific about the details of creation as well as the fulfilled prophecies from thousands of years ago and prophecies that are in the process of being fulfilled. God has revealed Himself in creation, through His written word, through history, archeology, and through fulfilled prophecies. He is the only true God, the Creator and the only Savior Jesus Christ.

"To whom then will ye liken me, or shall I be equal? saith the Holy One. Lift up your eyes on high, and behold who hath created these things, that bringeth out their host by number: he calleth them all by names by the greatness of his might, for that he is strong in power; not one faileth. Why sayest thou, O Jacob, and speakest, O Israel, My way is hid from the Lord, and my judgment is passed over from my God? **Hast thou not known? hast thou not heard,** *that the everlasting God, the Lord, the Creator of the ends of the earth,* **fainteth not, neither is weary? there is no searching of his understanding"** (Isaiah 40:25-28).

Chapter 12

The Circular Path of the Near-Sun

"And God said, Let there be lights in the firmament of the heaven to divide the day from the night; and let them be for signs, and for seasons, and for days, and years: And let them be for lights in the firmament of the heaven to give light upon the earth: and it was so. And God made two great lights; the greater light to rule the day, and the lesser light to rule the night: he made the stars also. And God set them in the firmament of the heaven to give light upon the earth, and to rule over the day and over the night, and to divide the light from the darkness: and God saw that it was good. And the evening and the morning were the fourth day" (Genesis 1:14-19).

"And they that be wise shall shine as the brightness of the firmament; and they that turn many to righteousness as the stars for ever and ever" (Daniel 12:3).

*"There are also celestial bodies, and bodies terrestrial: but the glory of the celestial is one, and the glory of the terrestrial is another. **There is one glory of the sun, and***

277

another glory of the moon, and another glory of the stars: for one-star differeth from another star in glory" (1 Corinthians 15:40-41).

"Immediately after the tribulation of those days shall the sun be darkened, **and the moon shall not give her light, and the stars shall fall from heaven,** *and the powers of the heavens shall be shaken: And then shall appear the sign of the Son of man in heaven: and then shall all the tribes of the earth mourn, and they shall see the Son of man coming in the clouds of heaven with power and great glory"* (Matthew 24:29-30).

"And it came to pass, as they fled from before Israel, and were in the going down to Bethhoron, **that the Lord cast down great stones from heaven upon them** *unto Azekah, and they died: they were more which died with hailstones than they whom the children of Israel slew with the sword. Then spake Joshua to the Lord in the day when the Lord delivered up the Amorites before the children of Israel, and he said in the sight of Israel,* **Sun, stand thou still upon Gibeon; and thou, Moon, in the valley of Ajalon. And the sun stood still, and the moon stayed, until the people had avenged themselves upon their enemies.** *Is not this written in the book of Jasher?* **<u>So, the sun stood still in the midst of heaven</u>, and hasted not to go down about a whole day.** *And there was no day like that before it or after it, that the Lord hearkened unto the voice of a man: for the Lord fought for Israel"* (Joshua 10:10-14).

"There was mention of a certain new astrologer who wanted to prove that the earth moves and not the sky, the sun, and the moon. *This would be as if somebody were riding on a cart or in a ship and imagined that he was standing still while the earth and the trees were moving...*

"So, it goes now. Whoever wants to be clever must agree with nothing that others esteem. He must do something of his own. This is what that fellow does who wishes to turn the whole of astronomy upside down. **Even in these things that are thrown into disorder _I believe the Holy Scriptures_, for Joshua commanded the sun to stand still, and not the earth.** *"* - Martin Luther of the Protestant Reformation

The first thing we should notice in Genesis 1 is that God did not mention the creation of extra-terrestrial planets and galaxies or that the moon is a reflector. According to Genesis, the only dry land mass that God created was earth. He made the water, the earth, the firmament, and the sun, moon, and stars. Then, He made man from the earth and woman from the rib of the man. There is absolutely nothing in the Bible about God making things like planets, comets, asteroids or blackholes, and to say or suggest that God created those things is pure conjecture based on the claims of modern astronomy. But here is something to understand: the only thing that can be known (through modern science) about the lights in the sky (which they claim are massive sun-stars, planets, spinning galaxies, supernovas, comets or meteorites) is that they are lights in the sky. It is quite humorous to hear the wild and elaborate stories about what these lights are based on seeing them slightly enhanced through telescopes. Yet most people just accept their descriptions and elaborate theories as facts because they come from the cult of scientism.

A Christian author from 1924 named E. Eschini comments and then quotes a renowned member of the Royal Astronomical Society and Professor of Astronomy at Oxford University H.H. Turner, *"**The results of recent research prove that the heavenly luminaries are not worlds, but lights**, and should cause all men who have been allowed to* *accept as proven Copernicus' theory of the motions of the earth to reconsider this subject.* **Professor H. H. Turner, of Oxford made the following statement regarding observations carried out on the brightest star in the constellation Orion: 'The most exciting discovery as a result of measuring this star in the winter of 1920, and 1921, in 1922 is that the diameter is changing and it looks as if the star is palpitating as a heart does.'"**[125] This quote confirms what flat earthers with their Nikon P900 and P1000 cameras have discovered about the nature of the stars and the alleged planets (that the ancients like Enoch and Jude called the "wandering stars"). They found that they are pulsating, shape-changing, semi-transparent, flickering lights in the sky. They are not like earth nor are they like the sun or the moon. Basically, they are not what the priests of the Copernican sun-worshipping cult have told us.

Concerning the sun, **"Heliocentrists' astronomical figures always sound perfectly precise, but they have historically been notorious for regularly and drastically changing them to suit their various models. For instance, in his time Copernicus calculated the Sun's distance from earth to be 3,391,200 miles.** *The next century Johannes Kepler decided it was actually 12,376,800 miles away. Isaac Newton once said,* **'It matters not whether we reckon it 28 or 54 million miles distant for either would do just as well!'** *How scientific!? Benjamin Martin calculated between 81 and 82 million miles, Thomas Dilworth claimed 93,726,900 miles, John Hind stated positively 95,298,260 miles, Benjamin Gould said more than 96 million miles, and Christian Mayer thought it was more than 104 million!"*[126]

---

[125] *Foundations of Many Generations* by E. Eschini ©1924 pp. 3-4
[126] *The Flat Earth Conspiracy* by Eric Dubay ©2014

Does this sound like people we can trust? What if this was a doctor who kept changing his diagnosis every time you visited him? Would you actually believe that he knew what he was doing or just guessing? Copernicus was only about 90 million miles off on his calculation about the distance of the sun, yet his theory on the nature of the cosmos is accepted.

For the Bible-believing Christian, there is no way to reconcile the claims of modern heliocentric astronomy with what the Bible actually teaches. We are told by the Big Bang, Copernican scientists that the (really just one of many stars as they allege) *"...mean radius of the sun is 432,450 miles (696,000 kilometers),* **which makes its diameter about 864,938 miles** *(1.392 million km). You could line up 109 earths across the face of the sun. The sun's circumference is about 2,713,406 miles (4,366,813 km).* **It may be the biggest thing in this neighborhood, but the sun is just average compared to other stars. Betelgeuse, a red giant, is about 700 times bigger than the sun and about 14,000 times brighter. 'We have found stars that are 100 times bigger in diameter than our sun. Truly those stars are enormous,'** *NASA says on its SpacePlace website. 'We have also seen stars that are just a tenth the size of our sun.' According to NASA's solar scientist C. Alex Young, if the sun were hollow, it would take about one million earths to fill it."*[127] But Jesus taught that the stars would fall to the earth just prior to His second coming. If stars are what modern scientists, astronomers and "space" agencies claim, then one star falling to earth would destroy the entire earth and all life on earth. That is not what Jesus said would happen. So, the stars that God created must be very different from what we are told by the Copernican priests.

[127] https://www.space.com/17001-how-big-is-the-sun-size-of-the-sun.html

Furthermore, they tell us that the sun is just an average star that is 93,000,000 miles away even though God made a distinct difference between the sun and stars in the Bible. They tell us that earth orbits the sun once per year at about 66,000 miles per hour as it flies through the vacuum of space. Yet, the Bible makes it quite clear that a much smaller and local sun moves in a circuit or circle over a motionless, flat earth. There are definitely conflicting stories here. In Psalms 19, the Holy Spirit revealed that the sun moves in a circuit like a man running a race, *"Their line is gone out through all the earth, and their words to the end of the world.* **In them hath he set a tabernacle for the sun, which is as a bridegroom coming out of his chamber, and rejoiceth as a strong man to run a race. His going forth is from the end of the heaven, and his circuit unto the ends of it: and there is nothing hid from the heat thereof"** (Psalms 19:4-6).

The Hebrew word for "circuit" in Psalms 19:6 is *tequwphah.* Its definition in the Strong's Greek Dictionary states that it is, **"...a revolution, that is, (of the sun) course, (of time) lapse: --circuit, come about."** Dictionary.com defines "revolution" as **"...a moving in a circular or curving course, as about a central point."** This Bible passage and the definitions of these words clearly teaches that the sun moves in a circular path over the earth. This is also the concept that we get from the event in Joshua 10 when Joshua commanded the sun and moon to stand still and God did just that. He caused the sun and the moon to stop their circular path over the earth. This is completely OPPOSITE of what is taught to children and college students in so-called "science" classes all over the world. And for the Christian, who claims to believe that all Scripture was God-breathed through His prophets and apostles and that the words of the Holy Bible are true and without error or

282

contradiction, you have a serious problem if you accept, believe, and teach the Copernican system as truth.

I once saw an elementary school teacher at a Christian school lead her students in their morning routine of her asking them a list of questions and the students responding back in unison. One of her questions was, *"Students, is every word of the Bible true?"* They chimed back, *"Yes, every Word of the Bible is true."* Well, not five minutes later she was telling the story in Joshua 10 and said, *"Science tells us that it really wasn't the sun and moon standing still."* What a mixed message those children received that day about the reliability of the Bible! Is it any wonder so many young people are leaving Christianity?

Dr. Henry M. Morris (Founder and President Emeritus of the Institute of Creation Research) attempts to interpret Psalms 19 and the circular path of the sun through the modern concept of "space" which is based on Big Bang cosmology. This cosmology was first proposed in 1931 by Jesuit-trained, Roman Catholic priest George Lemaitre. Before I address the ridiculous explanation of Psalms 19 by Dr. Morris, let's review what modern Big Bang cosmology teaches.

According to NASA our entire solar system, including the sun, orbit around the center of the Milky Way galaxy. They go on to say, *"We are moving at an average velocity of 828,000 km/hr. But even at that high rate, it still takes us about 230 million years to make one complete orbit around the Milky Way!"*[128] Then, Physics-Astronomy.com states that **"...the Milky Way Galaxy is travelling through space**

---

at an amazing speed of 2.1 million km/h, in the direction of the constellations of Virgo and Leo."[129]

A CNN article confirms the teaching of modern science that the Milky Way Galaxy is moving through the vast universe to another location, *"Think about it: Everything is moving. Earth is rotating on its axis and orbiting the sun. The sun and the rest of our solar system orbit the center of the Milky Way. **The Milky Way, along with other galaxies in the Laniakea Supercluster, is racing through space at about 2 million kilometers per hour**. But this is no aimless journey of motion. **Researchers have long believed that our galaxy was attracted to an area rich with dozens of clusters of galaxies 750 million light-years away, called the Shapley Concentration or Shapley Attractor. 'On average, galaxies are flying apart from one another due to the expansion of the universe,' Tully explained. 'However, each one is experiencing gravitational tugs from neighbors that cause deviant motions -- toward regions of high density and away from regions of low density.** Our solar system is a tiny part of a galaxy we call the Milky Way. As our galaxy participates in a flow, we go along for the ride.'"*[130]

Getting back to the explanation of creationist Dr. Morris (that was sent to me from a pastor), he states, *"His going forth is from the end of the heaven, and his circuit unto the ends of it: and there is nothing hid from the heat thereof"* (Psalm 19:6). **This verse is often derided by skeptics as teaching that the sun goes around the earth, instead of the earth rotating on its axis.** But the writer was more scientific then his critics. There is no fixed point of zero motion in the

---

[129] http://www.physics-astronomy.com/2017/07/the-milky-way-is-moving-through.html?m=1#.XYFNuhZOmEc

[130] https://www.cnn.com/2017/01/31/world/milky-way-dipole-repeller-space-trnd/index.html

universe, so far as astronomers know. **The sun indeed is moving in a gigantic orbit in the Milky Way galaxy, and the galaxy itself is moving among the other galaxies. So, the circuit of the sun is, indeed, from one end of the heavens to the other.**[131]

There are several problems with the explanation from Dr. Morris, chiefly, he automatically starts his interpretation of Scripture with the text of modern science, not the Bible. Thus, he immediately violates two of the primary laws of proper hermeneutics 1) he did not compare Scripture with Scripture and 2) he did not consider the historical, cultural (the known beliefs of the Hebrews), and background/situation behind the text. Dr. Morris claims that the "circuit of the sun" in Psalms 19 is the alleged orbital path of the sun around the center of the Milky Way galaxy. He also adds the idea that the sun along with the Milky Way galaxy is moving through the universe. However, when we compare what God inspired Solomon to write in Ecclesiastes 1:5 about the sun, his entire argument falls apart. The verse says, ***"The sun also ariseth, and the sun goeth down*** (Hebrew *bow* means to come and go like entering and then leaving a house), ***and hasteth to his place where he arose."***

In other words, the sun makes a circle right back to the same place where it first begins to shine each day. So, even if you want to cling to the Big Bang lie, this verse is about the sun setting and rising (breaking forth) each day over the earth. This passage does not even remotely refer to some alleged circuit of the sun (that takes millions and millions of years to complete) around the center of the Milky Way galaxy. Nor does it refer to any other alleged motion of the sun in the vastness of imaginary "space."

---

[131] https://www.icr.org/article/world-word-psalm-19

Furthermore, even if you want to believe the nonsense of Dr. Morris that the circuit of the sun is this alleged orbit around the Milky Way, the movement of the Milky Way through the universe would never allow the sun to return to the same place that it had been before as Scripture says it does. The present teaching from modern science that the Milky Way is constantly moving laterally through the universe would negate this passage in Ecclesiastes as it would not allow the sun to move in a circle (which is the definition of circuit) and return to the same starting point. Once again, the verse says, *"The sun also ariseth, and the sun goeth down* (Hebrew bow means to come and go like entering and then leaving a house), *and hasteth to his place where he arose"* (Ecclesiastes 1:5).

The Scripture says, *"...there is nothing hid from the heat thereof"* (Psalms 19:6). It is the continual circuit (circular path) of the sun over the flat earth and under the firmament dome that allows the sun's heat to touch everything that God made. Just based on that verse alone, there cannot be billions of galaxies billions of light years away from the heat of our sun. The Holy Spirit of God through King David also made it clear that the sun's circuit was from one end of heaven to the other, meaning that it covered the whole of His creation under the firmament dome (called heaven in Genesis 1:8). That would also be impossible in the Big Bang universe model as the sun could never reach one end and make it back in a universe that is supposedly billions of light years across.

The LORD even has David refer to the firmament dome as the "tabernacle for the sun." The Hebrew word translated "tabernacle" is *ohel* and means *"...a tent (as clearly conspicuous from a distance)—covering, dwelling place, home, tabernacle, tent."* *Ohel* is taken from the root word *ahal* which means "to shine." It is also the word used and translated "tent" in Isaiah 40:22, *"It is he that sitteth upon the circle of the earth, and the inhabitants thereof are as grasshoppers; **that stretcheth out the heavens as a curtain, and spreadeth them out as a tent to dwell in.**"* Again, confirming Genesis 1:14 that the sun is inside the firmament dome (tabernacle) that is spread out like a tent for us to dwell in.

Another ridiculous attempt to debunk this Biblical truth about the circuit of a very near-sun over God's flat earth is Dr. Danny Faulkner of Answers in Genesis. He did some photographic and distance experiments with the sun. This is ironic and hypocritical because when flat earthers show their long-distance photographs to prove there is no curvature, Dr. Faulkner is the first to try to discredit it crying, "REFRACTION!" I joke around and call him Danny "Stalkner" as it appeared that he followed our group to a restaurant during the Flat Earth International Conference in 2017 just to tell me that the things we saw and photographed across Mobile Bay were only seen due to refraction. Also,

Dr. Faulkner used an old flat earth assumption that the sun is 3,000 miles in altitude to base all of his calculations on, but after five years of looking into this, I am certain the sun is much, much lower than 3,000 miles high.

Furthermore, in the Biblical flat earth model, the sun circuit varies between 23.5° South around the Tropic of Capricorn and 23.5° North around the Tropic of Cancer. This movement of the sun from its inner path to the outer path creates the different seasons. The movement also creates the opposite seasons in the north and south parts of the world. *"The Solar Analemma also proves this movement and the two different paths of the sun. This is when the position of the sun in the sky is photographed at a fixed location every day throughout the year always at the same time of day. This produces a single, thin figure 8 pattern. The southern loop is much wider (five times larger) than the northern world. Sometimes, in illustrations, the loops will be drawn with an identical-sized loops - this is a deception. A round earth, with identical halves, should not have smaller and larger loops; the large and small loops are sometimes explained as a result of the overall path of the earth around the sun even though they will admit that the overpass is so minimal that it's almost a circle. A flat, enclosed earth is much wider past outward from the equator this is one of the southern loop is much larger the circuit diameter is larger. A flat earth explains the solar analemma shape - but not a round earth. And if you take a map of ocean temperatures and switch the map projection to the azimuthal equidistant* (aka flat earth map), *you will see that the warmest waters match this seasonal circular path. Also note, that if you can pair this to a spherical map, the warmest waters do not line up with the supposed tilt of the earth to the sun."*[132]

---

[132] *Circle of the Earth Investigation* by Daniel Valles ©2015

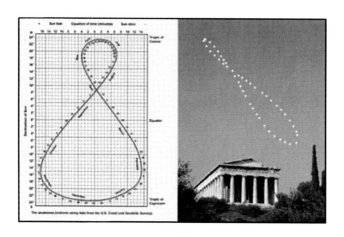

As I have already mentioned in this book, there are multiple witnesses to the nearness of the sun to the flat, firmament enclosed earth. One of the first things that I came across in my research was videos from multiple high-altitude balloon launches that have documented a bright sunspot directly under the sun on the cloud layer below. There is simply no way that a 93 million-mile-away sun could produce that. Furthermore, many people have videos and pictures of clouds behind the sun. Some even had solar filters on their cameras and used a negative filter to show the clouds that were in front and the one behind the sun. In fact, our family witnessed this on a trip back from Birmingham, Alabama one evening.

I saw a photographer post pictures on Facebook that clearly caught the clouds behind the sun but he didn't even realize what he had captured. I have also witnessed the clouds behind the moon on multiple occasions. Needless to say, this should NEVER be possible if the sun is 93 million miles away and the moon is 240,000 miles away, but we have been blinded to this by our years of brainwashing...I mean government education. There is a Bible verse that specifically mentions men not seeing the sun in the clouds:

"And now men see not the bright light which is in the clouds: but the wind passeth, and cleanseth them" (Job 37:21). The Hebrew word for "light" here was used all over the Bible to describe the light of the sun, the light of the morning or the light of day.

Perspective and the Horizon

While writing this chapter, I recalled a nasty email that I received from a South Carolina megachurch pastor on August 1, 2017. I only bring this up to show the kind of nonsense that I get from so-called "mainstream churches" that don't study the Bible in any depth. After mentioning on our Prophecy Quake radio show that I had been contacted by a South Carolina megachurch pastor, a member of his church emailed me. He said that the subject of flat earth and Biblical creation had come up in one of their Bible study groups and the pastor had shut it down. The pastor's first email called me a hypocrite for preaching Biblical cosmology (flat earth) and calling NASA a bunch of liars. He said that I was wrong for judging NASA. His big argument against flat earth was his assertion that the Bible teaches the sun literally goes down and comes up. Here's our exchange:

The megachurch pastor:

"Hypocrisy is hypocrisy. You don't believe in Biblical cosmology! You don't believe what Scripture says that the sun rises, and it goes down. You believe that it is just "perspective." So no, you don't believe in the literal words of the Bible. Your cosmology is yours; it is not from the Bible. As such, your sin remains...for accusing others what you

290

yourself do. Pray to God, don't answer me for your sinfulness regarding your twisting of the literal word of God.

You accuse others of lying while you lie yourself. You claim the sun spins above the earth and never goes down or comes up. The Bible literally says the sun rises and it sets; it comes up and it goes down. You say it's all 'perspective.' And then you accuse others of making Joshua lie when he stops the sun.

If Joshua stopped the sun, then the sun also rises, and it sets. But you deny that the sun comes up and that it sets. In that you deny the very words of Scripture, the exact Word of God. I said NOTHING about the earth being flat or globular. But I pointed out your hypocrisy of being a Biblical literalist when IT SUITS YOU.

IF YOU DON'T KNOW WHETHER THE SUN TRULY GOES DOWN AND COMES UP, and it's all a matter of perspective, then you are denying the plain word of God. Don't then accuse NASA's people of lying when YOU deny the very words of God.

NASA isn't right but neither are you! Two wrongs don't make a right LOL. Now just get on your knees, beg God's forgiveness for slandering NASA."

My Response:

"You need to study your Bible a little deeper before you accuse a brother of hypocrisy and twisting the Word of God. You accuse me of 'hypocrisy' for calling out the lies of a secular government agency, but you have no problem attacking a fellow Christian. You sir are the hypocrite and now an accuser of the brethren.

291

The very passages you bring up in Joshua 10 when it talks about the sun 'going down' is the Hebrew word 'bow' and has been defined in multiple Hebrew lexicons as 'to go or come in, depart; to enter. In fact, the KJV translation count is 2577 and only 23 times is that word translated down and that comes to 0.0089 % so the primary definition of 'bow' is to come in or got out.'"

I went on to send him screenshot pictures from the Blue Letter Bible app that showed the Strong's Hebrew Dictionary and Gesenius' Hebrew-Chaldee Lexicon definitions of the Hebrew word *bow*. Both lexicons define *bow* **"...to go or come in, to enter, to enter into a house or gates of a city, to go out and to come in, to reach, arrive at, to go, to cause to come in, to lead in, to bring in."** These definitions give the picture of coming and going in and out of a house not going up or down.

This pastor's ignorance of the issue of perspective does not negate the truth that perspective (the limits of our vision, distance, and how light works) is a real issue. In truth, the sun only appears to go up or down like an approaching airplane flying at 40,000 feet appears low on the horizon when it is in the distance, but higher when it is overhead or closer. I noticed this with clouds driving to Florida recently. There was a layer of clouds about 20,000 feet stretching as far as I could see. The ones in the distance seemed to come down and touch the highway, but when I got to that point in the highway, those clouds were at 20,000 feet like the others. This should be common knowledge, but years of brainwashing is difficult to overcome.

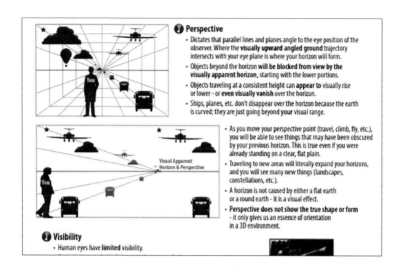

① Perspective
- Dictates that parallel lines and planes angle to the eye position of the observer. Where the **visually upward angled ground** trajectory intersects with your eye plane is where your horizon will form.
- Objects beyond the horizon **will be blocked from view by the visually apparent horizon**, starting with the lower portions.
- Objects traveling at a consistent height can **appear to** visually rise or lower - or **even visually vanish** over the horizon.
- Ships, planes, etc. don't disappear over the horizon because the earth is curved; they are just going beyond **your** visual range.

- As you move your perspective point (travel, climb, fly, etc.), you will be able to see things that may have been obscured by your previous horizon. This is true even if you were already standing on a clear, flat plain.
- Traveling to new areas will literally expand your horizons, and you will see many new things (landscapes, constellations, etc.).
- A horizon is not caused by either a flat earth or a round earth - it is a visual effect.
- **Perspective does not show the true shape or form** - it only gives us an essence of orientation in a 3D environment.

① Visibility
- Human eyes have limited visibility.

The law of perspective is observable. Our field of vision converges at a single point, which causes things to appear to shrink and go down as they approach that convergence point. The vanishing point at the horizon is not the result of the curvature of the earth, but rather, the limit of our vision. This is the reason that the sun only appears to set, and why things appear to vanish over the horizon with distance. This is also why a good set of binoculars or a telescope, or a quality high-zoom camera will bring things like ships that "disappeared" beyond the horizon back into view.

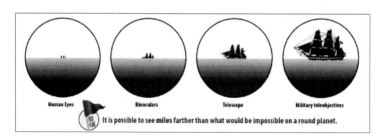

It is possible to see miles farther than what would be impossible on a round planet.

When we understand that the sun, moon, and stars are smaller and much closer than we have been told by the priests of Copernicus, it becomes clear why we can't see certain stars at different places on the earth – it is simply a

293

matter of distance and the limits of our vision, not the alleged curvature of the earth. This is why we can't see the Southern Cross from most of North America, *"For much of the Northern Hemisphere – including most of the United States – the Southern Cross never rises above the horizon, so it can never been seen from our middle and far northern skies. You can see see all of Crux from the U.S. state of Hawaii. In the contiguous U.S., you need to be in southern Florida or Texas (about 26 degrees north latitude or farther south). Even from the far-southern contiguous U.S., you have a limited viewing window for catching the Southern Cross. It has to be the right season of the year. It has to be the right time of night. And you have to look in the right direction: SOUTH!"*[133]

Thomas Winship describes this law of perspective concerning the North Star as well, ***"If we select a flat street a mile long, containing a row of lamps, it will be noticed that from where we stand the lamps gradually decline to the ground, the last one being apparently quite on the ground. Take the lamp at the end of the street and walk away from it a hundred yards, and it will appear to be much nearer the ground than when we were close to it; keep on walking away from it and it will appear to be gradually depressed until it is last seen on the ground and then disappears.*** *Now, according to the astronomers, the whole mile was only depressed about eight inches from one end to the other, so that this 8 in. could not account for the enormous depression of the light as we recede from it.* ***This proves that the depression of the Pole Star can and does take place in relation to a flat surface, simply because we increase our distance from it, the same as from the streetlamp. In other words, the further away we get from***

---

[133] https://Earthsky.org/favorite-star-patterns/the-southern-cross-signpost-of-southern-skies

any object above us, as a star for example, the more it is depressed, and if we go far enough it will sink (or appear to sink) to the horizon and then disappear. The writer has tried the streetlamp many times with the same result. "[134]

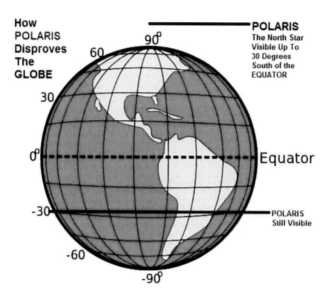

Above the Stars

Another Biblical passage that reveals the stars to be much closer than modern science wants us to believe is Isaiah 14:12-14, *"How art thou fallen from heaven, O Lucifer, son of the morning! how art thou cut down to the ground, which didst weaken the nations!* ***For thou hast said in thine heart, I will ascend into heaven, I will exalt my throne above the stars of God****: I will sit also upon the mount of the congregation, in the sides of the north:* ***I will ascend above the heights of the clouds; I will be like the most High.***"

---

[134] Zetetic Cosmogony by Thomas Winship ©1899 Durban Natal pg. 34

It is clear from Isaiah 14:12-14 that the location of heaven is just above the stars of God and the heights of the clouds. This gives the picture that the stars are at a certain level or altitude limit. Is heaven billions and billions of light years away from earth? Is that the picture the Bible gives us? Or does the Bible give us the picture of God viewing us from heaven and us appearing as small as grasshoppers to Him? Isaiah 40:22 gives the picture of heaven being high, and yet close to us, *"It is he that sitteth upon the circle of the earth, and the inhabitants thereof are as grasshoppers."*

Moses prayed, ***"Look down from thy holy habitation, from heaven,*** *and bless thy people Israel, and the land which thou hast given us, as thou swarest unto our fathers, a land that floweth with milk and honey"* (Deuteronomy 26:15). The Psalmist wrote, ***"For he hath looked down from the height of his sanctuary; from heaven did the LORD behold the earth;*** (Psalms 102:19). King David wrote by the Holy Spirit, ***"The LORD looked DOWN from heaven upon the children of men***, to see if there were any that did understand, and seek God"* (Psalms 14:2). Jeremiah wrote by the Holy Spirit, ***"Mine eye trickleth down, and ceaseth not, without any intermission, till the LORD look DOWN, and behold from heaven"*** (Lamentations 3:50-51).

How can there be a simple up and down on a sphere that is flying through an ever-expanding universe that is said to be billions and billions of light years in length in every direction? Is "up" only directly vertical from Israel? On the spherical earth up and down are different directions depending on where you are on the ball. Does God actually look down from heaven on the children of men or is that just a metaphor? Did Jesus ascend up to where He came from or would it be considered descending in relation to the Australians on the opposite side of the ball? It is obvious that

Lucifer (aka the Devil and Satan) knew the direction, altitude, and location of heaven directly above the heights of the clouds and the stars of God.

The Russian Documents: Near-Sun

During my research back in 2018 when I was going through the FOIA reading room at CIA.gov, I came across some declassified Russian documents. They were about the Russians studying the *"brightness of the firmament"* and creating a certain formula to calculate the brightness of the sky based on "a FLAT EARTH." This long study was done for a doctoral dissertation:

"Dissertations Defended in the Scientific Council of the Institute of Physics of the Earth, Institute of Physics of the Atmosphere and Institute of Applied Geophysics, Academy of Sciences USSR during the First Semester of 1957.

Ye. V. Pyaskovskaya-Fesenkova, **Investigation of the Scattering of Light in the Earth's Atmosphere - Doctoral dissertation.**

March 23, 1957 **The dissertation represents the result of many years of study of the clear, daytime sky.** *The observations were carried out in 12 locations at various altitudes above the sea, various climatic, and meteorological and synoptic conditions. The observations were carried out mainly during high-transparency of the atmosphere in the visual range of the spectrum in the absence of a snow cover.* **In the investigations, two instruments designed by V.G. Fesenkov were used; one of these was a visual photometer of the daytime sky intended for measuring the <u>brightness of the FIRMAMENT</u>; the other was a photo electric halo** *photometer for determining the brightness from <u>near-sun</u> halo and also from the sun on a surface perpendicular to these rays.* The dissertation contains a certain formula of the brightness of the sky, **taking into consideration only the brightness of the first order and <u>arrived on the assumption of a FLAT EARTH</u>** and giving some conclusions derived on the basis of this formula. "[135]

49-12-15/16

Dissertations Defended in the Scientific Council of the Institute of Physics of the Earth, Institute of Physics of the Atmosphere and Institute of Applied Geophysics, Ac.Sc. USSR during the First Semester of 1957.

Ye.V. Pyaskovskaya-Fesenkova - Investigation of the Scattering of Light in the Earth's Atmosphere (Issledovaniye rasseyaniya sveta v zemnoy atmosfere) - Doctor dissertation. Opponents: Doctor of Physico-Mathematical Sciences Ye.S. Kuznetsov, Doctor of Physico-Mathematical Sciences S.M. Polozkov, Doctor of Physico-Mathematical Sciences G.B. Rozenberg, Doctor of Physico-Mathematical Sciences I.S. Shklovskiy. March 23, 1957. The dissertation represents the result of many years of study of the clear, daytime sky. The observations were carried out in twelve locations at various altitudes above the sea, various climatic, meteorological and synoptic conditions. The observations were carried out mainly during high-transparency of the atmosphere in the visual range of the spectrum in the absence of a snow cover. In the investigations two instruments, designed by V.G. Fesenkov were used; one of these was a visual photometer of the daytime sky intended for measuring the brightness of the firmament; the other was a photo-
Card6/21 electric halo photometer for determining the brightness from

49-12-15/16

Dissertations Defended in the Scientific Council of the Institute of Physics of the Earth, Institute of Physics of the Atmosphere and Institute of Applied Geophysics, Ac.Sc. USSR during the First Semester of 1957.

near-sun halo and also from the sun on a surface perpendicular to these rays. The dissertation contains a certain formula of the brightness of the sky, taking into consideration only the brightness of the first order and derived on the assumption of a "flat" Earth and giving some conclusions derived on the basis of this formula. For a certain coefficient of transparency of the atmosphere, the brightness of the sky at any point is represented by derivation of two functions of which one is the function of the diffusion of light and the other is a function of the zenith distances of the sun and of the observed point of the sky. On changing of the zenith distances of the sun z from 90 to 0°, the brightness of the sky on the almucantar of the sun increases first, reaching a maximum for a certain value of z, and then decreases. A method is also proposed of determining the brightness of the clear daylight sky at any point based on measuring the brightness along the almucantar of the sun and of 5-6 points of the firmament located at various zenith distances. This method permits determination
Card7/21

---

[135] https://www.cia.gov/library/readingroom/docs/CIA-RDP86-00513R001343720008-3.pdf

If this document doesn't blow your mind, then I don't know what will. The Russian doctoral candidate gave his dissertation in front of four Russian Doctors of Physico-Mathematical Sciences. Does anyone believe that this doctoral candidate would get up and spout lunacy or anything that these other PhD scientists didn't agree was fundamentally true? How could an atheist, Russian scientist and PhD candidate use terms like "firmament," "near-sun" or "flat earth" if these things were not accepted as facts in echelons of Russian academia? After all, he wasn't seeking a PhD in religion or the Bible. Why would he waste years of study on coming up with a formula to calculate the brightness of the sky/firmament and base it on the assumption of a flat earth if the earth isn't flat? Well, because people at the highest levels of government and scientific agencies know the truth about creation, and they suppress those truths just like the Holy Spirit through the Apostle Paul said they would in Romans 1.

They know the sun is near and not millions of miles away. And they know that the earth is flat and enclosed by a firmament dome.

Chapter 13

The Moon, Eclipses & the Host of Heaven

*"At that time, saith the Lord, they shall bring out the bones of the kings of Judah, and the bones of his princes, and the bones of the priests, and the bones of the prophets, and the bones of the inhabitants of Jerusalem, out of their graves: **And they shall spread them before the sun, and the moon, and all the host of heaven, whom they have loved, and whom they have served, and after whom they have walked, and whom they have sought, and whom they have worshipped**: they shall not be gathered, nor be buried; they shall be for dung upon the face of the earth"* (Jeremiah 8:1-2).

*"If you think of feelings you have when you are awed by something - **for example, knowing that elements in your body trace to exploded stars - I call that a spiritual reaction, speaking of awe and majesty, where words fail you.**"* - Neil deGrasse Tyson, American astrophysicist, author, and science communicator.

"And he put down the idolatrous priests, whom the kings of Judah had ordained to burn incense in the high places in the

301

*cities of Judah, and in the places round about Jerusalem;
them also that burned incense unto Baal* (Satan), *to the sun,
and to the moon, and to the planets* (Hebrew word *mazzalah*
and means the constellations of stars that make up the
Zodiac*), and to all the host of heaven"* (2 Kings 23:5).

**"And God made two great lights; the greater light to rule
the day, and the lesser light to rule the night**: *he made the
stars also. And God set them in the firmament of the heaven
to give light upon the earth, And to rule over the day and
over the night, and to divide the light from the darkness: and
God saw that it was good"* (Genesis 1:16-18).

Modern science tells us the moon is a big, dark, rock
sphere that is 238,000 miles from earth and reflects the light
of the sun. Understandably, the vast majority of people have
accepted this idea because it has been programmed into their
heads since birth. They believe in the Apollo moon landing
and the rest of the "space" stories. Why wouldn't you simply
trust the "scientists" because after all – they're scientists.
Most people are so busy with day to day life that they never
take the time to really examine their claims. The really sad
thing is that most Christians, who claim to believe in the
Divine inspiration of the Bible and say that they believe
every word is true, also believe the scientists and the
testimonies of astronauts over what the Bible says about the
moon.

*God clearly stated in Genesis 1 that He made TWO great
lights.* He did not say that He made one great light and one
dark rock ball to reflect the one great light at nighttime. He
used the same Hebrew word for "light" when He said that
He made a greater LIGHT to rule over the day and a lesser
LIGHT to rule over the night. The Hebrew word translated

"light" in Genesis 1:16-18 is *ma'owr* and the Strong's Hebrew Dictionary defines it as ***"...a luminous body or luminary, i.e. light, brightness."*** This word *ma'owr* comes from *owr* which means *"...to be luminous."* The Oxford Dictionary defines the word "luminous" this way *"...full of or shedding light; bright or shining, especially in the dark."* Also, the Oxford Dictionary defines "luminary" as *"...a natural light-giving body, especially the sun or moon."*

This truth about the moon being and producing its own light can be seen in many other verses in the Bible. Here are a few:

*"Behold, the day of the Lord cometh, cruel both with wrath and fierce anger, to lay the land desolate: and he shall destroy the sinners thereof out of it. For the stars of heaven and the constellations thereof shall not give their light: the sun shall be darkened in his going forth, and **the moon shall not cause HER LIGHT to shine.** And I will punish the world for their evil, and the wicked for their iniquity; and I will cause the arrogancy of the proud to cease and will lay low the haughtiness of the terrible"* (Isaiah 13:9-11).

*"And when I shall put thee out, I will cover the heaven, and make the stars thereof dark; I will cover the sun with a cloud, **and the moon shall not give HER LIGHT"*** (Ezekiel 32:7).

*"Immediately after the tribulation of those days shall the sun be darkened, **and the moon shall not give HER LIGHT,** and the stars shall fall from heaven, and the powers of the heavens shall be shaken:"* (Matthew 24:29).

*"But in those days, after that tribulation, the sun shall be darkened, **and the moon shall not give HER LIGHT"*** (Mark 13:24).

"There is one glory of the sun, and ANOTHER glory of the moon, and another glory of the stars: *for one star differeth from another star in glory"* (1 Corinthians 15:41).

The word *"glory"* or *"doxa"* in Greek was often used in the New Testament to describe the bright light of God or one of His angels visibly shining. Here are a few examples:

*"And, lo, the angel of the Lord came upon them, **and the glory of the Lord shone round about them**: and they were sore afraid"* (Luke 2:9)

"And when I could not see for the glory of that light, *being led by the hand of them that were with me, I came into Damascus"* (Acts 22:11)

*"And after these things I saw another angel come down from heaven, having great power; **and the earth was lightened with his glory"*** (Revelation 18:1).

Thus, 1 Corinthians 15:41 clearly states that the sun has its own glory or light and the moon has *"another"* or *allos* in Greek. According to Thayer's Greek Lexicon *allos* means, **"...involves the secondary idea of difference of kind."** The sun has one kind of glory or light and the moon has a different kind of glory or light. Also, the stars are included in this verse. So, if the sun shining or producing its own light is called its glory, and the stars shining and producing their own light is called their glory, why would anyone assume that the moon is not producing its own light called its glory? The answer to that question is simple...it's called Satanic

304

indoctrination against God's Word and the reality of His creation. The Bible does not say that the moon borrows or uses the glory/light of the sun to be a reflector.

Another interesting Bible passage about the moon is Deuteronomy 33:13-14, *"And of Joseph he said, Blessed of the Lord be his land, for the precious things of heaven, for the dew, and for the deep that coucheth beneath, **And for the precious fruits brought forth by the sun, and for the precious things put forth by the moon.**"* This verse talks about the precious fruit brought forth by the sunlight referring to how it helps plants grow and flourish. But then, the verse says there are precious things *"put forth"* or in the Strong's Hebrew Dictionary *geresh* which means to *"produce (as if expelled)"* or in the Gesenius Lexicon it says *"propelled"* by the moon. In other words, the moon produces, expels or propels something that is beneficial, but different from the sun. This can be seen by the fact that two different Hebrew words are used for the phrase "brought forth" and "put forth." It just so happens that the Hebrew *geresh* only appears in the Bible this one time.

So, does the above passage mean that there is something different between the sun's light and the moon's light? Yes, it does. We know this because many people (including myself) have tested the moonlight with laser thermometers. Over and over, the temperature is always several degrees lower wherever the moonlight is shining. Even when measuring on the same surface, like a sidewalk, the temperature is cooler in the moonlight than where the "shade" is blocking the moonlight. This is opposite of the sun. Thus, it is obvious that moonlight has a cooling effect and sunlight a warming effect. Two different kinds of light, just like the Bible says.

What else are they wrong about when it comes to the moon? Well, NASA and modern scientists not only tell us that the moon is reflecting the light of the sun, but they also claim the moon is a sphere. One thing can be said with certainty, a sphere is not a good reflector of light and especially if it's made of dull, gray dust (as depicted in their fake moon landings). Simple experiments using a flashlight and a ball of some sort will never produce an even, bright reflection like we see when the moon is full. There would be a hot spot and then it would fade toward the edges. Furthermore, we have spent time looking at the moon through high-zoom cameras and there are places that look like cracks that have even brighter light breaking forth through them. It looks like there's a bright light inside of the moon escaping from these holes and cracks. Just more evidence that the moon is NOT reflecting the sun's light as we are told.

Eclipses and Full Moons

Of course, one of the first objections that comes up when someone brings up the possibility of flat earth or that the heliocentric model could be wrong is the subject of eclipses. Again, the reason for this is because we have had the Copernican model crammed into our brains since early childhood. However, the idea that the earth moves between the sun and the moon to cause a lunar eclipse is just not true. There is an eclipse called a "selenelion" that has been recorded throughout history. This occurs when there is a lunar eclipse while the sun is still well above the horizon of the earth. That means that the earth cannot be the object darkening of the moon's surface.

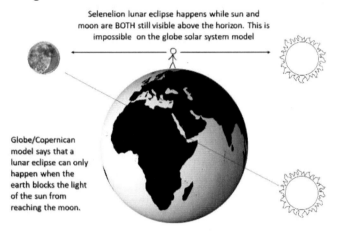

Selenelion lunar eclipse happens while sun and moon are BOTH still visible above the horizon. This is impossible on the globe solar system model

Globe/Copernican model says that a lunar eclipse can only happen when the earth blocks the light of the sun from reaching the moon.

Here's how Space.com explains away just about everything that disproves their precious system of flying, spinning balls (if you guessed refraction, then you are "smarter than the average bear" or you have been paying attention). Here's an excerpt from their 2011 article, *"For most places in the United States and Canada, there will be a chance to observe an unusual effect, **one that celestial geometry seems to dictate can't happen. The little-used*** *name for this effect is a "selenelion" (or "selenehelion") and occurs when both the sun and the eclipsed moon can be seen at the same time. But wait! How is this possible? When we have a lunar eclipse, the sun, earth and moon are in a geometrically straight line in space, with the earth in the middle. So, if the sun is above the horizon, the moon must be below the horizon and completely out of sight (or vice versa). And indeed, during a lunar eclipse, the sun and moon are exactly 180 degrees apart in the sky; so, in a perfect alignment like this (a "syzygy") such an observation would seem impossible. But it is atmospheric refraction that makes a selenelion possible."*[136]

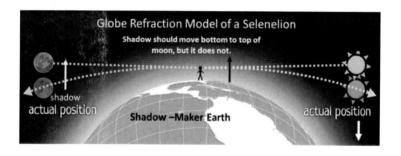

That's really all they have. When all else fails say "refraction," or "gravity," or use the word "quantum" a lot and the sheep will go back to sleep. We have been talked out of believing what we see, and most cannot think critically against the onslaught of "experts" in white science robes. However, when we look closely at the daytime selenelion eclipses, we notice that the "shadow" moves down from top of the moon to the bottom of the moon and not from the bottom to top as the atmospheric refraction argument would require. But who really considers these things? Someone said, *"REFRACTION! so it's debunked...move on folks, there's nothing to see here."*

[136] https://www.space.com/13856-total-lunar-eclipse-rare-senelion.html

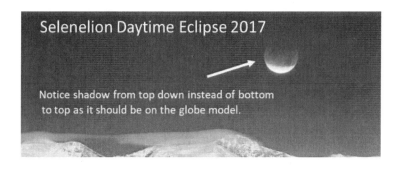

Selenelion Daytime Eclipse 2017

Notice shadow from top down instead of bottom to top as it should be on the globe model.

So, what causes lunar eclipses? One thing we can know for sure is that it is not caused by the earth. Lunar eclipses are caused by other luminaries that are opaquer and more translucent maybe even in the infrared spectrum (which could be why the Vatican and NASA have very powerful infrared telescopes). Regardless, eclipses do not prove a spherical Earth or that we live in a heliocentric solar system.

Another big problem the globe model has concerning the moon is that according to NASA data and their alleged videos of the moon transiting, every full moon should be a lunar eclipse. I discovered this back in 2016 and I shared it on YouTube in a video entitled, *"Pink Moon on Flat Earth."* On that particular full moon (April 22, 2016), we arrived home from the grocery store and I noticed that the moon was full and due east. I realized that according to the Copernican/globe model, the sun just went down behind the ball earth due west. That means the earth should be lined up with the sun and moon with the earth in the middle. According to the globe model some sort of lunar eclipse should have been happening. Of course, there wasn't a sliver or hint of any "shadow" on the full moon and I was even more shocked when I checked my Solar System Scope app based on NASA data. According to the exact date and time of that full moon, Solar System Scope showed the sun, the earth and the moon perfectly lined up with the moon dead center behind the earth. Then, I checked the date and time of the next full moon which was on May 21, 2016, then June, then July and for every single full moon the alignment of the sun, earth, and moon in the globe model was exactly the same as the full moons when there were eclipses.

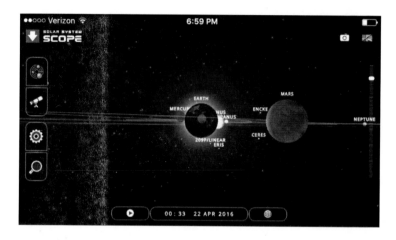

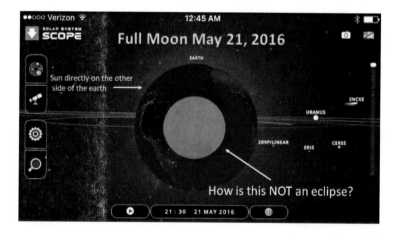

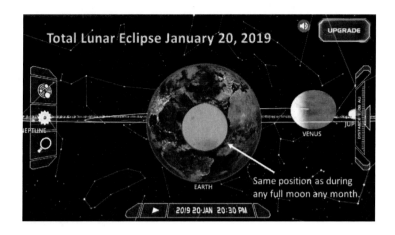

Total Lunar Eclipse January 20, 2019

UPGRADE

NEPTUNE

JUP

VENUS

Same position as during
any full moon any month.

EARTH

2019 20-JAN 20:30 PM

I pointed out this glaring flaw in the heliocentric model by using two different programs - Solar System Scope (based on NASA data) and Solar Walk made by the European Space Agency. Of course, a confident debunker showed up in my YouTube comments to share his knowledge in the cult of Copernicus. I have the screen shot from that day:

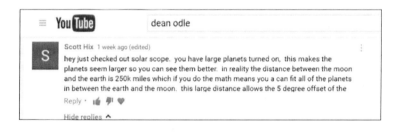

☰ You Tube   dean odle

Scott Hix 1 week ago (edited)
hey just checked out solar scope. you have large planets turned on, this makes the
planets seem larger so you can see them better. in reality the distance between the moon
and the earth is 250k miles which if you do the math means you a can fit all of the planets
in between the earth and the moon. this large distance allows the 5 degree offset of the

Reply · 👍 👎 ♥

Hide replies ︿

Basically, Scott was saying that the scale of the app was not right and because of the alleged great distance between the earth and moon, the 5-degree offset allowed for the same "apparent" alignment every full moon and on eclipses. I explained that regardless of the moon's alleged offset orbit, it still passes (according the heliocentric model) directly behind the center of their ball earth every month. I even explained to Scott that the Solar System Scope model was based on NASA data and that the ESA stated on their app information that - *"Solar Walk is a stunning model of the solar system that shows you all the planets and satellites with incredible detail and accuracy."* But what really silenced his argument about the app not showing the correct dimensions was when I pulled up the NASA video of the alleged transit of the moon across the earth. And what do you know, NASA's "video" from the EPIC "satellite" showed the exact same dimensions of both of my heliocentric solar system apps. Nothing but crickets after that. Here's a screenshot that compares the NASA moon transit to Solar System Scope app side by side:

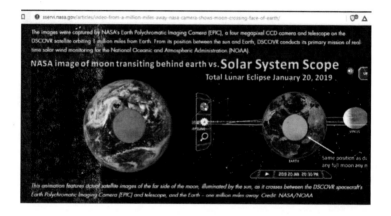

The Bible says in two places that God *"...taketh the wise in their own craftiness"* (1 Corinthians 3:19 and Job 5:13). In their craftiness to change the order and nature of God's creation to deceive mankind, the moon was a problem. To make the moon work in the heliocentric model, they had to say that the moon rotates and its rotation somehow (in the process of the Big Bang) became perfectly synchronized with its alleged orbit of the ball earth. They claim this is reason we always see the same side of the moon...talk about a fish story!

We are also told that the moon's rotation or spin is only 10.3 mph and that it doesn't have any real atmosphere (like they claim happens on earth) to drag anything along as it spins. Nevertheless, in their desperation to seal their deception with the fake moon landings, they showed us videos of astronauts jumping on the moon's surface. If you do the math, 10.3 mph comes to 15.1 feet per second. With virtually no atmosphere (apart from trace amounts of some gases) to pull the astronauts along with the moon so they could land in the same spot, they should have landed 15.1 feet away when they did the astronaut moon-hop. But that is not what we witnessed because we were watching the "moon landings" in movie sets. In fact, a NASA video from Apollo 16 shows astronaut John Young jump twice to salute the American Flag and then land in the exact same spot in front of the flag. He never moves out of the frame of the video camera.[137] The wise taken in their own craftiness.

---

[137] https://www.youtube.com/watch?v=efzYblYVUFk

The Very Close Moon

Like the sun, the moon is also much closer than government space agencies and scientists claim. The moon is not 238,000 miles away and our own eyes tell us this. We can see details, contours and color variations on the moon without a telescope or high-zoom camera. I have watched the moon often over the last few years and really paid attention. One of the things a group of us witnessed right after our Wednesday night prayer meeting was how the moon was only lighting up the clouds near it even though the sky was full of clouds that evening. Clouds just a short distance away were in darkness. If the moon was giving light from 238,000 miles away, it would light up all of the clouds in the sky that we could see. And like the sun, I have also witnessed clouds in front and BEHIND the moon on multiple occasions. This picture below from my friend Robert Foertsch shows the small area that the little nightlight in the sky illuminates and there are clearly clouds in front and behind the moon.

My next point is a great illustration that the moon is truly much closer than we have been told. It comes from a video that I saw years ago but can't remember who made the video, but I have tested it for myself. It has to do with the Tycho Crater on the moon. Even SkyandTelescope.com admits that it is one of the few craters that can be seen with the naked eye. The same article also states that it is 86 kilometers in diameter which is about 54 miles across.[138] Remember, they tell us that the Tycho Crater is 54 miles across and that the moon is 238,000 miles away, yet we can see and distinguish it with our unaided human eyes (and yes we can see it).

Just go open Google Earth and find the island of Jamaica. It is about 235 km (146 miles) long and 84 km (52 miles) wide which makes it somewhat bigger than the Tycho Crater on the moon. Google Earth states that it uses data from the Landstat and Copernicus "satellites." It also gives the altitude from which you are said to be viewing any given location depending on how much you zoom in or out. As you zoom out away from Jamaica, by the time you reach 8,000 miles in altitude, you cannot see Jamaica anymore and yet it is bigger than the Tycho Crater. And don't forget, you still have another 230,000 miles left to get as far as they claim the moon is from the earth.

Do you really believe any of us could see the Tycho Crater with our naked eye if it was 238,000 miles away? It's ridiculous nonsense that we have been taught all of our lives. But you may say, *"...but Pastor Dean, the Tycho Crater is lit up by the sun and Jamaica being green grass against the blue water is just too hard to see."* So, take the area of the Bahamas (which they have highlighted with a bright aqua green color) and start zooming out from there. That spot

---

[138] https://www.skyandtelescope.com/observing/full-moon-is-tycho-time/

stays visible on Google Earth to until you reach 39,252 miles in altitude (Google's limit). With my reading glasses on, I could barely make out tiny speck of that bright green Bahamas area, but to match the distance of the moon to earth, we have 200,000 more miles to go. By their own best scale of the earth made by satellite data, they show us that there's no way we could see the Tycho Crater from earth in their model. We should not be able to see any of the color or texture variations of the moon with our naked eyes, if it was really 238,000 miles away…but we do.

The Host of Heaven & the New Tower of Babel

God said that the sun, moon, and stars were put here to give light upon the earth. They were never to be worshipped or looked at like they were anything more than lights. We know that the stars are not massive suns nor are they even solid masses and there is no such thing as other planets either. The so-called planets were known by the prophets and the ancients as the "wandering stars." They are mentioned that way in the book of Jude. It is also apparent from the Bible that the stars are some type or class of angels.

"These are spots in your feasts of charity, when they feast with you, feeding themselves without fear: clouds they are without water, carried about of winds; trees whose fruit withereth, without fruit, twice dead, plucked up by the roots; Raging waves of the sea, foaming out their own shame; **wandering stars, to whom is reserved the blackness of darkness forever** *"* (Jude 1:13-14).

"And when I saw him, I fell at his feet as dead. And he laid his right hand upon me, saying unto me, Fear not; I am the first and the last: I am he that liveth, and was dead; and,

behold, I am alive for evermore, Amen; and have the keys of hell and of death. Write the things which thou hast seen, and the things which are, and the things which shall be hereafter; The mystery of the seven stars which thou sawest in my right hand, and the seven golden candlesticks. **The seven stars are the angels of the seven churches:** *and the seven candlesticks which thou sawest are the seven churches"* (Revelation 1:17-20).

"And the fifth angel sounded, **and I saw a star fall from heaven unto the earth: and to him was given the key of the bottomless pit. And he opened the bottomless pit;** *and there arose a smoke out of the pit, as the smoke of a great furnace; and the sun and the air were darkened by reason of the smoke of the pit"* (Revelation 8:1-2).

"In the end of the sabbath, as it began to dawn toward the first day of the week, came Mary Magdalene and the other Mary to see the sepulchre. **And, behold, there was a great earthquake: for the angel of the Lord descended from heaven,** *and came and rolled back the stone from the door, and sat upon it.* **His countenance was like lightning, and his raiment white as snow:** *And for fear of him the keepers did shake and became as dead men. And the angel answered and said unto the women, Fear not ye: for I know that ye seek Jesus, which was crucified. He is not here: for he is risen, as he said. Come, see the place where the Lord lay"* (Matthew 28:1-6).

"And of the angels he saith, Who maketh his angels spirits, and his ministers a flame of fire" (Hebrews 1:7).

"And he (Jesus) *said unto them,* **I beheld Satan as lightning fall from heaven"** (Luke 10:18).

I believe these and other passages are clear evidence that the stars are a class of angelic beings and the lights in the sky that are called comets, meteors, falling or shooting stars are angelic activity being witness (some good and some bad). Jesus even stated that when Satan fell from heaven that it had the appearance of lightning. That means there was a light show on the way down for the rebellious angel. I do believe that there are battles in the sky between God's angels and the fallen ones and sometimes we get to see a manifestation of it in the natural realm. God has cast down massive hailstones on ancient Israel's military foes. He has rained fire and brimstone from heaven and sent His angels to fight armies.

Thousands of years ago, mankind (assisted or at least influenced by the fallen angels) decided to build a tower that reached into heaven. They said, *"Come, let's make bricks and bake them thoroughly.' They used brick instead of stone, and tar for mortar.* **Then they said, 'Come, let us build ourselves a city, with a tower that reaches to the heavens, so that we may make a name for ourselves; otherwise we will be scattered over the face of the whole earth.'** *But the Lord came down to see the city and the tower the people were building. The Lord said, 'If as one people speaking the same language, they have begun to do this, then nothing they plan to do will be impossible for them. Come, let us go down and confuse their language so they will not understand each other.' So, the Lord scattered them from there over all the earth, and they stopped building the city. That is why it was called Babel—because there the Lord confused the language of the whole world. From there the Lord scattered them over the face of the whole earth"* (Genesis 11:3-8).

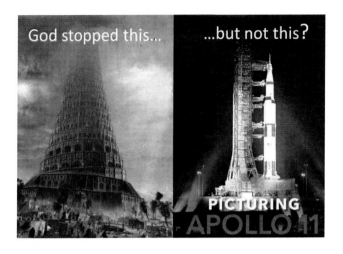

That rebellion to reach the heaven of heaven's was stopped in its tracks by God Himself, but somehow even Christians have come to believe that God has allowed moon landings, Mars rovers, and deep space probes higher than any ancient tower in Babel ever reached. God's word says that, ***"The heaven for height, and the earth for depth, and the heart of kings is unsearchable"*** (Proverbs 25:3). That means that heaven cannot be discovered or numbered, yet these so-called scientists want us to believe that they know the distances of stars and clusters of stars or the wandering stars. They assign these massive distances to them in an attempt to diminish the witness that the stars give us about a stationary earth. But the bigger problem is that most Christians just believe the white-coated priests without question and then get upset with Christians like me who point out how the Bible doesn't agree with modern Copernican cosmology. It is time to choose sides, Jesus or Mystery Babylon? God's Word or science textbooks? Biblical creation or Big Bang? The Antichrist Beast system or the Kingdom of our Lord and Savior Jesus Christ?

Chapter 14

NASA Deceptions & Project ISINGLASS

*"How art thou fallen from heaven, O Lucifer, son of the morning! how art thou cut down to the ground, which didst weaken the nations! For thou hast said in thine heart, **I will ascend into heaven, I will exalt my throne above the stars of God:** I will sit also upon the mount of the congregation, in the sides of the north: **I will ascend above the heights of the clouds; I will be like the most High.** Yet thou shalt be brought down to hell, to the sides of the pit"* (Isaiah 14:12-15).

*"And they said, Go to, let us build us a city and a tower, **whose top may reach unto heaven;** and let us make us a name, lest we be scattered abroad upon the face of the whole earth."* (Genesis 11:4).

"Because of what you have done, the heavens have become a part of man's world." - President Richard Nixon, July 21, 1969 phone call with the crew of Apollo 11

*"They just start making stuff up. Like that Neil Armstrong guy, have you seen him on talk shows? **Talk about a fish**

story...man and they're buying it." - Jim Carey talking to Jay Leno on the Tonight Show

The Lord Jesus Christ warned us that in the last days many false christs and false prophets would rise and deceive many. The Holy Spirit of Jesus Christ stated through the Apostle Paul that these end-time deceivers would come *"...after the working of Satan with all power and signs and <u>lying wonders</u>, And with all deceivableness of unrighteousness in them that perish; because they received not the love of the truth, that they might be saved"* (2 Thessalonians 2:9-10). It is important to note here that in the original Greek the phrase "lying wonders" is *pseudos teras*. The first Greek word *pseudos* means *"...a lie; a conscious and intentional falsehood."* The Greek word for wonders is *teras* and it means "...*something so strange as to cause it to be 'watched' or 'observed'; hence, 'a sign in the heavens.'"*[2]

The full meaning and weight of 2 Thessalonians 2:9-10 and the words of Jesus in Matthew 24 really come into focus when I think about the Apollo 11 launch toward the heavens and the fake moon landings that caused hundreds of millions of people to watch in awe and wonder. They watched an intentional lie in awe and wonder and were deceived into believing that it was the truth. And many believed this lie because they did not love the truth of God's word more than the false testimonies and fireworks shows of NASA and other government "space" agencies. Sadly, many were and continue to be blinded by their human pride in this alleged great achievement of mankind...so blinded, I might add, that they cannot see the glaring mistakes and impossibilities of NASA sending men to the moon even when those mistakes are pointed out to them.

Even though I have not believed that we landed on the moon since watching the movie *Capricorn One* as a preteen, I was not aware of the many blunders that exposed the entire Apollo program as a massive hoax. One of the first things that solidified the dishonesty of NASA for me was when I watched the documentary *A Funny Thing Happened on the Way to the Moon* by Bart Sibrel. To me, the most incriminating part of Sibrel's documentary was the Apollo 11 video footage that showed Neil Armstrong, Buzz Aldrin and Michael Collins faking a picture of earth from a high altitude and very stationary balloon capsule (much like the 2012 Felix Baumgartner Red Bull balloon carried capsule) while claiming to be halfway to the moon.

It is evident that these "astro-nots" are not halfway to the moon but rather in a stationary capsule (definitely carried by balloon) at a very high altitude. It took over an hour to stage a shot of the earth that should have just been a matter of taking a picture out of a window. But instead they had to turn out the lights in the capsule (to create the illusion of dark space around the earth) and use a circular window looking down on the earth to make it appear that they were far away in space taking a picture/video of a ball earth. This footage had never been shown to the public and I believe this particular gem was either leaked or sent to Sibrel by accident. Now NASA has somehow lost all Apollo 11 footage and data. How convenient.

To me, the footage of the Apollo 11 crew staging their deceptive shot of earth is the most damning piece of evidence that the moon landings were elaborate government hoaxes. There are other clues that the landing was staged like the fact that there was no blast crater on the surface of the moon from the 10,000lb thrust engine of the Lunar Lander. And somehow the engine didn't stir up any moon dust onto the feet of the Lunar Lander. This can be seen in NASA photos of the Apollo 11 mission even though Neil Armstrong stated, *"The exhaust dust was kicked up by the engine and this caused some concern in that it degraded our ability to determine not only our altitude and altitude-grade in the final phases, but also, and probably more importantly, our translational velocities over the ground."*[139] What's funny about this comment from Neil Armstrong is that there were only about ten seconds between the time they started kicking up dust and when the "Eagle landed." I know this from watching the video footage and hearing radio transmissions of that "landing" over and over. Though dust was being kicked up, it wasn't really a serious factor in the landing at all. This is just evidence that the Apollo "astronots" added nonexistent drama to their stories.

Nevertheless, in the made-for-TV drama (the moon landing), they forgot to put settled dust on the feet of the Lunar Lander, and they forgot to create a blast crater on the set under the Lunar Lander. I wish that I could take credit for discovering these two blunders, but that goes to Bill Kaysing. He authored the 1976 book, *'We Never Went to the Moon: America's Thirty Billion Dollar Swindle.'* Bill Kaysing was the head of the Technical Presentations Unit at the Rocketdyne Propulsion Field Laboratory from 1956 until 1963. That period encompassed the major planning period for the engine system and related components of the Apollo Project. During that time, Kaysing was cleared for U.S. Air Force "Secret" and Atomic Energy "Q" (levels of security clearance).

---

[139] We Never Went to the Moon: America's Thirty Billion Dollar Swindle by Bill Kaysing ©1976 & 2017 pp. 32-42

Between Kaysing's book and *NASA Mooned America* by Ralph Rene, no logical person could actually believe the fish-tale that we traveled 240,000 miles away to land on the moon. The problems with the alleged extreme temperatures, the vacuum of space, and the consistent photographic manipulation by NASA put nail after nail in the coffin. And you can add to those nails the fact that we did not have the technology or electrical power to broadcast a television signal 240,000 miles back to earth as they say we did during the Apollo missions. NASA has been busted so many times that believing anything they say about "space" or "space travel" would be like trusting Bill Clinton's, *"I did not have sexual relations with that woman…Ms. Lewinsky"* while you hold the dress with his DNA on it.

Another incident that confirms that "spacewalks" are filmed in NASA's big "training" pools (besides the many NASA videos showing air bubbles on alleged "spacewalks") was reported by Fox News on December 19, 2013. The article entitled, ***"Snorkels in space: NASA's 'MacGyver' solution to protect spacewalking astronauts"*** stated that an astronaut nearly drowned on a spacewalk when over a gallon of water leaked into his helmet. I'm not joking.

"After a spacewalking astronaut nearly drowned in his helmet in July, NASA has a plan to protect its crew when they venture into the vacuum of space this weekend: snorkels and absorbent towels.

NASA has determined that as many as four urgent spacewalks are necessary to fix a broken cooling line that led to the shutdown of several systems at the International Space Station, the space agency said during a press conference Wednesday afternoon. Station managers decided to send two American astronauts out as soon as possible to replace a pump with a bad valve...

During this spacewalk, Italian astronaut Luca Parmitano nearly drowned in July, when more than a gallon of water leaked into his helmet, filling it like a fishbowl*. Should water start pooling up again, NASA says it will be ready -- thanks to a hack worthy of TV's 'MacGyver'...Some smart engineers on the ground said,* **hey, this looks like a snorkel you'd use for scuba diving,' explained Allison Bolinger, NASA's lead U.S. spacewalk officer***. NASA realized that a water-line vent tube could be snipped down and attached with Velcro within the spacesuit, between a water restraint valve and the astronaut, she explained.* "[140]

Over a gallon of water leaked into an astronaut's helmet allegedly in the empty vacuum of "space." This where Dr. Evil would say, "Riiiiight." However, this is the level of absurdity that they expect us to believe. Sadly, most people just continue to blindly accept whatever lame excuses they offer for incidences like this. That much water leaking into a helmet is what would happen underwater in a pool, not in "outer space." This is not the only glaring example of faked "spacewalks."

The first ever "spacewalk" by astronaut Ed White during the Gemini 4 mission was clearly some kind of Claymation animation.[141] This was made clear when his fixed helmet[142] miraculously swiveled as he turned it to wave for the camera.

---

[140] https://www.foxnews.com/science/snorkels-in-space-nasas-macgyver-solution-to-protect-spacewalking-astronauts

[141] Ed White spacewalk footage https://youtu.be/cU2X4ysW5Jo

[142] Adam Savage's Tested How Astronauts Put on Space Suits https://youtu.be/VsdoJy8rzZg

Also, during the NASA documentary, the earth in the background was spinning left but shortly thereafter the earth is spinning to the right. Then, in more recent footage of an astronaut on a "spacewalk" from the ISS, he closes his sunshield on his helmet and it catches the reflection of the scuba diver camera man filming him in the pool. And don't even get me started on the NASA photograph from the Mars Rover that accidently included a dead prairie dog on "Mars."[143] - [144]

Fisheye Camera Lenses & NASA Artists

"A fisheye lens is a special type of ultra-wide-angle lens. ***They are small, ultra-wide, and show a distorted, spherical view of the world, most evident in the curved, outer corners of the photo, known as the 'fisheye effect.'*** *When reading about fisheye and regular wide-angle lenses, you will hear a term called barrel distortion.* ***This distortion causes curved lines at the edges of the photo****. This is a negative aspect of cheaper rectilinear wide-angle lenses at their widest settings. However, on fisheye lenses, this is their main feature. That is why they are called "fisheye" lenses, and the barrel distortion should not be viewed negatively* (unless a space agency or high-altitude balloon footage deceptively makes people think they captured the curve of the earth). *Land photographers will sometimes use software to correct the distortion of a fisheye lens. However, underwater this is rarely done, as the slight* (or not so slight) ***curvature of a fisheye*** *lens is often considered a desired effect."[145]*

[143] https://www.nasa.gov/mission_pages/msl/multimedia/pia16204.html

[144] https://www.foxnews.com/science/mars-rat-spied-by-nasas-curiosity-rover

[145] https://www.uwphotographyguide.com/fisheye-lenses-underwater

According to a Wikipedia article, these fish-eye camera lenses were first introduced in 1924, but were not mass-produced for photography until the 1960s. A few years ago I discovered that NASA and the U.S. government were using wide-angle, fish-eye camera lenses all the way back to the 1960s and maybe before. I was perusing Apollo 11 photographs on NASA's website when I saw a picture of the Apollo 11 Saturn V just as it was lifting off. The picture was taken from the tower next to the launch pad which was several stories high. In the picture, there was a massive fake curve on the horizon in the background clearly produced from a fisheye, wide-angle lens.

Nikon 7.5mm f/5.6
Fish-eye-NIKKOR (1966-1970)

I have watched footage and seen pictures of our U2 spy planes which show a massive curve of the earth from an altitude of 70,000 feet. But then, pictures from the ISS that claim to be 260 miles (1,372,800 feet) high in "low-earth-orbit" show less curve than the U2 pictures. How could less earth curvature be shown from the ISS when it is 1,302,800 feet higher than the U2 spy plane? Check out the comparison. NASA claims that the following image is a picture from the ISS on July 30, 2019 as it was *"...orbiting about 260 miles above the Earth, the crew of the*

International Space Station snapped this image of the Mediterranean coasts of Tunisia and Libya and the Italian island of Sicily, as the station flew over North Africa."[146]

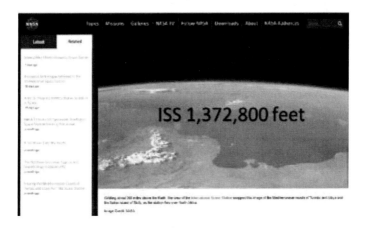

And here is a shot from the U2 Spy plane:

The next group of pictures are screenshots from NASA's Facebook page. They state that these were taken from the ISS and yet we see much less curve than the government gives us from 70,000 feet. Do you smell a rat?

---

[146] https://www.nasa.gov/image-feature/viewing-the-mediterranean-coasts-of-tunisia-and-libya-from-the-space-station

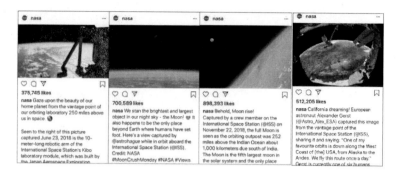

This fisheye manipulation was also used in the 2014 Red Bull Stratos jump from 127,851 feet (24 miles). Australian skydiver Felix Baumgartner and the Red Bull team used a gigantic helium balloon and a capsule (much like the Apollo capsule) to take Felix to that altitude. Somehow, they stopped the ascent of the balloon and the capsule to a hover and Felix stepped out and jumped. It was a great stunt and world records were broken, but I believe the ultimate goal was to plant the fish-eye images of what was supposed to be the earth's curvature into the minds of the rising YouTube audience (many of which were beginning to question things like 911 and the moon landing). Here's a picture of the Red Bull capsule and Felix with the fake curve and the earth "curve" going concave as he jumped and began to fall.

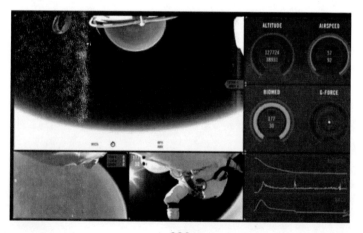

Most people don't question the images they see from NASA and other "space" agencies. They assume that what they are seeing are real photographs of the earth from "space" because with all of the satellites and "space" missions, why wouldn't we have actual photographs? Take for instance an image that was made famous when it was used as the default background for the early iPhones. This 2002 image of the ball earth was created by NASA "Lead Data Visualizer and Information Designer" Robert Simmon (aka Mr. Blue Marble). He was interviewed several years ago, and this is a direct transcript of what he said about the image of earth that he created.

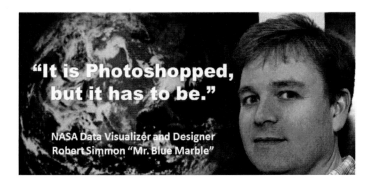

Interviewer: *2002 Blue Marble 2.0...NASA's Rob Simmon made this and it had wide appeal. For example, it ended up as the default background on the iPhone.*

Simmons: *I didn't even know until I bought an iPhone and turned it on and kinda did a little happy dance.*

Interviewer: *Simmon's job is?*

Simmons: **It's primarily taking data and making pictures out of it.**

Interviewer: **That's what this...a composite of data sets from several different instruments translated into a picture.**

Simmons: *To us the really cool thing was the data set.* **Up until that point, there was no REALISTIC color map of the globe anywhere.**

Interviewer: *So, the land layer here comes from?*

Simmons: The *Moderate Resolution Imaging Spectra Radiometer aboard TERRA.*

Interviewer: *And the tricky part here was the weather...*

Simmons: *So, we actually had to take clouds out...*

Interviewer: *...they stashed the clouds for later and went on to the ocean and that came from an instrument that measures phytoplankton in the sea.*

Simmons: *Where it was low,* **I colored it dark blue** *because they are low mostly in mid-oceans and then where it was a little bit higher, it was like a little bit brighter green.*

Interviewer: *Then add the clouds back in...*

Simmons: *There's a small problem with it because there's a very slight gap in between each orbit.*

Interviewer: **So, some of those are painted on...**

Simmons: **It is Photoshopped, but it has to be.**

Interviewer: *Then?*

Simmons: *There was another layer to sort of* **simulate** *the atmosphere.*

Interviewer: *And then there's this little bright spot.*

Simmons: *It's called the specular highlight. So, it's the reflection of sunlight off of water.*

Interviewer: **Those are the pieces, but you can't just slap them all together.**

Simmons: **It just didn't look realistic. It looks kind of flat or the clouds are sort of too see-through, so I just hit COMMAND Z a lot.**

Interviewer: **There's artistry to creating the world...**

Simmons: **What I imagine it to be.** *Unfortunately, I'm not an astronaut, haha. I've never been to space, but I've looked* *at these images over and over again trying to sort of get the essence of it.[147]*

The above interview should be quite eye-opening. The famous 2002 Blue Marble image of earth is NOT a picture from a satellite in "deep space." It is a composite image, created by some obscure high-altitude balloon pictures, Photoshop, and the imagination of a highly paid NASA artist. NASA claims that they have several "deep space" satellites and the Hubble telescope, but they are unable to get a real picture because they can't get high enough to get a shot of the entire earth.

That's why the Apollo 11 crew faked their famous shot of earth by darkening the cabin and using a circular window. And why the Apollo 17 picture of what was supposedly the entire illuminated side of the earth did not show everything that should have been lit up. It is also why North America is different sizes on alleged photographs of earth.

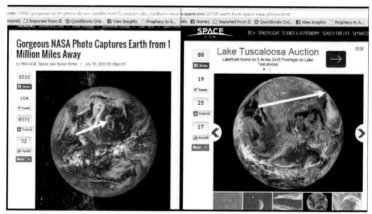

How big is North America?

[147] https://www.youtube.com/watch?v=u0I-H5VMBmY

Just take a closer look at the famous Apollo 17 "Blue Marble picture. NASA claims that it was the "Earth in Full View from Apollo 17." But really, it was not a full view of that sunlit side of the earth.

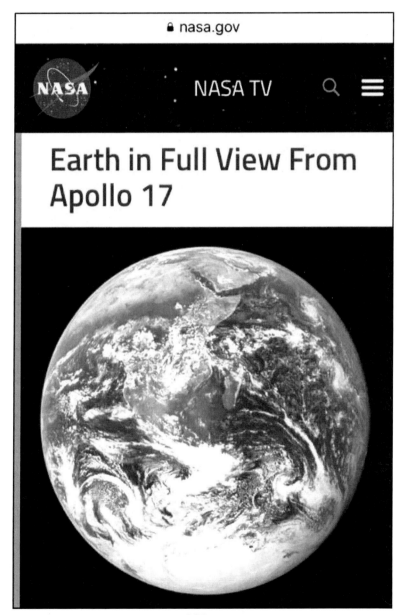

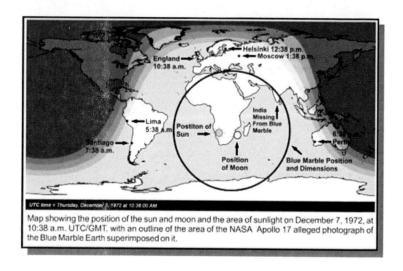

England → 10:38 a.m.

Helsinki 12:38 p.m.
Moscow 1:38 p.m.

Lima 5:38 a.m.

Postiton of Sun →

India Missing From Blue Marble

Perth

Santiago 7:38 a.m.

Position of Moon

Blue Marble Position and Dimensions

UTC time = Thursday, December 7, 1972 at 10:38:00 AM

Map showing the position of the sun and moon and the area of sunlight on December 7, 1972, at 10:38 a.m. UTC/GMT, with an outline of the area of the NASA Apollo 17 alleged photograph of the Blue Marble Earth superimposed on it.

It was 10:38 AM UTC/GMT in Greenwich, London, England when the Apollo 17 astronaut claims to have photographed the entire sunlit side of the earth. However, it was daylight in Greenwich, London, England at 10:38 AM UTC/GMT on December 7, 1972 and yet all of Europe was not in the picture at all. It was 12:38 PM in Finland or just after noon and the Apollo 17 photograph has them in darkness. It was 1:38 PM in Moscow, Russia, yet that city was depicted as in darkness as well by the famous Apollo 17 "Blue Marble" picture.

Needless to say, this is solid evidence that this was another manipulated picture that could not get the entire earth in the picture just like the Apollo 11 deception shown in *A Funny Thing Happened on the Way to the Moon*.

Here's another attempt at deception by Apollo 10:

Identical Cloud Formations On Earth Six Days Apart

Still frame from a video alleged by NASA to have been taken by astronauts aboard the Apollo 10 spacecraft on May 18, 1969, as the astronauts were traveling away from the earth toward the moon.

Still frame from a video alleged by NASA to have been taken by astronauts aboard the Apollo 10 spacecraft on May 24, 1969, as the astronauts were traveling away from the moon toward the earth.

On May 18, 1969, NASA claimed that the Apollo 10 astronauts took a video of the earth as they were on the way to the moon. Six days later, on May 24, 1969, NASA stated that the Apollo 10 astronauts took another video shot of the earth during their return to earth. However, when one examines the two pictures, they are exactly the same and have the exact same cloud formations even though NASA claimed the images were six days apart.

I could go on and on about NASA and their doctored images, CGI, Chromakey screens, augmented virtual reality, and harness mishaps. There is so much evidence that NASA and other "space" agencies are lying about almost everything that I could fill up another book with it. However, I want to move on to a more recent discovery that I made after hours of searching through FOIA documents on the CIA website.

Project ISINGLASS

ISINGLASS

The constantly improving Soviet radar and maximum intercept capability pose a threat to the life span of current aircraft reconnaissance programs such as the U-2 and the A-12. Project ISINGLASS has as its objective the development of a sophisticated aircraft capability to outdistance the possible Soviet intercept threat over the next five to ten years. It is envisaged that an aircraft capability of Mach 20 and altitudes of 200,000 feet must be developed. With this in mind, limited studies have been initiated and are proceeding.

Now, I am not saying that NASA and the governments of the United States, Russia, China, Europe and others don't actually have rockets, "space" capsules, fancy computers and "space" suits because those things are real. They are just not used for what they tell us, and they don't go to where they claim to go. For instance, the United States did have a fleet of "space" shuttles, but after spending a dozen or more hours going through CIA.gov FOIA declassified documents (some still partially redacted), I discovered the secret code name for the shuttle program and the real purpose and capabilities of the space shuttle. I shared that information in June 2018 in a two-hour presentation entitled, *"Isinglass, "Space" & the Firmament."*

Among the CIA declassified documents (of which I took screenshots) was a document with a phrase capitalized at the top of page 1 - "TOP SECRET ISINGLASS." It continued, "MEMORANDUM FOR THE RECORD," Subject: ISINGLASS Briefing with Dr. McMillion at Headquarters July 13, 1965. The briefing began with opening remarks from General Ledford. I discovered from a declassified document from January 11, 1966 (Memorandum for: Director of Reconnaissance, CIA Subject: ISINGLASS/Air Force Support of Pratt and Whitney High Pressure Rocket Program) that General Ledford was Jack C. Ledford a Brigadier General USAF and Director of Special Activities.

"Dr. McMillan interrupted with a barrage of questions. He asked, 'Had a detailed analysis been made of flight paths, with launch points and landing sites?' 'Had these analyses if done, included studies of targets per flight with specific target requirements?' (Redacted) answered in the affirmative and specifically referred to the west to east (redacted) mission which gives coverage of 300 COMAR targets. **Dr. McMillan Also question to what extent studies have been conducted on "throw away" boosters reminding (redacted) is that you could have a reusable vehicle without a reusable booster.** *"* The "reusable boosters" reference was the first clue to me that Isinglass was the code name for the shuttle program.

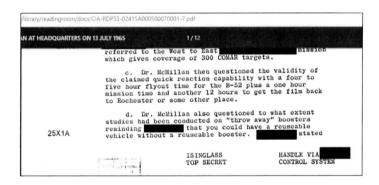

The briefing minutes continued, *"Dr. McMillan then wondered where the requirement for 7,000 nautical miles range came from and said that his back of the envelope calculation showed that a vehicle with 5,000 nautical mile*

range would have only half the launch weight. Dr. McMillan added that a 5,000-mile range vehicle could be launched over the Mediterranean Sea and recovered over the Indian Ocean for example. **(Redacted)** *answered that the 7,000 nautical mile range reduced to 5,000 miles for maneuver and relite missions. Dr. McMillan then commented that he didn't see the vulnerability advantage of these missions, but we would get to that later.* **At this point, he also referred to the Isinglass vehicle as an EXCUSE for a pilot to fly over the Soviet Union.** *Dr. McMillan also then repeated that this system had to be carefully analyzed based on a reasonable reconnaissance mission on a target per dollar basis. Dr. McMillan requested the flight Mach numbers for this vehicle over the Soviet Union on the west-east mission and* **(redacted)** *responded with the answers."*

Isinglass = "Space" Shuttle

Another CIA document about Isinglass gave several more vital clues that it was the "space" shuttle. *"The engine proposed would be a Pratt Whitney advanced rocket engine using liquid hydrogen oxygen fuel. The feasibility of engine concept has been proven by subscale test of major components and with extensive experience on the RL Dash 10.* **The plant aircraft would be lifted to a height of 25,000 feet by a B-52 mothership, released, and then boosted to an** *altitude of approximately 200,000 feet and attaining the speed of mach 20. A final horizontal range of 480 nautical miles is used in the landing maneuver, which should be by means of rear skids and a forward nose wheel similar to the X-15 system. Total range of the mission would be 7,500 nautical miles from start to finish including boost and landing maneuvers. Totally lapsed mission time would be one hour 15 minutes. Projected camera resolution is 1 foot on the ground and a 40 to 50 nautical miles swath. It would be capable of carrying film for 6,000 nautical miles of photography."*

The purpose of Isinglass (the "space" shuttle) was clearly revealed in this CIA document, *"The constantly improving Soviet radar and maximum intercept capability pose a threat to the lifespan of current aircraft reconnaissance program such as the U2 and the A-12. Project ISINGLASS has as its objective the development of a sophisticated aircraft capability throughout distance possible Soviet intercept through it over the next five to ten years. It is envisaged that an aircraft capability of Mach 20 and altitudes of 200,000 feet must be developed."*

341

Central Intelligence Agency

CATEGORY: MANNED HYPERSONIC
RECONNAISSANCE VEHICLE (ISINGLASS)

PROGRAM

REQUIREMENTS

Goals

	Total Money*	Personnel	Hardware	Capital Investment	R&D	Sponsor

To establish the
feasibility and initiate
development of a high
performance rocket engine,
hypersonic boost glide vehicle
and camera system capable of
providing quick reaction, wide
swath, high quality photography
of highly defended denied areas.
This system will perform at speeds
in excess of Mach 20.0 and at altitudes
over 200,000 feet.

*In Millions

25X

Encl. 3
Page 2

25

25X1

It is important to point out here that the world record holder for the fastest and highest-flying jet powered aircraft is the SR-71 Blackbird which was the replacement for the A-12. The SR-71 could fly between Mach 3 and Mach 4 and its maximum altitude for sustained level flight was under 90,000 feet. Flying at those speeds created such friction and heat that the SR-71 had to be built with panels instead of a solid outer shell so it could expand and not split open at the temperatures created by Mach 3+ speed. That is why the SR-71 leaked fuel while it was on the ground because the fuel tank was designed with gaps which would expand during flight.

Furthermore, air-breathing jet engines start being suffocated completely at about 100,000 feet. It takes a rocket engine to go higher and faster. Even the X-15 could not sustain flight at its alleged 317,000 feet pinnacle. So, can you imagine the type of aircraft/vehicle that would have to be built to fly five times faster than the SR-71 (Mach 20) and sustain an altitude over 200,000 feet for several thousand miles before starting its descent? It would take powerful rocket engines, "throw away" boosters, and very special heat-resistant outer panels (maybe called tiles) to accomplish such a task.

According to the Wikipedia article, *"The Space Shuttle thermal protection system or (TPS) is the barrier that protected the Space Shuttle Orbiter during the searing 3000-degree Fahrenheit heat of atmospheric reentry. A secondary goal was to protect from the heat and cold of space while in orbit."* Of course, as I learned from declassified documents, the purpose of ISINGLASS was never going into "outer space" which is allegedly higher than 73 miles (385,440 feet). The advanced Thermal Protection System tiles were for the friction and heat of a Mach 20 reconnaissance vehicle. It was a system of smaller panels that could expand under extreme temperatures just like the SR-71.

Wikipedia continued, ***"Much of the shuttle was covered with LI-900 silica tiles***, *made from essentially very pure quartz sand. The insulation prevented heat transfer to the underlying orbiter aluminum skin and structure. These tiles were such poor heat conductors that one could hold one by the edges while it was still red hot.* ***There were about 24,300 unique tiles individually fitted on the vehicle, for which the orbiter has been called 'the flying brickyard'*** *...The tiles were not mechanically fastened to the vehicle but glued. Since the brittle tiles could not flex with the underlying vehicle skin, they were glued to Nomex felt Strain Isolation Pads (SIPs) with room-temperature-vulcanisation silicone adhesive, which were in turn glued to the orbiter skin.* ***These isolated the tiles from the orbiter's structural deflections and expansions."***

Another 1966 CIA document reads: ***"Category: Man Hypersonic Reconnaissance Vehicle (ISINGLASS) GOALS: To establish the feasibility and initiate*** *development of a high-performance rocket engine, hypersonic, boost glide vehicle, and camera system capable of providing quick reaction wide swath, high-quality photography of highly defended denied **areas this system will perform at speed in excess of Mach 20 and at altitudes over 200,000 feet.** A few years later CIA document on Isinglass stated: Program Goals (FY 1970) Category: Manned Hypersonic Reconnaissance Vehicle (ISINGLASS) Goals: "To flight test three aircraft and produce eight operational aircraft and camera systems for deployment in FY 1971, capable of providing quick reaction, wide swath, high-quality photography of highly defended denied areas."*

As I was writing this portion of the book, I came across an article in 2010 about ISINGLASS. It played down what was really being identified and stated that the program was scrapped due to lack of funding in 1967. It went on to say that ISINGLASS never came to be. And then there are CIA memos in 1967 saying that a decision had been made not to pursue further investigation or development of the ISINGLASS system by the CIA. However, it is clear from later CIA documents that this program was picked back up in 1970-1971. The document reads, "Program goals FYI 1976 through 1981 Category: Manned Hypersonic Reconnaissance Vehicle Isinglass. GOALS: To use the ISINGLASS vehicle, including possible countermeasure techniques." It is interesting to note that the contract to build the first space shuttle was awarded to Rockwell International on July 26, 1972 and construction began in 1975. The first reusable, rocket-propelled, boost-glide vehicle with "throw away" boosters was launched on April 12, 1981. It was called the Space Shuttle Columbia.

The above-mentioned article claimed ISINGLASS was just another project like the X-15 or the SR-71 and was cancelled. Clearly this was media propaganda to hide something that had come to light through FOIA requests. They were trying to cover up the fact that the Top-Secret program ISINGLASS was indeed the Space Shuttle Program. You may ask, "But why try to hide or obscure the truth about ISINGLASS in 2010 when the Space Shuttle Program was being shut down in 2011?"

The answer to this question comes from going through dozens and dozens of FOIA CIA documents (that still contain many blacked-out and whited-out portions). The reason they want to obscure the truth about ISINGLASS being the Space Shuttle Program is because it is made clear in formerly Top-Secret documents that the "space" shuttle was NEVER about going to make believe "outer space" or resupplying the fake "space" station. The space shuttles were simply one-pass reconnaissance vehicles that would fly just over 200,000 feet (but not above 350,000 feet) in a 7,500-mile arc taking pictures over enemy territory. It was designed to fly faster and higher to avoid advancing Russian and Chinese anti-aircraft missiles. Thus, it had to be propelled by rocket engines to reach 200,000 feet, then use that momentum to glide at Mach 20 through altitudes where jet engines would not work. Then as it reached normal airliner altitudes the pilots would fire up the jet engines and land it just like any other jetliner. NASA claimed that the "space" shuttles were gliders from "reentry" to landing, but that was just another lie.

Also, while writing this chapter, I stumbled upon another article about Russia developing their own hypersonic boost-glide vehicle to deliver a nuclear warhead at Mach 20. Vladimir Putin was quoted as saying the following about Russia's Boost-Glide SATAN Missile: *"Large-scale and consistent the work has been in recent years to develop the army and the navy in a comprehensive manner and to saturate line units with advanced military equipment...* **For example, the Avangard missile system with a boost glide vehicle – our hypersonic intercontinental system – will considerably enhance the power of the Strategic Missile Forces.** *"* [148]And according to the Missile Threat Project, Russia's boost-glide vehicle can also reach 62 miles (one of several altitudes where "space" is said to begin) and a speed of Mach 20.

"Once boosted to its suborbital apogee of around 100 km (62.13 miles or 328,046 feet), *the glide vehicle separates from its rocket. It then cruises down towards its target through the atmosphere.* **In his March 2018 speech, Vladimir Putin claimed the HGV can maintain atmospheric speeds of up to Mach 20 (6.28 km/s) and can maneuver.** *This maneuverability could make Avangard's trajectory unpredictable, complicating intercept attempts after its boost phase."* [149]

It is also interesting to note that Mach 20 is 15,345.2 MPH which is close to the speed they claim the ISS and other "orbital" vehicles travel. However, I have viewed and documented quite a few videos from the International Space Station (taken by astronauts) that clearly show zero movement even though the ISS allegedly orbits the earth at 17,500 MPH. Some try to claim parallax as an excuse, but older NASA videos like Ed White's "spacewalk" show the fake ball earth spinning while Ed White and his "space" capsule allegedly orbit at 17,500 MPH.

[148] https://www.express.co.uk/news/world/1114363/russia-news-Satan-2-missile-world-war-3-hypersonic-ballistic-missile-USA
[149] https://missilethreat.csis.org/missile/avangard/

In the words of President George W. Bush, *"Fool me once…shame on you. Fool me…can't get fooled again."* The old saying Skull & Bones Bush was trying to quote was, *"Fool me once, shame on you. Fool me twice, shame on me."* Stop believing the lies of these New World Order Satanists like the Bush family, occultists like Jack Parsons, Nazi SS officers like Wernher von Braun and their Freemason astronauts over what the Bible has to say about creation and the way to the heaven of heavens which is repentance and faith in the Lord Jesus Christ.

Chapter 15

The Greatest Cover-Up in Modern Physics

"The heaven for height, and the earth for depth, and the heart of kings is unsearchable" (Proverbs 25:3).

*"**For the invisible things of him from the creation of the world are clearly seen, being understood by the things that are made,** even his eternal power and Godhead; so that they are without excuse:"* (Romans 1:20).

*"Of all the forms of nature's immeasurable, all-pervading energy, which ever and ever change and move, like a soul animates an innate universe, electricity and magnetism are perhaps the most fascinating... We know that electricity acts like an incompressible fluid; that there must be a constant quantity of it in nature; that it can either be produced or destroyed...**and that electricity and ether phenomena are identical.**"* - Nikola Tesla at the American Institute of Electrical Engineers (AIEE) at Columbia College, New York City, May 1891

*"And they answered the angel of the Lord that stood among the myrtle trees, and said, 'We have walked to and fro through the earth, **and, behold, all the earth sitteth still, and is at rest'** (Zechariah 1:11).*

"Outer space" and "space travel" are not at all what we have been programmed through movies and television shows to believe they are and neither are satellites, planets, or stars. Satan and his servants have truly deceived the entire world, but the Lord Jesus promised that everything done in secret or hidden would be made known, **"For there is nothing covered, that shall not be revealed; neither hid, that shall not be known"** (Luke 12:3). Another statement from Jesus puts it this way, *"For nothing is secret, that shall not be made manifest; neither anything hid, that shall not be known and come abroad"* (Luke 8:17). In the Amplified Bible it is worded, **"For there is nothing hidden that will not become evident, nor anything secret that will not be known and come out into the open"** (Luke 8:17). Thus, the "Truther" movement is really the fulfillment of a prophecy from the Lord Jesus Christ. That doesn't mean that everything in the "Truther" movement is true, but this is the reason so many real conspiracies and coverups are being exposed in these last days.

I also believe that God has given Satan certain guidelines that he and his servants must follow. We see this in the situation with Job when the Lord allowed Satan to attack Job, but forbade Satan to kill him, *"And the Lord said unto Satan, Behold, all that he hath is in thy power; only upon himself put not forth thine hand. So, Satan went forth from the presence of the Lord"* (Job 1:12) … *"And the Lord said unto Satan, Behold, he is in thine hand; but save his life"* (Job 2:6). God gave Satan "rules of engagement" or a guideline with Job. One of the guidelines that I believe Satan and his servants are required to follow now in this time is that they have to disclose suppressed truth and things that they plan and do.

In fact, one of their occultist cabal members named David Wilcock had to explain this to the public. Wilcock has appeared on the History Channel's *Ancient Alien Series* and teaches New Age occultism. He stated in an interview about an upcoming documentary, ***"One of the things that I learned from whistleblowers from the Cabal itself, is that they have to work within something they call "the rules."*** *This is very, very important. So, I really want to make sure that this gets into the film.* ***The rules are a body of spiritual principles that they must follow in order to be allowed to exist.*** *Now what do I mean by "allowed to exist"? I mean that they are aware that there are benevolent forces that will prevent them from achieving their goals unless we give them permission to enslave us.*

*Now, think about that. "I didn't give them permission."
So why did they put this plan for three world wars on display
in a book that's hanging there open behind glass in the
British Museum Library of London? And those three world
wars that they are outlining are exactly World War 1, World
War 2 and the War on Terrorism...**because the rules state
that they have to tell us what they are doing.** Therefore, if
we allow it to happen, we have consented to tyranny, we
have consented to enslavement.*

*Now, if you get into the secret history of the Cabal
(Illuminati, Satanists, Luciferians, Freemasonry, the Jesuits)
this was rediscovered by Queen Elisabeth, the original
Elisabeth that we have heard about from the 1500s. Queen
Elisabeth's royal astrologer, a man named John Dee (who
is the prototype of the wizard with the long beard, the hat);
and what he did was to rediscover through these ancient
documents that were in the Vatican the technology of how to
access what they considered to be spiritual beings that were
useful to them, but what we would consider to be demonic or
evil beings.*

*These beings need to be accessed through a very complex
set of rituals and ceremonies. You cannot just ask for them
to show up. You have to follow very elaborate and specific
protocols. If you follow those protocols, it's like having an
IP address which is what we use to go online in order to
notate a website. Every website has its own IP address.
These spiritual beings such as Baal and Moloch, which they
still do ceremonies for today such as in Bohemian Grove
there's a giant effigy, stone effigy of an owl, that's the god
Moloch. The god Moloch goes all the way back to Rome and
Carthage in which they were offering child sacrifices to this
god in exchange for power.*

352

So, John Dee rediscovered the technology of how to draw the magic circles, how to say the right incantations, how to actually do black magic on a governmental level. This is what people are going to have so much trouble with once disclosure happens (he told some truth, but he slips in their agenda) *is that these people actually practice black magic...and they are very, very good at it."*[150]

This is why we see leaked documents, the Freedom of Information Act, and truth in plain sight scattered throughout movies, TV shows, the Illuminati-controlled music industry and other media. They simply must disclose the truth and their plans (as they did with 9/11 years before it happened) because the Lord Jesus gave them that rule. And this is why some truthful messages are put forth from Satanic rock groups like the Red Hot Chili Peppers. In their song *Californication* they let you know that although some refer to space as the final frontier, it is actually made in a Hollywood basement. The actor Bill Nye the "Science Guy" shared this truth, ***"Now one thing I really want your generation to embrace is that the earth is a closed system. We cannot leave the earth. There's no place to go."***[151] And another example is Hillary Clinton saying, *"I know we have still not shattered that highest and hardest glass ceiling, but someday someone will and hopefully sooner than we might think right now."*[152]

Even NASA has admitted or let it slip at least five different times that they cannot go beyond low earth orbit which they claim is 99-1200 miles. Yet, they tell us that they

---

[150] https://www.youtube.com/watch?v=UHNd-eLe7VA&list=PLsPtgJfR9RVAjdEF897TBIbkeqDdC4Qy6

[151] Bill Nye on the Big Think YouTube Channel Bill Nye https://youtu.be/fjWGVrmuz74

[152] Hillary Clinton concession speech after losing the 2016 Presidential Election on Bloomberg YouTube https://youtu.be/ZAq8Mvs5I5Q

went to the moon 6 times from 1969-1972 which is allegedly 238,000 miles from earth in "outer space." And then when asked why we haven't been back to the moon, astronaut Don Pettit said, *"I'd go to the moon in a nanosecond. The problem is that we do not have the technology to do that anymore. We used to, but we destroyed that technology and it's a painful process to build it back again."* Upon hearing this and then considering the development of the space shuttle (especially with its technological advancements in thermal protection, guidance and computer systems), one must wonder why we could not have made several missions to the moon from 1981 to 2011. Wasn't the space shuttle a huge advancement for space travel? We were told that the space shuttles made 135 Space Transport System (STS) missions and yet not one went to the moon. Why? And how is it that the technology of the late 1960s and 1970s Apollo missions would be a "painful process" to rebuild in this time of incredible advancements in technology? If you don't smell a rat with all of this nonsense, then your "smeller" is broken.

The "space" program has never been to the fictional place called "outer space" with probes, or any of the Mercury, Gemini, or Apollo programs. Nor have they discovered the height of the dome firmament. They have only reached a height in our enclosed system that contains a very dense, gas-like almost water-like substance that they use to refer to as the aether (also spelled ether). From the visual evidence of high-altitude amateur rockets (like the Go-Fast), high zoom cameras/telescopes, and scientific study, it has become apparent that this dense aether realm starts at about 73 miles (385,440 feet) up. I also believe that this dense aether moves in a circular current above the flat circle of the earth and it takes rocket propulsion to be able to push into it. This is what the high-level government, "in-the-know" people are referring to when they talk about "space." They call this aether level "space" while leading the rest of us to believe in the science fiction of some vast, endless vacuum that goes on and on for millions and millions of light years.

The Aether (aka The Fifth Element)

What is the aether/ether? The ancient Greek philosopher Aristotle, *in his book "On the Heavens" (350 BC), introduced a new "first" element to the system of the classical elements of Ionian philosophy. He noted that the four terrestrial classical elements were subject to change and naturally moved linearly. **The first element however, located in the celestial regions and heavenly bodies, moved circularly and had none of the qualities the terrestrial classical elements had.** It was neither hot nor cold, neither wet nor dry. **With this addition the system of elements was extended to five and later commentators started referring to the new first one as the fifth and called it Aether.***"

The concept of the aether dominated physics for 2,000 years. It was used to explain many things about the natural world by various people from Aristotle to Sir Isaac Newton to Nikola Tesla (and even some modern scientists as we will see). The word "aether" comes from the Greek *"aither"* and means "upper air." The New Oxford Dictionary defines aether or ether as *"...the upper regions of air beyond the clouds, regarded as a medium for radio waves*, very rarefied and highly elastic substance formerly believed to permeate all space, including the interstices between the particles of matter, to be the medium whose vibrations constituted light and other electromagnetic radiation. **Originally, the word denoted a substance believed to occupy space beyond the sphere of the moon.*"

355

"Like their predecessors, nineteenth-century scientists recognized that all-pervasive space was filled to overflowing with somniferous Aether, the soul of the cosmos by which Divine thought manifest in matter and therefore the common origin of all matter, as Michael Faraday (1791-1867) believed."[153] Faraday was a devout Christian and a very ethical and moral man. He was also known as one of the greatest scientific discoverers of all time.[154]

James Strong was the valedictorian from Wesleyan University in 1844 and received a Doctor of Divinity (D.D.) from Wesleyan in 1856. From 1858 to 1861, Strong was both acting President and Professor of Biblical Literature at Troy University in New York. In 1868, he became Professor of Exegetical Theology at Drew Theological Seminary, where he remained for twenty-seven years.[155] In the Strong's Concordance and Hebrew Dictionary, this Bible scholar defines the word for "heavens" in Job 22:14 and many other passages as שָׁמַיִם *"...shâmayim, shaw-mah'-yim; dual of an unused singular שָׁמֶה shâmeh; from an unused root meaning to be lofty; the sky (as aloft; the dual perhaps alluding to the visible arch in which the clouds move, **as well as to the higher <u>ether</u> where the celestial bodies revolve):— air, × astrologer, heaven(-s)."***

In 1938, long after Albert Einstein had duped the world with his Theory of Relativity, Nikola Tesla (a contemporary scientist/inventor/genius and accurate critic of Einstein) stated this about the aether, ***"Only the existence of a field of force can account for the motions of the bodies as***

[153] *Under an Ionized Sky: From Chemtrails to Space Fence Lockdown* by Elana Freeland ©2018 Feral House pg. 91

[154] *Understanding Chemistry* by C.N.R. Roa ©2000 University Press pg. 281

[155] https://en.m.wikipedia.org/wiki/James_Strong_(theologian)

observed, and its' assumption dispenses with space curvature (Einstein's theory). *All literature on this subject is futile and destined to oblivion.* **So are all the attempts to explain the workings of the universe without recognizing the existence of the <u>ether</u> and the indispensable function it plays on phenomena."**

To demonstrate just how true Tesla's words were about the futility of trying to explain "…the workings of the universe without recognizing the existence of the ether," here is a quote from Astrophysicist Neil deGrasse Tyson (Harvard BA, Texas MA, Columbia PhD and recipient of the 2004 NASA Distinguished Public Service Medal):

"Dark Matter. I get asked what it is and my best answer is **'We don't know what it is.'** **We look out in the universe and 85% of all the gravity that's out there has some mysterious unknown force.** *We add up all the stars, the galaxies, the planets, the comets, the black holes,* **the dark clouds**—*everything out there that we can see, touch, smell or taste—and it doesn't add up to give us the gravity that we see operating in this universe.* **So really, we should be calling it the dark force because we don't know if it's made of matter.** *It could be a profound misnomer sending people off in thought directions that might not really be the right path.*

So, dark matter is just simply what we call this thing, about which we know nothing, yet is responsible for 85% of the gravity of the cosmos. *We've known about dark matter since the 1930s. Back then, it was called* **'missing mass.'** *That's what it was called. There's got to be some mass. Where is it? We can't find it. It's got to be here somewhere because we got the gravity. If you have the gravity, you have to have the mass…mass and gravity go*

357

together. It's really dark gravity. Actually, we shouldn't call it anything. **We should call it Fred...something that has no meaning because we don't know what it is to call it. But it is the longest standing unsolved problem in modern astrophysics.** *"[156]*

Einstein's Deception

The cause of this *"longest standing problem in modern astrophysics"* is that Einstein and his groupies did away with the long-standing concept of the aether. And the reason Einstein invented his theory of relativity was to cover up the very real discovery of the Michelson-Morley experiments in 1881 and 1887. These experiments revealed that the earth was not moving through aether-filled "space." But instead of accepting the results of the experiments (a stationary earth, still and at rest just as the Bible said), Einstein and his worshippers made the arbitrary decision that the zero velocity of the earth discovered by Michelson could not be correct and that meant the aether did not exist. So now almost every article or lecture you hear that mentions the Michelson-Morley experiments falsely claims that they proved the aether doesn't exist and never existed. All of this to guard their precious Copernican/heliocentric system.

*"And the man that stood among the myrtle trees answered and said, 'These are they whom the Lord hath sent to walk to and fro through the earth.' And they answered the angel of the Lord that stood among the myrtle trees, and said, We have walked to and fro through the earth, and, behold, **all the earth sitteth still, and is at rest"** (Zechariah 1:10-11).*

---

[156] Neil deGrasse Tyson on his podcast *StarTalk* published on YouTube 2-25-2015
https://youtu.be/kyKMvTu2oho

"The Lord reigneth, he is clothed with majesty; the Lord is clothed with strength, wherewith he hath girded himself: **the world also is stablished, that it cannot be moved"** (Psalms 93:1).

"Fear before him, all the earth: **the world also shall be stable, that it be not moved"** (1 Chronicles 16:30).

The following are excerpts from a well-documented article entitled *"Albert Einstein: The Earth-Mover"* by geocentric apologist Robert Sugenis:

"In his 1881 and 1887 experiments, Albert Michelson discovered the earth was not moving around the sun. As Michelson himself described the results of his own experiment: **'This conclusion directly contradicts the explanation...which presupposes that the earth moves.** '[157] *But since his colleagues, including Albert Einstein, were diehard Copernicans who didn't want to believe that Michelson had discovered a motionless earth, they proposed his experimental apparatus was distorted by the earth motion through space and thus, Michelson's apparatus only made it appear as if it was moving. In scientific parlance, we call this the fallacy of petitio principii, that is, using as proof (a moving earth) the very thing one is trying to prove (a moving earth).*

Other prominent physicists noted the same truth:

'There was just one alternative; the earths true velocity through space might happen to have been nil.' - Physicist, Arthur Eddington

---

[157] Albert A. Michaelson, "The Relative Motion of the Earth and the Luminiferous Ether" American Journal of Science, Volume 22, August 1881, pg. 125

*'The data of [Michelson-Morley] were almost unbelievable...**There was only one other possible conclusion to draw—that the earth was at rest.'** -* Physicist, Bernard Jaffe

*'**The failure of Michelson and Morley to observe different speeds of light at different times of the year suggested that the earth must be at rest**... It was therefore the "preferred" frame for measuring absolute motion in space. Yet we have known since Galileo that the earth is not the center of the universe. Why should it be at rest in space?'* - Physicist Adolph Baker

*'**The easiest explanation was that the earth was fixed in the ether and that everything else in the universe moved with respect to the earth and the ether**...Such an idea was not considered seriously, since it would mean in effect that our earth occupied the omnipotent position in the universe, with all the other heavenly bodies paying homage by moving around it."* - Physicist, James Coleman

*'**The Michelson-Morley experiment confronted scientists with an embarrassing alternative.** On the one hand, they could scrap the ether theory which had explained so many things about electricity, magnetism, and light. Or if they insisted on retaining the ether, they had to abandon the still more venerable Copernican theory that the earth is in motion. To many physicists, it seemed almost easier to believe that the earth stood still and that waves - light waves, electromagnetic waves - could exist without a medium to sustain them. Many new hypotheses were advanced and rejected. **The experiment was tried again by Morley and by others, with the same conclusion; the apparent velocity of the earth through the ether was zero.'** -* Historian, Lincoln Barnett, forward by Albert Einstein

360

'What happened when the experiment was done in 1887? That was never, never, in any orientation at any time of year, any shift in the interference pattern; none; no shift; no fringe shift; nothing. What's the implication? Here was an experiment that was done to measure the speed of the earth's motion through the ether. This was an experiment that was 10 times more sensitive than it needed to be. It could have detected speeds as low as 2 miles a second instead of the known 20 mps that the earth as in its orbital motion around the sun. It didn't detect it. **What's the conclusion from the Michaelson Morley experiment? The implication is that the earth is not moving.'** - Physicist, Richard Wolfson

'The 'null' result [of the Michelson-Morley experiments] *was one of the great puzzles of physics at the* **end of the 19th century.** *One possibility was that... v* (velocity of earth) *would be zero and no fringe shift would be expected. But this implies that the earth is somehow a preferred object; only with respect to the earth with the speed of light be c* (constant) *as predicted by Maxwell's equations.* **This is tantamount to assuming that the earth is the central body of the universe.'** - Physicist Douglas C. Giancoli

But the diehard Copernicans were not about to accept the prima facie results of Michelson's experiment. **They knew the catastrophic scientific, cultural, and religious implications if it was experimentally shown that the earth is fixed in space.** *In a word, the whole world would have been turned upside down, literally and figuratively.*

Since they insisted the earth is moving around the sun yet cannot detect it moving, they needed some physical and mathematical way of accounting for it since there is obviously a difference between motion and non-motion. So, length contraction became their convenient scapegoat. This is the essence of the special relativity theory that Einstein invented in 1905. It was invented solely to answer Michelson's experiment. As Einstein himself said: 'To the question whether or not the motion of the earth in space can be made perceptible terrestrial experiments...we have already remarked that all the attempts of this nature led to a negative result. **Before the theory of relativity was put forth, it was difficult to become reconciled to this negative result.'**

Whereas, in 1892, Hendrik Lorentz hypothesized that the ether of space was what caused the contraction, understanding this he decided to dispense with ether and attribute the cause to 'relative motion.' In effect, Lorentz at least proposed a physical cause for his claims of length contraction, but Einstein never explained how 'relative motion' could shrink objects. Hence, during his day, there were philosophers who accused him of violating the principle of 'cause-and-effect.'

So, whatever the cause of the contraction, in order to give the ad hoc theory some semblance of credibility, the required amount for the metal enclosure to contract was put into a mathematical equation called 'the Lorentz transform.'

It has become the most famous and most used equation in modern physics. Essentially, whatever test disagreed with their belief that the earth was moving around the sun could now be mathematically transformed into their desired result as well as give the semblance of being scientific.

Incidentally, we should know one more important facet of the Michaelson experiment before we move on. We saw above that the experiment showed only one-sixth of what was required for an earth moving around the sun. This one-sixth is important for another reason. It showed that space was composed of something substantive. The name given to it by Lawrence Maxwell, and all other scientists was ether. No one knew precisely what it was composed of, but they correctly deduced that space cannot be nothing, since metaphysically nothing cannot exist. Space must be a something composed of something physical although like air we cannot see it because it is invisible. It doesn't matter what you call it. The fact is that it must exist. Quantum mechanics has suggested that the ether's basic component is Planck particles, which are 20 orders of magnitude smaller than the electron. Another type of ether may be an electron–positron dipole particle, which was discovered in 1932 by Carl Anderson.

In any case, the substance of space, which we will call ether, was detected in Michelson's 1881 and 1887 experiments, as well as his 1897 experiment with an aboveground apparatus. Since light moves so fast, you can serve to measure the effect on something as small as ether particles. His interferometer was so accurate it could measure one hundred times more than it was required to measure. As such, Michelson's interferometer didn't measure enough ether to match an earth moving at 66,000 mph around the sun, but it did measure a little ether, otherwise his results would not have shown one-sixth, but zero-sixths of ether presence. Michelson noted this small presence in his 1887 paper.

This was not good for Einstein. He candidly admitted that if any ether was detected, even a little bit, this theory of special relativity would automatically be falsified. This was noted in Einstein's statement to Sir Herbert Samuel in Jerusalem: **"If Michelson-Morley is wrong, then relativity is wrong."** In other words, Einstein was forced to assume *that because Michelson did not find enough ether for an earth revolving around the sun, then Michelson couldn't have found any ether. But if this conclusion of Einstein's was wrong, then his whole relativity theory would be falsified automatically, since even a little ether would act as an absolute frame and then nullify relativity. Noted physicist Charles Lane Poor of Columbia University reiterated the problem:*

*'The Michaelson-Morley experiment forms the basis of the relativity theory: Einstein calls it decisive... **If it should develop that there is a measurable ether drift, then the entire fabric of the relativity theory would collapse like a house of cards.'***

So, Einstein was banking on the hope that since Michelson did not detect the required amount of ether for an earth moving around the sun, he could conclude that the ether simply didn't exist. Hence, the detection of one-sixth of the required either was conveniently chalked up to "experimental error."

The facts show otherwise, however. Every interferometer experiment performed from Michaelson in 1881 to 1930— which is 50 years of the same results from a dozen different experimenters—detected one-sixth to one-tenth. Einstein was so bothered by this fact that he hired what can be called a "scientific hit man." Robert Shanklin, to seek to discredit the experiments, especially the most comprehensive interferometer experiments performed by Dayton Miller between 1908 and 1921.

(Side note: Some have asked why Michelson-Morley detected one-sixth "movement" if the earth is stationary and at rest. The following from Sungenis answers this.) *'The simple answer is that since the universe, with its ether, is rotating around a fixed earth, some of that ether spilled into Michelson's 1887 interferometer when he was trying to check if the earth was moving around the sun. This is confirmed by the fact that Michelson did another experiment in 1925 in order to measure the ether movement for the daily rotation between space and earth. In that experiment, he found six-sixths of the required ether for daily rotation. Hence, it is logical to assume that the one-sixth found in 1887 came from the same ether he later detected in his 1925 experiment. Since the ether in the 1887 experiment hit the interferometer orthogonally instead of linearly, it would only pick up one-sixth of the total ether in space.'*

But at this point in time (the 1910s-1920s), the world was only too happy to accept Einstein's theories and reject anyone who challenged him. After all, Einstein was the Earth-Mover. He made the earth move around the sun and thus, saved mankind from having to admit that popular science had misled the world for the 500 years prior **(and the Bible was right all along about the earth being still and at rest (Zechariah 1:11 mine).**

You will often hear modern devotees of Einstein claim that he invented special relativity as an answer to Maxwell's equations of electrodynamics. They do this because they don't want to admit that Einstein invented special relativity for the express purpose of making it appear the earth was moving around the sun. They want to make it appear that Einstein invented special relativity out of pure motives and an independent thought process. The truth is far different. Einstein himself admits that the only reason he invented special relativity was due to Michelson's discovery. In 1922 he writes:

"Soon, I came to the conclusion that our idea about the motion of the earth with respect to ether is incorrect, if we admit Michelson's null result as fact. This was the first path which led me to the special theory of relativity."[158] & [159]

Although Sungenis did a wonderful job exposing Einstein's coverup of the Michelson-Morley experiments and the truth of the motionless earth, unfortunately, he has not broken free of the ball earth lie.

Tesla used to rant about the way in which Einstein had succeeded in pulling the wool over the eyes of the scientists of the world with his theories of special and general relativity. In fact, he stopped just short of calling Einstein the devil. Tesla like most classical physicists believed in the existence of an aether as the medium through which electromagnetic radiation propagated.[160]

Tesla stated, *"Today's scientists have substituted mathematics for experiments. They wander off through equation after equation and eventually build a structure that has no relation to reality* (like the heliocentric Copernican system). *Einstein's relativity work is a magnificent mathematical garb which fascinates, dazzles, and makes people blind to the underlying errors. The theory is like a beggar clothed in purple whom ignorant people take for a king...its' exponents are brilliant men, but they are metaphysicists rather than scientists."*

---

[158] Speech titled: *"How I Created the Theory of Relativity"* delivered at Kyoto University, Japan December 14, 1922 as cited in *Physics Today* August 1982 by Yoshimasa A. Ono

[159] https://web.archive.org/web/20190412005126/http://www.theprinciplemovie.com/wp-content/uploads/2016/08/Albert-Einstein-The-Earth-Mover.pdf

[160] https://www.quora.com/What-was-Teslas-opinion-on-Einsteins-theory-of-relativity-and-quantum-mechanics

Amazingly, the dishonest suppression of the results of the Michelson-Morley experiments (that proved both the existence of the invisible aether, and the Biblical truth of a geocentric, stationary earth) was clearly foretold in the New Testament. The Spirit of God inspired the Apostle Paul to write in Romans 1 that self-professed, wise men would suppress the truth about creation (specifically the "invisible things" of Him from the creation like the aether/ether):

*"For the wrath of God is revealed from heaven against all ungodliness and unrighteousness of men, **who *hold the truth in unrighteousness**; Because that which may be known of God is manifest in them; for God hath shewed it unto them. **For the invisible things of him from the creation of the world are clearly seen, being understood by the things that are made, even his eternal power and Godhead; so that they are without excuse:** Because that, when they knew God, they glorified him not as God, neither were thankful; but became vain in their imaginations, and their foolish heart was darkened. **Professing themselves to be wise, they became fools**"* (Romans 1:18-22).

*The Greek word for 'hold' in Romans 1:18 is *katéchō*, (pronounced kat-ekh'-o). **It means "to hold back, hold down (fast),** in various applications (literally or figuratively):—have, hold (fast), keep (in memory), let, × make toward, possess, retain, seize on, stay, take, **withhold**."

Author and researcher Elana Freeland confirms this "suppression" in her book *"Under An Ionized Sky"* when she writes, *"Somewhere between Darwinian evolutionary dogma, good-old-boy peer reviews, and powerful sub rosa occult societies, **a decision was made to eliminate Aether from the mainstream science and replace it with space as a vacuum** while scalar waves and the rest of Tesla's work and*

367

that of Maxwell and E.T. Whittaker (1873-1956) **were suppressed."** Again, the main reason for this suppression of the aether and the constant misrepresentations of the Michelson-Morley experiments was and is to continue hiding the fact that the earth is stationary and the center of the much smaller and closer sun, moon and stars that circle over our heads.

The occult societies and godless, unethical scientists had to be loyal to their master Lucifer/Satan to hide the truths about creation which would prove the Bible to be the inspired, infallible words of the One True God, Creator and Savior Jesus Christ. And these white-coat priests of the sun-centered cult of Hermes Trismegistus and their invention of magical "gravity" have deceived millions upon millions with tales of a vast, ever-expanding vacuum called "space," ETs, and galaxies far, far away. However, God is waking up a remnant to the Biblical truths of creation. Some are being snatched by the Holy Spirit out of the unbelief produced by this antichrist cult of Copernican, heliocentric nonsense.

Chapter 16

Space, the Aether & the Power of God

*"That they should seek the Lord, if haply they might feel after him, and find him, **though he be not far from every one of us:** **For in him we live, and move, and have our being;** as certain also of your own poets have said, For we are also his offspring"* (Acts 17:27-28).

*"Hast thou with him spread out the sky, **which is strong, and as a molten looking glass?"** (Job 37:18).*

*"**For now we see through a glass, darkly; but then face to face:** now I know in part; but then shall I know even as also I am known"* (1 Corinthians 13:12).

*"**Is not God in the height of heaven?** and behold the height of the stars, how high they are! And thou sayest, 'How doth God know? **can he judge through the dark cloud?** Thick clouds are a covering to him, that he seeth not; and he walketh in the circuit of heaven"* (Job 22:12-14),

Robert B. Laughlin is an American physicist with a PhD from Massachusetts Institute of Technology. He was one of

369

the recipients of the 1998 Nobel Prize in Physics and an endowed chair in physics at Stanford University. This is what Laughlin had to say about the existence of the aether and the so-called "vacuum" of space in light of contemporary theoretical physics:

"It is ironic that Einstein's most creative work, the general theory of relativity, should boil down to conceptualizing space as a medium when his original premise [in special relativity] was that no such medium existed. **The word 'ether' has extremely negative connotations in theoretical physics because of its past association with opposition to relativity.** *This is unfortunate because, stripped of these connotations,* **it rather nicely captures the way most physicists actually think about the vacuum**...Relativity *actually says nothing about the existence or nonexistence of matter pervading the universe, only that any such matter must have relativistic symmetry. [..]* **It turns out that such matter exists. About the time relativity was becoming accepted, studies of radioactivity began showing that the empty vacuum of space had spectroscopic structure similar to that of ordinary quantum solids and fluids. Subsequent studies with large particle accelerators have now led us to understand that SPACE IS MORE LIKE A PIECE OF WINDOW GLASS THAN IDEAL NEWTONIAN EMPTINESS.** *It is filled with 'stuff' that is normally transparent but can be made visible by hitting it sufficiently hard to knock out a part.* **The modern concept of the vacuum of space, confirmed every day by experiment, is a relativistic ether. But we do not call it this because it is taboo.** *"*[161]

It is almost unbelievable that this quote from Dr. Laughlin is coming from a modern-day scientist. His analysis of what

[161] *A Different Universe: Reinventing Physics from the Bottom Down* by Robert B. Laughlin ©2005 NY, NY: Basic Books. pp. 120–121. ISBN 978-0-465-03828-2.

they actually see through their telescopes is one of the most Biblically accurate descriptions of this region of dense aether located just below the glass/firmament dome that I have come across (I'm sure unbeknownst to him). It is worth repeating that he states that the so-called empty vacuum of "space" has "...*spectroscopic structure similar to that of ordinary quantum solids and fluids* (aka the aether, not dark matter*)"* and other studies have now led them to understand that "...*SPACE IS MORE LIKE A PIECE OF WINDOW GLASS* (God's firmament) *THAN IDEAL NEWTONIAN EMPTINESS."* Let that sink in!

"In 1982, Ioan-Iovitz Popescu, a Romanian physicist, wrote that the aether is 'a form of existence of the matter, but it differs qualitatively from the common (atomic and molecular) substance or radiation (photons).' The fluid aether is '...governed by the principle of inertia and its presence produces a modification of the space-time geometry.' Built upon Le Sage's ultra-mundane corpuscles, Popescu's theory posits a finite Universe 'filled with some particles of exceedingly small mass, traveling chaotically at speed of light" and material bodies "made up of such particles called etherons.'* From Popescu's Ether and Etherons,[162] he states in the conclusion, '*A new explanation of the Newtonian law of gravitation is given,* proceeding from the following statements: a) *the Universe is finite, and filled with particles of exceedingly small mass,* travelling chaotically at the speed of light; b) *all the material bodies in the Universe are made up of such particles,* which are here called "etherons;" c) the matter in the Universe is prevailingly under the form of etherons; d) the hydrodynamic mechanism of Lesage for gravitational*

---

[162] chrome-
extension://oemmndcbldboiebfnladdacbdfmadadm/https://editura.mttlc.ro/carti/Iovitz
%20-%20Etherons.CLP.pdf

interaction is valid, **and the cosmic background is the ETHER made up of etherons.** *"[163]*

Paul Adrien Maurice Dirac (1902-1984) was an English theoretical physicist who is regarded as one of the most significant physicists of the 20th century. He wrote in 1951:

"Physical knowledge has advanced much since 1905, notably by the arrival of quantum mechanics, and the situation [about the scientific plausibility of Aether] has again changed. If one examines the question in the light of present-day knowledge, one finds that the Aether is no longer ruled out by relativity, and good reasons can now be advanced for postulating an Aether... We have now the velocity at all points of space-time, playing a fundamental part in electrodynamics. It is natural to regard it as the velocity of some real physical thing. Thus, with the new theory of electrodynamics [vacuum filled with virtual particles] we are rather forced to have an Aether."[164]

In other words, "space" is not an empty vacuum. It is filled with an almost fluid-like yet gas-like substance the ancients called aether/ether. After much research, I now believe "space" is the area between the beginning of the upper region of dense aether (starting at about 73 miles high) and the molten glass/firmament dome to which the stars are attached. Above that aether region is the mysterious "missing mass" that Neil deGrasse Tyson mentioned. It is the solid firmament dome that Dr. Laughlin correctly described as being more like a *"...piece of window glass"* than the *"ideal Newtonian emptiness."* The Bible describes it as *"the molten looking glass"* and the *"terrible crystal."*

---

[163] Ioan-Iovitz Popescu's Romanian text *Ether and Etherons* originally appeared in the year 1982, in the Romanian Academy Journal of PhysicsStudii şi Cercetări de Fizică, vol. 34, 451-468.

[164] *"Is there an Aether?" by Paul Dirac Nature 168 (1951), p. 906.*

Why do I believe this? Well, it is a combination of things that has led me to this conclusion. The first evidence was the famous video from the onboard cameras of the 2014 GoFast Rocket. *"On July 14, 2014 the team repeated their accomplishment with a second successful space launch, which set new records for the highest and fastest amateur rocket ever launched. Analysis of the data from the recovered military grade Inertial Measurement Unit (IMU) that flew onboard shows that* **the 'GoFast' rocket reached an altitude of 385,800 feet (73.07 mi) (above mean sea level)** *and hit a top speed of 3,580 mph (5,800 km/h)."*[165]

Because the amateur rocket's climb and spin stopped abruptly, many early flat earth videos stated that it hit the firmament dome. However, the rocket did not disintegrate, nor did it even have a dented nose cone after allegedly hitting the solid, firmament. However, it did hit something that stopped its flight and upward momentum quite suddenly, but softly. The CSXT team claims that a device called Yo-Yo De-Spin mechanism was deployed to stop the spin of the rocket and that could be true, but that device would not have had any effect on the rocket's forward momentum especially 11 miles into space. The cameras on the rocket revealed that the top half of the rocket and even the bottom part that broke away appeared to experience a short season of "weightlessness" that slightly delayed its immediate fall back to earth.

Again, they claim that the GoFast rocket reached 11 miles above the "official" altitude of alleged "space" (around 62 miles) which is what they call the Kármán line. So, if it reached "space" (the realm of weightlessness where we begin to escape the earth's atmosphere), then what caused

---

[165] http://www.coloradospacenews.com/csxt-go-fast-rocket-confirms-multiple-world-records/ https://en.wikipedia.org/wiki/Civilian_Space_eXploration_Team#cite_note-12

373

the abrupt halt of the rocket? And don't say gravity! That overused, default, magical excuse for everything does not explain the sudden stop of a rocket that just made it 11 miles into "space." I believe it hit something very dense, gas-like, and almost liquid-like in the upper layer, yet still similar to air - the upper blue "air" called the aether. That would explain the rocket's abrupt but soft stop and why its immediate fall back to earth was slowed down.

This was confirmed to me when I watched the SpaceX launch of Falcon 9 on December 23, 2017. It was clear that it took the Falcon 9 close to the same amount of time to hit the thicker, blue aether level as it did the 2014 GoFast rocket. Of course, it took the Falcon 9 about 30 seconds longer to reach that altitude because it was much heavier than the GoFast. Nevertheless, it was evident that once the Falcon 9 reached an altitude comparable to the top altitude of the GoFast (73 miles), it was plowing through a dense layer of gas-like, liquid-like substance. As the rocket disturbed the aether, it glowed blue. The Falcon 9 looked like a boat pushing through water except it was in the sky.

Another interesting thing to consider is a detail given in the account of Swiss/Belgium physicist, inventor, and explorer Dr. Auguste Piccard. I shared his story and how I stumbled across him in chapter four. The account of Piccard's ascent to the stratosphere in the August 1931 Popular Science Magazine article entitled, *Ten Miles High in an Air-Tight Balloon* is quite amazing.

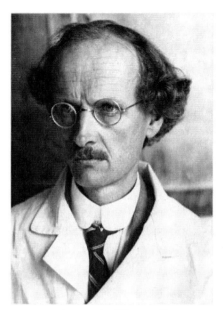

Auguste Piccard

However, while researching and writing about the aether, I remembered the article also mentioned that Auguste Piccard and his assistant trapped some of the "upper air." Here's how it reads, ***"The explorers trapped samples of the upper air, "<u>blue air</u>," as Piccard reported it to appear in the cylinders.*** *Analysis may prove it exceptionally rich in ozone, the intensely blue gas supposedly responsible for the Heaviside or 'radio roof.'"*[166]

Upper blue air...intensely blue gas used as a radio roof to bounce their radio signals off...could it be the aether? You bet it is! They renamed it the ionosphere because to admit the aether exists would mean that the Michelson-Morley experiments did prove that the earth is not moving. The following Wikipedia article describes this layer of "space" or anything above 62 miles (though the United States awards

---

[166] *"Ten Miles High in an Air-Tight Ball"* Popular Science Magazine August 1931 pg. 23

astronaut wings to anyone who reaches an altitude of at least 50 miles).

"The Heaviside layer sometimes called the Kennelly– Heaviside layer, named after Arthur E. Kennelly and Oliver Heaviside, **is a layer of ionized gas occurring between roughly 90 and 150 km (56 and 93 mi) above the ground** — one of several layers in the earth's ionosphere. **It is also known as the E region** (could that E stand for Ether?). It reflects (they should say carries) medium-frequency radio waves. Because of this reflective layer, radio waves radiated into the sky can return to earth beyond the horizon. This "skywave" or "skip" propagation technique has been used since the 1920s for radio communication at long distances, up to transcontinental distances.

Propagation is affected by time of day. During the daytime the solar wind presses this layer closer to the earth **(on a flat earth this alleged solar wind would be like a car traveling at a good speed and pushing and disturbing the air as it moves passes by. The sun is moving at around 1,000 mph in a circuit over a stationary earth and creates the solar wind and heat disturbance in the aether during the day)**, thereby limiting how far it can reflect radio waves. Conversely, on the night (lee) side of the earth, the solar wind drags the ionosphere further away, thereby greatly increasing the range which radio waves can travel by reflection. (I would venture to say that the moon's much cooler light has everything to do with this day and night variation of radio waves.) The extent of the effect is further influenced by the season, and the amount of sunspot activity."[167]

---

[167] https://en.wikipedia.org/wiki/Kennelly%E2%80%93Heaviside_layer

Furthermore, I came across a FOIA document on the CIA website during my research in 2018 that mentioned the aether and connected it to worldwide radio communications. The document was published January 1950 by the Russians and stated on the front page inside a black outlined box, *"This document contains information affecting the national defense of the United States within the meaning of the espionage act 50 U.S. C..31 and 32, as amended. It's transmission or the revelation of its contents in any manner to an authorized person is prohibited by law. Reproduction of this form is prohibited:"*

THE FAILURE OF U.S. ATTEMPTS TO ATTAIN SUPREMECY OF THE ETHER

"In accordance with international agreements, all countries register the frequencies used by them with the Bern Bureau of the International Communications Union, which regularly publishes a list of frequencies so used.

World War II made great changes in the state of radio communications in many countries. The 1947 radio communications conference reallocated frequency bands for various services (stationary, air, sea broadcasting), etc. and passed a resolution calling for a new international list for frequency distribution, Taking into consideration the requirements of each country and service.

For this purpose, a Provisional Frequency Bureau was created, composed of delegated and experts from 57 countries. It began work in Geneva in January 1948. Its' main object was to prepare a draft of new international frequencies from 14 to 27,500 kilocycles.

*If all delegations had been willing to cooperate, this difficult problem could have been solved. However, from the very first days of the conference, **the US put pressure on countries dependent upon her in an attempt to obtain passage of an allocation plan <u>which would give the US supremacy of the ether.</u>***

*The US delegation tried to mask its' insolent pretensions by prating about 'improving the utilization of the frequency spectrum,' 'preparing a list on scientific and technical principles,' etc. **However, there was no ambiguity in the practical proposals introduced by US delegates to further the imperialistic aims of the US.***

*They insisted on a complete redistribution of frequencies, allocating them not, as heretofore, by individual stations **but by assigning to each radio communications line a minimum set of frequencies selected on the basis of 'average' data, without regard for ionospheric variations.** Their claims, amounting to four times the prewar requirements of the US, **aptly illustrate their desire for world domination.** "*[168]

Sanitized Copy Approved for Release 2011/08/17 : CIA-RDP80-00809A000600310776-6

CLASSIFICATION CONFIDENTIAL **CONFIDENTIAL**

CENTRAL INTELLIGENCE AGENCY   REPORT   50X1-HUM

INFORMATION FROM
FOREIGN DOCUMENTS OR RADIO BROADCASTS   CD NO.

COUNTRY	USSR	DATE OF INFORMATION	1950
SUBJECT	Political; Scientific - International broadcasting		
HOW PUBLISHED	Monthly periodical	DATE DIST.	Jun 1950
WHERE PUBLISHED	Moscow	NO. OF PAGES	2
DATE PUBLISHED	Jan 1950		
LANGUAGE	Russian	SUPPLEMENT TO REPORT NO.	

THIS IS UNEVALUATED INFORMATION

SOURCE   Radio; No 1, 1950.

---

[168] https://www.cia.gov/library/readingroom/docs/CIA-RDP80-00809A000600310776-6.pdf

378

THE FAILURE OF US ATTEMPTS
TO ATTAIN SUPREMACY OF THE ETHER

I. Tsingovatov

In accordance with international agreements, all countries register the frequencies used by them with the Bern bureau of the International Communications Union, which regularly publishes a list of frequencies so used.

World War II made great changes in the state of radio communications in many countries. The 1947 Radio Communications Conference reallocated frequency bands for various services (stationary, air, sea, broadcasting, etc.) and passed a resolution calling for a new international list for frequency distribution, taking into consideration the requirements of each country and service.

For this purpose, a Provisional Frequency Bureau was created, composed of delegated and experts from 57 countries. It began work in Geneva in January 1948. Its main object was to prepare a draft of new international frequencies from 14 to 27,500 kilocycles.

If all delegations had been willing to cooperate, this difficult problem could have been solved. However, from the very first days of the conference, the US put pressure on countries dependent upon her in an attempt to obtain passage of an allocation plan which would give the US supremacy of the ether.

The US delegation tried to mask its insolent pretensions by prating about "improving the utilization of the frequency spectrum," "preparing a list on scientific and technical principles," etc. However, there was no ambiguity in the practical proposals introduced by US delegates to further the imperialistic aims of the US.

They insisted on a complete redistribution of frequencies, allocating them not, as heretofore, by individual stations but by assigning to each radio communications line a minimum set of frequencies selected on the basis of "average" data, without regard for ionospheric variations. Their claims, amounting to four times the prewar requirements of the US, aptly illustrate their desire for world domination.

Thus, it is evident that the Russians believed in the aether and that there is a concentration of it at higher altitudes. It is also clear that they renamed this aether layer the ionosphere because aether became a taboo term after Einstein and his groupies hid the fact that the earth doesn't move. As for the actual height of the firmament dome, I don't think that can be determined because the Bible says, *"The heaven for height, and the earth for depth, and the heart of kings is unsearchable"* (Proverbs 25:3). Based on this Scripture, I don't believe the Lord has allowed anyone to figure out the height, but it is not millions of miles. In fact, it's probably only several hundred miles at the most because several astronauts have stated, *"Low earth orbit is as far as we can go."*

So, where does "space" or this level of dense aether begin? As I have stated, I believe it is around 73 miles due to observing the 2014 GoFast rocket footage. Then, I came across an article at Space.com that confirms the EXACT SAME ALTITUDE, *"With data from a new instrument developed by scientists at the University of Calgary, scientists confirmed that space begins 73 miles (118 kilometers) above earth's surface...In the new study, an instrument called the Supra-Thermal Ion Imager detected the boundary by tracking the relatively gentle winds of earth's atmosphere and the more violent flows of charged particles in space, which can reach speeds well over 600 mph (1,000 kph)."*[169]

What is the Aether?

Let's go back to an earlier quote, *"Like their predecessors, nineteenth-century scientists recognized that all-pervasive space was filled to overflowing with somniferous Aether, the soul of the cosmos by which Divine thought manifest in matter and therefore the common origin of all matter, as Michael Faraday (1791-1867) believed."* Others have postulated that there are different manifestations of the Aether on our physical world. Dr. Marc J. Seifer put it like this, *"Concrete proof that relativity can be violated can be found in George Gamow's watershed book Thirty Years That Shook Physics. Gamow, one of the founding fathers of quantum physics, tells us that in the mid-1920's, Goudsmit and Uhlenbeck discovered not only that electrons were orthorotating, but also that they were spinning at 1.37 times the speed of light. Gamow makes it clear that this discovery did not violate anything in quantum physics, what it violated was Einstein's principle that nothing could travel faster than the speed of light. Paul Adrian Dirac studied the problem. Following in the footsteps of Herman Minkowski, who used an imaginary number i, (the square root of -1) to be equivalent to the time coordinate*

---

[169] https://www.space.com/6564-edge-space.html

in space-time equations, Dirac assigned the same number i to electron spin. In this way he was able to combine relativity with quantum mechanics and won a Nobel Prize for the idea in the process (1966, pp. 120-121). That was the upside. **The downside was that the finding that elementary particles spin faster than the speed of light as a matter of course went the way of the passenger pigeon. No physicist talks about this anymore.** *What this means is that the entire evolution of 20th and nascent 21st century physics is evolving ignoring this key Goudsmit and Uhlenbeck finding.* **The ramifications suggest that elementary particles, by their nature, interface dimensions. Because they are spinning faster than the speed of light, the idea is that they are drawing this energy from the ether, a pre-physical realm, and converting the energy into material form."**[170]

Though some of this may sound more metaphysical than physics, let's remember that, as Christians, we believe that the God of Abraham, Isaac, & Jacob, YHVH also known as the Lord Jesus Christ, the Word (Logos) made flesh or God in the flesh is all powerful and the Creator. We believe in a supernatural power beyond just the creation itself. And this Creator inspired His apostles to write these things in His Holy Bible.

*"**For the invisible things of him from the creation** of the world are clearly seen, being understood by the things that are made, **even his eternal power and Godhead**; so that they are without excuse:"* (Romans 1:20).

"God, who at sundry times and in divers manners spake in time past unto the fathers by the prophets, Hath in these last days spoken unto us by his Son, whom he hath appointed heir of all things, by whom also he made the worlds; **Who**

---

[170] https://www.newdawnmagazine.com/articles/tesla-vs-einstein-the-ether-the-birth-of-the-new-physics

being the brightness of his glory, and the express image of his person, and upholding all things by the word of his power, when he had by himself purged our sins, sat down on the right hand of the Majesty on high:" (Hebrews 1:1-3).

The Holy Spirit had the Apostle Paul write this, *"For by him* (Jesus Christ*) were all things created, that are in heaven, and that are in earth, visible and invisible,* whether they be thrones, or dominions, or principalities, or powers: all things were created by him, and for him: *And he is before all things, and by him all things consist"* (Colossians 1:16-17).

The Bible says invisible things from creation make it possible to understand two things:

1) God's eternal power.

2) The Godhead (The Father, Son/Word of God, and the Holy Spirit which are the three distinct parts of the One God, not three Gods).

Then, we are told that God upholds all things by the word of His power. In the original Greek the verb "upholding" is a Present Tense Greek verb which means that it is an ongoing and continuous action that is taking place in the present. Thus, God's Word that went forth to create all things is still the power and force behind and permeating all created things. The power or force of God's spoken word at creation continues to uphold all things (like the sun, moon, and stars) and by Him all things consist. The original Greek word for 'consist' is *synistáō* and it is defined in multiple Greek lexicons *"...to place together, to set in the same place, to bring or band together; to put together by way of composition or combination* (maybe like atoms...hmmm)*;*

to put together, unite parts into one whole; to be composed of, consist; to set together."[171]

While speaking to Greek students of Plato and Aristotle, the Apostle Paul gave some flat earth and aether truth in his gospel message, **"God that made the world and all things therein, seeing that he is Lord of heaven and earth,** *dwelleth not in temples made with hands; Neither is worshipped with men's hands, as though he needed anything,* **seeing he giveth to all life, and breath, and all things**; *And hath made of one blood all nations of men for to dwell on all* **the face of the earth, and hath determined the times before appointed, and the bounds of their habitation;** *That they should seek the Lord, if haply they might feel after him, and find him,* **though he be not far from every one of us: For in him we live, and move, and have our being;** *as certain also of your own poets have said, For we are also his offspring. Forasmuch then as we are the offspring of God, we ought not to think that the Godhead is like unto gold, or silver, or stone, graven by art and man's device.* **And the times of this ignorance God winked at; but now commandeth all men everywhere to repent: Because he hath appointed a day, in the which he will judge the world in righteousness by that man whom he hath ordained; whereof he hath given assurance unto all men, in that he hath raised him from the dead"** (Acts 17:24-31).

Think about the Apostle Paul's Holy Spirit inspired statement, "*…he (God) be not far from every one of us: For in him we live, and move, and have our being.*" THIS is what Satan, his demons and his followers have worked so hard to cover up and blind us to!

---

[171] https://www.blueletterbible.org/lang/lexicon/lexicon.cfm?Strongs=G4921&t=KJV

Chapter 17

Satellites, Balloons & GPS

"According to the Index of Objects Launched into Outer Space, maintained by the United Nations Office for Outer Space Affairs (UNOOSA), **there were 4,987 satellites orbiting the planet at the start of the year;** *an increase of 2.68% compared to end of April 2018."*[172]

"Orion is over 100 miles up and going over 17,000 mph. **Just as it passes over the Indian Ocean, we lose communication. This is expected. The communications link we have through satellites to Orion is momentarily lost,** *but Orion continues to receive and process data."*[173]
- Kelly Smith NASA Engineer Orion Trial by Fire video

"The SEALs made a number of attempts to contact their combat operations center with a multi-band radio and then with a satellite phone. The team could not establish

---

[172] https://www.pixalytics.com/satellites-orbiting-Earth-2019/
[173] https://www.youtube.com/watch?v=KyZqSWWKmHQ

consistent communication, other than for a period long enough to indicate that they were under attack."[174]
- Operation Red Wings (Lone Survivor) communication failure

The subject of satellites usually comes up when talking to someone who does not believe in Biblical cosmology (aka flat earth). Several years ago, a United States Air Force captain shared with me that he was informed while in the Air Force that satellites (as they have been explained to the public) do not exist. And a friend of mine that was a United States Army Ranger and Special Operations soldier told me an interesting story about a mission he was on years ago. He was part of the Ranger detachment assigned to the 101st Airborne Division at Ft. Campbell, Kentucky that was sent south of our border to extract a certain individual. Part of his job on the mission was to use his "satellite" phone to notify the team that would be picking them up about whether it would be a "hot extraction" (under enemy fire) or not. Long story short, the Rangers were spotted and under fire but when he tried to notify the pick-up team, he did not have a "satellite" signal to make the call. After successfully making it out, the commanders back at base questioned my friend about why he did not alert them to the "hot extraction." He told them that he never got a signal on the "satellite" phone. He said that they all looked at each other and smiled and then said, *"All communication is land-based, next time just make the call."*

In late 2015, I saw an article about a military airship that got loose from a base in Maryland, *"An unmanned Army surveillance blimp broke loose from its ground tether at a*

[174] *Victory Point: Operations Red Wings and Whalers - The Marine Corps' Battle for Freedom in Afghanistan* by Ed Darack ©2009 The Berkley Publishing Group

military base in Maryland on Wednesday and drifted over central Pennsylvania as two Air Force fighter jets tracked it. The blimp's long tether snapped power lines, causing outages. A North American Aerospace Defense Command spokesman confirmed to CBS News that the blimp landed in Montour County, Pennsylvania, CBS News national security correspondent David Martin reports. NORAD said the blimp detached from its station at Aberdeen Proving Ground, Maryland, at about 12:20 p.m., and initially traveled north at an altitude of about 16,000 feet."[175]

After hearing from ex-military and seeing articles like this, I started digging into the subject. I never thought that the current, modern U.S. military would be using any kind of balloons or airships. And the brainwashing and constant programming we receive from the media and movies like *Patriot Games* and *Enemy of the State* make us believe that our military and worldwide communications are done through these technical wonders called "satellites" that allegedly orbit a spherical, ball earth in "outer space." A 2005 technical note from the RAND Corporation entitled, *"High-Altitude Airships for the Future Force Army"* stated, *"The U.S. Army's combat operations in Afghanistan and Iraq in 2001 and 2003, respectively, showed that the forces lacked adequate intra-unit communications...Potential alternative platforms are solar-powered high-altitude airships and airplanes flying at or above 65,000 feet. Aircraft payloads could support communications suites, such as the Adaptive Joint C4ISR Node (AJCN), and surveillance suites similar to Global Hawk equipment and space-based radar.*"[176]

---

[175] https://www.cbsnews.com/news/military-blimp-maryland-fighter-jets-pennsylvania/

[176] https://www.rand.org/content/dam/rand/pubs/technical_reports/2005/RAND_TR423.pdf

SPENCER ACKERMAN   SECURITY 04.01.11 18:58 AM

Cameras, Spy Balloons Surge in Afghanistan

Share

f   SHARE

🐦   TWEET

💬   COMMENT

✉   EMAIL

Of course, RAND claimed that high-altitude balloon platforms are needed because "satellites" are too expensive and difficult to use. So, the troops needed high-altitude balloons for reconnaissance and communications over the battlefield. But, you will learn in this chapter that the real reason the military needs high-altitude balloons is because there are no "satellites" in make-believe "outer space," orbiting the earth at 17,000 mph as they transmit communication signals all around a ball earth.

An article from MIT Technology Review in 2018 entitled, ***"The US military is testing stratospheric balloons that ride the wind so they never have to come down"*** seems to have accidentally exposed that NASA's early "satellites" were actually balloons. The article states:

*"A sensor that can spot the wind direction from miles away will let DARPA's surveillance balloons hover at the very edge of space in one spot indefinitely...**It's not a new idea. Indeed, the original stratospheric balloons were flown by NASA in the 1950s, and the agency still uses them for***

science missions. And Project Loon, owned by Google's parent company Alphabet, successfully deployed such balloons to provide mobile communications in the aftermath of Hurricane Maria in Puerto Rico.

There's a major snag, though: current balloons shift with the wind and can only stay in one area for a few days at a time. At the height of the stratosphere, some 60,000 feet (18,300 meters) up, winds blow in different directions at different altitudes. In theory it should be possible to find a wind blowing in any desired direction simply by changing altitude. But while machine learning and better data are improving navigation, the progress is gradual.

DARPA, the US military's research arm, thinks it may have cracked the problem. It is currently testing a wind sensor that could allow devices in its Adaptable Lighter-Than-Air (ALTA) balloon program to spot wind speed and direction from a great distance and then make the necessary adjustments to stay in one spot. DARPA has been working on ALTA for some time, but its existence was only revealed in September.

'By flying higher we hope to take advantage of a larger range of winds,' says ALTA project manager Alex Walan. ALTA will operate even higher than Loon at 75,000 to 90,000 feet (22,900 to 27,400 meters or 14 to 17 miles), where the winds are less predictable. That shouldn't be a problem if the balloon can see exactly where the favorable winds are.

The wind sensor, called Strat-OAWL (short for "stratospheric optical autocovariance wind lidar"), is a new version of one originally designed for NASA satellites. Made by Ball Aerospace, OAWL shines pulses of laser light *into the air. A small fraction of the beam is reflected back, and the reflected laser light is gathered by a telescope. The wavelength of the reflected light is changed slightly depending on how fast the air it bounced back from is moving, a change known as doppler shift. By analyzing this shift, OAWL can determine the speed and direction of the wind."*[177]

Did you catch that? DARPA designed a new wind sensor so their high-altitude balloons can better navigate and stay aloft. Then, the article says that the new WIND SENSOR is just a new version of one originally designed for ***NASA satellites***. Why would NASA "satellites" (that are supposed to be in the weightless, empty vacuum of "outer space" where there is no wind) need a sophisticated WIND SENSOR to help them navigate and stay aloft? Because NASA "satellites" are nothing more than high-altitude balloons. That's why NASA needed wind sensors on their "satellites."

The following CIA document from the 1960s was declassified in 2004. It states that their "program goal" in 1969 was to develop a "PHOTO BALLOON" reconnaissance system capable of steerable and stationary flight up to 200,000 feet.[178] Again, if we had ball earth-orbiting "satellites" in "outer space," why would we need balloons to reach 200,000 feet? Why would we need to make them capable of steerable and stationary flight?

---

[177] https://www.technologyreview.com/s/612417/darpa-is-testing-stratospheric-balloons-that-ride-the-wind-so-they-never-have-to-come-down/

[178] https://www.cia.gov/library/readingroom/docs/CIA-RDP75B00159R000100010013-6.pdf

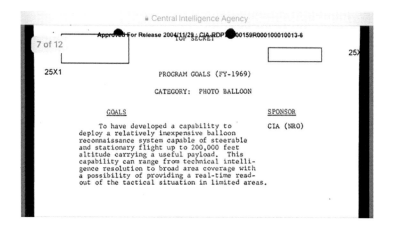

This is why NASA Engineer Kelly Smith is quoted saying they expect to lose communication over the Indian Ocean. This is also why a jet pilot with 30 years of experience told me there is a "communications gap" over the Atlantic Ocean. They lose communication when a ground-based cellular tower is not in range. It's that simple. Just like the rest of us lose cell signal when we get too far from a cell tower. The pilot also told me about tethered balloons (one 14,000 feet high) that they use to help with radar tracking and communications.

Google's Project Loon is another discovery that confirms there are not thousands of communications "satellites." Google planned to use high-altitude balloons in the stratosphere (11-20 miles high or between 58,000 and 105,000 feet) to provide internet access to rural and remote areas. This started in 2008 when they considered contracting with or acquiring Space Data Corp which is a company that uses high-altitude balloons as radio repeaters to extend communications to truckers, oil companies, and the military. However, Google decided not to do business with Space Data Corp and created their own version. From 2011 to 2016 they continued to test and perfect their Project Loon system.[179] In May 2017, Space Data Corp filed a lawsuit against Google for patent infringement and settled out of court in July 2019. The article reads, ***"Google has settled a singular intellectual property case that involves the deployment of balloons in the stratosphere to provide wireless communications on earth."***[180]

After a corporate restructuring of Google in 2015, Project Loon became Loon LLC which is a subsidiary of Alphabet Inc. located in Mountain View, California. Loon LLC's website reads, *"In 2011, Billions of people around the world are still without internet access. Loon is a network of balloons traveling on the edge of space, delivering connectivity to people in unserved and underserved communities around the world. In 2013, one of our balloons completes a lap around the world in 22 days and clocks the project's 500,000th kilometer as it begins its second lap. These learnings lead to major improvements in wind prediction models, balloon trajectory, forecast, and navigation. A sheep farmer in Canterbury, New Zealand is the first person to connect to balloon-powered internet through an internet antenna attached to the roof of his home. Project Loon is revealed to the public, which helps to explain some UFO sightings that were reported after testing around the world.*

In 2014, a local school in Agua Fria, in the rural outskirts of Campo Maior, Brazil is connected to the internet for the first time, through a balloon launched nearby. ***This marks Project Loon's first successful LTE connection. Loon balloons log a significant milestone of traveling 3 million***

---

[179] https://en.wikipedia.org/wiki/Loon_(company)

[180] https://www.law.com/therecorder/2019/07/29/google-settles-ip-case-over-high-altitude-balloons/?slreturn=20190701152031

kilometers through the stratosphere, a distance that would get you to the moon and back nearly 4 times. Millions of kilometers of test flights help us to more accurately predict wind patterns at different altitudes, giving us the best chance to keep our balloons where we need them.

In 2016, One of our Latin America flights manages to keep our balloon aloft in Peruvian airspace for a total of 98 days, making nearly 20,000 separate altitude adjustments. In 2017, Working together with Telefonica and the Peruvian Government, Project Loon delivers basic connectivity to tens of thousands of people in flood affected areas across the country. At 20 km up in the stratosphere, Loon balloons can provide connectivity where it's needed, regardless of what's happening below. ***And in 2017, Collaborating with the Federal Communications Commission, the Federal Aviation Authority, FEMA, AT&T, T-Mobile, and many others, Project Loon provides basic connectivity to 200,000 people in Puerto Rico after Hurricane Maria.*** *Project Loon launches balloons from Nevada, using machine learning algorithms to direct them over Puerto Rico."*[181]

Again, what happened to "satellite" communications? Don't we have "satellite" TV? The answer is…no we don't. At least not as we have been made to believe. Just take a look at **Space Data Corp** and their website. They call their high-altitude balloon communications system ***SkySat***. Do you catch the connection? They are calling the balloon system a "satellite." They are not hiding what "satellites" really are, but most people are not willing to give up the make-believe "satellites." The following confirms what my military sources have told me because the United States military currently uses this company and their ***SkySat*** system:

---

[181] https://loon.com/journey/

"Space Data's SkySat™ Repeater Platform extends the range of standard issue military two-way radios from 10 miles to nearly 500 miles. The SkySat™ Platform's cutting-edge technology is currently being used by the United States Air Force.

SkySat™ uses high-altitude radio repeaters which allow troops to instantly relay critical combat information and data to forward deployed troops or combat air support under any conditions, including rugged terrain, remote areas, and even sandstorms. This platform is a low-cost system that has many applications for a wide range of government programs, including border control and disaster response communications. The concept is simple: fill a balloon with helium or hydrogen and attach a Space Data radio repeater payload. Once launched and on its way to a roughly 80,000-foot float, a SkySat™ Platform provides users' portable radio systems with the same communications coverage previously available only via bulky and expensive satellite equipment.

The balloon-borne communications system has exceptional capability for continuous operations in rural and remote locations and provides users with the means for a rapid launch. With a weight of 12 pounds or less, the balloon payload can be quickly deployed with minimal effort and manpower.

The current production version SkySat™ Payload operates as a military-UHF repeater, covering 225-375 MHz. Other band coverage can be engineered to meet user needs.

Another increasingly common mission for the SkySat™ Payload is to serve as a means to carry another payload, *suspended beneath it, to altitudes above 65,000 feet to carry out a variety of special purpose missions, including intelligence, surveillance, and reconnaissance. The SkySat Platform provides a short-range two-way communication link between itself and the suspended payload to support command and control of, and low-rate telemetry from, the lower payload, all through the SkySat™ Platform's command and control link with its standard ground station."*[182]

Of course, this is just the tip of the iceberg. I have done hours of research; others have done similar research and you can do your own and connect the dots to discover that balloon "satellite" projects have been going on in the military and NASA for a very long time. In fact, NASA's first "satellites" were balloons with retrievable payloads. Here's a description from NASA's website:

*"**NASA launched the Echo I communications balloon satellite on Aug. 12, 1960. The 100-foot-diameter (30.5 meter) satellite, designed by the Space Vehicle Group of the NASA Langley Research Center** and constructed by General Mills of Minneapolis, Minnesota, was shown during ground inflation tests in 1959. Suspended from the ceiling of a hangar the sphere, named "Echo," was inflated by use of a blower connected to the satellite by a hose. Forty thousand pounds (18,144 kg) of air was required to inflate the sphere on the ground, **while in orbit it only required several pounds of gas to keep it inflated.***

Echo was a passive communications satellite which reflected radio and radar signals as a limited communications relay. It was also used, over a period of

———————————
[182] https://www.spacedata.net/government/skysat/

time and with accurate tracking, to plot the variations in air density at the top of the atmosphere by following the vagaries of its orbit. Weighing 150 pounds (68 kg), the satellite was inflated in space. It did not have a rigid skin and accordingly was used at high altitudes where it would be subjected to negligible aerodynamic drag force. To keep the sphere inflated in spite of meteorite punctures and skin permeability, a make-up gas system using evaporating liquid or crystals of a sublimimg solid were incorporated inside the satellite."[183]

It is hard to believe that NASA would release information identifying their first communication "satellite" as a balloon, but of course I believe they must in order to "play by God's rules." As I shared previously, they did launch a rocket that punched into the dense aether level of our sky at approximately 73 miles high. Then they deployed and inflated the balloon "satellite" into the circular current of the dense blue aether gas (I believe this aether current also

[183] https://www.nasa.gov/centers/langley/about/project-echo.html

moves the sun and moon in their circular orbits over the flat earth). But NASA makes the ridiculous claim that this balloon "satellite" reached an altitude of over 1,000 miles (5,280,000 feet) when they claim the International Space Station only reaches 250 miles high:

"Echo 1A (commonly referred to as just Echo 1) was put successfully into a 944-to-1,048-mile (1,519 to 1,687 km) orbit by another Thor-Delta, and a microwave transmission from the Jet Propulsion Laboratory in Pasadena, California, was received at Bell Laboratories in Holmdel, New Jersey, on August 12, 1960.

The 30.5-meter (100 ft) diameter balloon was made of 0.5-mil-thick (12.7 μm) metalized 0.2-micrometer-thick (0.00787-mil) biaxially oriented PET film ("Mylar") material, and it was used to redirect transcontinental and intercontinental telephone, radio, and television signals. The satellite also aided the calculation of atmospheric density and solar pressure due to its large area-to-mass ratio. As its shiny surface was also reflective in the range of visible light, **Echo 1A was easily visible to the unaided eye over most of the earth.** *The spacecraft was nicknamed a 'satelloon' by those involved in the project, as a portmanteau of satellite-balloon."*

Another laughable aspect of the story that this satelloon orbited at an altitude of 1,000 miles in the empty vacuum of "space" is that they claim it was visible to the unaided eye over most of the earth. This is just beyond ridiculous. An airplane flying at 40,000 feet (just over 7 miles high) looks like a small speck in the sky, but they say that we could see the reflection off of a balloon that is supposedly 1,000 miles away…ludicrous! However, if Echo 1 was actually "orbiting" over the flat earth at an altitude of 386,000 to

500,000 feet (73 to 95 miles high) in the aether current, then it makes sense that it could be seen with the unaided eye over most of the earth. It also explains how it was able to stay inflated that long, how it was able "...*to plot the variations in air density at the top of the atmosphere,*" and how it was used to "redirect" telephone, radio, and television signals much like the Project Loon and Space Data Corp balloon "satellite" systems.

Furthermore, a simple, repeatable experiment like placing a balloon into a vacuum chamber proves that NASA has been lying about what "space" really is and where they have been going ever since the very beginning. A balloon in a vacuum chamber bursts within seconds of the air is sucked out. They tell us that the vacuum of space is $1\times10\text{-}6$ to $<3\times10\text{-}17$ Torr (a unit of pressure used in measuring partial vacuums). If that were true, there is just no way that a man-made balloon of any kind could stay inflated in that strong of a vacuum. This is the strongest evidence that balloon "satellites" "orbit" in a much different atmosphere than what they call "outer space."

The following is from the NASA history page telling the story of the Echo 1 balloon: *"O'Sullivan, the scientific wizard of Langley's PARD, still sat at the hotel desk, perched on the horns of this dilemma. Finally, in the early hours of the morning, he arrived at a possible solution: **why not build the sphere out of a thin material that could be folded into a small nose cone? If the sphere could be packed snugly into a strong container, it could easily withstand the acceleration loads of takeoff and come through the extreme heating unscathed. After the payload container reached orbit, the folded satellite could be unfolded and inflated pneumatically into shape.** Finding a means of inflation should not be difficult. Either a small tank of* compressed gas such as nitrogen, or a liquid that would readily evaporate into a gas, or even some solid material that would evaporate to form a gas (such as the material used to make mothballs) could be used to accomplish the inflation. (He apparently had not yet thought of using residual air as the inflation agent, as in Shotput 1) Almost no air pressure existed at orbiting altitude, so a small amount of gas would do the job. 'Clearly then,' O'Sullivan concluded, *'that is how the satellite had to work.'*

Other critical questions still needed answers. Surely, if he presented his notion of an inflatable satellite to the prestigious scientific panel the next day, someone would ask him to specify its construction material. **The material had to be flexible enough to be folded, strong enough to withstand being unfolded and inflated to shape, and stiff enough to keep its shape even if punctured by micrometeoroids.** O'Sullivan reviewed the properties of the materials with which he was familiar and quickly realized that "no one of them satisfied all the requirements." Next he tried combining materials. The forming of thin sheet metal into certain desired shapes was a standard procedure in many manufacturing industries, but sheet metal thin enough for the skin of his satellite would tear easily during the folding and unfolding. **Perhaps, thought O'Sullivan, some tough but flexible material, something like a plastic film, could be bonded to the metal foil.**

Here was another critical part of the answer to O'Sullivan's satellite design problem: a sandwich or laminate material of metal foil and plastic film. *'I could compactly fold a satellite made of such a material so that it could easily withstand being transported into orbit, and once in orbit, I could easily inflate it tautly,* stretching the wrinkles out of it and forming it into a sphere whose skin *would be stiff enough so that it would stay spherical under the minute aerodynamic and solar pressure loads without having to retain its internal gas pressure.' Such a thin-skin satellite would be so aerodynamically sensitive that even a minute amount of drag would cause a noticeable alteration in its orbit. Researchers on the ground could track the sphere, measuring where and when it was being pushed even slightly off course, and thereby compute the density of the air in that part of the atmosphere."[184]*

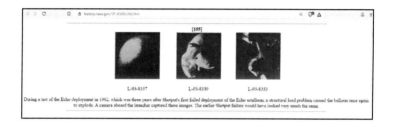

During a test of the Echo deployment in 1962, which was three years after Shotput's first failed deployment of the Echo satelloon, a structural load problem caused the balloon once again to explode. A camera aboard the launcher captured these images. The earlier Shotput failure would have looked very much the same.

CIA, NSA & NASA Documents on Balloon Satellites

Prior to NASA's Echo 1 and Echo 2, the following FOIA CIA document dated May 29, 1958 reveals a plan for a high-altitude balloon "satellite" equipped with what they call an Elint platform:

MEMORANDUM FOR THE RECORD

SUBJECT: High Altitude Power Balloon

REFERENCE: Memorandum for AC/TSS/R&D (research and development) dated 29 April 1958, from C/TSS/Engineering Division

[184] https://history.nasa.gov/SP-4308/ch6.htm

1. On 21 May the undersigned visited (redacted) of OSI for the purpose of discussing possible applications of a high-altitude power balloon in fields of interest to OSI. After a brief discussion Mr. (redacted) to join the discussion. The memorandum references the following possible uses for such an item were presented as probably worthy of further consideration:

(a) satellite research vehicle tracking

(b) **Elint platform**

(c) infrared scanning antenna combined with flame spectragraphy for missile tracking

2. (Redacted) mentioned and infrared antenna under development by the army at White Sands that might advantageously be operated at altitudes under consideration for the powered balloon.

3. It was suggested that the idea of the powered balloon be taken up directly with Mr. Bissell's staff.[185]

---

[185] https://www.cia.gov/library/readingroom/docs/CIA-RDP78-03642A001300040022-9.pdf

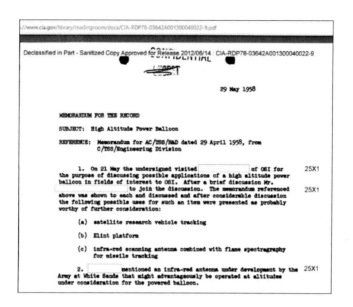

29 May 1958

MEMORANDUM FOR THE RECORD

SUBJECT: High Altitude Power Balloon

REFERENCE: Memorandum for AC/TSS/R&D dated 29 April 1958, from C/TSS/Engineering Division

1. On 21 May the undersigned visited [____] of OSI for 25X1 the purpose of discussing possible applications of a high altitude power balloon in fields of interest to OSI. After a brief discussion Mr. [____] to join the discussion. The memorandum referenced 25X1 above was shown to each and discussed and after considerable discussion the following possible uses for such an item were presented as probably worthy of further consideration:

(a) satellite research vehicle tracking

(b) Elint platform

(c) infra-red scanning antenna combined with flame spectragraphy for missile tracking

2. [____] mentioned an infra-red antenna under development by the 25X1 Army at White Sands that might advantageously be operated at altitudes under consideration for the powered balloon.

This document (two years before Echo 1) exposes the fact that early "satellites" were just special high-altitude balloons injected or inserted into the dense aether level/current by a rocket. I found further confirmation of this when I went digging to find out what "Elint platform" meant. That led me to the NSA website and an NSA PDF that explained it all. According to the NSA document entitled, *Electronic Intelligence (ELINT) at NSA*, ELINT is information derived primarily from electronic signals that do not contain speech or text (which are considered COMINT). The document goes on to say, ***"Since the early 1960s, NSA had been a participant in the NRO and US Navy-led GRAB and POPPY efforts to collect ELINT on Soviet air defense radar signals from an orbiting satellite.*** *Intelligence from GRAB and POPPY provided the location and capabilities of Soviet radar sites and ocean surveillance information to the U.S. Navy and for use by the USAF. This effort provided* *significant ELINT support to US forces throughout the war in Vietnam.*"[186]

Here's the NSA's information on the GRAB "satellite" which also reveals that they don't always tell the truth about "satellites," as they admit to the dual mission: ***"The GRAB II Elint Satellite or (Galactic Radiation And Background) satellite depicts one of the earliest signals intelligence satellites launched by the U.S. Government. The first GRAB satellite was launched on June 22, 1960 following the loss in May of the U-2 spy plane flown by Gary Powers.*** *The successful launch of the GRAB II satellite occurred on June 29, 1961.* ***The GRAB satellites had a dual mission. The unclassified mission was to gather solar radiation data. The secret mission gathered radar pulses within a specific bandwidth from Soviet equipment.*** *The data was then downloaded to ground stations, recorded on magnetic tape, and couriered to the NRL, whose engineers had designed and built GRAB. Following initial analysis, the tapes were duplicated and sent to Strategic Air Command and the National Security Agency (NSA). Based on the information NSA received, analysts determined that the Soviets had radars that supported the capability to destroy ballistic missiles.*"[187]

As I was researching the GRAB "satellite" and the ELINT system, I came across a picture of the GRAB "satellite" being loaded into the nose cone of the rocket that would punch it into its aether orbit. The picture clearly shows the Mylar tinfoil-looking balloon neatly folded and installed into the top of the rocket nose cone just slightly above the

---

[186] https://www.nsa.gov/Portals/70/documents/about/cryptologic-heritage/historical-figures-publications/publications/misc/elint.pdf

[187] https://www.nsa.gov/about/cryptologic-heritage/museum/exhibits/#grabii

"satellite." This picture of GRAB, the information from the 1958 CIA document on powered balloon "satellites" and the NASA information on the packing of the Echo 1 "satellite" balloon really put the "nail in the coffin." There should be no question about what "satellites" are or the true nature of the realm they call "outer space."

As I continued my research, I found another declassified CIA document dated January 4, 1971 that recounts the history of the CORONA program. The document title reads, **"CORONA: The First Photographic Reconnaissance Satellite."**[188]

And then a declassified document from the National Reconnaissance Office entitled, *"Space and Missile Systems Center Los Angeles Air Force Base, California SMC/HO Oral History Program Interview with LIEUTENANT COLONEL HAROLD E. MITCHELL CORONA PROGRAM (Interview No. 6),"* clearly reveals the Corona "satellites" to be balloons with gondolas.

Those gondolas were filled with Corona spy cameras, film, and the electronics to communicate with the balloons and even remotely bring them down to be retrieved by a specially-equipped aircraft. Lt. Col. Mitchell was the **"Recovery Pilot for the Drag Net/Genetrix Program (1954-1956) and the Discoverer/Corona Program (1958-1962)."** The date of the interview was October 1, 2003.

---

[188] https://www.cia.gov/library/readingroom/docs/CIA-RDP66R00546R000100060062-1.pdf

Space and Missile Systems Center
Los Angeles Air Force Base, California
SMC/HO Oral History Program

Interview With

LIEUTENANT COLONEL HAROLD E. MITCHELL

CORONA PROGRAM
(Interview No. 6)

*C-119 (Aircraft 818037) recovering a parachute and
capsule near Hawaii*

Mulcahy: Before Corona was declassified, did you ever say or hear the word "Corona" again after that briefing?

Mitchell: No.

Mulcahy: How did the C-119 recovery equipment change from Genetrix to Discoverer?

Mitchell: Those Genetrix gondolas weighed about 1400 pounds. When you tried to recover a 110-pound or 140-pound package with the steel cable on the winches, the cable all came winding back in on you; contact with the parachute would cause a backlash and snap the cable. In that regard, aerial recovery was like fishing. You get a backlash, and it comes all back in on your reel and that's what it did with the light payloads.

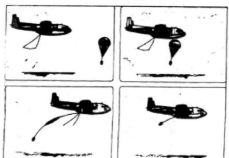

A C-119 performing a midair parachute and capsule recovery

21

"In 1954, Drag Net [Program, also called the Genetrix Program or Weapon System 119L] came along. That was the code name that we used for the program (as far as the crews were concerned) in our training at Charleston, South Carolina. There was a lot of speculation at that time about what was going on. If my memory serves me correctly, in March of 1955 we started sending our C-119s back to Hagerstown, Maryland to have them modified with the beavertail door, rather than the clamshell door that was the initial design for airborne support aircraft. In addition to that, the old airplanes had just a single nose wheel. They modified them and put on a co-rotating dual nose wheel system, so we wouldn't have the problems with the single nose wheel shimmying. We transitioned into two different models of the C-119 at that time, those built by Fairchild and those by Kaiser-Frazier.

I believe it was in November 1954, when we sent three crews to Langley AFB [Virginia] with an Air Force captain. I can't recall his name. He worked with All American Engineering, and he was the first Air Force pilot checked out in aerial recovery. These three crews were the initial crews checked out in air recovery for the Genetrix Program. After their training, they came home and started checking out more crews.

The gondola was probably about five feet high. It was just as wide, except the bottom of it was beveled on each lower corner so that your side-looking cameras were aimed out at an angle. The other camera was straight down. The top of the gondola had a compartment for the parachutes and all that stuff. A lot of it had to be the parachutes, but the whole capsule was 1450 pounds when it was airlifted. The gondola had a huge balloon. I mean a huge balloon! You could see it at 60,000 to 85,000 feet...once it was inflated. With the helium it carried, that balloon was designed to go, during the day, to about 85,000 feet. As nighttime came and the gas cooled down, it would come down' to around 60,000 to 65,000 feet.

We sighted the balloon at about 85,000 feet. After you sighted a balloon, you'd interrogate it. The balloon's radio signal would give you its code name, or code number. If you wanted to terminate its flight, you had a black box up on the flight deck at the navigator's station. He would dial in the code of the balloon we were trying to track, and the balloon would come back and answer. Then if we had clearance from the Charleston AFB command post to bring the balloon down, we would insert another code. This, then would ignite a blast from the gondola that would burst the balloon. After we terminated the flight of the balloon, it would do very much the same as the Discoverer did. It would fall so far and then the drogue chute would conic out. The chute would slow it down until it was at an acceptable altitude and airspeed, and then the parachute would get fully deployed. It was late in the evening when they authorized me then to terminate the balloon.

*The balloons were launched from Norway, Denmark, West Germany; and I think some from Turkey. In the winter [February] of 1956, there was an article in **Time Magazine** about the Russians complaining about our over flight of the Soviet Union with these **balloons.** They had any number of the gondolas stacked in the [Spiridonvka Palace] driveway of Foreign Minister [Vyacheslav] Molotov. It was just unbelievable. He had many of them. **An interesting fact, the airplane I flew during the Corona Program [C-119 #18037], had more recoveries of balloons than any airplane in our 456th Wing.** It was flown by Capt. Slaughter Minims, and I think Slaughter recovered three balloons near*

Japan. He got more than anybody else. Slaughter had a lot of success with #037, as I did.

We called it Drag Net. Genetrix was the classified code name for the program, like. Corona and Discoverer. Dr. [Alvin H.] Howell was the brains behind the balloon program. "[189]

Declassified U.S. government documents clearly identify the first photographic reconnaissance "satellites" as high-altitude balloons carrying CORONA spy cameras over Russia and other denied territories. "Satellites" are not tinfoil covered boxes orbiting a mythical spherical earth in the 3,100-degree Fahrenheit thermosphere of "outer space" or anywhere else in their imaginary endless vacuum.

However, here is the final and most amazing "smoking gun" that proves "satellites" are still carried on balloons. It is an old declassified document that I quoted from NASA's website in the chapter entitled *"The Secrets of Antarctica."* It tells of NASA launching balloons in Antarctica to take advantage of the special winds there. That 2012 article states, *"The Long Duration Balloons (LDB) site was established at Willy Field, McMurdo Station in order to take advantage of the stratospheric anticyclone wind pattern circulating from east to west around the south pole. **The stratospheric wind circulation combined with the sparsely populated continent of Antarctica allows for long duration balloon flight at altitudes about 100,000 feet. <u>One circumnavigation of the pole takes approximately 14 days.</u>** "*

[189] https://www.nro.gov/Portals/65/documents/foia/declass/WS117L_Records/129.PDF

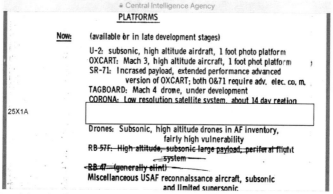

PLATFORMS

Now: (available or in late development stages)

U-2: subsonic, high altitude airdraft, 1 foot photo platform
OXCART: Mach 3, high altitude aircraft, 1 foot phot platform
SR-71: Incrased payload, extended performance advanced
version of OXCART; both O&71 require adv. elec. co. m.
TAGBOARD: Mach 4 drone, under development
CORONA: Low resolution satellite system. about 14 dav reation

25X1A

Drones: Subsonic, high altitude drones in AF inventory,
fairly high vulnerability
RB-57F: High altitude, subsonic large payload, periferal flight
system
RB-47 (generally elint)
Miscellaneous USAF reconnaissance aircraft, subsonic
and limited supersonic.

In this declassified CIA document from the 1960s, they are listing "available or in late development stages" reconnaissance platforms. First notice that they did not list "space satellites," but the CORONA "satellite" system that had a 14-day reation (Meaning 14 days to recover in mid-air. Reate is British for crowfoot which gives the picture of a bird grabbing something). Note that the 14 days to retrieve the CORONA "satellite" system just happens to be the exact same number of days that NASA says it takes to retrieve the balloon "satellites" they launched in Antarctica in 2012. Also, note that the part under the CORONA 14-day "satellite" system is still redacted which means there is something still classified about that because they are still using it.

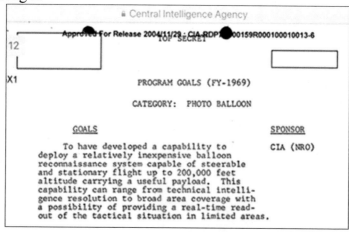

Approved For Release 2004/11/29 : CIA-RDP1●00159R000100010013-6
TOP SECRET

12

X1

PROGRAM GOALS (FY-1969)

CATEGORY: PHOTO BALLOON

GOALS   SPONSOR

To have developed a capability to   CIA (NRO)
deploy a relatively inexpensive balloon
reconnaissance system capable of steerable
and stationary flight up to 200,000 feet
altitude carrying a useful payload. This
capability can range from technical intelligence resolution to broad area coverage with
a possibility of providing a real-time read-
out of the tactical situation in limited areas.

Lights in the Sky

It is a fact that NASA/military possess high-altitude aircraft which include the U2, the SR-71, and the mysterious and highly secretive X-37B Space Plane Drone that acts much like the Space Shuttle except it is unmanned. Along with these aircraft, NASA/military also possess other very strange looking aircraft/spacecraft that (I believe) have been used in regularly repeated flight paths at various altitudes. These give the appearance of "orbiting satellites," so I think this could be some of what people see moving across the sky at night.

But let us not forget something else that I pointed out earlier in this book, the spiritual forces of Satan, his fallen angels and demons can and do create deceptive light shows in the sky like UFOs. Couldn't these same demonic forces create the very fast-moving lights people see shooting across the sky to perpetrate the "satellite/outer space" deception? Isn't it an obvious deduction to understand that these fallen angels and demons are in league with their Freemason/Illuminati/Jesuit/Nazi accomplices in governments and NASA?

X-37B "Space" Plane

Remember, the Bible calls Satan *"the god of this world"* (2 Corinthians 4) and *"the prince and power of the air"*

411

(Ephesians 2) and that he (Satan) and his ministers can also appear to be *"angels of light"* (2 Corinthians 11). In fact, the Bible states that stars and angels are one and the same (Revelation 1:20). Could these entities be pretending to be "satellites" or even the ISS in transit across the moon just like they pretend to be UFOs and "aliens?"

I bring this up because I saw where Dr. Danny Faulkner made an argument against flat earthers using his observation of "satellites" and different degrees and angles of perception. Here's his argument, *"Flat Earthers claim that satellites that we can see in the early evening or morning sky are drones. But have flat earthers worked out the details for this? Suppose that I see an eastward traveling satellite pass directly overhead. If the satellite is traveling at a little more than 17,000 mph (as it must in low-earth orbit), the satellite will pass overhead to an observer due east of me 0.2 seconds later. Can a drone explain this? How high is the drone? Suppose that the drone is 1,000 feet high. Then when I see it overhead, the observer to the east will see the drone 11 degrees up (tangent [1,000/5280]). But I will see the drone that high (11 degrees) just 0.2 seconds later. And the drone would have been only 11 degrees high in the other part of the sky just 0.2 seconds before it was high overhead. Thus, from my perspective, the satellite would take 0.4 seconds to go most of the way across the sky. I've seen many satellites. They don't travel nearly that fast. Making the drone lower only worsens the problem. Making it go higher helps, but then there is the speed problem. The drone must be moving 17,000 mph. Without a sonic boom.*

Maybe there are two drones, one for me, and one for the guy down the road. That way, the drones can fly lower and slower. That might work, but then how do the people running these drones know who will be looking and where they might be? And what of the other thousands of people over many miles who will see this satellite? Wouldn't that require thousands of drones? Then there are other satellites as well. You might say that people look these things up, say, on their cell phones, and then the fleet of drones are sent out to meet the expectations. But then many times people reverse engineer this. They see a satellite, and then they go online to see what satellite they just saw. That way, Big Brother can't intercept your searches and send out the fleets. No, the only way this would work is if there are many tens of thousands or millions of drones sent out every evening and morning to fake us all out. How many people are in on this? Wouldn't it require a huge number of people to be in the know?"

And what about those satellites that I saw over a half century ago, long before there were drones? Have any of you flat earthers spent any time thinking about what monumental problems this silly answer to what satellites are entails?"[190]

But again, I reiterate, has Faulkner considered that Satan and his forces could be deceiving him and the rest of the world with false signs and wonders in the heavens calling it technology when it is really something supernatural? Furthermore, does he really think that he has a full understanding of everything our government has done or is doing at very high altitudes? There could be many more drones and special balloons up there than we will ever know about. But (the alleged Christian astronomer), Dr. Faulkner doesn't understand another principle and that is when you choose not to believe any part of God's Word, then you are far more susceptible to be deceived by Satan and his servants (and many of Satan's servants are in positions of power and influence in all fields).

---

[190] Copied from a Facebook post on a Flat Earth page

"Global" Communications and GPS

An April 2, 2015 article in *Newsweek* reported, ***"In our wireless, satellite-broadcasted world, it's easy to forget that most of our electronic communications still run through wires. This includes the vast majority of international calls, text messages and Internet transmissions, which must be ferried through cables that stretch across continents at the bottom of the ocean.***

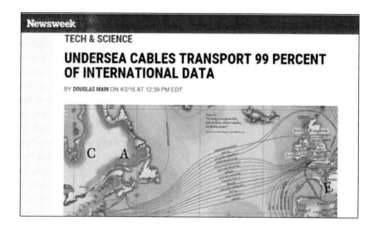

These undersea cables are easy to forget, since they are well out of sight and mind. ***But without them, the world as we know it would cease to exist,*** *and their history is fascinating, says Nicole Starosielski, an assistant professor of media, culture and communication at New York University. Starosielski first looked into the topic while in grad school at U.C. Santa Barbara, at her adviser's behest; she thought it would be boring, but she instead found herself enthralled, and ended up writing one of the first books on the topic called The Undersea Network.*

What is something most people don't know about undersea cables?

Most people probably don't know that 99 percent of all transoceanic data traffic goes through undersea cables, and that includes Internet usage, phone calls and text messages."[191]

That's right…you read it correctly that "…***99 percent of all transoceanic data traffic goes through undersea cables, and that includes Internet usage, phone calls and text messages.***" Most people live under the illusion that the vast, majority of world-wide communications are routed through orbiting or geosynchronous "satellites" circling the spherical earth in "outer space." Alas, it's just another fairytale from the government that the masses blindly accept. But as we have discovered, the truth always leaks out. This truth was reported by the New York Times, CNN and other news outlets in 2015 when the Russians gave the Pentagon a scare by getting close to those undersea cables.

Similarly, people have been led to believe that the GPS in their car or on their phone is coming from "satellites" in "outer space." But GPS was in existence long before we had the alleged "satellites." It really should stand for Ground Positioning System because it is all ground-based technology. GPS works using triangulation between cell towers or radio transmitters. Of course, when explaining this to someone who believes in "satellites" they might try to debunk it by pointing out that GPS still works for ships at sea. However, this is explained in old U.S. Navy and USAF documentaries on the LORAN system. A 1959 USAF training film called Radio Navigation Operational Techniques of LORAN Skywaves is a good place to start.[192]

---

[191] https://www.newsweek.com/undersea-cables-transport-99-percent-international-communications-319072

[192] https://youtu.be/B73yPnIweDs

"LORAN, short for long range navigation, was a hyperbolic radio navigation system developed in the United States during World War II. It was similar to the UK's Gee system but operated at lower frequencies in order to provide an improved range up to 1,500 miles (2,400 km) with an accuracy of tens of miles. It was first used for ship convoys crossing the Atlantic Ocean, and then by long-range patrol aircraft, but found its main use on the ships and aircraft operating in the Pacific theatre.

LORAN, in its original form, was an expensive system to implement, requiring a cathode ray tube (CRT) display. **This limited use to the military and large commercial users. Automated receivers became available in the 1950s, but the same improved electronics also opened the possibility of new systems with higher accuracy. The US Navy began development of Loran-B, which offered accuracy on the order of a few tens of feet but ran into significant technical problems.** *The US Air Force worked on a different concept, Cyclan, which the Navy took over as Loran-C. Loran-C offered longer range than LORAN and accuracy of hundreds of feet. The US Coast Guard took over operations of both systems in 1958...*

At a 1 October 1940 meeting of the US Army Signal Corps' Technical Committee, Alfred Loomis, chair of the Microwave Committee, proposed building a hyperbolic navigation system. He predicted that such a system could provide an accuracy of at least 1,000 feet (300 m) at a range of 200 miles (320 km), and a maximum range of 300–500 miles (480–800 km) for high-flying aircraft. This led to the 'Precision Navigational Equipment for Guiding Airplanes' specification, which was sent back to the Microwave Committee and formed up as "Project 3." Orders for initial systems were sent out at a follow-up meeting on 20

December 1940. Edward George Bowen, developer of the first airborne radar systems, was also at the 20 December meeting. He stated that he was aware of similar work in the UK but didn't know enough about it to offer any suggestions…

During early experiments with LORAN's skywaves, Jack Pierce noticed that at night the reflective layer in the ionosphere was quite stable. This led to the possibility that two LORAN stations could be synchronized using skywave signals, at least at night, allowing them to be separated over much greater distances. Accuracy of a hyperbolic system is a function of the baseline distance, so if the stations could be spread out, the system would become more accurate, so fewer stations would be needed.

A test system was first attempted on 10 April 1943 between the LORAN stations at Fenwick and Bonavista, 1,100 miles (1,800 km) away. This test demonstrated accuracy of ½ mile, significantly better than normal LORAN. This led to a second round of tests in late 1943, this time using four stations, Montauk, East Brewster, MA, Gooseberry Falls, MO, and Key West, FL. Extensive evaluation flights revealed an average error of 1–2 miles (1.6–3.2 km)."[193]

[193] https://en.m.wikipedia.org/wiki/LORAN

So, you see that we have had the Gee Positioning System long before the era of alleged "satellites" and it was very accurate. The real "GPS" was and still is the LORAN radio wave system, only now they have added microwave cell towers into the mix. All of these deceptions and facts are easy to uncover for those who seek the truth, but so many are more comfortable not knowing. And that is why they are able to keep perpetuating the lies about "satellites," GPS, "outer space," the ISS, "aliens," and the globe earth to keep people from believing the Bible account of creation and finding Jesus as their Lord and Savior.

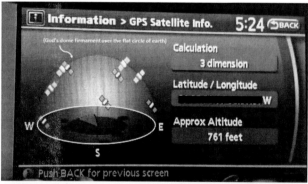

Real picture of a friend's GPS display in their car

Chapter 18

Government Documents Admit Flat Earth

"For there is nothing covered, that shall not be revealed; neither hid, that shall not be known. Therefore whatsoever ye have spoken in darkness shall be heard in the light; and that which ye have spoken in the ear in closets shall be proclaimed upon the housetops. And I say unto you my friends, Be not afraid of them that kill the body, and after that have no more that they can do. But I will forewarn you whom ye shall fear: Fear him, which after he hath killed hath power to cast into hell; yea, I say unto you, Fear him" (Luke 12:2-5).

"The Freedom of Information Act (FOIA) generally provides that any person has the right to request access to federal agency records or information except to the extent the records are protected from disclosure by any of nine exemptions contained in the law or by one of three special law enforcement record exclusions."[194] – Freedom of Information Act Website

---

[194] https://foia.state.gov/learn/foia.aspx

"A federal Court has concisely described the vital role of the FOIA in democracy:

'It has often been observed that the central purpose of the FOIA is to '...open up the workings of government to public scrutiny.' One of the premises of that objective is the belief that 'an informed electorate is vital to the proper operation of a democracy.' A more specific goal implicit in the foregoing principles is to give citizens access to the information on the basis of which government agencies make their decisions, thereby equipping the populace to evaluate and criticize those decisions.'"[195]

"The eyes of the LORD are in every place, beholding the evil and the good" (Proverbs 15:3).

As I stated in chapter 15, I believe that God has given Satan certain guidelines that he and his evil servants must follow. The example I gave of this is when the Lord allowed Satan to attack and test Job but forbade Satan to kill him. Now one of these guidelines Satan must follow is to disclose suppressed truths and their secret plans. He divulges things in ways that only seekers of truth will take the time to search out in order to "connect the dots." God even likes it when He sees someone diligent enough to search out obscure truths, *"It is the glory of God to conceal a thing: but the honour of kings is to search out a matter"* (Proverbs 25:2).

Thus, I believe that the Satanic "elite" (who have infiltrated and pretty much control every government, government agency, and major media outlet) do try to suppress and hide truth from the general public. However,

---

[195] https://en.wikipedia.org/wiki/Freedom_of_Information_Act_(United_States)

they are required to disclose those truths in subtle ways that most people miss or they reveal it in a way that seems like a joke. Like their father Lucifer, they mix some truth in with their lies. But when it comes to aircraft, ballistic missiles, artillery, helicopters, rockets, "space" shuttles, etc. they must build them to actually operate in the real world. This means they must function according to the true physics of the true heavens and earth. That's why Army, Navy, Air Force, FAA, NASA, MIT, and many other technical manuals and research base their equations and formulas on the assumption of a *"...flat, non-rotating earth."*

Of course, the most common excuse I have heard from the naysayers, failed debunkers, and NASA lovers about the phrases ***"non-rotating, flat earth," "based on a flat earth assumption"*** or ***"assuming a flat earth"*** is that those equations based on a flat, non-rotating earth are there to simplify the math. REALLY?! Should MIT or NASA rocket scientists need help to simplify math? Isn't that what they go to school for years and years to learn? Why would they waste time doing fancy equations and math relating to something that they claim doesn't exist? Don't they have to factor in the curve of the earth when designing or calculating how a supersonic aircraft, guided missile or artillery shell will fly and where they will land? Why would anyone ever waste time on a flat earth equation if the earth is a sphere curving 8 inches per miles squared? Sorry... but I call bull on that lame excuse.

This is not to say that the math for a spherical earth doesn't exist in some of their technical manuals and books, but flat earth equations and formulas should never exist in any of these manuals. Including "flat earth equations" in their manuals would be like including "Peter Pan flying equations" in manuals for helicopters. Why add the equations for a fairytale (something that allegedly doesn't exist) when trying to put forth a serious technical manual on aircraft, rockets, or artillery? Personally, I think the spherical math and equations are included just to keep those "without a need to know" in the dark.

One interesting thing to note before we get into these documents is something I discovered when I looked up the Freedom of Information Act. My Google search gave me a link for the U.S. State Department. The description of the FOIA law on that website states that the law generally provides any person the right to request access to federal agency records or information EXCEPT to the extent that the records are protected from disclosure by any of the nine exemptions.

In the process, I found it quite odd that Exemption #9 that authorizes government agencies to withhold information is "geological and geophysical information." Geological information would be about the solid earth and its' composition. Geophysical information would be about the physical processes and phenomena occurring especially in the earth and the earth's atmosphere. Why would any truth about the nature of the earth, its atmosphere, physics or composition have to remain classified by the government? Does that not tell you that they are hiding truth about God's creation?

422

Let's take a look at some of these government documents and technical manuals that base everything on a flat, non-rotating earth. As I stated in a previous chapter, the first government document I came across that admitted a flat, stationary earth (as the Bible always taught) was NASA Reference Publication 1207 from 1988. I used this document in one of my flat earth sermons in 2016 and in my presentation at the first Flat Earth International Conference in November 2017. Its title is: ***"The Derivation and Definition of a Linear Aircraft Model."*** [196]

NASA Reference Publication 1207

1988

Derivation and Definition of a Linear Aircraft Model

Eugene L. Duke,
Robert F. Antoniewicz,
and Keith D. Krambeer
Ames Research Center
Dryden Flight Research Facility
Edwards, California

NASA
National Aeronautics
and Space Administration

SUMMARY

This report documents the derivation and definition of a linear aircraft model for a rigid aircraft of constant mass flying over a flat, nonrotating earth. The derivation makes no assumptions of reference trajectory or vehicle symmetry. The linear system equations are derived and evaluated along a general trajectory and include both aircraft dynamics and observation variables.

INTRODUCTION

The need for linear models of aircraft for the analysis of vehicle dynamics and control law design is well known. These models are widely used, not only for computer applications but also for quick approximations and desk calculations. Whereas the use of these models is well understood and well documented, their derivation is not. The lack of documentation and, occasionally, understanding of the derivation of linear models is a hindrance to communication, training, and application.

This report details the development of the linear model of a rigid aircraft of constant mass, flying over a flat, nonrotating earth. This model consists of a state equation and an observation (or measurement) equation. The system equations have been broadly formulated to accommodate a wide variety of applications. The linear state equation is derived from the nonlinear six-degree-of-freedom equations of motion. The linear observation equation is derived from a collection of nonlinear equations representing state variables, time derivatives of state variables, control inputs, and flightpath, air data, and other parameters. The linear model is developed about a nominal trajectory that is general.

Whereas it is common to assume symmetric aerodynamics and mass distribution, or a straight and level trajectory, or both (Clancy, 1975; Dommasch and others, 1967; Etkin, 1972; McRuer and others, 1973; Northrop Aircraft, 1952; Thelander, 1965), these assumptions limit the generality of the linear model. The principal contribution of this report is a solution of the general problem of deriving a linear model of a rigid aircraft without making these simplifying assumptions. By defining the initial conditions (of the nominal trajectory) for straight and level flight and setting the asymmetric aerodynamic and inertia terms to zero, one can easily obtain the more traditional linear models from the linear model derived in this report.

Another significant contribution of this report is the derivation and definition of a linear observation (measurement) model. The observation model is often entirely neglected in standard texts. A thorough treatment of common aircraft measurements is presented by Gainer and Hoffman (1972), and Gracey (1980) provides a detailed discussion of speed and altitude measurements. However, neither of these references present linear models of these measurements. This report relies heavily on these two references and uses their results as one of the bases for the nonlinear measurement equations from which the linear measurement model is derived. Also included in this report is a large number of other measurements or variables for observation that have been found to be useful in vehicle analysis and control law design.

Duke and others (1987) describe a FORTRAN program called LINEAR that derives a linear aircraft model by numerical differencing (Dieudonne, 1978). The program LINEAR produces a linear aircraft model (both state and observation matrices) that is equivalent to the linear models defined in this report.

This report is divided into two main sections that define the reference systems and nonlinear state and observation equations (section 1) and derive a linear model presented in the appendixes (section 2). The appendixes contain a definition of the linear aerodynamic model used in this report (app. A), a derivation of the wind axis translational acceleration parameters (app. B), generalized linear derivatives of the nonlinear state and observation equations (app. C), and the individual derivatives of the state and observation equations (app. D). The details of the principal results of this report are presented in appendix D.

NASA document 1207 states in the summary and the conclusion of a manual full of very complicated, mathematical equations:

"This report documents the derivation (mathematical origin) *and definition of a linear aircraft model for a rigid aircraft of constant mass **flying over a FLAT, NON-ROTATING EARTH…This report details the development of the linear model of a rigid aircraft of constant mass, flying over a fiat, nonrotating earth.** This model consists of a state equation and an observation (or measurement) equation. The system equations have been broadly*

424

formulated to accommodate a wide variety of applications. The linear state equation is derived from the nonlinear six-degree-of-freedom equations of motion. The linear observation equation is derived from a collection of nonlinear equations representing state variables, time derivatives of state variables, control inputs, and flight path, air data, and other parameters. The linear model is developed about a nominal trajectory that is general."

The conclusion of this report after all of their very complicated math equations was this:

3   CONCLUDING REMARKS

This report derives and defines a set of linearized system matrices for a rigid aircraft of constant mass, flying in a stationary atmosphere over a flat, nonrotating earth. Both generalized and standard linear system equations are derived from nonlinear six-degree-of-freedom equations of motion and a large collection of nonlinear observation (measurement) equations.

This derivation of a linear model is general and makes no assumptions on either the reference (nominal) trajectory about which the model is linearized or the symmetry of the vehicle mass and aerodynamic properties.

Ames Research Center
Dryden Flight Research Facility
National Aeronautics and Space Administration
Edwards, California, January 8, 1987

"This report derives and defines a set of linearized system matrices for a rigid aircraft of constant mass, flying in a stationary atmosphere (not spinning with the Earth like they tell us) *over a FLAT, NONROTATING EARTH."* Those are NASA's words in a technical manual, not mine or some other "crazy" flat earther. And there's much more!

The following is one of my favorite technical manuals that also comes from NASA.gov:

General Equations of Motion for a Damaged Asymmetric Aircraft

Barton J. Bacon[*] and Irene M. Gregory[†]

NASA Langley Research Center, Hampton, VA, 23681

There is a renewed interest in dynamic characteristics of damaged aircraft both in order to assess survivability and to develop control laws to enhance survivability. This paper presents a set of flight dynamics equations of motion for a rigid body not necessarily referenced to the body's center of mass. Such equations can be used when the body loses a portion of its mass and it is desired to track the motion of the body's previous center of mass/reference frame now that the mass center has moved to a new position. Furthermore, results for equations presented in this paper and equations in standard aircraft simulations are compared for a scenario involving a generic transport aircraft configuration subject to wing damage.

I. Introduction

There is a renewed interest in control of aircraft that have sustained damage. This interest is driven by diverse factors such as advances in adaptive flight control, threats from shoulder-fired missiles, mid-air collisions, aging aircraft, and undetermined lifecycles of new composite transport aircraft. Illustrative examples are shown in figure 1. In order to analyze the dynamics of damaged aircraft the dynamic equations of motion must properly reflect the underlying physics. This is not a novel problem from the dynamic perspective. Since the first payloads have been delivered from aircraft in flight, the equations of motion describing these dynamics have been derived from first principles.[1] With the renewed interest in the problem, the authors hope to provide a convenient reference for the dynamic equations of motion that properly account for non-collocation of the center of mass and the body axes reference point.

If you will notice, starting on page one and the fourth line under the heading **"Introduction"** it states, *"In order to analyze the dynamics of damaged aircraft the dynamic EQUATIONS of motion MUST properly reflect the UNDERLYING PHYSICS."* Did you read that? Equations MUST properly reflect the underlying physics. Then, on page two, the manual states, *"In this paper, the rigid body equations of motion over a flat non-rotating earth are developed."*[197]

Why would they say that equations of motion must properly reflect the underlying physics and then present equations based on a flat, non-rotating earth if there is no such thing as a flat, non-rotating earth? You can read the entire document and it does not change the fact that they stated that the equations that properly reflect the underlying physics are equations based on a flat non-rotating earth.

---

[197] https://ntrs.nasa.gov/archive/nasa/casi.ntrs.nasa.gov/20070030307.pdf

Another technical manual comes from the Army Research Laboratory. The title is *"Trajectory Prediction of Spin-Stabilized Projectiles with a Steady Liquid Payload."* Notice that it says "Trajectory Prediction" which means that they are trying to figure out the path and destination of these projectiles flying through the air.

It stands to reason that the curvature rate of the spherical earth should be a big part of the equations to figure these things. However, this Army manual states clearly that, *"A typical 6-DOF rigid projectile model is employed to predict the dynamics of a projectile in flight. **These equations assume a flat earth.**"*[198]

ARMY RESEARCH LABORATORY

Trajectory Prediction of Spin-Stabilized Projectiles With a Steady Liquid Payload

by Gene R. Cooper

ARL-TR-5810   November 2011

---

[198] https://www.arl.army.mil/arlreports/2011/ARL-TR-5810.pdf

2. Projectile Flight Dynamic Model With a Liquid Payload

A typical 6-DOF rigid projectile model is employed to predict the dynamics of a projectile in flight. These equations assume a flat Earth. The well-known 6-DOF states comprise the three translational components describing the position of the projectile's center of mass and the three Euler angles describing the orientation of the projectile with respect to the Earth. Figures 1 and 2 provide a visualization of the degrees of freedom.

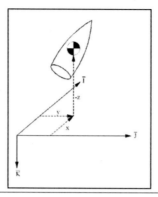

NASA Technical Memorandum 100996 entitled, *"Flight Testing a V/STOL Aircraft to Identify a Full-Envelope Aerodynamic Mode"* states on pages 4-5, *"For aircraft problems, the state and measurement models together represent the kinematics of a rigid body **for describing motion over <u>a flat, nonrotating earth.</u>"**[199]*

The RCC or Range Commanders Council Telemetry Standards document which is for the Navy, NASA, the Pacific Missile Range Facility and Arnold Engineering Development Complex and others states, ***"Although the equations for the two-ray model can be rather daunting, in its simplest form, one uses <u>flat-earth trigonometry</u> to compute the difference in path lengths between the direct and reflected signals."***[200]

[199] https://ntrs.nasa.gov/archive/nasa/casi.ntrs.nasa.gov/19880014378.pdf

[200] http://www.irig106.org/docs/106-17/106-17_Telemetry_Standards.pdf

An old declassified CIA document (also a NASA document) from 1961 entitled, *"CALCULATION OF WIND COMPENSATION FOR LAUNCHING OF UNGUIDED ROCKETS"* by Robert L. James, Jr., and Ronald J. Harris states, *"The advent of high-altitude-performance missiles has made the consideration of factors causing trajectory deviations or dispersion a necessity. One of the main contributors to the dispersion of an unguided vehicle is wind, and the purpose of this paper is to present a method for minimizing this effect on the trajectory."* On page 7 of the document it says, *"A trajectory simulation incorporating the above requirements is presented in reference 8. In addition to the above requirements, this simulation assumes a vehicle with six degrees of freedom and aerodynamic symmetry in roll and the missile position in space is computed relative to a flat nonrotating earth.*

429

This trajectory simulation was programmed on the IBM 704 electronic data processing machine <u>and is the basis for all trajectory computations made in this paper.</u>"[201]

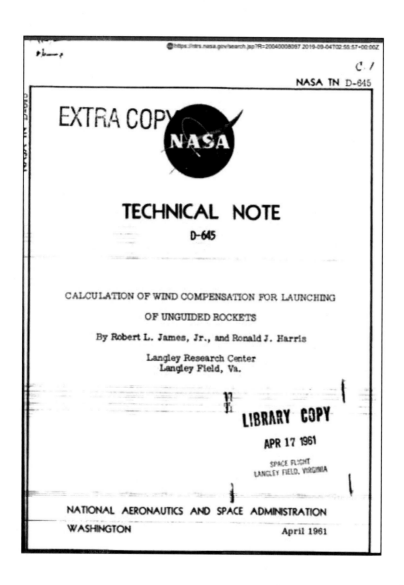

[201] https://ntrs.nasa.gov/archive/nasa/casi.ntrs.nasa.gov/20040008097.pdf

NATIONAL AERONAUTICS AND SPACE ADMINISTRATION

TECHNICAL NOTE D-645

CALCULATION OF WIND COMPENSATION FOR LAUNCHING

OF UNGUIDED ROCKETS

By Robert L. James, Jr., and Ronald J. Harris

SUMMARY

A method for calculating wind compensation for unguided missiles is derived which has a greater degree of flexibility than the previously proposed methods. Most of the earlier theories were based on a common set of assumptions which are (1) vehicle motions in pitch and yaw are independent, (2) linear aerodynamic coefficients with respect to flow incidence angle are used, (3) launch angles for wind compensation are the dispersion angles computed by using the weighted wind, and (4) factors used to determine azimuth correction are computed for the standard launch-elevation angle.

Elimination of the first two limitations is the result of using a three-dimensional trajectory simulation with arbitrary wind and nonlinear aerodynamic coefficients with respect to flow incidence angle. The last two limitations were removed by the unique analytical methods used in the present paper.

Utilization of the wind-compensation technique is demonstrated by using the Shotput vehicle as a model. Postflight simulations of four of these missiles with the use of measured winds show that if the winds are known, very good accuracy can be obtained by using the proposed method.

A wind-compensation system for the unguided Scout-SX-1 is presented in the appendix. This system was developed by using the assumptions and methods presented in this paper. The errors obtained are of about the same magnitude as those found for the Shotput system; yet the missile configurations and performance histories are very different.

A trajectory simulation incorporating the above requirements is presented in reference 8. In addition to the above requirements, this simulation assumes a vehicle with six degrees of freedom and aerodynamic symmetry in roll and the missile position in space is computed relative to a flat nonrotating earth. This trajectory simulation was programmed on the IBM 704 electronic data processing machine and is the basis for all trajectory computations made in this paper.

I find all of these documents amazing, but this NASA Technical Note from 1961 should make everyone stop and think. Notice that the spin of the earth was not even considered as a factor on unguided missiles reaching "space" or very high altitudes. They stated that their biggest problem

431

was compensating for the wind. They computed the missiles position in "space" relative to a flat, nonrotating earth and that data was programmed on the IBM 704 and was the basis for ALL trajectory computations made in a NASA technical paper. Remember, this paper was published by these NASA scientists two years AFTER the first U.S. "satellite" (1958 Explorer 1) was sent into the alleged vacuum of infinite "space" to fly around the spinning, sun-orbiting ball earth. This paper was released a year after NASA allegedly sent the first communications balloon "satellite" (Echo 1) over a thousand miles into "space" to orbit the ball earth. And yet, these two NASA rocket scientists set up a computer program for unguided missiles going into "space" in 1961 based on a flat, nonrotating earth. If that doesn't help convince someone that they have been lying to us about the shape of the earth and the true nature of "space" and the sun, moon, and stars then I don't know what will.

And just in case some might question the credibility of Robert L. James Jr. and Ronald J. Harris who authored the above technical note, I found them elsewhere. A NASA Technical Note from 1965 authored by these same two men confirms that they were clearly top-notch, NASA rocket and computer scientists. In it they explained the results of a *"...flight-test investigation of a "space" vehicle upper stage employing a rotating-solid-rocket attitude control system. Experimental data received from an onboard telemetry system are presented and discussed."*[202]

So, let's fast-forward to 1971 and another NASA Technical Note dated June 1971 - ***"A METHOD FOR REDUCING THE SENSITIVITY OF OPTIMAL NONLINEAR SYSTEMS TO PARAMETER***

---

[202] https://ntrs.nasa.gov/archive/nasa/casi.ntrs.nasa.gov/19660011640.pdf

UNCERTAINTY" by Jarrell R. Elliott of Langley Research Center and William F. Teague of the University of Kansas. This particular document confirms NASA and university scientists were still using the idealizing assumptions of a flat, nonrotating earth when working through problems with "...*a single-stage rocket vehicle starting from rest and going to specified terminal conditions of altitude and vertical velocity which will maximize the final horizontal velocity.*"[203]

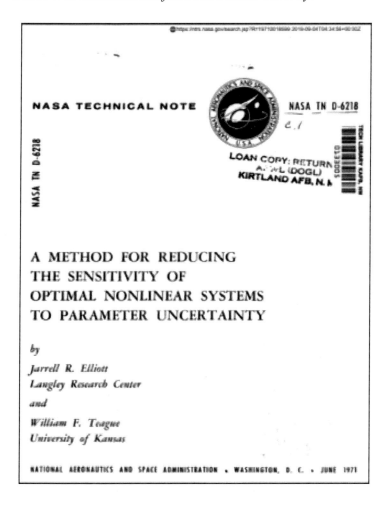

A METHOD FOR REDUCING
THE SENSITIVITY OF
OPTIMAL NONLINEAR SYSTEMS
TO PARAMETER UNCERTAINTY

by

Jarrell R. Elliott
Langley Research Center

and

William F. Teague
University of Kansas

NATIONAL AERONAUTICS AND SPACE ADMINISTRATION . WASHINGTON, D. C. . JUNE 1971

[203] https://ntrs.nasa.gov/archive/nasa/casi.ntrs.nasa.gov/19710018599.pdf

433

1. Report No. NASA TN D-6218	2. Government Accession No.	3. Recipient's Catalog No.
4. Title and Subtitle A METHOD FOR REDUCING THE SENSITIVITY OF OPTIMAL NONLINEAR SYSTEMS TO PARAMETER UNCERTAINTY		5. Report Date June 1971
		6. Performing Organization Code
7. Author(s) Jarrell R. Elliott and William F. Teague (University of Kansas)		8. Performing Organization Report No. L-7485
9. Performing Organization Name and Address NASA Langley Research Center Hampton, Va. 23365		10. Work Unit No. 125-17-06-03
		11. Contract or Grant No.
12. Sponsoring Agency Name and Address National Aeronautics and Space Administration Washington, D.C. 20546		13. Type of Report and Period Covered Technical Note
		14. Sponsoring Agency Code

15. Supplementary Notes

16. Abstract

Mathematical relationships are derived and used to establish a procedure for reshaping the optimal solution so as to reduce the statistical uncertainty in the terminal conditions of the system due to system parameter uncertainties of known statistical properties. The procedure introduces the use of an augmented performance index which contains a scalar measure of the system sensitivity partial derivatives. A nonlinear multiparameter optimal-rocket-trajectory problem was solved by using an algorithm based on the method of steepest descent to illustrate the procedure.

17. Key Words (Suggested by Author(s)) Sensitivity Optimal control Nonlinear systems	18. Distribution Statement Unclassified — Unlimited		
19. Security Classif. (of this report) Unclassified	20. Security Classif. (of this page) Unclassified	21. No. of Pages 40	22. Price* $3.00

*For sale by the National Technical Information Service, Springfield, Virginia 22151

A NUMERICAL EXAMPLE

Problem Statement

The example problem is a fixed-time problem in which it is required to determine the thrust-attitude program of a single-stage rocket vehicle starting from rest and going to specified terminal conditions of altitude and vertical velocity which will maximize the final horizontal velocity. The idealizing assumptions made are the following:

(1) A point-mass vehicle
(2) A flat, nonrotating earth
(3) A constant-gravity field, $g = 9.8$ m/sec^2 (32.2 ft/sec^2)
(4) Constant thrust and mass-loss rate
(5) A nonlifting body in a nonvarying atmosphere with a constant drag parameter $K_D = \frac{1}{2}\rho C_D S$, where S is the frontal surface area.

The coordinate system and pertinent geometric relations and terms are shown in figure 1. The differential equations of motion needed in the algorithm setup are

$$\left.\begin{aligned}
\frac{du}{dt} &= \frac{1}{m}\left(T\cos\theta - K_D u V\right) = \dot{x}_1 = f_1 \\
\frac{dy}{dt} &= v = \dot{x}_2 = f_2 \\
\frac{dv}{dt} &= \frac{1}{m}\left(T\sin\theta - K_D u V\right) - g = \dot{x}_3 = f_3
\end{aligned}\right\} \tag{12}$$

434

It is interesting to note that the word "idealizing" means to *"...regard or represent as perfect or better than in reality."* In NASA's case, they know the flat, nonrotating earth is perfect and true and that it conflicts with their lies about reality. It is that reality that we can go out and prove for ourselves with high-zoom cameras and much simpler math. We can observe this flat, nonrotating earth reality with high-altitude balloons of our own as we disregard the fisheye, wide-angle, fake-curve-producing camera lens. We can now use lasers like the U.S. Navy and discover that there is zero earth curvature over dozens and dozens of miles.

Another NASA Technical Memorandum March 1972 entitled, *"DETERMINATION OF ANGLES OF ATTACK AND SIDESLIP FROM RADAR DATA AND A ROLL-STABILIZED PLATFORM"* by John S. Preisser of Langley Research Center states, *"Equations for angles of attack and sideslip relative to both a rolling and nonrolling body axis system are derived for a flight vehicle for which radar and gyroscopic-attitude data are available. **The method is limited, however, to application where a flat, nonrotating earth may be assumed.** The gyro considered measures attitude relative to an inertial reference in an Euler angle sequence. In particular, a pitch, yaw, and roll sequence is used as an example in the derivation. Sample calculations based on flight data are presented to illustrate the method. Results obtained with the present gyro method are compared with another technique that uses onboard-camera data.*"[204]

Why is this method that includes radar and GYROSCOPIC-attitude data limited to application where a flat, nonrotating earth may be assumed? It is because

_____

[204] https://ntrs.nasa.gov/archive/nasa/casi.ntrs.nasa.gov/19720012071.pdf

gyroscopes are instruments that prove the earth is flat. In fact, my friend who is a 30-year commercial jet pilot told me that it was thinking about the gyroscope that gave him the over-the-top confirmation that he had been flying over a flat earth all those years. Here is yet another NASA document about aircraft that assumes a flat, nonrotating earth.

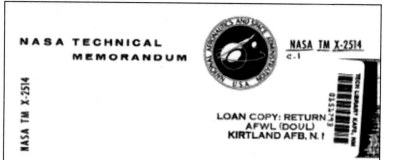

DETERMINATION OF ANGLES OF ATTACK
AND SIDESLIP FROM RADAR DATA
AND A ROLL-STABILIZED PLATFORM

by John S. Preisser

Langley Research Center
Hampton, Va. 23365

NATIONAL AERONAUTICS AND SPACE ADMINISTRATION • WASHINGTON, D. C. • MARCH 1972

DETERMINATION OF ANGLES OF ATTACK AND SIDESLIP FROM
RADAR DATA AND A ROLL-STABILIZED PLATFORM

By John S. Preisser
Langley Research Center

SUMMARY

Equations for angles of attack and sideslip relative to both a rolling and nonrolling body axis system are derived for a flight vehicle for which radar and gyroscopic-attitude data are available. The method is limited, however, to application where a flat, non-rotating earth may be assumed. The gyro considered measures attitude relative to an inertial reference in an Euler angle sequence. In particular, a pitch, yaw, and roll sequence is used as an example in the derivation. Sample calculations based on flight data are presented to illustrate the method. Results obtained with the present gyro method are compared with another technique that uses onboard-camera data.

INTRODUCTION

Roll-stabilized platforms have been used for many years for vehicle-attitude determination on various flight projects. Recently, a miniature attitude-reference system has found use in several flight programs at NASA Langley Research Center. (See ref. 1.) The system consists of two two-degree-of-freedom gyroscopes which are mounted on a common gimbal. The gimbal is roll stabilized; thus, the platform is isolated from the rolling motion of the vehicle. An inertial axis system is set up at the time of gyro uncaging. The orientation of the body axes relative to the inertial axes at any time during the flight is determined from the angular displacements measured by the platform after uncaging in the sequence pitch, yaw, and roll.

In order to properly analyze flight-test data for obtaining aerodynamic parameters, such as force and moment coefficients and stability derivatives, it is necessary to know the orientation of the flight vehicle to the airstream. The purpose of this paper is to obtain the equations needed to determine vehicle orientation relative to the airstream using an inertial-reference gyro platform in conjunction with radar and wind data. Total angle of attack between the longitudinal vehicle axis and the vehicle velocity vector as well as the angle between a vector perpendicular to the longitudinal axis and the velocity vector has been calculated before from radar data and gyro-platform data using a direction-cosine approach. (See ref. 2.) The present method, using an Euler angle

DETERMINATION OF ANGLES OF ATTACK AND SIDESLIP FROM
RADAR DATA AND A ROLL-STABILIZED PLATFORM

By John S. Preisser
Langley Research Center

SUMMARY

Equations for angles of attack and sideslip relative to both a rolling and nonrolling body axis system are derived for a flight vehicle for which radar and gyroscopic-attitude data are available. The method is limited, however, to application where a flat, non-rotating earth may be assumed. The gyro considered measures attitude relative to an inertial reference in an Euler angle sequence. In particular, a pitch, yaw, and roll sequence is used as an example in the derivation. Sample calculations based on flight data are presented to illustrate the method. Results obtained with the present gyro method are compared with another technique that uses onboard-camera data.

This is a NASA Technical Memorandum entitled, *"A Mathematical Model of the CH-53 Helicopter"* by William

R. Sturgeon and James D. Phillips of Ames Research Center in Moffett Field, California. It states, *"The help of the following persons in obtaining this mathematical model is acknowledged: Dean E. Cooper, Thomas H. Lawrence, and Phil Gold of Sikorsky Aircraft Division of United Technologies, Stratford, Connecticut; and J. D. Shaughnessy of Langley Research Center. The model was programmed on the Sigma 9 computer by Boris Voh of Computer Science Corporation. Validation was performed with the help of George Tucker and Ron Cerdes of Ames Research Center...The helicopter equations of motion are given in body axes with respect to a flat, nonrotating earth."*[205]

[205] https://ntrs.nasa.gov/archive/nasa/casi.ntrs.nasa.gov/19810003557.pdf

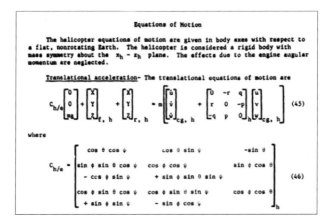

Equations of Motion

The helicopter equations of motion are given in body axes with respect to a flat, nonrotating Earth. The helicopter is considered a rigid body with mass symmetry about the x_h - z_h plane. The effects due to the engine angular momentum are neglected.

Translational acceleration- The translational equations of motion are

$$C_{h/e}\begin{bmatrix}0\\0\\g\end{bmatrix} + \begin{bmatrix}X\\Y\\Z\end{bmatrix}_{f,h} + \begin{bmatrix}X\\Y\\Z\end{bmatrix}_{r,h} = m\begin{bmatrix}\dot{u}\\\dot{v}\\\dot{w}\end{bmatrix}_{cg,h} + \begin{bmatrix}0 & -r & q\\r & 0 & -p\\-q & p & 0\end{bmatrix}_h\begin{bmatrix}u\\v\\w\end{bmatrix}_{cg,h} \quad (45)$$

where

$$C_{h/e} = \begin{bmatrix} \cos\theta\cos\psi & \cos\theta\sin\psi & -\sin\theta \\ \sin\phi\sin\theta\cos\psi & \cos\phi\cos\psi & \sin\phi\cos\theta \\ -\cos\phi\sin\psi & +\sin\phi\sin\theta\sin\psi & \\ \cos\phi\sin\theta\cos\psi & \cos\phi\sin\theta\sin\psi & \cos\phi\cos\theta \\ +\sin\phi\sin\psi & -\sin\phi\cos\psi & \end{bmatrix}_h \quad (46)$$

I also discovered an interesting MIT thesis issued in 2006 from the Department of Aeronautics and Astronautics by Brian E. Mihok entitled, *"A Property-Based System Design Method with Application to a Targeting System for Small UAVs."* It clearly shows that they are teaching flat earth equations at the esteemed Massachusetts Institute of Technology. The Abstract of this paper says, *"The method was demonstrated on the design of a targeting system for small UAVs. **Three targeting methods were considered: assuming a flat earth, using DTED data, and using range data**. The evaluation revealed a descending utility order of DTED, **Flat Earth**, and Range based upon the system's stated requirements."*[206]

---

[206] https://dspace.mit.edu/handle/1721.1/35571

the method translates component properties into system properties, which are then turned into scores. A utility function is used to create a total system utility for the alternative, which serves as the basis for comparison. A Python-based tool was written to facilitate the method, encapsulating the process in a high-level, easily configurable script. The method was demonstrated on the design of a targeting system for small UAVs. Three targeting methods were considered: assuming a flat Earth, using DTED data, and using range data. The evaluation revealed a descending utility order of DTED, Flat Earth, and Range based upon the system's stated requirements. While the Range method produced the most accurate results by far, its unit cost was well beyond the allocated budget, as was its power. DTED data was found to be a beneficial addition to small UAVs. In the evaluation, the method was able to elucidate the key information required to shape the design and thus showed promise.

Thesis Supervisor: Jeff Miller
Title: Charles Stark Draper Laboratory

Thesis Supervisor: Brent Appleby
Title: Lecturer in Aeronautics and CSDL Technical Supervisor

Again, why use flat earth equations in a targeting program (that needs to be very accurate) if the earth is a sphere, curving 8 inches per miles squared or 66.6 feet in ten miles? Why wouldn't they assume the earth is curved and create programs with equations that take that curve into account? Why waste time on flat, nonrotating earth equations? Are these MIT aerospace engineers and NASA rocket scientists not able to do the math for a spherical earth? Why do people keep saying that they only use flat earth equations to simplify the math? If the earth is not flat, they should NEVER assume that it is in ANY equation, computer program, or targeting/guidance system.

I think back to the NASA Technical Note from 1961 where two NASA scientists were programming NASA computers to work based on a flat, nonrotating earth. Their work and calculations did not have anything to do with short distances or anything that wouldn't be affected by simplified flat, nonrotating earth equations. Their work had to do with missile trajectories and positions at high-altitude "...*the missile position in space is computed relative to a **flat, nonrotating earth**. This trajectory simulation was programmed on the IBM 704 electronic data processing*

440

machine and is the basis for all trajectory computations made in this paper." So, again I ask, why would NASA scientists base everything in their computer simulation programs on a flat, nonrotating earth if there is no such thing?

And it's not just the "crazy Americans" factoring a flat earth into their equations. The Russian scientists that conducted the light study on "the brightness of the firmament" also based that formula on the existence of a flat earth. Why do that if the earth is a ball? The Russian doctoral thesis study did not have anything to do with aviation or short distances, yet they based their formula for measuring/analyzing the brightness of the firmament on a flat earth and a near-sun.

It stated, " *In the investigations, two instruments designed by V.G. Fesenkov were used; one of these was a visual photometer of the daytime sky intended for measuring the <u>brightness of the FIRMAMENT</u>; the other was a photo electric halo photometer for determining the brightness from <u>near-sun</u> halo and also from the sun on a surface perpendicular to these rays. The dissertation contains a certain formula of the brightness of the sky, taking into consideration only the brightness of the first order and <u>arrived on the assumption of a FLAT EARTH</u> and giving some conclusions derived on the basis of this formula."*

49-12-15/16

Dissertations Defended in the Scientific Council of the Institute of Physics of the Earth, Institute of Physics of the Atmosphere and Institute of Applied Geophysics, Ac.Sc. USSR during the First Semester of 1957.

Ye.V. Pyaskovskaya-Fesenkova - Investigation of the Scattering of Light in the Earth's Atmosphere (Issledovaniye rasseyaniya sveta v zemnoy atmosfere) - Doctor dissertation. Opponents: Doctor of Physico-Mathematical Sciences Ye.S. Kuznetsov, Doctor of Physico-Mathematical Sciences S.M. Polozkov, Doctor of Physico-Mathematical Sciences G.B. Rozenberg, Doctor of Physico-Mathematical Sciences I.S. Shklovskiy. March 23, 1957. The dissertation represents the result of many years of study of the clear, daytime sky. The observations were carried out in twelve locations at various altitudes above the sea, various climatic, meteorological and synoptic conditions. The observations were carried out mainly during high-transparency of the atmosphere in the visual range of the spectrum in the absence of a snow cover. In the investigations two instruments, designed by V.G. Fesenkov were used; one of these was a visual photometer of the daytime sky intended for measuring the brightness of the firmament; the other was a photo-electric halo photometer for determining the brightness from

Card6/21

49-12-15/16

Dissertations Defended in the Scientific Council of the Institute of Physics of the Earth, Institute of Physics of the Atmosphere and Institute of Applied Geophysics, Ac.Sc. USSR during the First Semester of 1957.

near-sun halo and also from the sun on a surface perpendicular to these rays. The dissertation contains a certain formula of the brightness of the sky, taking into consideration only the brightness of the first order and derived on the assumption of a "flat" Earth and giving some conclusions derived on the basis of this formula. For a certain coefficient of transparency of the atmosphere, the brightness of the sky at any point is represented by derivation of two functions of which one is the function of the diffusion of light and the other is a function of the zenith distances of the sun and of the observed point of the sky. On changing of the zenith distances of the sun z from 90 to 0°, the brightness of the sky on the almucantar of the sun increases first reaching a maximum for a certain value of z, and then decreases. A method is also proposed of determining the brightness of the clear daylight sky at any point based on measuring the brightness along the almucantar of the sun and of 5-6 points of the firmament located at various zenith distances. This method permits determination

Card7/21

Here's another military technical manual from the Defense Technical Information Center or dtic.mil website which is a U.S. Department of Defense website. This document was protected under the U.S. Espionage Law. The contents of this report were not to be transmitted or revealed in any manner to an unauthorized person:

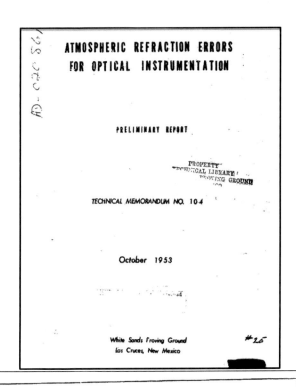

The abstract of this document explains that *"...Differences are brought out between guided-missile refraction geometry and astronomical refraction geometry. A simple relationship between angular refraction of light, refraction error for ground observer, and refraction error*

443

for aerial observer is demonstrated...Present equations hold for any altitude." Then, in the introduction, it says this:

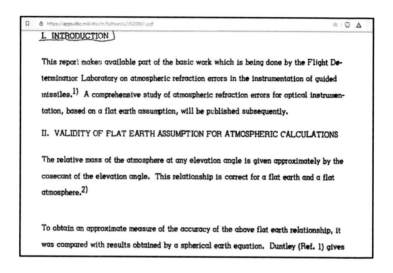

First, they say that they are working on the problem of atmospheric refraction errors in the instrumentation of guided missiles. They go on to explain that a comprehensive study of this problem will be based on *"a flat earth assumption."* Then, they proceed to affirm the **VALIDITY OF FLAT EARTH ASSUMPTION** for atmospheric calculations. The definition of the word 'validity' according to the Oxford Dictionary is *"...the quality of being logically or factually sound; soundness or cogency also the state of being legally or officially binding or acceptable."* And then they follow that up by saying, *"The relative mass of the atmosphere at any elevation angle is given approximately by the cosecant of the elevation angle. **This relationship is CORRECT for a FLAT EARTH and a FLAT ATMOSPHERE. To obtain an approximate measure of the accuracy of the above flat earth relationship, it was***

444

compared with results obtained by a spherical earth equation."[207]

That last line is both amazing and irrefutable; they are plainly saying that to understand the measure of the ACCURACY of the flat earth relationship to their equations, they compared it to the results of spherical earth equations. This document is simply a huge admission that the flat earth equations are the valid and accurate way to address equations of motion and atmospheric refraction errors in guided missile instrumentation at any altitude rather than the equations of the fictitious spherical earth. It also further debunks the excuse that these flat earth equations only exist to simplify the math for rocket scientists.

Let's look at another Army Research Laboratory document that discusses their desire to create a more *Scale-Insensitive Algorithm for FLIR Imagery.*"[208]

Army Research Laboratory
Adelphi, MD 20783-1197

ARL-TN-175   February 2001

Scale-Insensitive Detection Algorithm for FLIR Imagery

Sandor Der, Chris Dwan, Alex Chan, Heesung Kwon, and Nasser Nasrabadi
Sensors and Electron Devices Directorate

Before going further into this document, let's first understand what an algorithm is and why they are used:

[207] https://apps.dtic.mil/dtic/tr/fulltext/u2/020861.pdf

[208] https://www.arl.army.mil/arlreports/2001/ARL-TN-175.pdf

algorithm

Posted by: Margaret Rouse WhatIs.com

 in

Contributor(s): Fouad Tawfiq and Ali

An algorithm (pronounced AL-go-rith-um) is a procedure or formula for solving a problem, based on conducting a sequence of specified actions. A computer program can be viewed as an elaborate algorithm. In mathematics and computer science, an algorithm usually means a small procedure that solves a recurrent problem.

On this same webpage, their video tutorial on algorithms asked, "What makes a good algorithm?" The answer was 1) That it solves a problem and is correct and then 2) It does so efficiently. Now, understanding the purpose of an algorithm, let's get to an important fact stated in the ARL document from 2001 about the types of algorithms being used for targeting enemy equipment down range. They wrote on page one, *"While most automatic target detection/recognition (ATD/R) algorithms use much problem-specific knowledge to improve performance, the result is an algorithm that is tailored to specific target types and poses. The approximate range to target is often required, with varying amounts of tolerance. For example, in some scenarios, it is assumed that the range is known to within one meter from a laser range finder or a digital map. **In other scenarios, only the range to the center of the field of view and the depression angle is known, so that a flat-earth approximation provides the best estimate.**"*

So, this 2001 document admits that some military targeting algorithms were based on a "flat-earth approximation" which "provided the best estimate" of a target down range. Remember, an algorithm must solve a problem and do so efficiently. It is obvious that the United States military uses flat earth algorithms to solve the problem of hitting enemy targets down range. But once again, it is not only the United States, but also the Russians that base many things on a flat, nonrotating or still earth. While writing this chapter, I had a phone conversation with my friend retired Lieutenant Colonel Bryan Read (who taught Russian at West Point) and he told me about a World War II Russian bombing document that states:

В дальнейшем рассмотрим только движение центра массы бомбы, причем примем:
а) земля неподвижна и поверхность ее плоская;
б) сила тяжести постоянна по величине и направлению;

Translation to English:

In the following we consider only the center of mass of the bomb, using these precepts:

A) **the land is still and its surface is flat;**

B) *the force of gravity is constant in magnitude and direction;*

Глава I

ОСНОВНЫЕ СВЕДЕНИЯ ИЗ БАЛИСТИКИ

1. Общие сведения о движении бомбы

Движение бомбы после отделения ее от самолета определяется системой шести дифференциальных уравнений: три уравнения определяют движение центра массы бомбы и три уравнения — колебания бомбы вокруг центра массы.

Силы, действующие на бомбу в полете, полностью не изучены, и до настоящего времени задача одновременного интегрирования всех шести уравнений не решена. Обычно система шести уравнений разбивается на две отдельные системы, по три уравнения в каждой. Одна система определяет движение центра массы при условии, что ось бомбы совпадает с касательной к траектории. Другая система определяет колебания бомбы вокруг центра массы при условии, что движение центра массы известно из решения первой системы.

В дальнейшем рассмотрим только движение центра массы бомбы, причем примем:

а) земля неподвижна и поверхность ее плоская;
б) сила тяжести постоянна по величине и направлению;
в) атмосфера неподвижна относительно земли;
г) сила сопротивления направлена по касательной к траектории центра массы в сторону, противоположную скорости.

Начнем с простейшего случая — с движения центра массы бомбы в пустоте.

2. Движение центра массы бомбы в пустоте

При движении бомбы в пустоте на бомбу действует только сила тяжести.

Напишем уравнения движения центра массы. Возьмем прямоугольную левую систему координат и начало ее расположим в той точке, в которой сбрасывается бомба (рис. 1).

Оси направим следующим образом: ось x — горизонтально в сторону полета самолета; ось y — вертикально вниз; ось z — горизонтально, перпендикулярно к направлению полета.

1*

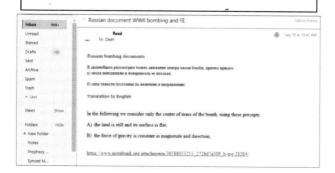

The Russians stated that their bombing calculations were based on the land (or earth) being still (not moving) and the land (or earth) surface being flat. Some skeptics might throw out excuses like *"The Russians bombed at lower altitudes, so the rotation of the earth and the curvature of the earth didn't come into play."* Yet, these same people will claim that snipers have to compensate for the spin of the earth when shooting long distances, but somehow bombs that are dropped from airplanes (which make it to their targets much slower than sniper bullets) don't have to account for the rotation of the earth. The contradictions in their spherical earth model and the mental gymnastics that must be done to defend the spinning ball earth is amazing.

Here is another Russian scientific document from 1959 about antennas in "space" over a flat earth:

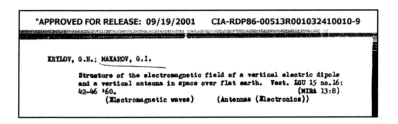

"APPROVED FOR RELEASE: 09/19/2001   CIA-RDP86-00513R001032410010-9

KRYLOV, G.N.; MAKAROV, G.I.

Structure of the electromagnetic field of a vertical electric dipole and a vertical antenna in space over flat earth. Vest. LGU 15 no.16: 42-46 '60.   (MIRA 13:8)
(Electromagnetic waves)   (Antennas (Electronics))

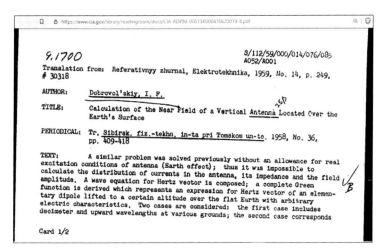

9.1700   3/112/59/000/014/076/085
                                          A052/A001
Translation from: Referativnyy zhurnal, Elektrotekhnika, 1959, No. 14, p. 249,
30318

AUTHOR: Dobrovol'skiy, I. F.

TITLE: Calculation of the Near Field of a Vertical Antenna Located Over the
           Earth's Surface

PERIODICAL: Tr. Sibirsk, fiz.-tekhn, in-ta pri Tomskom un-te, 1958, No. 36,
            pp. 409-418

TEXT: A similar problem was solved previously without an allowance for real
excitation conditions of antenna (Earth effect); thus it was impossible to
calculate the distribution of currents in the antenna, its impedance and the field
amplitude. A wave equation for Hertz vector is composed; a complete Green
function is derived which represents an expression for Hertz vector of an elementary dipole lifted to a certain altitude over the flat Earth with arbitrary
electric characteristics. Two cases are considered: the first case includes
decimeter and upward wavelengths at various grounds; the second case corresponds

Card 1/2

As I was writing this chapter on September 10, 2019, I did another extensive search in the CIA Freedom of Information Act (FOIA) Reading Room. My original research on these government websites took place in June of 2018. I spent hours going through documents searching key words and phrases like flat earth, firmament, balloon satellites,

Antarctica, ice wall, geocentric and many more. In my most recent search, I came across a few more formerly TOP-SECRET documents that are real "smoking guns." The first is a document dated January 31, 1969. Keep in mind that this was the same year of the alleged Apollo 11 moon landing and yet TOP SECRET government documents are still talking about a "flat earth."

This particular document has a list of 7 different aerial photography missions and contains the number of passes, frames, and the type of camera used. These passes came from their balloon spy "satellites" (known as satelloons) which they injected into the very dense aether level (just above 73 miles) with rockets. Those satelloons were equipped with the Corona cameras and would make multiple passes over restricted areas as they were moved in a circular path by the ether current over our flat earth. At the bottom of the page, the document states, *"The above scales were computed using 15 degrees of pitch **and assuming a flat earth (tangent plane).** The error at a nominal altitude of 100 NM* (nautical miles which is 115.08 miles) *is 0.68 percent* (which is almost nothing)."[209]

[209] https://www.cia.gov/library/readingroom/docs/CIA-RDP78B04555A000100030041-2.pdf

The last document that I will share is also about aerial photography and resolution issue. The document is dated August 12, 1964 and is a CIA Memorandum for the Record entitled, *"The Change in Ground Resolution as a Function Obliquity."* It discusses changing the aiming angle of their high-altitude, balloon carried spy cameras and then states, *"A flat earth is assumed—using a spherical earth increases the discrepancy in size between the resolvable dimensions of ground objects as a function of target orientation."*[210] In other words…"trying to use a spherical earth model messes everything up, so we use a flat earth model to get things right."

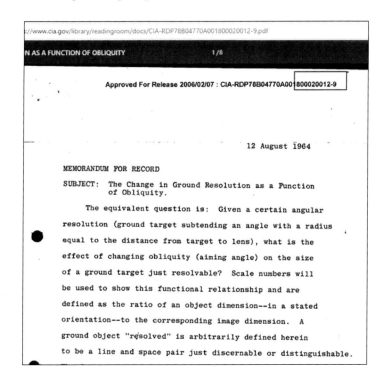

---

[210] https://www.cia.gov/library/readingroom/docs/CIA-RDP78B04770A001800020012-9.pdf

defined as the ratio of an object dimension--in a stated
orientation--to the corresponding image dimension. A
ground object "resolved" is arbitrarily defined herein
to be a line and space pair just discernable or distinguishable.
The following brief analysis shows that the orientation
of a ground object is most important in determining whether
it can be resolved, and this orientation is of great
importance in determining system capability.

Assumptions and Comments

a. Only geometric effects are considered--
atmospheric seeing is not included.

NGA review(s) completed.

b. A flat earth is assumed--using a spherical
earth increases the discrepance in size between the
resolvable dimentions of ground objects as a function
of target orientation.

c. Camera dynamics (including image motion
are considered to be 0).

There are many other government documents that I could add to this chapter, but I don't believe it is necessary. The point here is clear: Equations, algorithms, computer programs, cameras, antennas pertaining to high-altitude satelloons, airplanes, helicopters, rockets in "space," artillery shells, targeting programs, light studies to determine the brightness of the firmament, and a technical manual on damaged asymmetric aircraft were all based on a flat, nonrotating earth. It's just that simple. It is a fact that U.S.,

NASA and Russian scientists created formulas, programmed their computers, and wrote technical notes based on a "flat, nonrotating earth." Those that believe in a flat earth in today's society are mocked and considered ignorant or even crazy, and yet some of the "top minds" in our "top agencies" seem to agree with flat earthers. Just let that sink in for a while.

Chapter 19

The Day the Sky Falls

"And the third angel followed them, saying with a loud voice, If any man worship the beast and his image, and receive his mark in his forehead, or in his hand, The same shall drink of the wine of the wrath of God, which is poured out without mixture into the cup of his indignation; and he shall be tormented with fire and brimstone in the presence of the holy angels, and in the presence of the Lamb: And the smoke of their torment ascendeth up for ever and ever: and they have no rest day nor night, who worship the beast and his image, and whosoever receiveth the mark of his name" (Revelation 14:9-11).

"And the beast was taken, and with him the false prophet that wrought miracles before him, with which he deceived them that had received the mark of the beast, and them that worshipped his image. These both were cast alive into a lake of fire burning with brimstone" (Revelation 19:20).

"And I beheld when he had opened the sixth seal, and, lo, **there was a great earthquake; and the sun became black as**

sackcloth of hair, and the moon became as blood; And the stars of heaven fell unto the earth, even as a fig tree casteth her untimely figs, when she is shaken of a mighty wind. And the heaven (FIRMAMENT) *departed as a scroll when it is rolled together;* and every mountain and island were moved out of their places. And the kings of the earth, and the great men, and the rich men, and the chief captains, and the mighty men, and every bondman, and every free man, hid themselves in the dens and in the rocks of the mountains; And said to the mountains and rocks, Fall on us, and hide us from the face of him that sitteth on the throne, and from the wrath of the Lamb (JESUS CHRIST): For the great day of his wrath is come; and who shall be able to stand? (Revelation 6:12-17).

"Everything is NOT a conspiracy!" That is what I heard from some Christians recently when we were debating about Biblical cosmology and the lies and deceptions that abound today. It seems to be the "mantra" of Christians who don't want to the face reality. However, the Bible foretold a massive conspiracy by the wealthy, the world leaders, and the scientific elite to turn people away from believing the God of the Bible and the only Messiah Jesus Christ. Psalms 2:1-2 says, *"Why do the heathen rage, and the people imagine a vain thing? The kings of the earth set themselves, and the rulers take counsel together, against the LORD, and against his anointed."* The Bible foretold the end-time conspiracies that would 1) suppress the truth of creation, 2) undermine the freedom of sovereign nations in order to create a world government, 3) take over the economy of the world, and 4) impose the death penalty to take care of nonconformists.

It stands to reason that conspiracies on that grand of a scale would require a great number of people and a long period of time to accomplish. Even though the Bible warns of this and the world around us is filled with signs that it has and is occurring, somehow many Christians refuse to open their eyes. Some stay blind because of fear, some ignorance and others because of their pride.

Georgia Congressman Larry McDonald (1975-1983) was known for his staunch opposition to communism and believed in long standing covert efforts by Trilateral Commission and other powerful US groups to bring about a SOCIALISM and WORLD GOVERNMENT. He was the second president of the John Birch Society and also a cousin of General George S. Patton.

"The drive of the Rockefellers and their allies is to create a one-world government combining super capitalism and communism under the same tent, all under their control.... Do I mean conspiracy? Yes, I do. I am convinced there is such a plot, international in scope, generations old in planning, and incredibly evil in intent."

Sadly Congressman Larry P. McDonald was killed in the Korean Airlines 007 flight that was shot down by the Soviet fighter pilots over international waters.

The Holy Spirit through the prophets of the Old Testament and the Apostles of the New Testament spelled out Satan's end time conspiracies. According to God's Word here is some of what we can expect to see in the coming years:

- A worldwide financial collapse.
- A world government led by a man the Bible calls the Antichrist.
- A new monetary system controlled by something implanted in the forehead or right hand.
- Mass imprisonment and killings of true, Bible-believing Christians (beheading being one of the preferred methods according to Revelation 13 & 20).

- A third world war starting in the Middle East (Ezekiel 38-39 & Revelation 9).
- Great deception from very visible religious leaders.
- Government disclosure of UFOs and "extraterrestrials" (the "alien" deception).
- Intense hatred for the state of Israel, culminating in a movement of the Antichrist world armies to annihilate them at the battle of Armageddon.

When the world moves to wipe Israel off the map (a coalition of Muslim nations with Russia), that is when the Lord Jesus Christ (the True God and Creator) will physically return to earth. He will defeat the armies of the Antichrist and the false prophet and set up His kingdom (Revelation 16-19). These prophecies range from before 3,000 B.C. to 95 A.D. when the final book of prophecy was written by the Apostle John.

EXPRESS Home of the Daily and Sunday Express

LOGIN   Apps

HOME | NEWS | SHOWBIZ & TV | SPORT | COMMENT | FINANCE | TRA

UK WORLD SCIENCE WEIRD POLITICS NATURE WEATHER ROYAL SUNDAY SCOTLA

Home > News > World

World War 3: Turkey's Erdogan calls for 'ARMY of Islam' to ATTACK Israel on all sides

TURKEY'S President Recep Tayyip Erdogan and his ruling Justice and Development Party (AKP) have announced they want to create an "army of Islam" to wage war against Israel, it has been revealed.

By MATT DRAKE
PUBLISHED: 06:15, Tue, Mar 27, 2018 | UPDATED: 07:46, Tue, Mar 27, 2018

One of the most amazing of the Hebrew prophets was Daniel. He served in the court of King Nebuchadnezzar of Babylon and later King Cyrus of Persia. During the reign of Cyrus, Daniel was shown several visions of the future, particularly the end time when the Messiah would return. In the visions, the Lord God of Abraham showed Daniel four great kingdoms that would rise in the last days and provided him with great detail about each. God did this by revealing them as different beasts. The angel told Daniel, ***"These great beasts, which are four, are four kings, which shall arise out of the earth"*** (Daniel 7:17).

First, Daniel saw a lion that had the wings of an eagle until the wings were plucked. We now understand that this lion represents the great British Empire because the symbol for England is a lion and the eagle (the United States) came out of the lion (England). Another beast was a bear with three ribs in its mouth that was told to arise and devour much flesh. The bear is the symbol of Russia. This prophecy came to pass as Russia rose up and killed millions of people through its Communist revolutions across Europe, Asia, and Central and South America. We see that the Russian bear is still on the move; taking over Crimea in 2014 and getting ready for a broader war. The four-headed leopard with wings represents the fourth German-dominated European Union (see picture below). And then the ten-horned beast will be unlike all the others because it will unite all nations under a ten-region world government. There is more Scripture and information to explain these interpretations, but for our purposes I only want it to be clear that the prophets referred to kingdoms as beasts. Some traditional teachings on Daniel 7 state that Babylon was the lion and Persia was the bear, however, those nations already existed. The Scripture says that the four kingdoms "shall arise" which means that they did not exist at the time of the prophecy.

The German-made Leopard 2A5 Tank

The main battle tank of European countries like Austria, Denmark, Sweden, Switzerland, Norway, Greece, Spain, Portugal, Finland, and Poland to name a few.

The book of Revelation was written around 700 years after Daniel's prophecies by John, the beloved disciple of Jesus. His vision of the resurrected Jesus Christ was identical to the one Daniel had seven centuries before. John was also shown a vision of how the end times would play out. In Revelation we also see many of the same things Daniel foretold except with more explanation. For instance, Revelation 13 tells us that in the last days these four beasts (nations) spoken of in Daniel 7 will be united into one beast with seven heads and ten horns. That means that 2000 year ago, God revealed that during the time of the great tribulation and the second coming of Jesus Christ there would be a United Nations. The Apostle John goes on to say that this "United Nations Beast" would speak blasphemous things against the God of the Bible and move to make war against Christians and the nation of Israel. The Bible also tells us that this beast will worship Satan (the Dragon/Lucifer). This also agrees with what Daniel saw concerning the last days.

"It is the sacred principles enshrined in the UN Charter to which we will HENCEFORTH pledge our allegiance."

President George H.W. Bush addressing the United Nations

As I have studied the Bible, researched history, and watched current events since the 1980s, it has become clear that what these prophets foretold has been and is still unfolding to the letter. I discovered that the goal of the United Nations is to become the world government and that it also has a spiritual side that was adopted from the writings of occultist Alice Bailey. Once I knew that, I had no doubt that the United Nations is the beginning of the world government beast spoken of by Daniel and the Apostle John.

Alice Baily

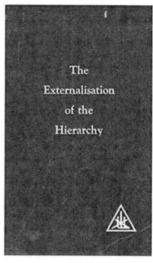

The Externalisation of the Hierarchy

The name of Alice Bailey's organization (that has been embedded in the United Nations for decades) is presently called the *Lucis Trust*. However, when Bailey founded it in 1922, the Lucis Trust was named Lucifer Publishing Company. Alice Bailey was the disciple of occultist Helen Blavatsky who originally founded the magazine called Lucifer. As you may remember, Blavatsky was a very dedicated witch and wrote in her book *The Secret Doctrine* that *"Lucifer is God and the Light."* She even taught that Satan is the Logos (a Greek term used in the Bible to describe the Lord Jesus Christ as God in the flesh) and she calls Lucifer the Holy Spirit. This is blasphemy of the true God and His ONLY Messiah Jesus Christ to the highest degree. Nevertheless, the Lucis Trust is a recognized NGO (Non-governmental Organization) of the United Nations and sits on the board of UN's economic and social council.

Here are several quotes from Helen Blavatsky's book *The Secret Doctrine:*

"One of the most hidden secrets involves the so-called fall of Angels. Satan and his rebellious host will thus prove to have become the direct Saviors and Creators of divine man. Thus Satan, once he ceases to be viewed in the superstitious spirit of the church, grows into the grandiose image. It is Satan who is the God of our planet and the only God. Satan (or Lucifer) represents the Centrifugal Energy of the Universe, this ever-living symbol of self-sacrifice for the intellectual independence of humanity." pages 215, 216, 220, 245, 255, 533 (VI)

"Lucifer represents... Life... Thought... Progress... Civilization.'. Liberty... Independence... Lucifer is the Logos, The Serpent, the Savior" (pp. 171, 225, 255 Volume II).

"The Celestial Virgin which thus becomes the Mother of Gods and Devils at one and the same time; for she is the ever-loving beneficent Deity...but in antiquity and reality Lucifer or Luciferius is the name. Lucifer is divine and terrestrial Light, 'the Holy Ghost' and 'Satan' at one and the same time" (Pg. 539).

So, it is clear that Alice Bailey's mentor was dedicated to Lucifer (or Satan) and his fallen angels. And now the Satanic writings of Alice Bailey and her organization are deeply embedded in the United Nations. Her writings are also the spiritual foundation of the UN-sanctioned, Robert Muller World Core Curriculum taught in his more than thirty schools throughout the world, including Arlington, Texas. In fact, in the preface to Robert Muller's World Core Curriculum, it states, *"The underlying philosophy upon which the Robert Muller School is based will be found in the teachings set forth in the books of Alice A. Bailey... The school is now certified as a United Nations Associated School providing education for international cooperation and peace."* Robert Muller was the Assistant Secretary General of the UN for over 40 years and he was an advocate for a world government via the UN for many decades. He was also a very devoted disciple of Alice Bailey who taught her followers to pray for the coming of the Antichrist to lead them into the Age of Aquarius or the New Age.

The Two Beasts

As we continue on in Revelation 13, the Apostle John saw two different "beasts" that will work together in the last days to fulfill Satan's plan for the world. They are two men representing two large entities; one political and the other religious. Both "beasts" will promote and enforce a totalitarian world government, a "global" economic system, and a new religion that rejects Jesus Christ as the only way to heaven.

Of course, the technology is now available to accomplish controlling all financial transactions in the world with the use of a tiny implantable RFID microchip, undersea cables and the internet. And make no mistake, the coming world government authority will soon control who "buys or sells" just as the Bible warned. This is another reason Americans have witnessed several of our Presidents, including Obama, push for more submission to UN treaties and things like Agenda 21. This is also why our rogue government defies our Constitution with NSA spying, has brainwashed Federal and local law enforcement into thinking that Christians and patriots are "domestic terrorists," funded FEMA and DHS to build prison camps throughout America as they prepare to implement martial law and the unlawful detainment of American citizens...it is all part of the bigger agenda.

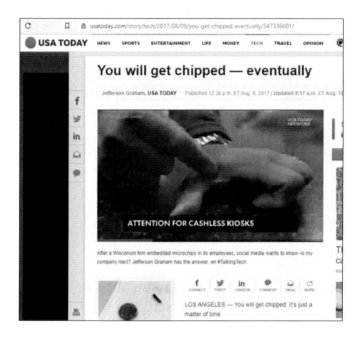

The Bible goes on to tell us that these two world leaders in Revelation 13 will deceive the majority of people in the world with promises of peace, social/economic justice, and the working of great demonic miracles. The first beast is the UN world government and the coming "moderate Muslim" that will arise to lead it. The second beast is referred to as having "two horns like a Lamb" but he speaks as a Dragon or the Devil. That means that the second beast of Revelation 13 is like a Lamb (appearing to be gentle and harmless) but he will be the mouthpiece of Satan. He will speak deceptive things that sound good to the world, but they will be in direct opposition to God and the truth of the Bible. He will also push the world to worship or be loyal to the first beast (the New World Order of false peace pushed by the UN).

465

Thus, we will have a political leader of a beast world government and a religious leader who appears to be a Lamb (the symbol of Jesus Christ and His followers) who will work together to deceive the entire world. After much study, research and prayer I know that this second beast that looks like a lamb can be none other than the last Pope of the Roman Catholic Church. I find it interesting that horns in Scripture can represent leaders and so I wonder if this second beast that has "two horns" might be referring to the fact that Rome would have two popes alive during this end time prophecy. We shall see!

The Great Whore

Some people think it is speculation to say the Roman Catholic Church is the Great Whore Mystery Babylon. They have been duped by Rome or they bought into the false idea that America is Mystery Babylon. If you look at Revelation 17, it shows the same two entities working together that we read about in Revelation 13 except in a slightly different way. We see the seven-headed beast with ten horns (the UN world government) but then it says there is another entity riding the beast. That entity is depicted as a harlot wearing scarlet and purple and holding a golden cup in her hand full of idolatry. Then, the passage goes on to give many identifying clues about Mystery Babylon that clearly identify her as the Roman Catholic Church.

*"And there came one of the seven angels which had the seven vials, and talked with me, saying unto me, Come hither; **I will shew unto thee the judgment of the GREAT WHORE that sitteth upon many waters: With whom the kings of the earth have committed fornication, and the inhabitants of the earth have been made drunk with the***

wine of her fornication (in Greek this word also means idolatry). So he carried me away in the spirit into the wilderness: and I saw a woman sit upon a scarlet coloured beast, full of names of blasphemy, having seven heads and ten horns. **And the woman was arrayed in PURPLE and SCARLET colour**, *and decked with gold and precious stones and pearls, having a golden cup in her hand full of abominations and filthiness of her fornication: And upon her forehead was a name written,* **MYSTERY, BABYLON THE GREAT, THE MOTHER OF HARLOTS AND ABOMINATIONS OF THE EARTH. And I saw the woman drunken with the blood of the saints, and with the blood of the martyrs of Jesus:** *and when I saw her, I wondered with great admiration. And the angel said unto me, Wherefore didst thou marvel?* **I will tell thee the mystery of the woman, and of the beast that carrieth her, which hath the seven heads and ten horns... And here is the mind which hath wisdom. The seven heads are seven mountains, on which the woman sitteth."** (Rev. 17:1-7, 9).

The Bible describes this "Mother of Harlots" as being clothed in scarlet and purple, drunk with the blood of the saints it killed, and a city on seven mountains/hills. Just the clue that this entity is "drunk with the blood of the saints" would rule out the USA as Mystery Babylon. Furthermore, Mystery Babylon is said to be very wealthy and deeply involved in the world economy. This is one of the main reasons the U.S. is thought to be the Great Whore, but when we look at reality, we see that America is broke. We are over $22 trillion in debt and that is not even counting derivatives. Karen Hudes (attorney for twenty years at the World Bank who turned into a "whistle-blower") while sharing about the worldwide economic corruption stated that 40% of US tax dollars go to the European bankers and the other 60% goes to the Jesuits at the Vatican. There is no doubt who controls the world's wealth/economy and it is NOT the United States of America. (If you are wondering where the U.S. gets money to pay our own bills, the answer is simple: we print it and make up the difference with drug money from CIA and DEA drug sales...but that's another story).

Just a little research of the history of the Roman Catholic Church will leave you with no doubt that they are the "great whore" that will work with the Beast at the time of the end. Popes have even referred to Rome as the "Mother Church." And a quick search of an encyclopedia will reveal that Rome is most famously known as "the city on seven hills." The colors of the two ruling branches of the Roman Catholic priesthood are purple and scarlet red. Bishops wear purple and Cardinals wear red. In fact, the popes wore red until the 1500's, and at times still do.

It is also a historical fact that the Roman Catholic Church has slaughtered millions of true Christians and Jews over the centuries in their inquisitions and by supporting people like Hitler and other communist regimes. Even Pope Francis supported the slaughter of innocent people in Argentina during the seven-year reign of its brutal communist dictator. And Pope Benedict's legacy is years as a Nazi Youth and allowing pedophile priests to continue raping children. The evidence is solid that the Roman Catholic Church is the great whore of Revelation. And the sitting pope in the end WILL BE the false prophet who works with the Antichrist throughout the tribulation period.

This is something that I have believed and taught since the late 1980's. And now, after more than 32 years of studying the Bible and watching the events of our time unfold, I am convinced that Pope Francis is most likely the last pope. If this is true, that means we should see him trying to appear as sweet and gentle as a lamb while he speaks things straight from the mouth of Satan. Well, over the last several years since his election, Pope Francis has wasted no time as he began speaking some of Satan's favorite false teachings. When asked a question about the sin of homosexuality his response was, *"Who I am to judge?"* Then, he stated that even atheists would go to heaven if they were good people.

This statement alone is one of the greatest blasphemies of Satan! It totally negates the entire reason that Jesus Christ (God in the flesh) came to earth as a man and shed His sinless blood on the cross for our sins. It is a total rejection of what Jesus and the Apostles taught in the New Testament regarding the requirements of faith in Jesus Christ and repentance from sin in order to be saved from an eternity in hell. And then recently, Pope Francis spewed out his most evil attack on true Bible-believing Christians. He stated that those who are "rigid" in their beliefs have an "illness" and are no longer disciples of Jesus. Truly, this pope appears to be a gentle, loving, tolerant lamb, but he speaks the ideologies of Satan the Dragon.

Rome & Islam: The Iron and the Clay

In the days ahead, you will see more and more confirmation in the headlines that the pope is departing from the fundamentals of the Christian faith. He will continue to say that heaven is open to all people whether they accept Jesus Christ as Lord or not. He will continue to reach out to Muslims even more than Pope John Paul II (who revised the Catholic Catechism to include Muslims in salvation). He will do this because he and the coming Muslim Antichrist will work together to influence the masses. In fact, on June 8, 2014 Pope Francis allowed Muslim prayers and readings from the Quran to be performed at the Vatican for the first time ever. That is why I believe this pope will soon perform some "amazing miracles" that will greatly increase his influence over the deceived people of the world. And he will convince many that the new world government and moving away from physical money to the implanted RFID chip is a good thing.

The pope's campaign to get the world to pledge allegiance to the new "man of peace" and his one-world government will certainly carry more weight if we have experienced a devastating nuclear war and economic collapse. Also, as I have mentioned several times in this book, I believe the fallen angels will appear during that time or right before and claim to be "aliens." They will work with the Vatican and the United Nations to influence the deceived masses into accepting the man they have chosen to be the "mediator" of their New World Order. Sadly, the entire world has been set up for this "alien" deception of Satan through the entire heliocentric/Big Bang/Copernican cosmology and faked space missions.

Vatican linked to United Nations Video on Integrating Extraterrestrial Life.

Once the final pope and the "alien chosen" Muslim world leader gain control, they will redistribute the wealth of the world to those who will go along with their plan. Then, the Bible tells us that in the middle of the last seven years the Antichrist will break the peace treaty he negotiated with Israel and then later he will even turn on Rome and destroy it with fire. She (Rome) will then realize that she was used like a whore by the Antichrist and then discarded. It is easy to see why this would happen since Islam has an old grudge to settle with the Roman Catholic Church from the Crusades. Revelation 17-18 states that it is God who puts it into the heart of the Beast to destroy the Great Whore of Rome. Amazingly, even some old Roman Catholic prophecies from their own people foretell this coming destruction of Rome.

What Should You Do?

Four or five years ago, my friend who used to work and live in Hollywood sent me a very interesting email. He stated that some very well-known people in Hollywood had been offered great wealth and diplomatic immunity if they would help influence the public into accepting the coming New World Order through the United Nations and the "alien agenda." He said that to join in they would have to take an oath and pledge loyalty to the United Nations and to certain New Age religious beliefs. This plan also includes total control over the world economy and banking system. In other words, EXACTLY what the Bible foretold in Revelation.

The world is full of evil and deception and it is not getting better. The Luciferian cabal will be making their final moves in these last days. After reading this book, hopefully you understand the evil behind the deception and most importantly, the power behind the One, true God and Creator. So, what is the answer for the storm that is coming?

The only answer is to trust the God of the Bible and His Holy Word and turn to Jesus Christ for salvation from sin and eternal life in heaven. Do not take any kind of mark or implant in your hand or forehead that controls buying and selling. And do not pledge allegiance or make any oath to the new world government of the UN or any man that leads that government. If you do "worship" their new government/leader or take their mark for buying and selling, God Almighty, the Lord Jesus Christ considers that the ultimate betrayal. According to God's Word, there is no forgiveness or escaping eternal judgment in hell if you submit to this coming Antichrist system:

*"And the third angel followed them, saying with a loud voice, **If any man worship the beast and his image, and receive his mark in his forehead, or in his hand, The same shall drink of the wine of the wrath of God**, which is poured out without mixture into the cup of his indignation; **and he shall be tormented with fire and brimstone in the presence of the holy angels, and in the presence of the Lamb: And the smoke of their torment ascendeth up for ever and ever: and they have no rest day nor night, who worship the beast and his image, and whosoever receiveth the mark of his name.** Here is the patience of the saints: here are they that keep the commandments of God, and the faith of Jesus"* (Revelation 14:9-12).

Give your life to the Jesus of the Bible, confess your sins and turn from them. He will forgive your sins, cleanse your heart, and make an eternal place for you in the real heaven. He is truly the ONLY way! If you haven't already, I hope you choose a relationship with Jesus Christ before it is too late. He does love you, but gives you the choice to love Him or follow Satan.

"Choose you this day whom ye will serve...but as for me and my house, we will serve the LORD." (Joshua 24:15)

At the very end of these last days, the Bible says the sky will fall (Revelation 6:12-17 & 16:17-21). Every eye will see as Jesus Christ returns to destroy the Antichrist, the Pope who deceived the world and all those who decided to take the mark and follow them. Which side will you be on when the sky falls?

"John to the seven churches which are in Asia: Grace be unto you, and peace, from him which is, and which was, and which is to come; and from the seven Spirits which are before his throne; ***And from Jesus Christ****, who is the faithful witness, and the first begotten of the dead, and the prince of the kings of the earth.* ***Unto him that loved us and washed us from our sins in his own blood****, And hath made us kings and priests unto God and his Father; to him be glory and dominion for ever and ever. Amen.* ***Behold, he cometh with clouds; and every eye shall see him, and they also which pierced him: and all kindreds of the earth shall wail because of him.*** *Even so, Amen. I am Alpha and Omega, the beginning and the ending, saith the Lord, which is, and which was, and which is to come, the Almighty"* (Revelation 1:4-8).

474

**Dean Odle Ministries &
Fire & Grace Church
P.O. Box 4275
Opelika, Alabama 36803**

deanodle.org

fireandgracechurch.org

Other books by Pastor Dean Odle:

Grace Abuse: One of the Greatest Hindrances to Revival
(1998)

The Holy Spirit: Tongues of Fire
(2007)

The Polluted Church: From Rome to Kansas City
(2012)

Appendix 1

The Impossible Flight of the ISS
jasonthegrey   Empirical Science July 8, 2015

I was looking at some additional sites from NASA that try to explain the nature of gravity at certain altitudes. https://www.grc.nasa.gov/www/K-12/airplane/wteq.html

The final sentence of the explanation is "…But the high orbital speed, tangent to the surface of the earth, causes the fall towards the surface to be exactly matched by the curvature of the earth away from the shuttle. In essence, the shuttle is constantly falling all around the earth."

As mentioned in my previous posts, the centripetal force only makes sense for something that is tethered to the spinning body (If you feel that the centripetal force *does* have special powers, please provide a clear empirical example that can be tested). Neither the space shuttle nor the ISS are tethered to the earth unless we grant the centripetal magical grappling abilities (see hammer throw). https://www.youtube.com/watch?v=KnHUAc20WEU

As well, for the shuttle to be constantly "falling" but not actually falling downwards, a constant acceleration would need to be applied (ie. rockets) plus a continual adjustment of direction or the shuttle would fly off into space (see what happens when the hammer is released). Again, for apparent "weightlessness" in space, it would require objects to be falling at a rate of 9.8N/kg (or m/s/s) which would mean a constant counter-force of equal value would need to be applied or they would rapidly fall to earth. So the "floating" objects and people in space would need to be in a free fall all the time. This is obviously not the case since the ISS would have crashed to earth a long time ago. In essence the ISS is just like a airplane at a higher altitude and would require constant thrust to stay in "orbit". If you turn off the engines of an airplane at 30,000 feet will it stay in "orbit" because "...the high orbital speed, tangent to the surface of the earth, causes the fall towards the surface to be exactly matched by the curvature of the earth away from the [airplane]? " I don't think any scientist would want to be in that airplane at 30,000 feet. It should be noted that the standard equation for centrifugal force for any object at the equator great than ~317kg would have a centrifugal force greater than gravity. Unless the centripetal force is magically grappling those objects, they should all start floating and since objects like elephants weigh ~4000-7000kg, they should all be floating thousands of miles above the earth.

If we grant the ISS a value of 3217N/kg (centrifugal force) due to its orbit around the earth (@ 17,150 miles/h & 4200 miles & ~331,000kg) – what force was initially used to get it to that speed?), then an equivalent (but opposite direction) for it must be present via the centripetal force. In order for a centripetal force to be present the object must be tethered to the earth. However, to obtain 3217N/kg, this would require the object to be traveling at a faster rate than the earth's rate of spin. So an object that travels faster than the earth's rate of spin *must* be under its own propulsion and not tethered to the earth. Since the ISS is traveling at such a high rate of speed and is not tethered to the earth, then it *must* be under its own propulsion and heading. This is plainly not the case. If the centripetal and centrifugal forces are equal but opposite directions, then we are left with 9.8N/kg (the force of gravity) on all objects.

In conclusion, if the centripetal force only applies to objects that are tethered to a spinning object (ie. earth) then objects above the earth's surface must be constantly under their own propulsion (like an airplane) to stay above the earth's surface. In other words, the ISS should be falling out of the sky.[211]

---

[211] https://eternalworldorder.com/2015/07/08/the-impossible-flight-of-the-iss/